The publisher gratefully acknowledges the generous support of the Ahmanson Foundation Humanities Endowment Fund of the University of California Press Foundation.

Polemics and Patronage in the
City of Victory

SOUTH ASIA ACROSS THE DISCIPLINES

Edited by Muzaffar Alam, Robert Goldman, and Gauri Viswanathan

Dipesh Chakrabarty, Sheldon Pollock, and Sanjay Subrahmanyam, Founding Editors

Funded by a grant from the Andrew W. Mellon Foundation and jointly published by the University of California Press, the University of Chicago Press, and Columbia University Press.

For a list of books in the series, see page 213.

# Polemics and Patronage in the City of Victory

*Vyāsatīrtha, Hindu Sectarianism, and the
Sixteenth-Century Vijayanagara Court*

Valerie Stoker

UNIVERSITY OF CALIFORNIA PRESS

University of California Press, one of the most distinguished university presses in the United States, enriches lives around the world by advancing scholarship in the humanities, social sciences, and natural sciences. Its activities are supported by the UC Press Foundation and by philanthropic contributions from individuals and institutions. For more information, visit www.ucpress.edu.

University of California Press
Oakland, California



Suggested citation: Stoker, Valerie. *Polemics and Patronage in the City of Victory: Vyāsatīrtha, Hindu Sectarianism, and the Sixteenth-Century Vijayanagara Court*. Oakland: University of California Press, 2016. doi: http://doi.org/10.1525/luminos.18

Library of Congress Cataloging-in-Publication Data

Names: Stoker, Valerie, author.
    Title: Polemics and patronage in the city of victory : Vyāsatīrtha, Hindu sectarianism, and the sixteenth-century Vijayanagara Court / Valerie Stoker.
    Other titles: South Asia across the disciplines.
    Description: Oakland, California : University of California Press, [2016] | Series: South Asia across the disciplines | Includes bibliographical references and index.
    Identifiers: LCCN 2016032554 | ISBN 9780520291836 (pbk. : alk. paper) | ISBN 9780520965461 (ebook)
    Subjects: LCSH: Vyāsatīrtha, 1460–1539—Influence. | Hinduism and state—India—Vijayanagar (Empire)—History—16th century. | Vijayanagar (Empire)—Religion—16th century.
    Classification: LCC BL1153.2 .S76 2016 | DDC 294.50954/809031—dc23
    LC record available at https://lccn.loc.gov/2016032554

25   24   23   22   21   20   19   18   17   16
10   9   8   7   6   5   4   3   2   1

# CONTENTS

ILLUSTRATIONS

FIGURES



MAPS

PLAN

ACKNOWLEDGMENTS

This book is the product of many years' labor. One of the great pleasures of seeing it completed is the opportunity it provides me to thank all those individuals and agencies that have supported it.

My initial research for this project was funded by a 2008–2009 American Institute of Indian Studies (AIIS) Senior Short-Term Fellowship. While I was in India, the AIIS staff also supplied much practical assistance, for which I am extremely grateful. Later support came in the form of a generous National Endowment for the Humanities Fellowship in 2012–2013. The College of Liberal Arts at Wright State University granted me an extended professional leave to write the manuscript, while the Office of Research and Sponsored Programs covered the costs of several trips to South Asian research libraries in the United States and England. Portions of this book have appeared in other publications, all of which are cited in the bibliography under my name. I thank *History of Religions* for allowing me to reuse material I published with them in 2011 (vol. 51, no. 2). Portions of a chapter I published in an edited volume entitled *Krishnadevaraya and His Times* (2013) appear here courtesy of the K. R. Cama Oriental Institute of Mumbai. Taylor and Francis granted me permission to reuse material that appeared in an edited volume, published by Routledge in 2015, entitled *Scholar-Intellectuals in Early Modern India: Discipline, Sect, Lineage and Community.*

This book has benefited from the informed expertise of many individuals whose assistance has proven invaluable. I am extremely grateful to Dr. D. Prahladachar for generously reading Vyāsatīrtha's works with me in Bangalore and for explaining, in masterful detail, their many subtleties. I am also grateful to Dr. K. T. Pandurangi who, over the course of several trips to India, read the works of other

Mādhva philosophers with me. Together with his family, especially his daughter, Sudha, Dr. Pandurangi helped me forge valuable connections with local scholars in Bangalore and procure published copies of important texts. Madhav Deshpande, Frederick Smith, Ludo Rocher, and Rosane Rocher each offered me valuable feedback and encouragement when I first began to consider undertaking this project. Colleagues at Columbia University's Institute for Religion, Culture, and Public Life helped shape my thinking on my work's broader implications; I thank Sudipta Kaviraj and Rajeev Bhargava for including me in those conversations in 2009 and 2011. I am also grateful to the Oxford Early Modern South Asia workshop, particularly Rosalind O'Hanlon and Christopher Minkowski, for including me in an equally enlightening set of dialogues in 2013. In 2012, Anila Verghese and the K. R. Cama Institute in Mumbai afforded me the opportunity to meet with many other Vijayanagara scholars from India, Europe, and the United States during a fascinating two-day conference on Kṛṣṇadevarāya. At various stages of this project, Dr. Verghese also generously supplied much practical assistance, including taking some photographs for me during one of her own research trips to Hampi as I was in the final stages of preparing my manuscript. Kathleen Morrison and Ilanit Loewy Shacham took the lead in assembling an international roster of Vijayanagara specialists at the University of Chicago in 2015 to discuss the connections between the empire's symbolic and material cultures; I thank them for their efforts. I am additionally grateful to Ilanit for many informative conversations on Kṛṣṇadevarāya and for sharing her work on the *Āmuktamālyada* while it was still in progress. Also in 2015, Caleb Simmons and the Department of Religion at the University of Arizona organized and funded a workshop on *maṭha*s in Indian history that clarified my thinking on this subject in several important ways. I thank him and his collaborator, Sarah Pierce Taylor, for pursuing this important line of inquiry. Leslie Orr, whose historical studies of South Indian religion have been a long-standing source of inspiration, read and commented on several of the book's chapters. I am grateful for her acute insights and her encouragement.

Less formally, but just as significantly, my work has benefited from the input of Yigal Bronner, Elaine Fisher, V. N. Rao, Ajay Rao, Prithvi Datta Chandra Shobhi, Gil Ben-Herut, Jon Keune, John S. Hawley, Chakravarthi Ram-Prasad, Anand Venkatkrishnan, Michael Williams, Nabanjan Maitra, and Sucharita Adluri. Colleagues in the Department of Religion at Wright State University, especially David Barr and Ava Chamberlain, have provided a stimulating and supportive intellectual environment. This book benefited from the extensive support and technical expertise of Reed Malcolm, executive editor at the University of California Press; I thank him, Rachel Berchten, Zuha Khan, and the rest of the UC Press staff for their consistent professionalism. Ann Donahue improved this book greatly through her attentive copy-editing as did Jonathan Peterson through his proofreading of the Sanskrit transliterations. Bill Nelson worked patiently with me on drawing the maps on which several of my arguments hinge. Phillip Wagoner and Richard Eaton, whose work is cited frequently in what follows, also helped hone my thinking about maps and shifting borders. I am extremely grateful to the anonymous reviewers of the manuscript for recommending critically important revisions. Lawrence McCrea deserves special recognition for his comments on the manuscript and for his support and encouragement of this project at several key stages. While all of the above individuals have enriched my thinking, and several have edited my prose, any errors in this book are fully my own.

It is certainly gratifying to finish a long project, but it is more gratifying still to have lived a full life while doing so. For this abundance, my heartfelt thanks go to all of my friends and family who, often from great distances and in the midst of their own busy lives, routinely give me generous portions of their time. In particular, I would like to acknowledge several people in India whom I have come to regard as my extended family and who have been extremely helpful to me over the years. K. Marulasiddappa, G. S. Jayanthi, Radika Makaram, and K.M. Chaitanya have not only been generous hosts to me on numerous (and often lengthy) occasions, they have also been endlessly entertaining conversationalists, deep wells of information, and ideal travel companions. Zakhia Siraj, Gita Shivalingaiah, Poornima Prasad, and Shiva Prasad have each given up portions of their precious free time to eat, chat, and travel with me. It was through S.N. Sridhar that I was first introduced to many of these fine people. I thank them all for their sustained friendship. A bit closer to home, one of my oldest friends, K.M. Tiro, also happens to be a deft American cultural historian. I thank him for reading the entire manuscript and for asking all the necessary, challenging questions that only an insightful nonspecialist can ask.

Finally, I would like to acknowledge all the inspiration I have drawn over the years from Alex and Sylvie. These two have not only accommodated, supported, and enhanced this project in more ways than they are likely aware of, they have done so with their characteristic curiosity, patience, and enthusiasm. I thank them for cultivating these qualities and for sharing them with the lucky people in their lives.

# ABBREVIATIONS

ARIE        *Annual Report on Indian Epigraphy*
ARSIE       *Annual Reports on South Indian Epigraphy*
ARMAD       *Annual Report of the Mysore Archaeological Department*
EC          *Epigraphia Carnatica*
EI          *Epigraphia Indica*
SII         *South Indian Inscriptions*
TDI         *Tirupati Devasthanam Inscriptions*

## NOTE ON TRANSLITERATION AND TRANSLATION

In general, I have retained the diacritical marks for historical, religious, and philosophical terms taken from texts and inscriptions (e.g., "mokṣa," not "moksha"; "maṭha, not "matha") and for the names of historical figures (e.g., "Kṛṣṇadevarāya," not "Krishnadevaraya"; Vyāsatīrtha, not "Vyasatirtha"). In the case of foreign terms that have been assimilated into English, I have generally omitted the diacritics (e.g., "sufi," "brahmin," "sultan"). I have also omitted diacritics for the names of contemporary South Asian authors. In general, I have avoided diacritics when transliterating place or language names (e.g., "Sringeri," not "Śṛṅgeri"; "Kannada," not "Kannaḍa") I have, however, retained the diacritics when referring to deities and their eponymous temples. On occasion, this has required retaining the diacritics for a particular place named after a temple; for example, the neighborhood within the Vijayanagara capital known as "Viṭṭhalapura" is written with diacritics because the name of the deity "Viṭṭhala" is in its name. When quoting passages from other modern authors' works, I have preserved their spelling and use of diacritics. Unless otherwise noted, all translations are my own.

1

_______

# Hindu Sectarianism and the City of Victory

This book explores the ways in which the patronage activities of a major precolonial South Indian polity, the Vijayanagara Empire (c. 1346–1565), influenced the articulation of Hindu sectarian identities. Named after its capital, "the City of Victory," as a testament to its rulers' military prowess, this empire eventually encompassed most of the Indian peninsula south of the Krishna River. However, the empire's historic significance is not limited to India; for a little over two centuries, the empire sat at the center of an emerging global economy. It attracted foreign merchants, dignitaries, and mercenary soldiers who had arrived in India from Europe, Africa, and the Middle East.[1] By 1500, the City of Victory had one of the largest, most diverse urban populations in the world,[2] and it engaged in trade, diplomatic, and military relations with polities both within and beyond South Asia. Ultimately, the empire's military prowess was unable to withstand an alliance to the north of rival states, which sacked the city in 1565, effectively ending Vijayanagara rule in the south. The capital's ruins, which currently consist of about sixteen hundred identified structures, cover roughly thirty square kilometers along the Tungabhadra River in the Deccan Plateau's dramatic, boulder-strewn landscape. Impressive enough to be declared a United Nations Educational Scientific, and Cultural Organization World Heritage site in 1986, the Vijayanagara capital, and the empire it ruled, loom large in the collective imagining of India's precolonial past. And religion has featured prominently in that image.

Because of Vijayanagara's ongoing military engagements with a variety of sultanates to the north, the empire has been presented in older scholarship as a Hindu bulwark against further southern incursions of Islam.[3] More recent scholarship challenges this view by citing the many examples of the Vijayanagara court's cultural eclecticism, particularly its stylistic borrowings from the northern sultan-ates, as well as its ecumenical patronage of a variety of religious institutions.[4] In this view, the Vijayanagara Empire was a tolerant haven for many religious tradi-tions including Islam, Jainism, Christianity, and diverse forms of Hinduism. While this emphasis on religious diversity is refreshing and, to a great extent, warranted, it ignores both the court's privileging of certain forms of religiosity over others and the impact that this had, not only on religious identity and expression, but also on South Indian society more broadly.[5]

This book argues that, in fact, the Vijayanagara court was selective in its pa-tronage of primarily Hindu religious institutions, but the motivations behind this selectivity were not always religious. Rather, Vijayanagara patronage of Hindu sectarian groups responded creatively to a variety of incentives in ways that re-flected the particular circumstances of specific locations. This opportunistic flex-ibility of Vijayanagara patronage, coupled with its generosity, galvanized Hindu sectarian leaders to pursue certain kinds of intellectual projects as well as to form different intersectarian alliances and rivalries. Because these alliances and rival-ries demarcated areas of overlap and distinction in doctrinal and practical mat-ters, they simultaneously articulated a shared religious sensibility and significant sectarian divisions.

Thus, by examining Hindu sectarian responses to Vijayanagara patronage, this book documents important developments in religion and philosophy while locat-ing the proponents of these systems socially and historically. Such location delin-eates not only how specific sociopolitical factors implicated Hindu religious for-mations but also how philosophical argumentation and religious practice shaped social and political reality. Certainly, this shaping was subtle and indirect, but it was not nonexistent. In fact, it is essential to our understanding of early modern South India.

To shed light on the dynamic interaction of royal and religious institutions in this period, I focus my analysis on the career of the important Hindu intellectual and religious leader Vyāsatīrtha (1460–1539). Vyāsatīrtha was the monastic head of the Mādhva Brahmin sect under a succession of Vijayanagara rulers, most notably, the great monarch Kṛṣṇadevarāya (r. 1509–29). Prior to Vyāsatīrtha, Mādhva Brah-minism was dominant mainly in the coastal South Kanara region around Udupi, where the movement's eponymous founder, Madhva, lived in the thirteenth cen-tury. A Smārta Brahmin by birth and education, Madhva (1238–1317) eventually rejected nondualist or Advaita Vedānta to put forward a new reading of canoni-cal Vedānta texts like the *Brahma Sūtra*s and the *Upaniṣad*s.[6] Because this new reading emphasized the abiding reality of difference, particularly that between the ultimate reality Brahman (whom Madhva identified with Viṣṇu) and individual human souls, Madhva's system is often labeled "Dvaita" or "dualist" Vedānta. But perhaps the more significant feature of Mādhva Vedānta was its realistic pluralism, which lent eternal significance to many of the structures of everyday life. By authoring manuals for distinctive Mādhva forms of devotionalism, ritual practice, and initiation rites, as well as rules governing daily routines that implicated both monks and laypeople, Madhva inaugurated a new religious movement in South Kanara.[7] While adherents of his pluralistic ontology, realist epistemology, and distinctive form of Vaiṣṇava devotionalism established communities and institutions in other parts of Karnataka as early as the fourteenth century, the sect does not seem to have achieved much prominence.[8] It was not until the sixteenth century that, under Vyāsatīrtha's direction, Mādhva Brahminism became a major intellectual, social, and political force throughout South India. This was due to a variety of factors, the most notable of which were Vyāsatīrtha's polemics and Vijayanagara's patronage.

To be sure, Madhva's positioning of his system at the opposite pole of Advaita Vedānta's idealistic monism, in which any experience of difference or plurality was deemed illusory, made his thought polemical from its inception. Philosophical debate was a long-established tradition in India by Madhva's time, and he was certainly not the first Hindu thinker to criticize the views of his predecessors. But Vyāsatīrtha took Madhva's polemics against his intellectual and religious rivals to new heights. Drawing upon the "new dialectics" or *navya-nyāya* that were increasingly embraced by Sanskrit intellectuals of his era,[9] Vyāsatīrtha's most famous works closely parse a variety of opponents' arguments to reveal a multitude of logical inconsistencies. Vyāsatīrtha's discussions, which focus on alternative forms of Vedānta, are marked by what McCrea has identified as a new type of doxography, one that presents the historical evolution of ideas within rival philosophical systems.[10] McCrea rightly argues that, through this historical presentation, Vyāsatīrtha identifies the emergence of significant internal divisions within these intellectual communities.[11] As I will demonstrate, Vyāsatīrtha's exposure of intrasectarian intellectual fault lines often revealed intrasectarian social divisions as well.

Indeed, Vyāsatīrtha's concern with critiquing his opponents' ideas is deeply entangled with the social and political status of those opponents and the relationships they enjoyed with the Vijayanagara court. In his polemical works, Vyāsatīrtha identifies two main intellectual rivals. First are the Smārta Brahmins, proponents of Advaita Vedānta, who managed the court temple of Virūpākṣa—a form of Śiva and the empire's tutelary deity. Their dominance at court begins with the empire's founding in the fourteenth century. Second are the Śrīvaiṣṇavas, who advocated Viśiṣṭādvaita Vedānta or qualified nondualism and who, by the sixteenth century, seem to have controlled many of the royally funded Viṣṇu shrines in the empire. That Vyāsatīrtha's criticisms of these rival Vedānta systems proved to be incisive is evident in the fact that, for the duration of the sixteenth century (and even into the seventeenth), both direct and indirect responses to his works were being composed. This was true not only in South India but as far north as Varanasi, where the Advaitin intellectual Madhusūdana Sarasvatī (fl. 1550) composed a line-by-line refutation of one of Vyāsatīrtha's most polemical texts, the *Nyāyāmṛta*.

But Vyāsatīrtha was more than just a polemicist. One of the central themes of this book is that Vyāsatīrtha's arguments elicited such a strong response from his intellectual opponents because he was head of a network of sectarian monasteries that was significantly expanded by Vijayanagara patronage. The inscriptional and monumental records indicate that, throughout the empire's holdings, Vyāsatīrtha received several land grants for the construction of *maṭha*s or monasteries and the establishment of related *agrahāra*s or settlements of Brahmin households. Vyāsatīrtha also used royally bequeathed wealth to install icons and subsidiary shrines at prominent Vaiṣṇava temples and patronize large-scale public works, such as irrigation projects, in strategically significant locations. As I will demonstrate, Vyāsatīrtha used such means to spread Mādhva Brahminism's distinctive doctrines, iconography, and rituals into Tamil- and Telugu-speaking regions while also implementing key features of the royal court's agenda. Other sources on Vyāsatīrtha considered in this book include sectarian biographies that, while diverse in genre and content, share an emphasis on Vyāsatīrtha's close relationship with the court. These biographies also attest to the sectarian leader's interactions with a wide range of other social agents, including tribal peoples, foreign dignitaries, and emissaries from North Indian peer polities. Such interactions are substantiated in other sources, including travel accounts of Portuguese traders.

These diverse multilingual sources documenting Vyāsatīrtha's life attest to the dynamic pluralism that characterized the early sixteenth-century Vijayanagara capital, a pluralism that shaped the nature of religious identity in this period. The reign of Kṛṣṇadevarāya, which is considered the empire's apex, is particularly famous for its lavish patronage of a variety of Hindu religious institutions that encouraged new styles of temple art and architecture. While it receives fewer accolades, Kṛṣṇadevarāya's reign was also a period of intense military activity that both consolidated the empire's holdings in rebellious areas in the south and expanded the empire northward.[12] Maps 1 and 2 below, which depict the empire's boundaries in 1500, 1510, and 1520, respectively, document the empire's growth to its largest size under Kṛṣṇadevarāya's rule. This territorial expansion occasioned much foreign trade, technological exchange, migration, and other forms of cross-cultural interaction.

For instance, the Vijayanagara army consisted of mercenary soldiers from throughout the subcontinent, as well as recent transplants from Africa, Europe, and the Middle East. The court's military activities depended on its horse trade with Arabia, trade into which Europeans had effectively inserted themselves as middlemen by the end of the fifteenth century. The Portuguese state of Goa, established in 1511 to protect its economic interests in India, added a new polity to the subcontinent that both competed and collaborated with Vijayanagara. That Kṛṣṇadevarāya received emissaries from Goa at court is well documented.[13]

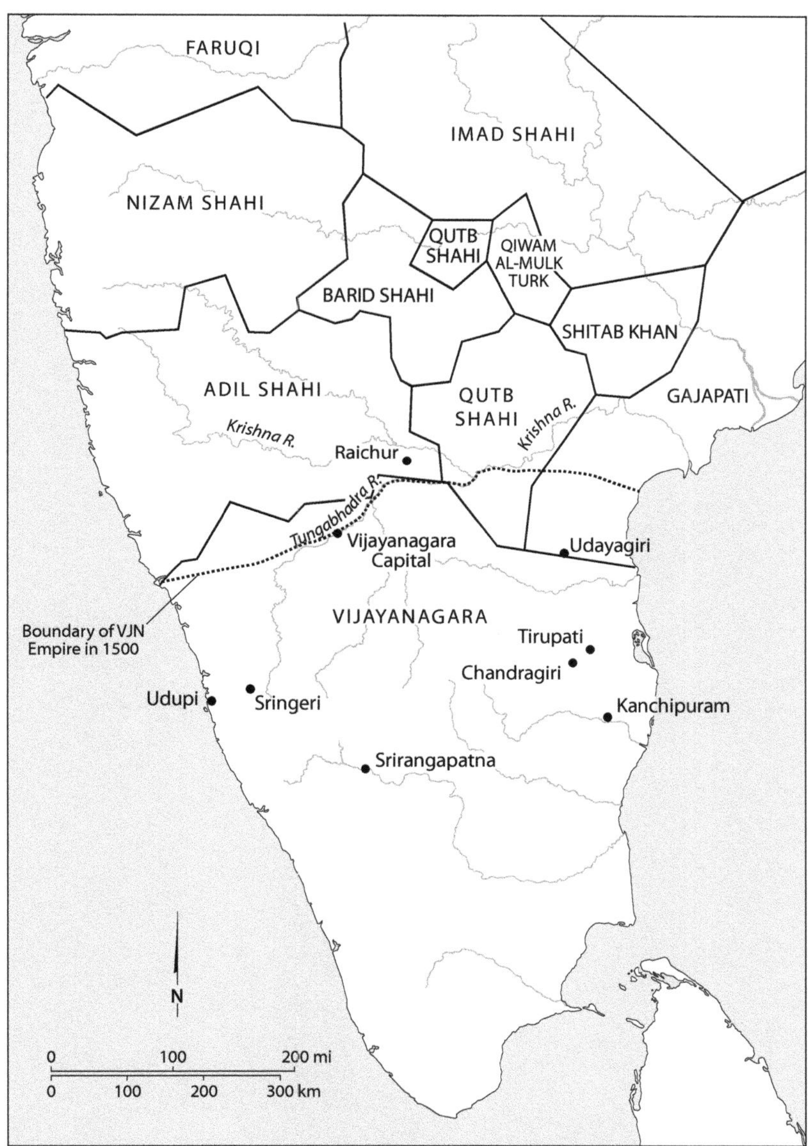


MAP 1. Vijayanagara Empire, 1510 (1500 border also shown).

Moreover, contingents of Portuguese musketeers assisted Kṛṣṇadevarāya in his successful 1520–21 military campaign against the Adil Shahi dynasty of the Bijapur sultanate, with which Vijayanagara shared a border. The Vijayanagara economy depended in part on its textile trade with Southeast Asia; many of its

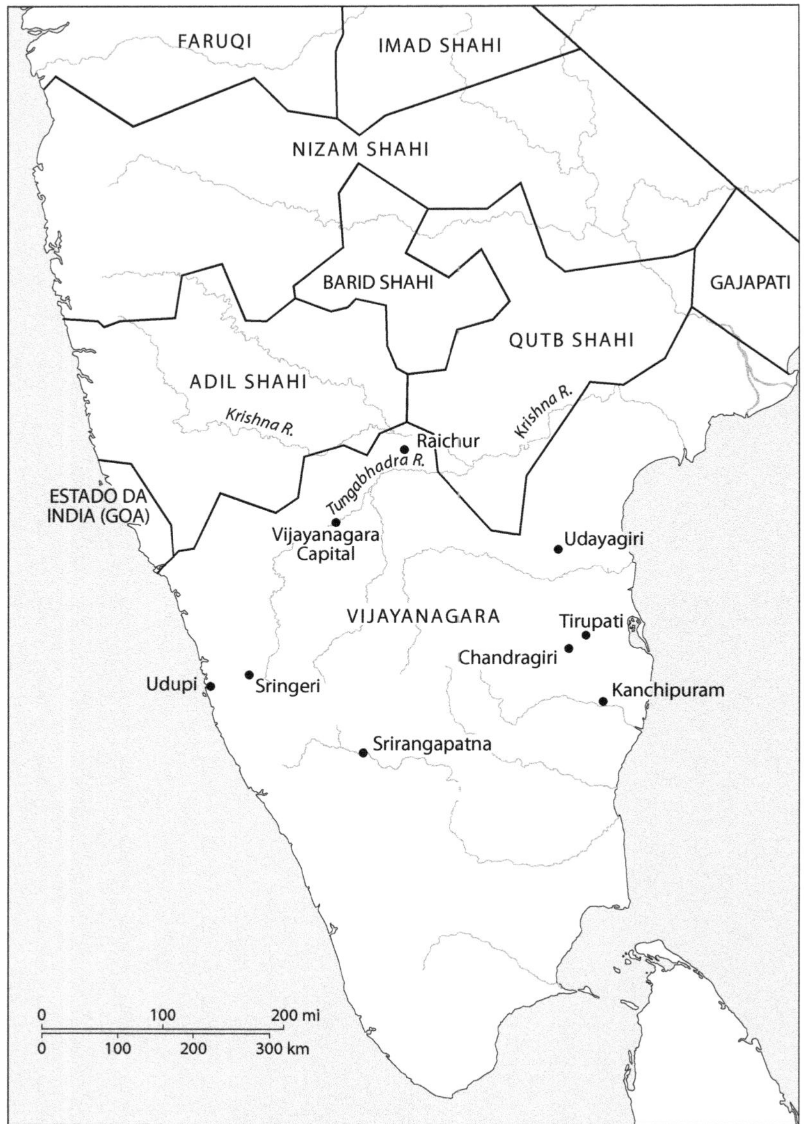


MAP 2. Vijayanagara Empire, 1520.

military campaigns in the Tamil country were undertaken to protect this. Thus, Kṛṣṇadevarāya presided over a cosmopolitan capital of roughly 250,000 people[14] and a region of approximately 140,000 square miles[15] that was marked by geographic and social mobility. At the same time, it maintained an economic and

sphere of activity also enabled new kinds of transregional religious interaction. Such interactions, which were often facilitated directly by Vijayanagara patronage, encouraged new articulations of relative religious identity that mapped out varying degrees of affinity and difference between sectarian groups. Finally, the fact that Vijayanagara stood at the center of a global trade network, one that increased the ethnic and religious diversity of its capital city and major towns, reshaped the economy in ways that increased social mobility. This, in turn, stimulated new conceptions of identity that implicated Hindu monastic leaders and their relationships with their constituencies, their rivals, and the state.

There has been almost as much debate over the use of the term *Hindu sect* as over the use of the term *Hinduism*.[28] One of the problems with the term *sect* is that it presumes the existence of a shared set of core religious doctrines and practices that are then interpreted variously by different subgroups. If no such core doctrines defining a Hindu community existed in precolonial India, then it follows that there was also no community to be subdivided into sects. This argument is further supported by the fact that there is no clear indigenous counterpart to this English term. The one most often resorted to is *sampradāya* or *tradition,* with its connotations of *guru-śiṣya* lineages used to transmit specific sets of teachings. But *sampradāya* arguably does not successfully convey a breaking off from a larger shared tradition and could just as easily refer to an entire religion in its own right.[29]

If we are looking for a term that conveys Indian conceptions of religiosity that coalesce with the English word *sect,* perhaps the most efficacious for the Vijayanagara period would be the Sanskrit term *maṭha.* Often translated as "monastery" and used in many vernacular Indian languages, the term *maṭha* carries a host of connotations (so many, in fact, that one could argue that it lends little clarity to the debate to use it). The term *maṭha* refers in part to an architectural space that typically housed Hindu ascetics and implicated the surrounding area in significant ways, not unlike the Hindu temple. But the term *maṭha* also transcended these spaces to refer to conceptual entities, in much the same way that a church is both a building that one goes to and the religious community to which one belongs. *Maṭha*s of a particular sectarian community constituted a network of interrelated institutions with shared practices and ideals; their residents were typically initiates into an order. Like the monasteries of medieval Europe, they performed many intellectual, religious, social, and political functions and, as such, were engaged both with the state and the local population.

The main virtue of using *maṭha* for *sect* is that it is largely in terms of the Vijayanagara court's relationship to *maṭha*s that the state fomented both a generic Hindu religious sensibility and Hindu sectarian divisions. Some scholars maintain that *maṭha*s functioned as universities and taught a variety of students and subjects.[30] While this is true to an extent, there is ample evidence from this period that *maṭha*s typically endorsed a particular system of thought and a specific devotional orientation. *Mathas* established and maintained *guru-śiṣya* lineages and codified not only intellectual practices within the community but religious rituals for iconographic worship, rules governing daily routines such as bathing and food consumption, and techniques for marking the body with emblems of sectarian affiliation.[31] To be sure, *mathas* functioned differently within their respective communities. The Śrīvaiṣṇavas, for instance, had monastic institutions but also had prominent householder religious leaders, meaning that *mathas* in that community did not hold exclusive claims to religious authority.[32] Moreover, *mathas* could themselves be the locus of expressing intrasectarian differences and rivalries. Different branches of monastic lineages within a given sectarian community could observe slightly different practices and engage with slightly different doctrinal and textual traditions.[33] But because *mathas* also performed similar functions in South Indian society, were organized according to similar administrative patterns, and were often placed by the court on the same temple premises, they ended up enacting shared religious identities, even as they promoted their distinctiveness. To be sure, these shared religious identities and their internal divisions do not correspond exactly to today's formulations of "Hinduism" and "Hindu sects."[34] But they are important historical antecedents to some of the later developments. Thus, while the semantic overlap between the terms *matha* and *sect* is not exact, studying the various connotations of the word *matha* and the nature and role of these institutions in sixteenth-century South India helps us to delineate a bit more precisely the contours of religious unity and difference.

Vyāsatīrtha's life story is an ideal vantage point from which to consider the dynamic interactions between the Hindu *matha,* the Vijayanagara court, and broader South Indian society. His relations with the court suggest that the court was increasingly dependent on Hindu *mathas* for implementing certain aspects of its statecraft. As chapter 2 of this book will demonstrate, the inscriptional record indicates that, particularly when it came to integrating newly conquered or rebellious territories, the court regularly donated land in these regions to Hindu sectarian leaders to found freestanding monasteries. The construction of a *matha* in a given location was often accompanied by the irrigation of land whose increased harvest benefited both the monks and the local population.[35] A *matha*'s reliance on local laborers to supply other necessities also created new economic opportunities that helped to promote political integration. Furthermore, by taking on courtly emblems and titles, the monastery symbolically linked its authority to that of the Vijayanagara court.

While my study of Vyāsatīrtha's ties to the Vijayanagara court thereby reveals a symbiotic relationship between the royal court and the sectarian Hindu *matha,* it also provides evidence that the court sometimes felt uneasy about its reliance on these institutions. To rein in the increasing local power of monastic leaders like Vyāsatīrtha, the court fostered competition between sects. One way it did this was by placing rival monastic institutions on the premises of large and popular temples, a cohabitation that fostered intersectarian competition for prominence at the temple. At the same time, the court's facilitation of multiple sectarian presences at a given temple could expand that temple's appeal across diverse constituencies of the empire. Such expansion not only increased outreach opportunities for the court but also encouraged intersectarian collaboration in the ritually based implementation of imperial gifts. Indeed, despite being famous as a sectarian polemicist, Vyāsatīrtha often collaborated with his intellectual rivals at the practical level of material and honorific exchanges in shared temple environments. Because a broad swath of Vijayanagara society was typically implicated in these exchanges, royal patronage of sectarian leaders had the potential to affect religious identity at many social levels.

The multifaceted role played by *matha*s and their leaders in Vijayanagara society influenced the intellectual production of these religious institutions. Monastic institutions' increasing sociopolitical prominence inspired new genres and modified existing genres of Hindu literature. Much of this literature reflects increased sectarian competition over courtly resources. Biographies of sectarian leaders detailing their exclusively close ties to various kings, doxographic mappings of the philosophical landscape offering a historical yet hierarchical presentation of opponents' ideas, and even the use of inscriptional records on the part of religious leaders to argue for their sect's historical prominence all reflect sectarian concerns about the royal rationing of resources. While I focus primarily on sources pertaining directly to Vyāsatīrtha, I also examine sources relating to other early sixteenth-century communities such as the Smārtas and Śrīvaiṣṇavas as a result of Vyāsatīrtha's engagement with these other sectarian groups.

From a doctrinal standpoint, the era's emphasis on debate and polemics strongly suggests that these groups were looking to convert others to their systems of thought. Certainly, "conversion" from one school of Brahminical Vedānta thought (and its related ritual practices) to another did not necessarily require the radical rejection of one's former identity and affiliations that conversion has historically connoted in traditions like Christianity.[36] But the doctrinal and ritual differences between various Brahmin Vedānta sects were often significant and convincing others of the unique correctness of one's own system was undoubtedly a principal motivation behind the period's polemical literature.[37] However, while Vijayanagara patronage fostered a more bounded sense of sectarian identity, evident in intersectarian polemics, it also provided new social frameworks for philosophical dialogue and intellectual exchange. Brahmin intellectuals like Vyāsatīrtha simultaneously criticized and borrowed ideas from their intellectual rivals, reflecting the intersectarian competition and collaboration that Vijayanagara patronage inspired.

Of course, Brahmin intellectual and religious pursuits were not simply a reflection of the court's agenda and of sectarian leaders' desire to excel within it. While sectarian doctrines and practices could be modified in response to political

circumstances and were, therefore, socially located, they were not infinitely malleable. As I show, through a detailed analysis of Vyāsatīrtha's polemics against rival schools, the doctrines themselves provided a framework for sectarian identities that in many ways was nonnegotiable. Religious doctrines and philosophical
commitments imposed certain limits on sectarian interactions that took place at
temples and at court. In this sense, such commitments blocked incursions of the
sociopolitical realm into religious and philosophical activity. Nevertheless, insofar
as they exercised an important influence over the sociopolitical behavior of sectarian institutions, religious beliefs and intellectual practices played an active role in
shaping the sociopolitical sphere.

My efforts to contextualize Vyāsatīrtha's polemical writings in terms of his
quotidian interactions with his sectarian rivals and with the royal court depart
from other studies of Vyāsatīrtha that tend to locate their analyses mainly in the
Sanskrit intellectual tradition.[38] Recent projects, such as Nicholson's, that examine
Hindu philosophical literature in light of broader social and historical realities, do
not necessarily examine how the authors of such literature acted upon their environments to shape them in important ways. This book draws on collections edited by Rosalind O'Hanlon and David Washbrook (2012) and Rosalind O'Hanlon,
Christopher Minkowski, and Anand Venkatkrisnan (2015), as well as additional
work by Christopher Minkowski (2010), Elaine Fisher (2013), and others who have
considered the intersection of Indian scholar-intellectuals' different roles and how
these roles affected social reality.[39] By studying Vyāsatīrtha's multiple identities
as an intellectual, a monastic administrator, a public works patron, an economic
stimulator, a temple donor, and a state agent, I aim to illuminate how this important historic figure contributed to a variety of related social processes.

My argument that Vyāsatīrtha's multifaceted roles both affected and furthered
his philosophical program is not intended to undermine the cogency of his arguments or the incisiveness of his polemics. One of this book's main goals is to
demonstrate Vyāsatīrtha's thorough familiarity with other systems of thought and
his creative use of new argumentation techniques to buttress his school's realistic
pluralism and distinctive form of Vaiṣṇava devotionalism. Significant portions of
chapters 3 and 5 examine various arguments in Vyāsatīrtha's magnum opus, the
*Nyāyāmṛta* or "Nectar of Logic." In these chapters, I offer a close reading of certain passages of that text in order to elucidate Vyāsatīrtha's polemics against other
forms of Vedānta. But I am also interested in how Vyāsatīrtha's arguments were informed by his context, not merely to demonstrate the obvious point that philosophy is influenced by culture but to show that we can better understand some of the
arguments Vyāsatīrtha was making if we know more about how those arguments
were related to his daily interactions. For example, Vyāsatīrtha's polemics against
Viśiṣṭādvaita Vedānta read very differently when you know that Vyāsatīrtha was
actively collaborating on temple rituals with this alternative Vaiṣṇava group. In

many instances, we can greatly improve our understanding of Vyāsatīrtha's philosophical position precisely by historically contextualizing it.

In the past decade, there has been some discomfort with biographical accounts of historically important Indians. In cases where the individual in question was a religious leader, contextualizing his life and thought can seem to ascribe worldly motivations to his behavior that contradict his status as a spiritual icon. My study of Vyāsatīrtha's significant connections to the Vijayanagara court is intended, in part, to clarify why royals entrusted wealth to religious men, as well as to show how such connections to royalty may have abetted religious and spiritual interests. The fact that Vyāsatīrtha, and men of his ilk, received so much royal patronage and, by extension, power, attests to their self-abnegating status. In an analysis of a twentieth-century utopian movement in Bengal, Raphaël Voix argues that its founder, Prabhat Ranjan Sarkar, aspired to a world governed by ascetics precisely because they were, in his view, the least self-interested.[40] This attitude has evidently been long held in India, where men like Vyāsatīrtha were considered ideal recipients of royal wealth and political power precisely because they were above exploiting them. Thus, exploring the sociopolitical role and economic power of a *maṭhādhipati* under Vijayanagara rule does not require arguing that the court cynically used religion to further its interests; rather, such study can show how the court respected religion's social value and how that respect influenced political decisions.

Furthermore, the extensive sixteenth-century biographical literature focusing on sectarian leaders like Vyāsatīrtha offers its own theories as to why these men were of value to the state. A key theme of the biographies of Vyāsatīrtha is that Vyāsatīrtha interacts with the political realm somewhat reluctantly out of magnanimous concern for its dharmic well-being. By considering this literature in some detail, chapter 2 showcases indigenous sixteenth-century perspectives on the relationship between religion and politics. The proliferation of biographies of sectarian leaders in the sixteenth century indicates that the lives of these figures had become increasingly important, not just to royal courts but to sectarian identities. Part of the goal of this book is to understand more fully which factors in the sixteenth century contributed to this new importance.

A compelling counterargument to criticism of the biographical treatment of a figure like Vyāsatīrtha is that contemporary understandings of precolonial India tend to dismiss the role of individual human agency. This leaves us with a very static account of Indian history that sustains the Orientalist legacy. Colonial-era historians cited Indian culture's lack of linear progress and social dynamism as evidence of its inferiority and as partial justification for "enlightened" colonial rule.[41] A great deal of literature on precolonial India (particularly precolonial Indian religion) has failed to examine the role of individual agents operating in specific circumstances marked by historical contingency. This has resulted in a presentation of Indian culture and religion as monolithic; static; beholden to doctrinal imperatives; and allowing for almost no social, intellectual, or economic mobility. As Eaton has demonstrated in his book *A Social History of the Deccan (1300–1761): Eight Indian Lives,* biographical studies of precolonial Indian agents can recover the fluidity, dynamism, change, diversity, and mobility that have been constitutive features of Indian society for centuries.

Following Eaton's approach, I have narrowed my focus to a relatively short period of time and a few main protagonists while also consulting a wide variety of sources from contemporaneous social contexts. By being attentive to the different types of institutional discourse in the extant sources, I hope to create a dynamic portrait of the early sixteenth-century Vijayanagara society in which Vyāsatīrtha lived and worked. Such a portrait would allow for inherited conceptual and structural frameworks, historical contingency, and individual initiative. I show that interactions both among *maṭhādhipati*s and between them and Vijayanagara kings were not based purely on age-old entitlements or static conceptions of dharma. Rather, the nature of royal and religious interactions depended upon a variety of factors that included personal religious sentiment and respect for established institutions, as well as practical considerations such as warfare, resource management, and strategic innovations in statecraft. The plethora of sources on Vyāsatīrtha and his environment have opened up new possibilities for understanding not just Vyāsatīrtha's specific life but the lives and interactions of a variety of social groups and agents. They also reveal the underlying patterns of sixteenth-century South Indian society and the significant changes that were taking place.

In addition to this introductory chapter, this book is divided into four main chapters and a conclusion. Chapter 2, entitled "Royal and Religious Authority in Sixteenth-Century Vijayanagara: A *Maṭhādhipati* at Kṛṣṇadevarāya's Court," explores the relationship between Vyāsatīrtha and the royal court as documented in a variety of sources. These include the Mādhva biographical tradition, the inscriptional records documenting material and honorific exchanges between Vyāsatīrtha and various agents, the monumental and topographical remains of several structures associated with Vyāsatīrtha, and, finally, Emperor Kṛṣṇadevarāya's own writings on statecraft. These sources demonstrate that, while kings and sectarian leaders did enjoy a mutually beneficial relationship, there were boundaries between courtly and monastic life. Precisely because these boundaries delimited the relative power of royal and religious leaders, they were occasionally subject to contestation.

Chapter 3, "Sectarian Rivalries at an Ecumenical Court: Vyāsatīrtha, Advaita Vedānta, and the Smārta Brahmins," links Vyāsatīrtha's role as an institutional administrator of *maṭhas* to his intellectual activities with respect to other Vedānta sects. In particular, it examines how Vyāsatīrtha's critique of Advaita Vedānta's doctrine of *jīvanmukti,* or liberation from *saṃsāra* (the cycle of rebirth) while still embodied, reflects Vyāsatīrtha's challenge to Smārta Brahmin dominance at court. The doctrine of *jīvanmukti* implied that some ascetic Smārta leaders had achieved a special spiritual state granting them access to otherwise unknowable truths. Vyāsatīrtha's claim that this traditionally Advaita concept made more sense in his own system of thought could be read as an attempt to undercut the authority of the Advaitin Smārta gurus at court and make a bid for that authority for Mādhva teachers.

In addition to including a detailed discussion of Vyāsatīrtha's philosophical arguments against *jīvanmukti* in Advaita, this chapter considers the historical arc of the Smārtas' relationship with the Vijayanagara court by examining the inscriptional, monumental, and literary records that document it. In particular, it considers the claim, widely accepted in Vijayanagara studies, that Rāmacandra Bhāratī, Vyāsatīrtha's exact contemporary as the head of the Sringeri Smārta *maṭha*, fabricated inscriptions attesting to the Sringeri *maṭha*'s role in the empire's founding. I argue that this act may be interpreted as a response to a marked shift in patronage away from Smārta-dominated Śaiva institutions and toward Mādhva and Śrīvaiṣṇava ones during Vyāsatīrtha's lifetime. It also reflects an increasing historical consciousness, wherein historical claims of courtly prominence were understood to benefit sectarian communities.

Chapter 4, entitled "Allies or Rivals? Vyāsatīrtha's Material, Social, and Ritual Interactions with the Śrīvaiṣṇavas," focuses on Vyāsatīrtha's interactions with his intellectual rivals, the Śrīvaiṣṇavas, at three prominent sites of Vijayanagara patronage: the capital itself, especially the Viṭṭhala and Kṛṣṇa temples there; the Varadarāja temple in Kanchipuram; and the ritually related Śrī Veṅkaṭeśvara and Govindarājasvāmi temples in Tirupati-Tirumala. The inscriptional and monumental records at these sites document Vyāsatīrtha's efforts to forge a mutually beneficial alliance with the Śrīvaiṣṇavas even as he used this alliance to import distinctive features of Mādhva Brahminism into new regions. These records also indicate that the Vijayanagara court actively supported this alliance but also, on occasion, stirred up competition between these two communities. In some instances, the inscriptions describe royal gifts made to Vyāsatīrtha at Śrīvaiṣṇava-dominated temples as punishment for infractions on the part of temple leadership. In other instances, the court used its donations to encourage the ritual collaboration of the two sects at these large temple complexes. In this way, the court strove to cultivate a "big tent" Vaiṣṇavism that would appeal to a variety of regional, linguistic, and devotional publics.

The fifth chapter, "The Social Life of Vedānta Philosophy: Vyāsatīrtha's Polemics against Viśiṣṭādvaita Vedānta," considers Vyāsatīrtha's polemics against Viśiṣṭādvaita Vedānta, the system of thought advocated by the Śrīvaiṣṇavas. It focuses on the final section of the *Nyāyāmṛta*, entitled "The Defense of a Hierarchical Ordering of Brahmā and Other Souls in the State of *Mokṣa*." In this section, Vyāsatīrtha argues against Viśiṣṭādvaita's doctrine of *paramasāmya* or parity of souls in the state of liberation (*mokṣa*) from *saṃsāra*; in contrast to this parity,

Vyāsatīrtha advocates for eternal spiritual hierarchies among souls in the liberated state. This latter doctrine was one of Mādhva Vedānta's most controversial. I argue that Vyāsatīrtha's defense of it exhibits an interesting reconstruction of its basic premises that reflects his efforts to reach his contemporary audiences. In some important ways, Vyāsatīrtha's arguments in this section reflect his ongoing collaboration with the Śrīvaiṣṇavas at royally patronized temples. Vyāsatīrtha consistently maintains that Viśiṣṭādvaita premises are conducive to Dvaita conclusions. He thereby demonstrates what the two sects have in common, even as he argues for the superiority of Dvaita. Yet there is also evidence in this section of Vyāsatīrtha holding the line against too much blurring of sectarian boundaries. Indeed, while Vyāsatīrtha may have been willing to collaborate with Śrīvaiṣṇavas, particularly those of the northern and more Sanskrit-oriented faction, he also makes the case for Dvaita's unique doctrinal correctness. Thus, while sociopolitical realities influenced the articulation of philosophical doctrines, these doctrines also set limits on incursions of the political into the religious sphere. Doctrinal differences demarcated a boundary between sects even when those sects collaborated ritually at temples and shared in royal wealth.

The book's concluding chapter, "Hindu, Ecumenical, Sectarian: Religion and the Vijayanagara Court," highlights key features of our exploration of Vyāsatīrtha's life and work and analyzes what they tell us about the links between religion, society, politics, and economy under sixteenth-century Vijayanagara rule. It also addresses in a more sustained way those themes, such as the relationships between elite and popular religious formations and between religious doctrine and practice, that received somewhat fragmentary treatment in the individual chapters. But the conclusion primarily explores the implications of taking a more dynamic view of India's precolonial religious history by focusing on individual agents. It restates the advantages of attempting to locate philosophical and religious practitioners in their social and historical environments, not merely to discern how they were affected by those environments but also how they acted upon them. It also reemphasizes that a historically informed reading of Vyāsatīrtha's polemics actually highlights the precise contours of his arguments. Finally, while it is perhaps a cliché to speak of Hinduism as a religious system of unity-in-diversity, studying Vijayanagara patronage practices delineates more precisely the social and historical mechanisms by which one version of such unity-in-diversity emerged. Understanding this version as a social and historic phenomenon both clarifies and problematizes scholars' inherited vocabulary on religion under Vijayanagara rule, especially the terms *Hindu, ecumenical,* and *sectarian.*

# 2

# Royal and Religious Authority in Sixteenth-Century Vijayanagara

## *A* Maṭhādhipati *at Kṛṣṇadevarāya's Court*

As an institutional leader in charge of a network of sectarian monasteries that was significantly expanded by Emperor Kṛṣṇadevarāya's patronage, Vyāsatīrtha was more than just a sectarian polemicist; he was an agent of the Vijayanagara state and a powerful regional authority. Not only did Vyāsatīrtha display his intellectual acumen in oral and literary Sanskrit debates, he also forged productive relationships with a variety of social groups and, in doing so, expanded the empire's economic and social networks. The inscriptional records indicate that Vyāsatīrtha installed icons and covered pavilions (*maṇḍapas*) at prominent Vaiṣṇava shrines, patronized large-scale public works such as irrigation projects in strategically significant locations, and collaborated with other sectarian communities at large temple complexes so as to articulate a big tent Vaiṣṇavism that was favored by the court. In these and other ways, Vyāsatīrtha spread Mādhva Brahminism's distinctive doctrines, iconography, and rituals into new territories while also implementing key features of the royal court's agenda.

Thus, studying Vyāsatīrtha's role as a *maṭhādhipati* or head of a monastic institutional network illuminates key connections between Brahmin intellectual and religious activity and various social and political formations of early sixteenth-century South India. This chapter explores some of these connections by focusing on the relationship between Vyāsatīrtha and the royal court as documented in the following four sets of sources: First, the Mādhva biographical tradition that has produced three known accounts of Vyāsatīrtha's life, one of which seems to be contemporary with the sectarian leader; second, fifteen inscriptional records that document a significant set of material and honorific exchanges between the Vijayanagara court, especially that of Kṛṣṇadevarāya and Vyāsatīrtha; third, the monumental and topographic remains of several religious structures and irrigation projects that Vyāsatīrtha had constructed, often using resources given to him by Kṛṣṇadevarāya, throughout the empire; and, finally, Kṛṣṇadevarāya's own writings on the role of religious leaders in his statecraft as presented in his Telugu *mahākāvya* or "great poem," the *Āmuktamālyada*.

While many of these sources documenting the relationship between Vyāsatīrtha and Vijayanagara royals have not been studied in any detail, their content has nevertheless influenced modern scholarly conceptions of the role of religious leaders at the Vijayanagara court. For instance, the traditional biographies' claim that Vyāsatīrtha was Kṛṣṇadevarāya's *kuladevatā* or "family deity" has been picked up by several scholars. B. N. K. Sharma, historian of the Mādhva school, identifies Vyāsatīrtha as Kṛṣṇadevarāya's *rājaguru* or personal spiritual guide.[1] Anila Verghese, who rejects the idea that Vyāsatīrtha had such an official advisory role, describes Vyāsatīrtha in more symbolic terms as the empire's "guardian saint."[2] Writing more extensively on the role of sectarian heads at the Vijayanagara court, Burton Stein refers to Vyāsatīrtha as Kṛṣṇadevarāya's "preceptor."[3] Somewhat in contrast to Sharma, who seems to view Vyāsatīrtha's position as distinctive, Stein takes Vyāsatīrtha's status to be representative of the prominence enjoyed by *maṭhādhipati*s (literally, "leaders of monasteries") in Vijayanagara times:

> The *mathadipati* toured the areas where his followers lived, and his progress was conducted in the manner of a king, on elephants, with the royal paraphernalia of umbrellas and drummers, and with large retinues. And like the Vijayanagara [kings], these heads sent their agents to where their followers lived to advise them in matters spiritual and secular, to collect funds for the order, sometimes to initiate new members, to arbitrate disputes among them, and to preach the doctrines of the sect.[4]

Stein elsewhere maintains that the offices of the king and the *maṭhādhipati* were nearly identical:

> These religious leaders may thus be viewed as personages whose religious roles conferred command over substantial and redistributable resources; considering the evidence of . . . 16th century Tirupati, they were not very different from the great political notables of the time.[5]

Thus, the leaders of *maṭha*s figure prominently in the scholarship on the sixteenth-century Vijayanagara court. However, the precise nature, not only of their role, but that of the institutions they headed merits further analysis. In particular, the claim that kings and *maṭhādhipati*s enjoyed a similar status, had similar accoutrements, and played similar roles in South Indian society needs to be reassessed.[6] While many of the relevant sources support such a view, they also indicate that courts and monasteries were very different types of institutions and that the men who ran such institutions lived in many ways qualitatively different lives.

Those *maṭhas* most heavily patronized by the Vijayanagara court were generally headed by Brahmin ascetics who had renounced worldly trappings, such as families and personal wealth, in the pursuit of special knowledge linked to particular nonworldly goals, including liberation (*mokṣa*) from the cycle of rebirth (*saṃsāra*).[7] Such ascetics were also guardians of complex intellectual and ritual traditions that required intensive study and practice. Typically, *maṭhas* also functioned as schools and libraries, attesting to the centrality of education to their existence. They were also constituted in this period by specific sectarian identities.[8] The doctrines and customs associated with these identities were passed down from guru to student, after the latter had been properly initiated into the order. Thus, a *maṭhādhipati* like Vyāsatīrtha was an institutional administrator, a religious leader, and an intellectual. He performed the role of teacher to his students and was an author and public polemicist against other sectarian groups. That Vyāsatīrtha was highly effective in performing all of these roles will be demonstrated throughout this book.

Meanwhile, kings had to marry and sire sons, send troops into war, manage the economy, quell rebellion, integrate far-flung regions of the empire, and engage in diplomacy with other states both within and beyond the subcontinent. In Kṛṣṇadevarāya's case, he expanded the already large Vijayanagara Empire northward through a series of spectacular military conquests that were almost unceasing between the years of 1509 and 1523.[9] He then had to manage this culturally, environmentally, and linguistically diverse kingdom, which found itself situated in an increasingly large and complex world.[10] That Kṛṣṇadevarāya was highly effective in doing so is evident in his reign's association with an unprecedented period of artistic, cultural, and intellectual efflorescence.

All this is to say that kings and *maṭhādhipati*s had distinct domains and performed different functions in early sixteenth-century Vijayanagara society. Yet, just as it is indisputable that Kṛṣṇadevarāya and Vyāsatīrtha had much interaction, there is no doubt that the court and the monastery were linked in a variety of critically important ways. Using sources from both the courtly and monastic contexts, this chapter aims to present a more detailed description of the various links between Kṛṣṇadevarāya and Vyāsatīrtha than has previously been available, so as to enrich our understanding of the *maṭhādhipati*'s role in early sixteenth-century Vijayanagara. By examining the inscriptional and monumental records alongside the biographical traditions surrounding Vyāsatīrtha, as well as Kṛṣṇadevarāya's own writings on statecraft, I aim to expose the variety of conceptions of royal and religious authority articulated in the relevant sources. Studying these sources reveals a general consensus that Hindu sectarian leaders played an important role at the sixteenth-century Vijayanagara court. However, the sources define that importance in different ways.

Taken together, the sources present a picture of mutual dependence between royal and religious authorities, with royals relying on *maṭhādhipati*s to enact certain features of their socioeconomic agenda and *maṭhādhipati*s benefiting from royal patronage that promoted their respective sects' social positions. However, precisely because of that mutual dependence, there is also evidence of tension between these two spheres. The inscriptional records indicate that Kṛṣṇadevarāya kept his religious options open and perhaps even used his patronage to manipulate relationships between the leaders of different Hindu communities. Furthermore, he expresses some resentment toward these *maṭhādhipati*s in his *Āmuktamālyada*, perhaps because their prestige in a given location could upstage his own. Meanwhile, the biographical tradition surrounding Vyāsatīrtha portrays Vijayanagara kings as utterly dependent on this sectarian leader for their successful rule, with religious concerns and motivations consistently trumping political ones in depictions of royal behavior. Thus, this chapter will show that, while kings and *maṭhādhipati*s did enjoy a mutually beneficial relationship and shared certain roles and honors in early sixteenth-century South Indian society, there were boundaries between courtly and monastic life. Precisely because these boundaries delimited the relative power of royal and religious leaders, they were frequently renegotiated.

## COURT AND *MAṬHA* IN TRADITIONAL BIOGRAPHIES OF VYĀSATĪRTHA

The notion that Vyāsatīrtha was Kṛṣṇadevarāya's personal guru has an old history, dating perhaps to Vyāsatīrtha's own lifetime. The poet Somanātha's biography of Vyāsatīrtha, the *Vyāsayogicarita*,[11] portrays Kṛṣṇadevarāya as having worshipped Vyāsatīrtha as though he were his *kuladevatā* or "family deity."[12] This text, of which we have three printed editions, is considered by its editors to be contemporary with Vyāsatīrtha, a perspective that has influenced later scholarship on this sectarian leader.[13] The editors base this understanding on four internal features of the text, the first of which is that the text itself makes this claim. In the concluding chapter, the author, Somanātha, has his finished product read aloud to Vyāsatīrtha and gains the sectarian leader's approval.[14] Second, the text is relatively devoid of miraculous occurrences in its presentation of Vyāsatīrtha's life story.[15] Third, the text contains many references to specific historical events and people that can be corroborated by other sources. Finally, the text does not mention Vyāsatīrtha's death but culminates with him continuing to advise Kṛṣṇadevarāya's successor, Acyutarāya, after the former's demise.[16] While the text's exact date cannot be firmly established, it does seem to be the oldest biography we have of Vyāsatīrtha and to provide a template for later versions of his life story.

By choosing to write a *carita* about Vyāsatīrtha, Somanātha may have been participating in what V. N. Rao, David Shulman, and Sanjay Subrahmanyam have identified as a newly emergent historical consciousness in sixteenth-century South India that produced many such texts, particularly in regional languages.[17] Such consciousness was directly indebted to courtly culture as it was primarily the *karaṇam*s or court (and, by extension, temple or village) record keepers who were responsible for this new literary production. These texts, according to Rao, Shulman, and Subrahmanyam, aimed to be more factual and less idealistic, placing a greater emphasis on causal links between events. They often favored prose over poetry or were composed in the style of a *campū*, which mixed the two literary forms together. Indeed, the *Vyāsayogicarita* is written in this *campū* form.

As Rao, Shulman, and Subrahmanyam also point out, the term *caritra* or *carita* originally meant "biography," even if it later came to have historiographic connotations.[18] Somanātha presents his work as contemporary with Vyāsatīrtha by showing the sectarian leader himself approving it, which indicates that he is writing a biography, not a history of an earlier period, as many *caritra* authors were attempting to do. Furthermore, Somanātha writes in Sanskrit and, as we shall see, privileges a religious sensibility throughout the text. At the same time, he is clearly concerned with establishing the veracity of his account. Thus, his *carita* seems to fall somewhere between the term's earlier meanings and its sixteenth-century connotations.

The *Vyāsayogicarita* that Somanātha produces is different in many ways from the better known type of biography for religious leaders, the *digvijaya* or "conquest of all directions."[19] In such biographies of religious leaders, the protagonist, who is typically a world renouncer, embarks on a tour in all directions of India and debates with proponents of rival systems of thought. His "conquest" of all directions is thus a religious and philosophical one, but it has worldly implications since such victories often enable him to establish communities of converts and related institutions throughout the subcontinent. Somanātha's decision not to write in this vein may be significant, given that the *digvijaya* genre seems to have been gaining in popularity as the typical life narrative for religious leaders in this period.[20] For example, the son of a direct disciple of Madhva, founder of Vyāsatīrtha's system of thought, composed the *Sumadhvavijaya* sometime in the fourteenth century, roughly coincident with the Vijayanagara Empire's founding.[21] There is also an extensive collection of *digvijaya*s pertaining to Śaṅkara, (c. eighth century), the South Indian nondualist Vedānta philosopher, whose system of thought is portrayed throughout the *Sumadhvavijaya* as Madhva's philosophical nemesis. These Śaṅkara *vijaya*s are notoriously difficult to date, but they seem to have spanned the fourteenth to nineteenth centuries;[22] many were apparently composed in South India, although Śaṅkara figures in narratives from as far north as Nepal.[23] On the basis of this time frame and regional emphasis, as well as on some of the shared features of these Śaṅkara *vijaya*s, it is likely that many of them were based on legends that would have been in circulation during the period of

Vijayanagara rule. Indeed, the two texts, Anantānandagiri's *Śaṅkaravijaya* and Cidvilāsa's *Śaṅkaravijayavilāsa,* that Bader (2000) and Clark (2006), respectively, identify as the oldest seem to date from the sixteenth century. Moreover, both texts explicitly attribute the founding of the Advaita *maṭha* at Śṛṅgeri, which features prominently in both legendary and inscriptional records of the Vijayanagara Empire, to Śaṅkara.[24] Other Śaṅkara *digvijayas* mention his association with other socially and historically prominent *maṭhas* in South India. Indeed, the problem of dating these texts with any precision is related in part to competing claims about their antiquity that have been made by those monastic institutions that consider Śaṅkara to be their founder.[25] Yet while these *digvijayas* often differ in their specifics, with the significance of one Śaṅkara *maṭha* privileged over another, they share a concern common to all *digvijaya* literature: that of historicizing their sectarian institutions through biographical accounts of their founder as a world conqueror.

These *digvijaya* texts are notable not only because they are quite combative regarding rival systems of thought (or even rival *maṭhas* advocating the same system) but also because they often give a miraculous tinge to the protagonist's life story.[26] For these reasons, modern scholars often dismiss these texts as sectarian myths or as hagiographies with little historical value. Yet, the texts' very emphasis on all-India conquest to establish their sect's doctrinal and institutional preeminence does tell us something about the historical situation of the texts' authors. Christian Lee Novetzke's 2007 study of various genres of South Asian hagiography provides a helpful overview of recent scholarship on this material that seeks to address the question of hagiography's historical veracity.[27] Novetzke points out that hagiographic literature encompasses within it both theographic, or religiously didactic elements that are "transhistorical," and historiographic elements that seek to establish facts about a given religious community's history. He advocates reading these elements as collaborative rather than competitive features of the genre.[28] Such a reading, he suggests, would enable scholars to understand not only a given religious community's actual history but also how that community has invested its history with sacred meaning.

Taking a slightly different approach to this material, William Sax charts the history of the *digvijaya* genre and argues that it originated in the period of the composition of the Hindu epics as a life narrative for kings. It was only later, Sax argues, in about the thirteenth century, that the *digvijaya* narrative came to be applied to religious leaders, particularly those world-renouncers who were credited with founding new religious movements and institutions. In Sax's view, in the epics, the "political" power enacted by a king's *digvijaya* was always linked to "religious" ideas about establishing a specific notion of dharma within certain conquered territories. By the same token, the religious power enacted by a renunciant's *digvijaya* exhibited clear sectarian striving for sociopolitical prominence. Thus, according to Sax, the *digvijaya* genre always documented important links between religious and philosophical belief systems, on the one hand, and the social and political order, on the other.[29]

Sax's historical overview also indicates that the thirteenth to sixteenth centuries witnessed a proliferation of such narratives among different Hindu sectarian communities. His explanation for this is that Hindu kings had had to cede their power to Muslim rulers, leaving religious leaders as the only vestiges of Hindu authority:

> The emphasis of the *digvijaya* had changed: now it was not so much an imperial conquest by kings as a dharmic conquest by renouncers.
>
> This should come as no surprise. After all, much of India was by now occupied by Muslim rulers. The age of world-conquering Hindu kings was long gone and Hindu leaders were now renouncers, not kings.[30]

Sax's research focuses on North India, where the political situation was much as he describes it. However, this explanation does not fit South India, where many (if not most) *digvijaya* texts were composed. Rather, in South India during this period, narratives of strong sectarian leadership, typified by these *vijaya* texts, likely resonated with Hindu courts because this genre had originated as an archetypal narrative for victorious kings. In the context of the Vijayanagara Empire, it would seem that sects attempted to use convincing *digvijaya* narratives, in which their leader disposes of rival systems of thought, to edge out their competitors for courtly attention. Large polities like Vijayanagara often exercised their authority by exploiting the social capital of locally authoritative institutions and networks. Such authority could be documented—and amplified—in sectarian hagiographic histories. Thus, the growing popularity of the *digvijaya* genre during the period of Vijayanagara rule in South India was likely due to the empire's increasingly complex interactions with Hindu sectarian institutions. The proliferation of the *digvijaya* narrative and the movement of this genre away from the court and into the sectarian monastery reflect the increasing interdependence of these two spaces under Vijayanagara rule.

In fact, there is a later biography of Vyāsatīrtha, called the *Vyāsa Vijaya,* which is more in the *digvijaya* vein than the *Vyāsayogicarita.*[31] By presenting Vyāsatīrtha as going on a long pilgrimage throughout the subcontinent and successfully debating with various individuals he meets, this text presents Vyāsatīrtha as conquering all directions.[32] The *Vyāsayogicarita's* very different manner of presentation may be evidence that Somanātha himself was not a member of the Mādhva school. The *Vyāsa Vijaya* is attributed to Śrīnivāsatīrtha, who was a direct disciple of Vyāsatīrtha, but Venkoba Rao disputes the veracity of this claim and makes plausible arguments for why the *Vyāsa Vijaya* must be a later text.[33] Because of the text's emphasis on sectarian conquest, however, he does take it for granted that the *Vyāsa Vijaya* was composed by a member of the Mādhva community. In contrast, both Venkoba Rao and B.N.K. Sharma assert that the author of the *Vyāsayogicarita,*

Somanātha, was a Smārta Brahmin. Furthermore, each argues that this confirms the *Vyāsayogicarita*'s historical accuracy by ridding it of sectarian bias.[34]

Certainly, while there is overlap between the manner in which events are portrayed in the *Vyāsa Vijaya* and the *Vyāsayogicarita*, the version in the *Vyāsa Vijaya* often seems embellished or is more miraculous in tone.[35] It may also be significant that the *Vyāsa Vijaya*'s presentation seems to have had greater influence on contemporary Mādhva understandings of Vyāsatīrtha. The third biography known to exist, a brief set of verses encapsulating the major events of Vyāsatīrtha's life composed in the early twentieth century by Śrī Vidyāratnākara, then head of the Vyāsatīrtha *maṭha*,[36] recapitulates the sectarian leader's life largely in terms of the *Vyāsa Vijaya*'s presentation. Events like the *kuhuyoga,* or a brief inauspicious period of time in which Vyāsatīrtha ascended to Kṛṣṇadevarāya's throne in order to protect the king from harm, or Vyāsatīrtha's installation of 732 icons of the Hindu deity Hanumān throughout the empire are often related by twenty-first-century Mādhvas when recounting Vyāsatīrtha's significance.[37] Neither event is mentioned in the *Vyāsayogicarita.*

Yet while the *Vyāsa Vijaya* and the *Vyāsayogicarita* thereby seem to belong to different literary genres and possibly reflect distinctive insider and outsider perspectives, neither text is without verifiable facts nor free of generic conventions. Furthermore, it is not entirely clear that the *Vyāsayogicarita* is without sectarian bias, regardless of the author's religious affiliation.[38] While Vyāsatīrtha's specific sectarian identity as a Mādhva is arguably downplayed in the text and while he reigns at court as a kind of ecumenical emblem of Hindu piety,[39] the text nevertheless extols Vyāsatīrtha's superiority over other *saṃnyāsin*s and sectarian leaders. Indeed, by presenting Vyāsatīrtha as Kṛṣṇadevarāya's *kuladevatā,* or family deity, the text at once places Vyāsatīrtha beyond the limits of circumscribed worldly identities and highlights the Mādhva sect's particular worldly importance.

Furthermore, while the *Vyāsayogicarita* exhibits a self-conscious attention to veracity and refers to many events that can be corroborated by other records, the text can also be formulaic in its presentation of Vyāsatīrtha's life story.[40] Vyāsatīrtha is conceived by long-barren parents after the intervention of Brahmaṇyatīrtha, the Mādhva ascetic who would become Vyāsatīrtha's initiator into the sect and whom Vyāsatīrtha acknowledges as one of his teachers in the colophons of all of his writings. Brahmaṇyatīrtha has Vyāsatīrtha's parents consume a three-part fire offering (*havis*) so that they might produce three children, the last of whom is Vyāsatīrtha.[41] According to the text, Vyāsatīrtha is born "Yatirāja," literally "King of Ascetics" in the village of Bannur, which is called "Vahnipura" in the text.[42] (See map 3 for its location.)

Yatirāja's/Vyāsatīrtha's childhood in his natal village consists of the typical Brahmin male upbringing. At age seven, he is sent to the *gurukula* to study sacred rituals and related texts with the village's elder males. At age eleven, he returns to

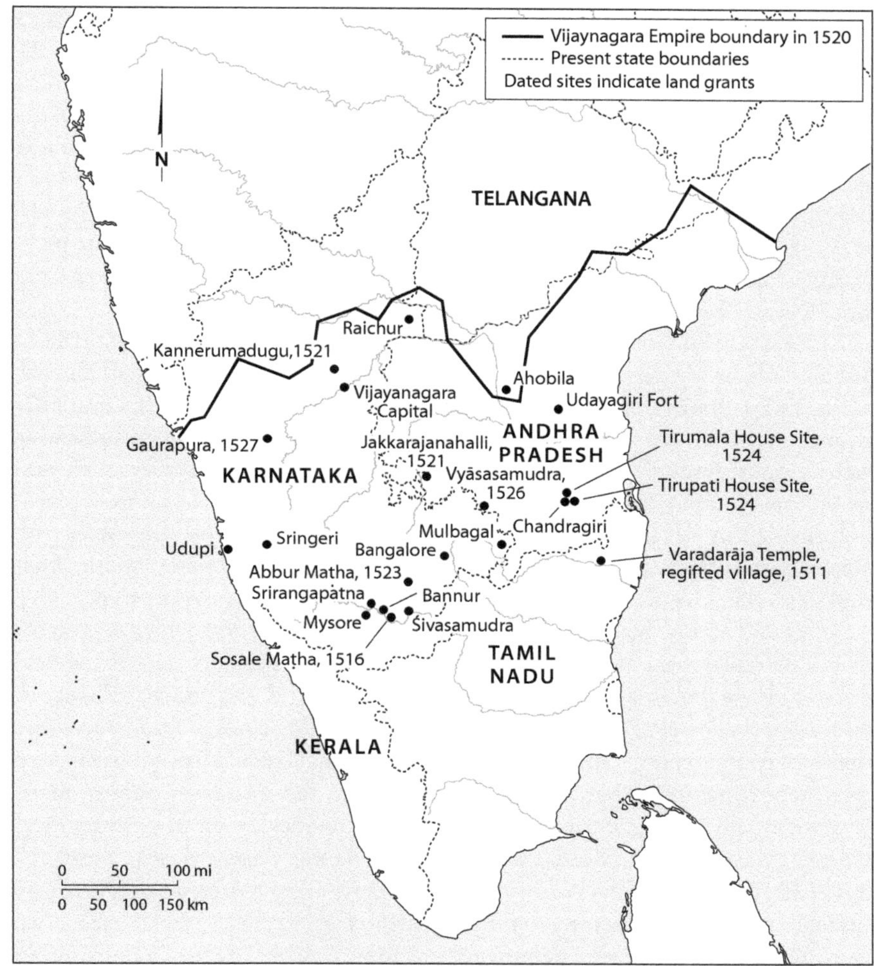



MAP 3. Land grants made by Kṛṣṇadevarāya to Vyāsatīrtha.

his parents' home for further study; after an unspecified time has elapsed, he is sent for by Brahmaṇyatīrtha, the ascetic who brought about Vyāsatīrtha's conception and who wishes to initiate Yatirāja into the Mādhva order. The text does not say so explicitly, but it is likely that Brahmaṇyatīrtha was living at Abbur, located near the place where an inscriptional record tells us Vyāsatīrtha later installed thirty-two students, on land given to him by Kṛṣṇadevarāya, in honor of his late teacher whose tomb is located there (see map 3).[43] The boy's parents bravely surrender their child to his new life, which will be quite different from his old one and in which they will have no role.[44] While the reluctance of families to give their sons over to an ascetic life is a stock (and understandable) feature of South Asian religious biographies,[45] it is also historically informative. The poignancy with which this moment is depicted suggests that entering a monastic order was a radical life change and not merely a matter of pursuing further religious education. The text indicates that Yatirāja himself was reluctant to make this radical change and ran away from Brahmaṇyatīrtha's hermitage. However, after Viṣṇu and Lakṣmī appear to him in a dream, he returns of his own volition to take up the ascetic path. Brahmaṇyatīrtha initiates Yatirāja as a *saṃnyāsin* of the Mādhva order and renames him "Vyāsa" (the "tīrtha" being an appended honorific title.)[46]

Chapter 4 of the text indicates that, after studying with Brahmaṇyatīrtha in Abbur for a brief time, Vyāsatīrtha goes on a pilgrimage.[47] In marked contrast to the *Vyāsa Vijaya*'s presentation, this pilgrimage is dispensed with summarily in one sentence.[48] No specific places are mentioned and only general indicators such as "dense forests," "tall cloud-topped mountains," "cities with palaces, art, and music," and "*maṭha*s wherein many impressive displays of asceticism took place" are provided. Apart from its brief allusion to a long voyage, the *Vyāsayogicarita* situates Vyāsatīrtha's life exclusively in the Deccan Plateau and points south, often in places where the inscriptional and monumental records also locate him.

At the end of this voyage, Vyāsatīrtha arrives at Kanchipuram, which is presented as a pluralistic seat of learning.[49] Here, Vyāsatīrtha reportedly stays for several years, studying the six systems of Hindu thought and exhibiting much brilliance in learning and debate.[50] He is so brilliant at the latter that he poses a threat to some intellectual opponents. One such opponent poisons Vyāsatīrtha, who survives because he learns of an antidote in a dream.[51] Here, the *Vyāsayogicarita* overlaps somewhat with the *digvijaya* tradition, wherein conquest, even in philosophical debate, involves some risk of physical harm. While the *Vyāsayogicarita*'s miraculous claim that Vyāsatīrtha received vital assistance from a dream might damage the text's credibility in some scholars' eyes, the earliest inscriptional record we have referring to Vyāsatīrtha definitely dates from 1511 and involves a donation to the Varadarāja Temple at Kanchi. This seems to substantiate Vyāsatīrtha's presence in that city early in his life.[52]

After his stint in Kanchi's religiously and philosophically pluralistic environment, Vyāsatīrtha goes to Mulbagal, then a major center of Mādhva learning. There, he studies with Lakṣmīnārāyaṇa Yogi,[53] also known as Śrīpādarāja, who, in addition to being renowned for his knowledge of Madhva's teachings, is also famous for having authored popular Vaiṣṇava devotional songs in Kannada. After several years of studying under Śrīpādarāja, whom he also acknowledges to have been one of his teachers in all of his writings, Vyāsatīrtha, according to the *Vyāsayogicarita*, goes to the court of Sāḷuva Narasiṃha I.[54] This Vijayanagara emperor was then ruling from the empire's erstwhile capital at Chandragiri, about sixteen kilometers southwest of the major Vaiṣṇava religious complex at Tirupati-Tirumala (see map 3).

At this point in the *Vyāsayogicarita*'s narrative, a dominant theme takes over: that of Vyāsatīrtha's close relationship, not just with Kṛṣṇadevarāya, but with a series of Vijayanagara emperors beginning with Sāḷuva Narasiṃha I (r. 1485–91) and ending with Acyutarāya (r. 1529–42), during whose reign Vyāsatīrtha's own life ended (1539). According to Somanātha's text, Vyāsatīrtha was encouraged by his second great teacher, Śrīpādarāja, to go to Sāḷuva Narasiṃha's court at Chandragiri precisely to serve as the king's spiritual guide and to help establish dharma throughout his reign. The text repeatedly invokes epic metaphors to justify such a relationship between ascetic Brahmin advisors and worldly royal leaders.[55] Somanātha reports Śrīpādarāja's speech to Vyāsatīrtha as follows:

> Thus, you are like the sun dutifully awakening the elephant of Vedic comportment which was like a lotus flower that had gone to sleep for too long a time at the close of day, deluded by the false enjoyments offered by unrighteous people. Following the rule that a king ought to be a bridge to all righteousness, it becomes your duty to stay always [near a king]. Those *yogis* of olden times, such as Dattātreya and others, even though they were indifferent [to the affairs of the world], for the sake of benefitting that very world, adorned the courts of kings.[56]

This idea that the sectarian leader could offer worldly guidance to the king, despite his own detachment from worldly affairs, is a central theme of the text. The text consistently underscores Vyāsatīrtha's worldly detachment by referring to him in terms that emphasize his asceticism. Indeed, Somanātha does not generally refer to him as "Vyāsatīrtha" but as, for example, "Vyāsayogī" or "Vyāsa, adept at yoga"; "Vyāsabhikṣu" or "Vyāsa, the mendicant"; "Vyāsamuni" or "Vyāsa, the sage"; and, finally, "Vyāsatāpasamaṇi" or "Vyāsa, jewel of asceticism." At the same time, Somanātha explicitly mentions how each Vijayanagara royal consulted Vyāsatīrtha regularly for guidance. For instance, "[King Narasa, Kṛṣṇadevarāya's father], out of devotion [to Vyāsatīrtha] went on a daily basis to get secret instruction [from him] in *dharma*."[57] The text also states that "[Vyāsatīrtha] was waited upon daily by [Narasa's son and Kṛṣṇadevarāya's older brother, Vīra Narasiṃha] just as a lotus-filled lake is visited [daily] by geese."[58]

According to the text, the kings showed their appreciation of Vyāsatīrtha's advice by honoring him in various ways. For instance, after shifting the capital of the empire away from Chandragiri and back to its original home near Hampi, the founder of the Tuḷuva dynasty, King Narasa, went out to receive Vyāsatīrtha on the latter's arrival in the city. The king did so with all of his nobles and many troops present.[59] According to the text, King Narasa then provided Vyāsatīrtha with a lavish *maṭha* in which to live and seated Vyāsatīrtha on a *mudrāsana* or some kind of "seat" with royal insignia, that is, a throne.[60]

> After that, [Vyāsatīrtha] came to dwell, like the lord of beasts on a great mountain, in a *maṭha* that had been appointed by the king with a large lustrous staircase in-laid with crystals and jewels and that had a large golden altar and an arbor of coral-bearing trees arranged in rows like columns. There, that complete destroyer of darkness [Vyāsatīrtha] ruled as a *muni* over the earth, seated in a *mudrāsana*. He, [bright] like the reflection of the sun, slowly took his path at will, just as the heavenly river Ganga, after she had descended to earth [meandered] amidst the sandbanks. The king immediately worshipped [Vyāsatīrtha] just as the son of Pāṇḍu worshipped Bādarāyaṇa. [Vyāsa], having been honored with the first offering, transformed [that offering] himself into the blessed portion.[61]

Thus, the *maṭha* is likened to both a temple and a palace in the above passage, and its main occupant, Vyāsatīrtha, is likened to both a deity and a ruler, although the text specifies that he is, as a leader, a *muni* or sage. Images of Vyāsatīrtha being "enthroned" are picked up in the two later biographies, which speak of a period known as the *kuhuyoga*. For Kṛṣṇadevarāya to occupy the throne during this inauspicious astronomical formation was considered dangerous.[62] Despite his initial demurral, Vyāsatīrtha was prevailed upon to assume the throne during this period and, in that manner, protected the king from harm.[63] The *Vyāsayogicarita* makes no reference to this event, but the claim in chapter 5 that "the kings who put the sacred ash that was sanctified by his mere sight, on their forehead, showed extraordinary valour in battles and became victorious" is evidence of Vyāsatīrtha's protective capacity for kings.[64] Furthermore, in a possible display of *carita* realism, the *Vyāsayogicarita* alludes to Vyāsatīrtha's being honored by various foreign dignitaries or "prominent men sent by rulers from other continents,"[65] who are portrayed as giving the sage valuable offerings as one does to a deity in a *pūjā*. In addition to being a possible reference to the presence of Portuguese and other foreigners in the empire's capital, this description of foreigners' interaction with Vyāsatīrtha simultaneously highlights the religious basis of the *saṃnyāsin*'s authority at court and implicates him in Vijayanagara diplomacy.

One way in which the *Vyāsayogicarita* makes explicit connections between Brahmin intellectual and religious activity and political challenges facing the court is by linking Vijayanagara royals' veneration of Vyāsatīrtha to his acumen in philosophical debates. Such acumen certainly reflects Vyāsatīrtha's fame as a Dvaitin or "dualist" polemicist against other systems of Vedānta, a feature of his identity that I will discuss at length in subsequent chapters. Of the three major works Vyāsatīrtha authored, two are polemical critiques of both Advaita or nondualist Vedānta, advocated by the Smārta Brahmins, and Viśiṣṭādvaita or "qualified nondualist" Vedānta, advocated by the Śrīvaiṣṇavas.[66] These rival sectarian groups were not only active at the Vijayanagara court alongside Mādhva proponents of Dvaita Vedānta but were also established recipients of the court's patronage. Moreover, there is evidence to suggest that philosophical debates between these three sects actually reflect intersectarian competition for royal favor, as will be discussed in this book's later chapters.

However, the *Vyāsayogicarita* does not present philosophical debates as indicative of rivalry *within* the empire. Instead, the text emphasizes Vyāsatīrtha's defeat of Advaitin opponents emanating from outside the empire's territories, particularly the much contested region of Kalinga. Indeed, in the *Vyāsayogicarita*, the three major debates in which Vyāsatīrtha participates at successive courts of Vijayanagara royals are all initiated by members of the court of the Gajapatis, Kalinga's rulers, with whom Vijayanagara shared both a border and a long history of military conflict. The fact that the Udayagiri fort, often held by the Gajapatis, had been conquered, lost, and reconquered several times over the course of the Sāḷuva and Tuḷuva dynasties attests to the region's strategic, economic, and symbolic significance.[67] The inscriptional record indicates that Kṛṣṇadevarāya considered his recapture of this fort in 1514 to be one of his greatest military achievements.[68] For further evidence of the importance of this region to Kṛṣṇadevarāya's military strategy, see maps 1 and 2 in chapter 1, which show how much territory this monarch ultimately took from Kalinga's Gajapati rulers.

The *Vyāsayogicarita* echoes the political arena's emphasis on this region's significance but subsumes this worldly perspective into its religious idiom. Chapter 4 of the text states that, while he is still at the court of Sāḷuva Narasiṃha, Vyāsatīrtha participates in an eighteen-day debate with several opponents, among whom someone named "Bhaṭṭa" is said to be the most prominent. In the next chapter, this "Bhaṭṭa" is identified as Basava Bhaṭṭa, an Advaitin emissary from Kalinga. When Vyāsatīrtha is victorious, Sāḷuva Narasiṃha invites him to stay at his court for several years.[69] The implication of this seems to be that the king had a vested interest in the debate's outcome and perhaps himself became an advocate of Mādhvaism. Yet it also attests to sectarian communities' hopes that political capital could be gained by victory in such debates. Indeed, despite the prominence given to spiritual concerns over political ones in the *Vyāsayogicarita*, the text takes for granted the value to religious communities of strong ties to the court. It does this even as it consistently presents the court as benefiting much more from the presence of religious leaders like Vyāsatīrtha than the other way around.

The next debate, which takes place at the court of King Narasa, Sāḷuva Narasiṃha's successor who was both the founder of the Tuḷuva dynasty and Kṛṣṇadevarāya's father, is even more spectacular. In this case, a thirty-day debate takes place between Vyāsatīrtha and several opponents, who have been organized and led by the same Basava Bhaṭṭa from Kalinga. That the king has a vested interest in the debate's outcome is indicated by textual references, first to his nervousness and then to his relief and inspiration on witnessing Vyāsatīrtha's eloquence and easy win.[70] Shortly after this philosophical victory, the *Vyāsayogicarita* makes an explicit connection between royal victories in battle and religio-philosophical victories in debate. According to the text, there is an isomorphic relationship between Vyāsatīrtha's defeat of his philosophical opponents and King Narasa's defeat of more worldly enemies:

> The Lord of Yogis [i.e., Vyāsatīrtha], victorious against philosophical opponents, and the Lord of Men, [i.e., the king], victorious against enemies, were each so munificent that they were could have changed places, being mutually endowed with increasing compassion, taste, and devotion.[71]

The most significant debate between Vyāsatīrtha and an opponent from Kalinga occurs during Kṛṣṇadevarāya's reign, when the King of Kalinga himself sends an Advaita or monist Vedānta text for Vyāsatīrtha to respond to. Vyāsatīrtha immediately comments on it, pointing out its various logical flaws.[72] In response to this, Kṛṣṇadevarāya worships Vyāsatīrtha with a *ratnābhiṣeka* or a ritual bathing with jewels. This *ratnābhiṣeka,* which occurs in the last chapter of the six-chapter text, is considered by the Mādhva tradition to be one of the greatest gifts that Kṛṣṇadevarāya bestowed on Vyāsatīrtha. It is also the biography's climactic moment. The *ratnābhiṣeka* ties together many of the text's themes, including Vyāsatīrtha's status as the empire's *kuladevatā* and the intimate connection between Vyāsatīrtha's conduct and the successful functioning of the Vijayanagara court. The text's description of the *ratnābhiṣeka* is also important for how it references various political realities while subsuming them into a religious framework.[73]

Kṛṣṇadevarāya's feelings for Vyāsatīrtha are expressed in this section by his insistence that he do the *abhiṣeka* himself as an act of devotion to Vyāsatīrtha. The passage in which Kṛṣṇadevarāya invites Vyāsatīrtha to come have the *ratnābhiṣeka* performed by him again refers to Vyāsatīrtha as Kṛṣṇadevarāya's "kuladevatā" or "family deity."[74] The king performs the ritual himself at his palace, placing Vyāsatīrtha on a seat of gold "like a Rājahaṃsa on a lotus in Autumn."[75] The text presents Vyāsatīrtha as acquiescing to the whole notion of a bathing by jewels out of kindness to the king, who is his devotee, but emphasizes that Vyāsatīrtha does not agree out of any personal desire for material wealth: "Having thought for just a moment, [Vyāsatīrtha], with a heart full of compassion, out of affection for his devotee, came to the King's court from his ascetic abode."[76] Vyāsatīrtha's lack of interest in material wealth is further evidenced by what he does with the gems once the king has completed the ritual:

> Having had collected into a pile [those gems] that remained after diligently giving many away to Brahmins,[77] [Vyāsatīrtha] the most generous among *bhikṣu*s, distributed those collected [jewels] to [rulers] who had come from all directions, giving earrings to chiefs and warriors, upper-arm bracelets to those from Kerala, strings of pearls to the Persians, crowns to the Lāṭas,[78] rings to those from Kalinga, bracelets to those from Konkan, gold coins to the Turuṣkas (Turks), crest jewels to the Gauḍas,[79]

rubies to the Coḷas, jeweled girdles to the Pañcālas[80] as well as [other jewels] to rulers from other places.[81]

This redistribution of the lavish wealth bestowed on him by Kṛṣṇadevarāya is a vivid illustration of Vyāsatīrtha's personal indifference to material concerns and deepens the impression that Vyāsatīrtha's guidance of the Vijayanagara kings is purely spiritual. Indeed, by giving back what has been offered to him in such a magnanimous way, Vyāsatīrtha arguably takes on the role of a deity in a *pūjā*, transforming what was offered to him into *prasād* to be distributed among the devotees.

Yet, the very inclusiveness of Vyāsatīrtha's redistribution of the jewels also highlights Vyāsatīrtha's political function at court, even as it makes religiosity more prominent. While the list of recipients of these jewels is fairly imprecise, perhaps even anachronistic (e.g., the reference to the "Coḷas"),[82] it does echo actual political concerns of the empire. By including rulers and chieftains from conquered areas, some of whom we know resented Vijayanagara rule and balked at paying taxes,[83] the list implies that Vyāsatīrtha played a role in diplomacy. Indeed, other recipients include possible members of various sultanates and kingdoms to the north, with which the empire had important, if somewhat unstable, diplomatic relations. By showing that Vyāsatīrtha gives away wealth to these various constituents of the empire, the *Vyāsayogicarita* again presents his role at court as essential to the empire's effective functioning.

Thus, the *Vyāsayogicarita* references actual political realities, even as it subsumes such worldly activities into its religious idiom. While such a rhetorical tactic gives prominence to Vyāsatīrtha's spiritual authority, that very authority is clearly enhanced by its associations with the state. By emphasizing Vyāsatīrtha's long-standing and centrally significant connection with the Vijayanagara court, the *Vyāsayogicarita* underscores the importance of such a connection to the Mādhva sect's history. In this way, the text acquiesces to the very political realities it aims to present as subservient to religious concerns.

## VYĀSATĪRTHA AND THE VIJAYANAGARA COURT IN THE INSCRIPTIONAL RECORD

While there is a temptation to measure a traditional biography's truth claims against the apparently more disinterested and empirical inscriptional/monumental record, a study of these two types of sources on Vyāsatīrtha actually reveals important points of convergence.[84] Many claims in Somanātha's biography regarding Vyāsatīrtha's importance to the court of Kṛṣṇadevarāya are substantiated, albeit with different specifics and emphases, in the inscriptional record. Of course, the inscriptions reveal other aspects of this relationship that are critical to our understanding of it. But it is not only the inscriptions' presumed factuality that differentiates them from the biographies. It is also that reading the inscriptions against the biographies illuminates their distinctive institutional discourse and agenda.

Inscriptions as a genre are often viewed as the most empirical documents we have from precolonial India because they record a variety of specific, dated material and honorific exchanges between identifiable social agents. Such transactions had bearing on individual and communal rights to basic resources such as land and water and stipulated other valuable arrangements, such as tax exemptions, that obtained between individuals or communities and the state. That the bulk of South Indian inscriptions were carved into the walls of religious structures such as temples and *maṭha*s or were written on copper plates housed in such institutions attests to the central role played by religious organizations in such transactions.[85] This means that inscriptions provide important data about the interconnections between precolonial South India's social, political, religious, and economic landscapes.

Furthermore, while Leslie Orr (2000), Talbot (2001), Mack (2001), and others have effectively demonstrated the value of macrostudies of inscriptions to document systemic patterns in precolonial South Indian society, inscriptions also have biographical value. They can locate a specific individual fairly precisely within his or her social, geographic, and monumental landscape.[86] For instance, the fifteen inscriptions in which Vyāsatīrtha appears between 1511 and 1532 establish a time line of major events in his life by placing him at particular locations. His receipt and redistribution of gifts of land and *prasād* to specific individuals, who are often identified by name and relevant status markers, illuminates his relationships with the royal court, his own disciples, and even members of other sectarian groups. Furthermore, by documenting Vyāsatīrtha's arrangement for the construction of *maṭha*s; the establishment of related *agrahāra*s, or Brahmin settlements; and the installation of icons at established temples throughout the empire, the inscriptions chart the Mādhva sect's geographic expansion under Vyāsatīrtha's direction. In inscriptions where Vyāsatīrtha uses royally bequeathed resources to fund irrigation projects or to pay various local laborers such as basket weavers and oil-lamp suppliers to benefit temple worship, we see how religious institutions and their leaders shaped economic development in certain regions. Thus, the inscriptional record pertaining to Vyāsatīrtha highlights both his complex personal relationship with the Vijayanagara court and, more broadly, the *maṭhādhipati*'s multifaceted role in sixteenth-century South Indian society.[87]

Yet while inscriptions provide us with many valuable data, they are also a literary genre with fixed formulae for presenting events. As Talbot has demonstrated, established conventions (or subversions thereof) for self-presentation in inscriptions reveal important information about a society's values as well as a particular donor's social aspirations.[88] For instance, while inscriptions recording royal donations typically praise the martial prowess of the king's entire lineage in a formulaic manner, they also reveal which conquests were of particular significance to a given king's conception of his authority and efforts to establish his legitimacy in a certain region.[89] Inscriptions referring to Kṛṣṇadevarāya clearly show that his conquest of Kalinga was particularly significant to his donations to the temple at Tirupati, a significance that, as we have seen, is echoed in the *Vyāsayogicarita*.[90]

That the *praśasti* or panegyric portion of Kṛṣṇadevarāya's inscriptions almost always tacks back and forth between praising his martial prowess and praising his generosity in supporting religious institutions is also significant. The list of these institutions is fairly consistent throughout the inscriptional record and includes an array of Śaiva and Vaiṣṇava temples, most of which are located in what is now Tamilnadu and in southern Andhra Pradesh, that are still well known today, in large part because they were royally patronized. While such inscriptional rhetoric has been generally interpreted as attesting to Kṛṣṇadevarāya's much-vaunted ecumenism, it also underscores Kṛṣṇadevarāya's double-sided stewardship as being rooted in both military might and constructive donations to religious institutions. This is evident in the following inscription:

> Overcome by his glory, the sun sinks into the western ocean as if quite unable to endure the distress of mind. As if fearing that the seven oceans would provide a refuge to his enemies, they were dried up by the clouds of dust raised by the earth, trampled to pieces by his horsemen, but were formed again by the measureless streams poured out with his great gifts—*brahmāṇḍa, svarṇameru* and others. As though, in order that the foundations and wealth he had given might be long enjoyed, he sought to stay the chariot of the sun and to provide resting places for the gods, by erecting pillars stretching like mountain-peaks in the sky, filled with the accounts of his victorious expeditions to each point of the compass and with the names of his titles. Going round and round Kanchi, Srisailam, Sonachala, Kanakasabha, Venkatadri and other places, often and in various temples and holy places, for his well-being in the present and future, did he again and again bestow, in accordance with the *śāstra*s, various great gifts like man's weight in gold, together with the other grants associated with such gifts.[91]

The fact that the above inscription balances out the destructive side of Kṛṣṇadevarāya's rule with the constructive nature of his donations to religious institutions is not mere rhetoric in that these seemingly distinct royal activities were two sides of the same coin. Kṛṣṇadevarāya's patronage of temples and other religious institutions such as *maṭha*s helped to rebuild and integrate conquered areas by developing these regions economically in ways that also linked them culturally to the state. The irrigation of dry land or of land negatively affected by warfare, alluded to in the above inscription, was a significant part of this economic and cultural integration. In fact, the account of Portuguese traveler Nunes of the movement of Kṛṣṇadevarāya's cavalry speaks of the desiccating impact this had on waterways throughout the Deccan. Speaking of the movement of Kṛṣṇadevarāya's troops toward the famous siege of "Rachol" (Raichur), Nunes had this to say: "On which route was seen a wonderful thing, namely that on passing a river which, when they reached it, came half-way up to the knee, before half the people had passed it was totally dry without a drop of water; and they went about in the sand of it making pits to find some water."[92] Thus, the *praśasti* portions' consistent references to Kṛṣṇadevarāya's horses' hooves drying up oceans by kicking up too much dust are not mere hyperbole. Nor is their claim that Kṛṣṇadevarāya rectified this situation by commissioning *abhiṣeka*s, or the ritual bathing of icons of temple deities, that is, by patronizing religious activity at temples that often included irrigating dry land.

Furthermore, while Kṛṣṇadevarāya's inscriptions typically list several temples located in territories that were already somewhat integrated into the empire and which had an established history of Vijayanagara patronage, they likely publicize this facet of Kṛṣṇadevarāya's stewardship precisely to quell rebellion. Indeed, while many of Kṛṣṇadevarāya's most impressive military achievements involved a northward expansion of the empire, he was also concerned about the rebellious local chieftains and heavily militarized *nāyaka*s, or overlords, throughout his holdings, particularly those in Andhra Pradesh and the northern Tamil country.[93] As map 4 indicates, a few of the temples that Kṛṣṇadevarāya is typically praised for visiting and supporting through donations are located along or within the contested northern border zone. But the rest are within the Tamil and Telugu country.[94] The economic significance of this region, linked as it was to overseas trade routes with Southeast Asia and inhabited by productive weaving communities who drove a thriving textile industry, required the Vijayanagara court's constant surveillance. Furthermore, Mack has shown that several of these royally patronized temples were situated along important military routes that linked major forts throughout the southern peninsula.[95] Thus, the connection between Kṛṣṇadevarāya's might as a conqueror and his generosity as a donor to temples speaks of the actual role that royal temple donation played in conflict prevention and resolution in this period. At the same time, this connection hints at the multifaceted role that a sectarian leader like Vyāsatīrtha, who managed some of these donations, would have played in sixteenth-century Vijayanagara society.

Indeed, it was not only at temples that *maṭhādhipati*s performed their role of implementing certain features of the royal court's agenda. Royal donations to *maṭhādhipati*s often resulted in the construction of new monastic institutions or *maṭha*s and the establishment of subsidiary *agrahāra*s, or settlements of nonascetic Brahmin families, who could interface with the *maṭha* and the local community. Particularly when the integration of newly conquered or rebellious regions took place, Kṛṣṇadevarāya regularly donated land to sectarian leaders to found freestanding *maṭha*s or to establish a *maṭha* on an existing temple's premises. Such

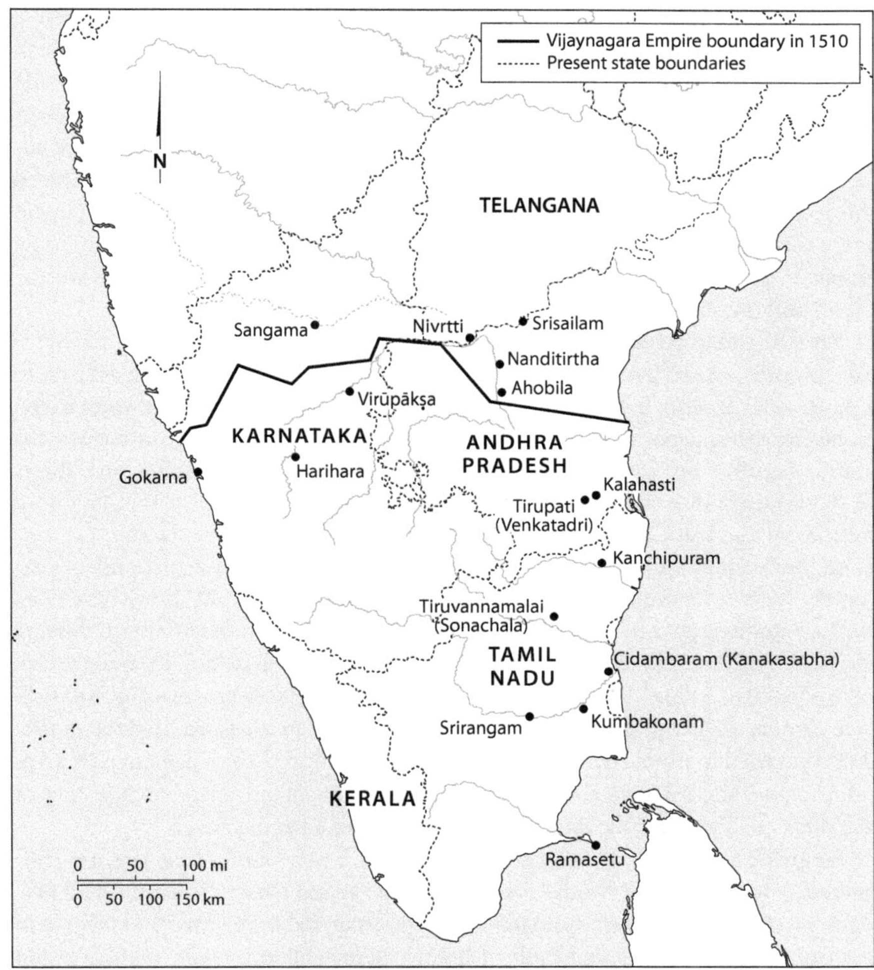



MAP 4. Religious sites listed in the Praśasti of Kṛṣṇadevarāya's inscriptions.

gifts simultaneously expanded a given sect's institutional network into new territories and created unofficial outposts of the empire.

In Vyāsatīrtha's case, the inscriptional record indicates that over the course of many years, he received much land from the court within an established orbit of Mādhvaism, that is, the region between Mysore and Bangalore where Vyāsatīrtha himself was born and raised.[96] By dividing up these royally gifted lands among his disciples in the establishment of sectarian institutions, Vyāsatīrtha consolidated his inner circle of followers and shored up the institutional underpinnings of his specific community. For instance, in 1523, Vyāsatīrtha used royally bequeathed land in the region of his teacher Brahmaṇyatīrtha's *bṛndāvana,* or tomb, to install thirty-two of his students. In the process, he renamed the village "Brahmaṇyapuri" after his teacher and thereby laid claim to the territory in the name of his sect.[97] (This gift is identified on map 3 as "Abbur Maṭha.") The fact that these gifts of villages brought with them perpetual rights to natural resources basically guaranteed the sect's continued existence in a given area. Indeed, a refrain found in almost every inscription recording such gifts is that the land and all its wealth are to be enjoyed "by [Vyāsatīrtha's] students and their students so long as there are the moon and the stars."[98]

Yet while this region between Mysore and Bangalore was of historic and symbolic significance to the Mādhva community, it was also strategically significant to Kṛṣṇadevarāya who, between 1509 and 1511, seized several important forts there, including Srirangapatna and Śivasamudra, from the chiefs of the powerful Ummattur family.[99] By helping Vyāsatīrtha shore up his institutional network there, Kṛṣṇadevarāya also created loyalist strongholds. Vyāsatīrtha also received land from Kṛṣṇadevarāya in more far-flung locations, often subsequent to a recent conquest. For instance, in 1511, Vyāsatīrtha received a village and several hamlets near Kanchi, only four months after Kṛṣṇadevarāya successfully put down rebellions by the Śambuvarāyas in that region.[100] In 1521, a couple of months after defeating the Adil Shahis of the Bijapur Sultanate at the battle of Raichur, Kṛṣṇadevarāya gave Vyāsatīrtha land in the Raichur doab for the establishment of a *maṭha.*[101] (See Kannerumadugu on map 3.) Later sources indicate that the Mādhva *maṭha* that Vyāsatīrtha established north of the capital enjoyed the allegiance of a local nonmonastic Mādhva elite with explicit positions of authority, such as that of *deśpāṇḍe* or "revenue collector," in the Vijayanagara administration.[102]

By giving land to a *maṭhādhipati* to construct a new *maṭha* in a recently conquered or reconquered area, the court helped to expand the sect's institutional network precisely by placing loyal subjects in these unstable regions.[103] Smaller and less ornate than temples and built of lighter, perishable materials, *maṭha*s could be constructed quickly. Many of their residents could be transplanted easily into new locations because they had severed family ties in becoming *saṃnyāsin*s and because, unlike temple servants, they were not charged with the care of a deity installed in a specific location. While ascetics by this period were typically organized into orders affiliated with specific institutions, *maṭha*s were still fairly mobile. They could branch off from their central organizations and put down roots, banyan-like, in new localities. In doing so, they could import not only religious sensibilities and intellectual practices but also new economic and political structures into conquered regions. Thus, the *maṭha*'s mobility was highly useful to the court.

Yet while these features of the *maṭha* distinguished it from the temple, *maṭha*s were advantageous to the court in part for the way in which they replicated some of the temple's functions.[104] Not only would articles needed by the *matha* for daily life be supplied by the local labor force but the construction of a *matha* in a given area was often accompanied by the irrigation of land and by arrangements with local farmers to supply some of this increase in produce to the *matha*. While irrigation and increased farming had the potential to displace some individuals and privileged elite patterns of food consumption,[105] they also enabled the development of new economic networks. Furthermore, the food generated this way would have been used to feed the *matha*'s residents and as offerings in rituals that would have been partially returned to the local population in the form of *prasād*.[106]

Indeed, *matha*s in this period took on many of the ritual trappings of temples but transformed them in subtle ways that made them more sectarian. Not only did *matha*s conduct the worship of icons of deities installed on their premises (such as one sees at the Mādhva-run "Kṛṣṇa" *matha* in Udupi)[107] but they also encouraged the worship of *bṛndāvana*s (also known as *samādhis*) or tombs containing the mortal remains of prominent *saṃnyāsin*s in the sect's lineage.[108](See ch. 4, figs. 2 and 4–9.) By taking on some of the temples' functionality but connecting it to their sectarian identity, *matha*s simultaneously increased their local prominence and implemented the court's agenda of economically developing and culturally integrating these regions.

If the *matha* came to function somewhat as a temple, it also mimicked certain features of the royal court. Inscriptional records indicate that many of the emblems of the royal court's power and authority were replicated in the *matha*s that Vyāsatīrtha established. For example, Vyāsatīrtha is referred to as "Vyāsarāya," or "King Vyāsa" (as he is more popularly known throughout Karnataka even today), in a 1513 Kannada inscription from the Viṭṭhala Temple in the Vijayanagara capital.[109] This is only the second inscription in which Vyāsatīrtha appears. His teacher Śrīpādarāya, head of the Mādhva *matha* in Mulbagal, is also referred to in this way, indicating that it was the office of the *mathādhipati* and not Vyāsatīrtha himself that was likened to the sovereign.[110]

While titles such as "Lord" and "Ruler" had long been used to refer to religious leaders in South India,[111] Vijayanagara-era *matha*s further established an explicit connection between themselves and the court by taking on tutelary deities of royal significance. Inscriptions documenting Kṛṣṇadevarāya's gifts to Vyāsatīrtha habitually mention one of two possible witnessing deities, Virūpākṣa or Viṭṭhala, who were the respective signatory deities of the empire.[112] But there is often a third deity mentioned in those inscriptions where Vyāsatīrtha establishes a *matha*: the deity Rāmacandra, whose protection is often sought for the arrangements detailed in the inscription and who is often given shares in the land grant.[113] This choice of Rāmacandra as a tutelary deity for these Mādhva *matha*s seems significant. A large Rāmacandra temple, the first of its kind, was built in the Vijayanagara capital in the fifteenth century near the living quarters of the royal family. While this was likely a private temple, it played a conspicuous role in public festivals such as the Mahānavamī, in which royal and divine authority were explicitly linked.[114]

Thus, by using courtly emblems and titles, *maṭhādhipati*s like Vyāsatīrtha asserted both their power in a given region and their ties to the Vijayanagara court. *Maṭhas'* similarities to temples enabled them to foster a certain type of economic development in the local community that bore the imprint of Vijayanagara courtly tastes, while their small size, simple construction, and mobile residents made it possible to implement this economic development fairly quickly. *Maṭhas* and their leaders had no official courtly roles, but their presence in a given area was often accompanied by the development of a local secular power structure that was affiliated with both the *maṭha* and the court. In all these ways, royal gifts of land to Vyāsatīrtha fostered a certain type of economic growth that facilitated political integration of recently conquered or rebellious territories while also spreading Mādhvaism into new regions.

Despite these intimate connections between the Vijayanagara court and the sectarian *maṭha,* the extent to which the court was invested in the intellectual practices and doctrinal particularities that were central to the *maṭha's* existence is unclear. The inscriptional records praise sectarian leaders not just in a generic manner for their knowledge of the Vedas or their erudition but also specifically for their doctrinal stance. Vyāsatīrtha is referred to in royal edicts by such epithets as "*tattvavādi*" or one who espouses a realist epistemology as well as a pluralistic ontology. He is also regularly called "a jewel in the lotus of Madhvācārya's teachings" in reference to his *guru-śiṣya* lineage. Finally, the most commonly repeated epithet in the inscriptions invokes Vyāsatīrtha's devotional orientation towards Viṣṇu: "*Vaiṣṇavāgamasiddhāntasthāpana.*" This Sanskrit compound, meaning "establisher of Vaiṣṇavism's true philosophy," attests to Vyāsatīrtha's identity as a polemicist against other systems of thought, including other forms of Vaiṣṇavism.[115]

Through such epithets detailing specific features of the recipient's identity, the court acknowledged the importance of Brahmin sectarian formations and implied that these formations lent meaning to royal gifts. But we also know that the Vijayanagara court, especially that of Kṛṣṇadevarāya, patronized a variety of Vyāsatīrtha's sectarian rivals and praised these leaders in different but just as robust terms. Moreover, the broad use of the term *guru* in the royal inscriptions to refer to many recipients of royal patronage suggests that the court kept its religious options open.[116] This openness in part attests to the court's ecumenism, but it may also imply that the court was aware of potential intersectarian rivalries that its patronage could foster. Indeed, some inscriptional records indicate that the court not only acknowledged but also occasionally manipulated such intersectarian dynamics when circumstances warranted it.

One possible example of this can be seen at the large Vaiṣṇava temple complex at Tirupati-Tirumala. Here, in 1524, Kṛṣṇadevarāya gave Vyāsatīrtha three house sites on which to construct two *mathas*. Two of these sites are located on top of the hill in Tirumala, near what was then the most important Vaiṣṇava shrine in South India, the Śrī Venakaṭeśvara *mandir*.[117] The third site is at the hill's bottom, in the town of Tirupati, near the ritually related (and also royally patronized) Govindarājasvāmi temple.

The significant implications of this gift will be explored in depth in chapter 4. The main thing to acknowledge here is that, by giving Vyāsatīrtha this land, Kṛṣṇadevarāya inserted Mādhva Brahmins, who had no previous official role at Tirupati, into the affairs of one of the most important redistributive centers of wealth and honors in the Vijayanagara Empire. That he did so at some cost to the Śrīvaiṣṇavas, who had long controlled the temples' ritual programs and related wealth and prestige, illuminates both the competitive nature of Hindu sectarian relations in this period and the role royal patronage played in that competition.

The region in and around Tirupati was one with which the Tuḷuva dynasty in general and Kṛṣṇadevarāya in particular worked to solidify alliances. The establishment of strong relationships with the local community in southern Andhra enabled Vijayanagara kings to monitor both rebellious local populations and the empire's own heavily militarized but occasionally rogue *nāyaka*s or overlords. Establishing footholds in this region also enabled Vijayanagara kings to remain within striking distance of those sites in modern-day Andhra Pradesh and Telangana that were often contested by the Gajapati kingdom ruling in Kalinga. To these ends, the Tuḷuva dynasty (1505–65) extended Sāḷuva Narasiṃha's policy of funneling economic developments through the Vaiṣṇava temples at Tirupati, the facilitation of which was placed mainly in the hands of Śrīvaiṣṇava sectarian leaders. Thus, royal patronage of these temples at Tirupati simultaneously increased the temples' importance and consolidated Śrīvaiṣṇava control over them.

Yet it is also in this region that some of the most important material transactions between Vyāsatīrtha and Kṛṣṇadevarāya are documented. Whatever Kṛṣṇadevarāya's reasons were for inserting the Mādhvas into the power structure at Tirupati-Tirumala, the inscriptions go on to indicate that, subsequent to receiving this gift and constructing his two monasteries, Vyāsatīrtha took steps to promote an active role for Mādhvas in temple affairs.[118] He constructed *maṇḍapas* or covered pavilions in front of both of his *mathas* at which the Mādhvas regularly distributed *prasād*. Vyāsatīrtha thereby replicated temple rituals at his *mathas* in a manner that explicitly linked these activities and their attendant religious and social implications to his particular sect.

Yet, while such gestures undoubtedly increased Mādhvaism's prominence in the region, an achievement of lasting significance to the Mādhva sect, they did so in large part by benefiting various local groups. This was exactly what the king intended. Vyāsatīrtha's arrangements to irrigate land and to supply produce and other items, such as lamps and oil, to the temples established long-standing economic relationships between Mādhva Brahmins and various labor groups in this region. Insofar as this promoted economic vitality and political stability, it was in the king's best interests.

However, there are some inscriptional indications that Vyāsatīrtha was so successful at building up local support that Kṛṣṇadevarāya actually worked to rein him in and remind the local populace of who was behind Vyāsatīrtha's munificence. This is evidenced in a land endowment in the Chittoor district (where Tirupati is also located) given by Kṛṣṇadevarāya to Vyāsatīrtha in 1526. This gift is recorded on a Sanskrit copper plate inscription, referred to in *Epigraphia Indica*, vol. 31 as the *Kamalapur Plates of Krishnadevaraya*. This inscription documents Kṛṣṇadevarāya's gift to Vyāsatīrtha of the village of Bettakonda, together with several lesser hamlets.[119] It indicates that the village was popularly known as "Vyāsasamudra," or "Vyāsa's Ocean," in reference to a large tank that Vyāsatīrtha had earlier constructed in the area (see map 3). It may be that the earlier Tirupati inscription (from November 1524), which records that Vyāsatīrtha arranged for the excavation of tanks and channels in the temple villages for the purpose of producing more goods to be donated to the deity, refers to what was to become Vyāsasamudra. The 1526 Kamalapur copper plates imply that Kṛṣṇadevarāya gave this land to Vyāsatīrtha as a reward for his having developed it. However, the inscription also documents the fact that the village will now be called Kṛṣṇarāyapura, after the king.[120] This may indicate that, although Kṛṣṇadevarāya was rewarding Vyāsatīrtha for his work to irrigate the area and thereby promote its economic well-being, he was also putting Vyāsatīrtha in his rightful place. The tank of Vyāsasamudra would not exist were it not for the king's patronage and, therefore, the village popularly known as Vyāsa's Ocean should also be called King Kṛṣṇa's Town.

Thus, the inscriptional record suggests that kings relied on sectarian leaders to manage gifts intended to develop strategic locations of the empire economically but that kings also felt somewhat anxious about this reliance. This anxiety was due to the fact that the sectarian leaders who managed these gifts could become quite prominent locally, potentially increasing their autonomy and eclipsing the fame of the king. The Kamalapur copper plate inscription suggests that the king could be uneasy about the extent to which *maṭhas* functioned as alternative institutions of power. He was therefore willing to exert his influence over sectarian religious activity, if the circumstances warranted it.

Yet it is also true that the inscriptional record documenting Kṛṣṇadevarāya's gifts to Vyāsatīrtha supports much of what the traditional Mādhva biographies say about the relationship between royal and religious authority. For example, the redistribution of royal wealth that sectarian leaders routinely implemented according to the inscriptional record is echoed in the *ratnābhiṣeka* that takes place in the *Vyāsayogicarita*. Of course, the inscriptional record documents a much more limited version of this than the *Vyāsayogicarita*, wherein Vyāsatīrtha redistributes jewels to an array of constituents that encompasses almost the entirety of the empire's territorial holdings and diplomatic spheres. However, this is not such an exaggeration if we regard the map of places where Vyāsatīrtha receives royally bequeathed land (map 3) nor if we take into account the increasing significance of the Tirupati region and its religious institutions to the empire's statecraft.

## THE ROLE OF MAṬHĀDHIPATIS IN KṚṢṆADEVARĀYA'S CONCEPT OF NĪTI

Our final source that sheds light on the role of sectarian leaders at Kṛṣṇadevarāya's court is the Telugu-language[121] poem the *Āmuktamālyada,* a text that seems to have been authored by the emperor himself.[122] This text arguably displays Kṛṣṇadevarāya's Śrīvaiṣṇava leanings in that the *Āmuktamālyada* concerns the life stories of two significant Āḷvārs, or Śrīvaiṣṇava saints, who are considered among the founders of this Viṣṇu devotional tradition. Meanwhile, the text makes no specific mention of Vyāsatīrtha or the Mādhvas, undercutting some of the sectarian sources' claims in favor of Vyāsatīrtha's preeminence at Kṛṣṇadevarāya's court. However, Kṛṣṇadevarāya makes some important generalized statements about the proper role of religious leaders to an effective king's statecraft. These statements reveal that the emperor saw all Hindu sectarian leaders in a similar light, thereby explaining the prominence of Vyāsatīrtha in the courtly inscriptional record despite the king's Śrīvaiṣṇava leanings.

The chapter of the *Āmuktamālyad*a that is most relevant to our purposes is the one on Rājanīti or "royal leadership/statecraft." This chapter appears in a much longer framing story that involves, in part, the famous Śrīvaiṣṇava teacher Yāmunācārya; in this portion of the text Yāmunācārya has taken on the role of king.[123] The premise of this chapter is that Yāmunācārya has decided to renounce the world and turn his kingdom over to his son. Before doing so, he wants to impart some of his hard-earned political wisdom. In a recent study of the text, V. N. Rao, Shulman, and Subrahmanyam suggest there is a "constant preoccupation in the work with the desire of the king to renounce,"[124] attesting perhaps to the simultaneous intimacy and tension between renunciants and royals that we have noted in our other sixteenth-century sources. While some might argue that this tension between dharma and *mokṣa* is perennial in Indian history, Rao, Shulman, and Subrahmanyam maintain that, in the *Āmuktamālyada,* "[a] distinction is drawn—perhaps for the first time in South India—between the king as individual, with his individual inclinations and exigencies, and the kingship as institution (which has to go on at all costs)."[125] Furthermore, while the context in which this political wisdom is proffered is somewhat mythical and the Rājanīti chapter invokes many established literary tropes and inherited conceptual frameworks in making its points, Rao, Shulman, and Subrahmanyam also note that the chapter is replete with realistic and often quite personal observations about the king's role:

> This is no arm-chair pontificating but a largely practical synthesis reflecting the political, economic and institutional changes of the early sixteenth century. Still, highly individualized statements that can be attributed directly to the book's author do alternate with verses that seem to be lifted from standard *nīti*-texts about politics and kingship. Nonetheless, we are left with a total impression of a unique concoction of pragmatic wisdom, specific constraints, an inherited normative politics, and a meditative sensibility capable of formulating something entirely new.[126]

In terms of what he has to say about traditional religious leaders in the *Rājanīti* chapter, Kṛṣṇadevarāya draws a distinction between Brahmins of a more *laukika* or worldly bent and those who are more explicitly involved in religious matters. With respect to the former, Kṛṣṇadevarāya advocates relying heavily on such Brahmins to command his forts, a documented Vijayanagara practice that Stein has portrayed as an innovative and effective means for preventing the increasingly militarized *nāyakas,* or overloads in the empire's employ, from getting too powerful.[127] Kṛṣṇadevarāya discusses this practice in the following verse:

> Make trustworthy Brahmins
> The commanders of your forts
> And give them just enough troops,
> To protect these strongholds,
> Lest they become too threatening.[128]

Stein's analysis of this practice highlights the practical benefits of installing in these positions nonlocal Brahmins, who had a limited sense of personal entitlement to rule and fewer local connections. Hence, they had a greater sense of allegiance to the king. However, Kṛṣṇadevarāya's justification for this practice, articulated in the Rājanīti chapter, invokes fairly generic notions of dharma and thus a somewhat conventional view of Brahminical identity. Kṛṣṇadevarāya maintains that Brahmin commanders will conduct themselves admirably precisely because they have studied the *dharmaśāstra*s and want to avoid being shamed before those they consider their social inferiors, the Kṣatriyas and Śūdras:

> The king will often benefit by putting a Brahmin in charge,
> For he knows both the laws of Manu and his own dharma.
> And from fear of being mocked
> By Kshatriyas and Sudras,
> He will stand up to all difficulties.[129]

Kṛṣṇadevarāya's discussion of what constitutes dharmic knowledge of Brahmin commanders and how this might actually influence statecraft remains vague, despite his specific reference to the *Laws of Manu*. However, it does support the general notion, expressed rhetorically in both Somanātha's biography of Vyāsatīrtha and the inscriptional records documenting Vyāsatīrtha's relationship with the Vijayanagara court, that the inherited ideals of kingship articulated in Sanskrit texts did influence practical reality on some level.

In terms of the role of the more explicitly religious Brahmins in Kṛṣṇadevarāya's conception of Nīti, the text makes the following, disparaging remarks:

> If you are partial to learning,
> and give lands and money away to the learned,
> mendicants, monks and men with matted hair
> will become swollen-headed.
> Famines, sickness and infant deaths will increase.
> Just show devotion to the learned,
> and if they resent their poverty—don't be concerned.[130]

Here, Rao, Shulman, and Subrahmanyam surmise that Kṛṣṇadevarāya is referring to the *maṭhādhipati*s. However, despite the text's disparagement of those religious men who might become "swollen-headed" from receiving too much royal patronage, Kṛṣṇadevarāya elsewhere advocates giving money to Brahmins and temples as money that is "well spent" (v. 262). He also talks about bad omens requiring gifts to Brahmins as well as publicly displayed patronage of Brahmin-controlled forms of religiosity such as "fire rites" (v. 271).

Thus, while Rao, Shulman, and Subrahmanyam argue rightly that Kṛṣṇadevarāya draws a distinction between two sets of Brahmins, that distinction is in some ways porous. In Kṛṣṇadevarāya's estimation, Brahmins who are engaged in more secular pursuits apparently still adhere to conventional notions of dharma, while those who are more overtly religious, such as *maṭhādhipati*s, may be power hungry. Indeed, we know from the inscriptional record, that Kṛṣṇadevarāya relied on both sets of Brahmins for implementing his statecraft. We also know, from the Kamalapur copper plate inscription of 1526 and from inscriptions in Tirupati, that Kṛṣṇadevarāya acted to regulate those sectarian leaders who he felt might be developing autonomous spheres of power and influence.

Thus, while the king speaks disparagingly about the *maṭhādhipati*s getting "swollen heads" if they are too heavily patronized, he does in fact make them powerful by placing a tremendous amount of wealth in their hands through donations to temples and *maṭha*s under their control. This is exactly why Kṛṣṇadevarāya expresses concern about them in the Rājanīti chapter of his *Āmuktamālyada*. Like our other sources, the *Āmuktamālyada* portrays the royal and religious realms as distinct but intimately linked in terms of the authority each holds. For that very reason, relations between the two forms of authority could be fraught.

## CONCLUSION

The inscriptional, biographical, monumental, and literary sources discussed in this chapter offer up different perspectives on the relationship between Kṛṣṇadevarāya and Vyāsatīrtha and, by extension, the relationship between royal and religious authority in sixteenth-century Vijayanagara. The *Vyāsayogicarita* sublimates its concerns with worldly affairs and the dependence of the sectarian leader on the court's largesse by placing all such references into a predominantly religious framework. In such a framework, the religious leader is indifferent to worldly matters and receives royal gifts only to share them with others, even as the text presents Vyāsatīrtha's relationship with the court as central to his life story. Meanwhile, the inscriptions present religious institutions as a critically important arena for Vijayanagara statecraft but not always for the same reasons provided by the biographical tradition. Kṛṣṇadevarāya's gifts to sectarian leaders seem to have been motivated by a variety of factors, some of which were religious and devotional while others had to do with managing his political and economic relations with various constituents. Indeed, on some occasions, the king seems to have used his patronage to assert his authority over religious leaders and their institutions, either to manage or stir up conflicts between them. Finally, Kṛṣṇadevarāya's own statements on statecraft in his *Āmuktamālyada* support the general impression, common to all the sources, that royal support of religious activity was not only beneficial to Brahmin sectarian groups but also a key component of the king's statecraft. Precisely because of this, however, the king had to be judicious regarding how much patronage he gave, and to whom, in order to avoid ceding too much authority to alternative institutions of power.

The fact that the sources discussed above hold somewhat different perspectives on the relationship between royal and religious authority reflects the distinctive social locations of the texts' producers and intended audiences. At the same time, where the sources share perspectives and display mutual influences, they reveal the complicated links between Kṛṣṇadevarāya's court and the religious communities he patronized. Thus, reading these sources in light of each other highlights the variety of perspectives held by different historical agents and, hence, the complex relationship between religious and royal institutional cultures during this period.

Finally, while my reading of the extant records implies that Vyāsatīrtha was particularly adept at situating his sect advantageously in this system, I have also alluded to the important role played by other sectarian groups, such as the Smārtas and the Śrīvaiṣṇavas, at the Vijayanagara court. Since the court relied on religious institutions to implement key features of its statecraft, its patronage of many different sectarian groups is not surprising. Yet this very ecumenism also seems to have created a competitive environment that affected the formulation of distinct sectarian identities and the dynamics of intersectarian relationships. In the following chapter, we turn to an examination of such issues.

3

---

# Sectarian Rivalries at an Ecumenical Court

## *Vyāsatīrtha, Advaita Vedānta, and the Smārta Brahmins*

In the previous chapter, we saw that *maṭhas* and their leaders performed various economic, political, and social functions for the royal court. Both as freestanding institutions and through their affiliations with temples, *maṭhas* irrigated and developed land, redistributed its produce as *prasād*, engaged in economic transactions with local laborers, and took on courtly emblems and titles. Through such activities, *maṭhas* and their leaders integrated newly conquered and rebellious territories more firmly into the empire while increasing their own social prominence.

But *maṭhas* were also educational and religious facilities, and their leaders cultivated qualities that were valued by their constituents for reasons having little to do with the court and its agenda. These qualities could include knowledge of sacred texts, ritual aptitude, devotional fervor, and intellectual prowess displayed in debates with proponents of rival systems of thought. Certainly Vyāsatīrtha's fame is rooted not only in his reputation as an advisor to several Vijayanagara kings but also in the intellectual project articulated in his writings. This project was multifaceted. It consisted, in large part, of a revamped presentation of Madhva's teachings that bolstered the system's realistic pluralism and distinctive form of Vaiṣṇava devotionalism through new methods of argumentation developed in the *navya-nyāya* or the "new dialectics."[1] It also consisted of an incisive polemic against the two alternative forms of Vedānta being advanced by other Brahmin sects in Vyāsatīrtha's milieu and, not coincidentally, of a historical doxography of the arguments internal to those systems.[2] Of the three major works Vyāsatīrtha authored,[3] two are centrally concerned with criticizing the Advaita or nondualist Vedānta advocated by the Smārta Brahmins and the Viśiṣṭādvaita Vedānta or qualified nondualism advocated by the Śrīvaiṣṇavas. These sects held established positions of power at the Vijayanagara court; that of the Smārtas was particularly long-standing. A central goal of this chapter will be to explore the ways in which Vyāsatīrtha's polemics against his Vedāntin intellectual rivals, especially the Smārtas, were related to his increasingly close ties to Vijayanagara royals.

Indeed, royal patronage not only enhanced the regional authority of *maṭhādhipati*s and the social prominence of their institutions, it also facilitated the spread of their ideas. As we saw in chapter 2, biographies of sectarian leaders assume the importance of strong ties to the court for a sectarian community's success, even as such texts deny worldly motivation to religious mendicants. This "success" could be measured in part by the spread of a given sect's teachings into new regions. The *digvijaya* genre's emphasis on all-India philosophical conquest attests to the fact that sectarian communities sought to convert others to their systems of thought. Of course, the dominance of this literary motif does not mean that actual "conversion" required radically rejecting one's former religious identity and intellectual affiliations. As I will show in this and subsequent chapters, Brahmin sectarian communities shared boundaries that were not only porous, but malleable. However, the *digvijaya* literature's glorification of doctrinal debate suggests that convincing others of the unique correctness of one's own system was important.[4] Indeed, this literature portrays these doctrinal victories as a form of "world conquest," implying that the spread of a given sect's ideas also promoted that sect's worldly stature. While the philosophical literature of the period is much more reticent about the social and political contexts in which its authors operated, its general preoccupation with polemics (and even to some extent with doxography) indicates that sectarian leaders sought to challenge the philosophical standing of other sectarian groups. These leaders were often receiving royal patronage and, in that capacity, acting as state agents, which implies that ties to the royal court encouraged sectarian doctrinal competition. This is suggestive of an intimate relationship between a *maṭha*'s worldly activities and its intellectual ones.

Thus, while our previous chapter focused on Vyāsatīrtha's role as an institutional administrator of *maṭha*s and as an advisor to a series of Vijayanagara kings, this chapter will link those roles to his intellectual activities with respect to other Vedānta sects. In particular, it will examine Vyāsatīrtha's critique of Advaita Vedānta, especially its doctrine of *jīvanmukti* or liberation from *saṃsāra* while still embodied, and how this critique reflects Vyāsatīrtha's challenge to the Smārta Brahmins' historical dominance at court. As will be discussed in some detail below, the Smārta Advaita *maṭha* at Sringeri enjoyed a close relationship with the Vijayanagara court from a very early date. This patronage enabled Sringeri Smārta Advaitins to establish an affiliation with the Virūpākṣa temple, which was the imperial capital's most prominent shrine because it housed the empire's tutelary deity. The Advaita Vedānta doctrine of *jīvanmukti* or "liberation while living" may have helped to buttress the Smārtas' worldly standing, by implying that some ascetic

Smārta leaders had achieved a special spiritual state that granted them access to otherwise unknowable truths. Vyāsatīrtha's claim that this traditionally Advaita concept makes more sense in his own system of thought could have been a way of undercutting the authority of the Smārta *gurus* at court and making a bid for that authority on the part of Mādhva teachers.

The effectiveness of Vyāsatīrtha's doctrinal criticisms of Advaita is evident in the extensive response they elicited. For the duration of the sixteenth and well into the seventeenth centuries, proponents of Advaita Vedānta composed both direct and indirect responses to Vyāsatīrtha's works. As far north as Varanasi, the Advaitin intellectual Madhusūdana Sarasvatī (fl. 1550) composed an innovative form of commentary: a line-by-line response opposing the anti-Advaita arguments in Vyāsatīrtha's magnum opus, the *Nyāyāmṛta*. In the South, the late sixteenth century witnessed some particularly vituperative criticisms of Dvaita thought, as Advaitin authors like Appayya Dīkṣita composed the *Madhvatantramukhamardana* or *Crushing the Face of Madhva's System.*[5]

While these responses attest to the acuity of Vyāsatīrtha's anti-Advaita polemics, the intensity and duration of Advaitin responses to Vyāsatīrtha's philosophical arguments also represent a reaction to the Dvaitin's social prominence at Vijayanagara. This prominence is substantiated by the inscriptional and monumental records examined in the previous chapter, which indicate that Vyāsatīrtha used courtly patronage to expand the Mādhva sect's geographical reach and, correspondingly, its social significance. If we consider that some of Vyāsatīrtha's philosophical arguments against Advaita were made almost verbatim by the earlier Mādhva author Viṣṇudāsācārya (1390–1440?),[6] it seems likely that Vyāsatīrtha's courtly eminence, insofar as it spread the Dvaita school's institutional network and, in turn, its doctrines, contributed to his intellectual fame. This fame made his cogent, detailed criticisms of other forms of Vedānta impossible to ignore.

Yet while royal patronage clearly shaped and promoted Vedānta *maṭhas'* intellectual production, the extent to which intersectarian doctrinal debates influenced royal behavior, including royal patronage of sectarian institutions, is less clear. Evidence that the Vijayanagara court was invested in Brahminical intellectual activity can be found in scattered references to royal support in Brahmin texts, a notable example being the Sringeri Smārta Brahmin Sāyaṇa's claim that Vijayanagara kings patronized his commentary on the Vedas. (This will be discussed in greater depth below.) There are also inscriptional records in which royals praise *maṭhādhipati*s for their doctrinal affiliations, knowledge, and erudition, thereby implying there was royal awareness of doctrinal divisions between sectarian communities. That philosophical debates between sectarian groups were witnessed by royals and, to some extent, performed for them is also attested to in many literary sources, such as Somanātha's biography of Vyāsatīrtha. While such sources have their biases, other less partisan sources, such as debate manuals, indicate that these intellectual engagements were regulated by established rules.[7] This suggests not only a degree of public scrutiny of these events but also that real stakes could be attached to a given debate's outcome.[8]

The "real world" implications of these doctrinal debates may be seen in the Vijayanagara court's eventual shift in patronage away from historically Smārta-dominated institutions and toward both Mādhva and Śrīvaiṣṇava ones over the course of the sixteenth century. While the complete exclusion of Smārta and Śaiva institutions from royal patronage did not occur until Rāmarāya's regency (1542–65), the seeds of this process were arguably planted during Kṛṣṇadevarāya's reign.[9] Vyāsatīrtha's rivalry with the Smārtas, manifested in his incisive polemics against their doctrines, as well as his alliance with the Śrīvaiṣṇavas (discussed in the next chapter), may have contributed to this shift. This would help to explain why Vyāsatīrtha's anti-Advaita arguments received so much more attention than those of his predecessors, such as Viṣṇudāsācārya.

That royal patronage responded to intersectarian doctrinal debates is not so far fetched, if we consider the influence such arguments had on sectarian institutions' behavior. Insofar as intellectual debates changed people's minds about which guru's teachings were superior,[10] they shaped social reality in various ways. The adoption of new religious identities on the part of religious elites could change the power structure and, correspondingly, the ritual activity at temples, whose economic importance in a given area implicated a broad swath of local society. The increased local prominence of a particular intellectual and religious community, organized into an institution such as a sectarian *matha,* was often consolidated through new forms of local patronage that reshaped regional economic, social, and even linguistic networks. Thus, while polemical and doxographic literature certainly served the purely philosophical purposes of mapping the intellectual landscape and identifying the most cogent responses to a range of competing arguments, there were social and political implications to presenting doctrinal positions in particular ways. Because the Vijayanagara court often exercised its authority precisely by affiliating with local institutions with established power, shifts in that power brought about by doctrinal debates could affect how the court would allocate its resources.

One of the reasons it is difficult to discern whether doctrinal debates and other competitive displays of intellectual prowess influenced Vijayanagara statecraft is the court's famous ecumenism, apparent in its patronage of a variety of religious groups. Recent scholarship on the Vijayanagara Empire has emphasized its religious diversity, presenting it as a tolerant haven for a variety of religious traditions, including Islam, Jainism, and Christianity, and highlighting the ecumenical manner in which its rulers patronized disparate Hindu sects.[11] Such scholarship offers an important corrective to older scholarly depictions of Vijayanagara as a monolithic Hindu bastion against the northern Islamic polities.[12] However, this emphasis on the court's religious diversity overlooks the fact that royal patronage did tend to benefit Hindu communities almost exclusively,[13] especially those with an orthodox and Vedānta orientation.[14] It also ignores the period's Hindu sectarian competition, which manifested itself most conspicuously among those very Brahmin elites who not only held competing interpretations of Vedānta literature, but were recipients of royal patronage.

It may be ironic that Brahminical sectarian tensions heightened precisely in the context of Vijayanagara's generous and reputedly ecumenical patronage system. The fact that many Brahmin sects came to establish *maṭhas* and other institutions within the empire's capital likely increased the interaction of these groups, which held competing Vedānta views.[15] Indeed, Vijayanagara patronage in the sixteenth century created multisectarian "mega-temples"[16] that encouraged both intersectarian collaboration and competition for prominence. Thus, it is plausible that the ecumenical patronage of the Vijayanagara rulers generated a certain give-and-take across Hindu sectarian lines. But that very familiarity may have also enabled a competitive striving for sectarian eminence. Furthermore, as our survey of inscriptions pertaining to Vyāsatīrtha in the previous chapter demonstrates, Vijayanagara donations of land to religious institutions expanded their geographical reach in ways that dramatically increased their social prominence. This, coupled with the fact that courtly generosity had tremendous implications for local control over basic resources such as land and water, may have engendered a greater sense of bounded sectarian identity and a desire to show one's sect off to advantage.

Ignoring sectarian competition among Brahmin sects who were receiving royal patronage from the Vijayanagara court has skewed our understanding of Vijayanagara ecumenism. Scholarship on the empire's ecumenism tends to portray it either as a deliberate policy of conflict avoidance or, in Pollock's view, as evidence of religion's lack of importance to Vijayanagara statecraft.[17] I would argue that the Vijayanagara court was careful to avoid playing favorites (at least until the late Tuḷuva dynasty), but it was not ecumenical in the way scholars have typically conceived it. In fact, Vijayanagara patronage of religious institutions looks ecumenical from our vantage point mainly because we have more records documenting the (mostly) Hindu groups who were patronized by a given king. We have comparatively fewer records of those religious communities who were not recipients of royal patronage. This means that our records leave out the true variety of religious options available, masking the selective aspect of Vijayanagara patronage.[18] While courtly patronage may have been generous and, in some ways, evenhanded, it could not have been infinite. Choices were made about which religious communities would receive royal gifts. These choices likely reflected many practical considerations. But the court's consistent privileging of Brahmin Vedānta *maṭhas* does suggest that something about this particular religious, intellectual, and institutional formation resonated with Vijayanagara royals. Furthermore, precisely because these *mathas* served many pragmatic imperial purposes, the court certainly would have been aware of their relationships. Because these intersectarian relationships were not merely practical but also doctrinal, doctrinal debate likely affected royal giving.

By examining Vyāsatīrtha's interactions with Smārta Brahmin advocates of Advaita Vedānta, through a contextualized study of his polemics against their doctrine of *jīvanmukti,* this chapter will explore how royal patronage practices influenced sectarian identities, as articulated through doctrinal disputes. But it will also consider how sectarian groups pursued their own distinctive goals through their ties to the court and the role such pursuits played in shaping social and political reality. Through this double-sided approach, I aim to examine both the influence of courtly culture on developments in Vedānta philosophy and the influence of such developments, particularly polemical argumentation, on sectarian sociopolitical positioning throughout the empire.

## SRINGERI SMĀRTAS AND
## THE FOURTEENTH-CENTURY VIJAYANAGARA COURT

Perhaps the Hindu sectarian institution most emblematic of Vijayanagara patronage practices is the Smārta *matha* at Sringeri. Inscriptional, legendary, and literary sources consistently link the empire's founding dynasty, the Saṅgamas, to this *matha.*[19] Intellectually affiliated with Śaṅkara's Advaita Vedānta, this Brahmin community is famous for its involvement in the Vedic commentarial project undertaken or, perhaps, overseen by Sāyaṇa. On the basis of several inscriptions and the colophons of Sāyaṇa's works, many scholars believe that this large-scale, and likely collaborative, project was directly funded by the early Saṅgamas. Indeed, in the introductory passages to various sections of his Vedic commentaries, Sāyaṇa often identifies himself as the king's minister and implies that Bukka himself, reputed cofounder of the Saṅgama dynasty, supported his commentarial work. Sāyaṇa refers to himself in the preamble to *Ṛgsamhitabhāṣya* [*RSBh*] 7.3 as "Sāyaṇa, the king's minister and one of unimpeded understanding,"[20] and, in the preamble to *RSBh* 7.4, as "Sāyaṇa, the minister knowing the true essence of the Śruti."[21] Such claims about an author's status in religious and literary texts can be problematic sources of historic information in part because they may be later insertions by other authors interested in advancing the text's agenda. However, Galewicz's recent study of Sāyaṇa's commentary argues that inscriptional records in which the early Saṅgama kings gave land grants to several Brahmins in the Sringeri region and in which Sāyaṇa's name appeared first attest to the court's support of Sāyaṇa's intellectual project.[22]

In terms of the legendary accounts of the Sringeri Smārtas' significance, they vary in their specifics.[23] But they are nearly unanimous in giving pride of place to Vidyāraṇya,[24] eventual head of the Sringeri Smārta-Advaita *matha.* According to many of these accounts, a meeting between Vidyāraṇya and the Saṅgama brothers inspired not only the founding of the empire but the location of its capital in the region of the Virūpākṣa temple in Hampi. Virūpākṣa, a form of Śiva, served as the empire's tutelary deity for its entire duration.[25] Inscriptions indicate that at some point prior to 1515, the Sringeri Smārta community established an offshoot *maṭha* on the premises of this temple in the empire's capital.[26] This undoubtedly enhanced the Sringeri Smārtas' prominence at court.[27]

Of course, the legendary, literary, and inscriptional sources do not always match up in their presentation of events. This is most evident in the role ascribed in these sources to Vidyāraṇya. Vidyāraṇya is not mentioned in the inscriptional record documenting royal patronage of Sringeri until 1375. The Saṅgama dynasty was clearly patronizing this community as early as 1346, when the five Saṅgama brothers held their *vijayotsava* or "festival of victory" at Sringeri to inaugurate their reign. The inscription documenting this event also records a royal donation of nine villages to Bhāratītīrtha, who is identified in later *maṭha* records as one of Vidyāraṇya's teachers. In 1356, Bukka I made an additional gift of land honoring Vidyātīrtha, who is identified as the head of the Sringeri *maṭha* and, elsewhere, as one of Vidyāraṇya's predecessors.[28] However, by the year 1384, there is a lengthy reference to Vidyāraṇya, and specifically to Harihara II's[29] devotion to him, for his knowledge: "By the glances full of love of Vidyāraṇya, the chief of ascetics, he acquired the empire of knowledge [*jñāna-samrājya*] unattainable by other kings."[30]

This explicit royal affinity for the intellectual activities of the Sringeri Smārta community is substantiated, as we have seen, by inscriptions recording royal donations of land to Sāyaṇa, his sons, and his Brahminical community.[31] This royal support for scholarly activities continues in 1381, when Harihara's son Cikka Rāya gave three other scholars associated with Sāyaṇa even larger land grants.[32] In a 1380 inscription, Harihara II confirms all the previous grants; in 1384, he made a donation to the disciples of the sage Vidyāraṇya.[33] After Vidyāraṇya's death, some time in 1386 or 1387, Harihara II made a donation of land near Sringeri in honor of the *guru*.[34] Furthermore, in 1406, Bukka II gave an endowment for the renovation and proper maintenance of a library belonging to the *maṭha*.[35]

Thus, it is indisputable that the Saṅgamas placed many resources at the disposal of the Sringeri Smārta Brahmin community and, in doing so, supported that community's intellectual pursuits as well as its institutionalization. In fact, Kulke argues that it was not the Sringeri Smārta *maṭhādhipati*, Vidyāraṇya, who founded the Vijayanagara Empire but the Saṅgama dynasty that founded the Sringeri Smārta *maṭha*. Kulke bases this argument on early fourteenth-century inscriptions that refer to Sringeri as a *tīrtha*, or holy pilgrimage place, but do not mention a *maṭha*; the oldest inscriptional reference to the *maṭha*'s existence dates from 1356, ten years after the empire's likely founding.[36] Kulke also mentions references in the Vidyāraṇyapura inscription of 1386 to several *samādhi* shrines or temples housing the tombs of famous saints in the monastic community's lineage.[37] The names of these temples are Vidyāśaṅkara, Bhāratīrāmanātha, and Vidyāviśveśvara, all of whom were part of the early Vijayanagara-era cohort of Sringeri Smārtas. That both a *maṭha* and related *guru* shrines were established in Sringeri within a thirty-year period suggests not only a rapid but a very deliberate institutionalization of this Brahmin intellectual community into a monastic and religious order.

While Kulke's theory is appealing and has enjoyed a general scholarly approval, the various historical and theoretical implications of the Sringeri Smārtas' ties to the court remain unclear. There has been much scholarly speculation regarding the influence of this community on the political proceedings of the Saṅgama court but very little consensus. Older scholarly tradition, represented in part by Nilakanta Sastri's work, has used the legend of Vidyāraṇya's interactions with the Saṅgama brothers as evidence of the "Hindu" nature of the Vijayanagara Empire. Nilakanta Sastri draws primarily on a legend, according to which the five Saṅgama brothers had been captured by the Sultan of Delhi and converted to Islam during their imprisonment before being dispatched by the sultan back to the Hampi region to put down a rebellion on his behalf. Upon arriving in the region of the Virūpākṣa temple in Hampi, future site of the empire's capital, they witness the miraculous sight of a hare attacking a dog. Nilakanta Sastri maintains that this sight, combined with the Saṅgamas' subsequent encounter with Vidyāraṇya in this location, simultaneously inspired the brothers' reconversion to Hinduism and political break with Delhi:

> Their meeting with Vidyāraṇya ("Forest of Learning") thus probably furnished them with the best and perhaps only means of following the promptings of their hearts; it needed a spiritual leader of his eminence to receive them back from Islam into Hinduism and to render the act generally acceptable to Hindu society. Thus it happened that the trusted Muslim agents of the sultan of Delhi, who were sent to restore his power in the Deccan, turned out to be the founders of one of the greatest Hindu states of history.[38]

More recent scholarship has criticized this notion of the empire as a "Hindu state," established to resist the further spread of Islam, by citing the multiple stylistic borrowings on the part of Vijayanagara rulers from the northern sultanates of art, architecture, dress, and military tactics.[39] Further evidence contradicting a Hindu identity to the court can be found in the court's own religious diversity and its ecumenical patronage.[40] While some scholars maintain that this policy was a deliberate attempt to avoid religiously motivated conflict, Pollock offers a different reading. He argues that the Vijayanagara court was in fact indifferent to religion and that "religious distinctions were simply irrelevant to the exercise of power."[41]

Kulke's study of the Sringeri *matha* and the early Saṅgamas is an example of the type of analysis with which Pollock takes issue because it assumes the legitimating capacity of religion without explaining it. In doing so, it overstates the role of religion in precolonial Indian politics. Kulke emphasizes the necessity of the newly minted Saṅgama dynasty to gain religious elites' approval in order to legitimate their reign. But he also acknowledges the court's pragmatic concerns when discussing why the Sringeri Smārtas would have been singled out for this purpose. In Kulke's view, Sringeri's location near the old Hoysaḷa capital enabled the Saṅgamas to lay claim to a transfer of the mantle of power from this dying kingdom to its successor state. This idea is substantiated by the 1346 inscription in which the Hoysaḷa queen, widow of the last Hoysaḷa king, participates in the Saṅgamas' inaugural festival of victory held at Sringeri. At the same time, Kulke does assert that the intellectual and religious "reforms" of the Sringeri Smārtas offered a compelling vision of Hindu "orthodoxy" with which the Vijayanagara court sought to link itself in order to promote its empire as a new seat of orthodoxy. Here, Kulke emphasizes the tradition of Śaṅkara's having founded the Sringeri *matha,* putatively articulated in the *Śaṅkaradigvijaya.* While this text has often been attributed to the Sringeri Smārta Mādhava,[42] its date and authorship are in dispute and there is strong evidence that the Śaṅkara affiliation with the Sringeri *matha* was not established until the sixteenth century.[43] But for present purposes, the important thing is that Kulke's reading of events assumes that elite religious activity had real-world implications in its power to attract royal patronage.[44]

Drawing largely on Kulke's analysis, Galewicz's study of Sāyaṇa's commentary on the Veda claims that the empire was concerned with questions of Hindu orthodoxy owing to its practical aim of unifying diverse centers of power that were controlled by religious elites. Galewicz sees Sāyaṇa's royally funded Vedic commentary as being "in the service of the empire," insofar as it helped to unite these different centers of elite religious authority throughout the empire's territories into a common cause of preserving and enacting dharma.[45] Clark argues that the Vijayanagara court privileged orthodox, Vaidika Brahminism in a manner that departed from the previous era of South Indian kings, such as the Hoysaḷas, Kalachuris, and Kākatīyas, who had supported Śaiva and other institutions that were less concerned with Vedic Brahminical orthodoxy.[46] His findings support Galewizc's argument that something about Vedic orthodoxy seems to have resonated with the Vijayanagara court in a new and potent way. But Clark refrains from theorizing as to why this was so.

Thus, despite the emblematic status of the Sringeri *matha* to Vijayanagara patronage, the reasons why this Brahminical community was singled out by the state and what this implies about the "religious" sensibilities of the Vijayanagara court remain ambiguous. The possibilities, and their underlying assumptions, identified in the scholarly literature, can be enumerated as follows: 1. Sringeri Smārtas were singled out because of Sringeri's location; 2. the Sringeri Smārtas' religious reforms impressed the Saṅgamas, who thought aligning themselves with these reforms would legitimate their reign; 3. the court was actually concerned about articulating Hindu orthodoxy either to stand united against Islam or because such presumed sociocultural unity could enable more efficient rule; and 4. the Sringeri Smārtas' expression of orthodoxy, articulated in their Vedic commentaries and other texts, was somehow more legitimate and more unifying than that of other groups.

Adding to the above list Pollock's view that Vijayanagara patronage of religious institutions carried no political meaning whatsoever presents an almost untenable array of options for interpreting Saṅgama patronage of the Sringeri Smārtas. While it is beyond the scope of this book to address this issue definitively, concerned as I am with the sixteenth century, I would argue that this very ambiguity surrounding the Vijayanagara court's patronage of the Sringeri Smārtas suggests that royal patronage took into account a variety of factors. Only some of these factors were under the control of religious elites. The random luck of a religious community's location in a politically or strategically significant area played as much, if not more, of a role as that community's literary and religious pursuits. But this is not to say either that royal patronage did not influence Brahmin intellectual and religious activity or that such activity went unacknowledged by the court. Indeed, as Clark and others have argued, royal patronage favored—and, thereby, fomented—a certain type of religious and intellectual institutionalization, one that was Vedic, Brahminical, and often Vedāntin and organized into monastic institutions or *mathas*. In fact, the emblematic status that the Sringeri Smārta *matha* came to have for the court's religious sensibilities may reflect the court's privileging not merely of Smārta Advaita intellectualism but also of that community's institutional structure. It is here that Kulke's argument about Saṅgama patronage founding the *matha* is most important. Given that many religious communities that were not recipients of royal patronage organized themselves into *mathas* and codified their doctrines, practices, and intellectual lineages during this period, one could argue that Vijayanagara patronage of religious institutions fostered a generic institutionalization process that became standard for a variety of South Indian Hindu communities.[47] Because the nature of the Hindu *matha* was sectarian for all of the reasons discussed in chapters 1 and 2, Vijayanagara patronage encouraged religious diversity while formalizing Hindu sectarianism.

While the Sringeri Smārta community of the fourteenth century may have been privileged within the Vijayanagara patronage system, ample evidence in its literary production shows that it was also confronting intellectual and religious pluralism and attempting to reconcile this pluralism in ways advantageous to itself.[48] Sāyaṇa's nearly comprehensive Vedic commentary was not sectarian per se, but its totalizing agenda exhibited a desire both to assert and command a compelling symbol of Brahminical authority.[49] Furthermore, fourteenth-century Sringeri Smārta intellectuals also wrote a doxography of many of the systems of Indian thought called the *Sarvadarśanasaṅgraha*.[50] As Halbfass argued, this text is unique, not for its efforts to enumerate the arguments of major philosophical systems, but because it devotes entire chapters to systems that were of relatively recent origin and often prevalent in the Sringeri Smārtas' milieu. These would include chapters on Rāmānuja's thought, Madhva's thought, and several different systems of Śaivism. The inclusion of these more recent and locally prominent systems deviates from the more conventional format of these doxographies, which typically limit their discussion of *āstika* systems to what Halbfass called "the classical systems" (i.e., Sāṃkhya, Yoga, Nyāya-Vaiśeṣika, Mīmāṃsā, and Vedānta).[51] Furthermore, as Halbfass's survey of these doxographic works also notes, "the Advaita Vedānta doxographic texts are usually based upon a hierarchical classification at whose apex stands the Vedānta."[52] *The Sarvadarśanasaṅgraha* does not do this at any length, but it does conclude with the following statement: "The system of Śaṅkara, which comes next in succession [i.e., last], and which is the crest-gem of all systems, has been explained by us elsewhere; it is therefore left untouched here."[53] Thus, in a more explicit way than the *Vedabhāṣya,* the *Sarvadarśanasaṅgraha* attempts to privilege the Sringeri school by positioning its doctrinal system at the pinnacle of a philosophical hierarchy.

Finally, the reputed "inspirer" of the founding of the empire, Sringeri Smārta Vidyāraṇya, wrote a treatise on the Advaita concept of *jīvanmukti* called the *Jīvanmuktiviveka* or *The Examination of the Doctrine of Liberation while Living.* This text is a syncretism of Advaita theories of liberation with yogic ascetic and meditation practices. But it is also, as Goodding has argued, an attempt to critique Viśiṣṭādvaita's rejection of the *jīvanmukti* doctrine. Goodding maintains that Vidyāraṇya was seeking to establish the authority of his Advaita tradition of thought over that of Viśiṣṭādvaita precisely by emphasizing the special spiritual status of his religious gurus as *jīvanmuktas*, or those who had been liberated in life. He dates the crafting of Vidyāraṇya's *Jīvanmuktiviveka* to the period when the Vijayanagara Empire had acquired more territory in regions of South India that were typically dominated by Śrīvaiṣṇava groups, the proponents of Viśiṣṭādvaita Vedānta. Thus, Goodding theorizes that the *Jīvanmuktiviveka* could have been Vidyāraṇya's attempt to win over some of these groups to Advaita Vedānta.[54]

Goodding's argument is significant mainly because many of the fourteenth-century Sringeri Smārtas' intellectual projects, such as the *Sarvadarśanasaṅgraha* and Sāyaṇa's commentary on the Vedas, have been taken as evidence of a South Indian Hindu response to the challenge posed by sociopolitical incursions of Islam.[55] However, they could just as easily reflect a response to religious diversity within South India. While unifying against Islam or articulating a shared Hindu orthodoxy may have been features of Brahmin religiosity in this period, showing one's own sect to advantage in a milieu in which the court singled out sectarian institutions to act as recipients of royal patronage for a variety of reasons was also considered desirable. These reasons may have been religious, utilitarian, or some combination thereof, depending upon the circumstances. Sectarian leaders had limited control over these circumstances. Nevertheless, because the benefits of receiving such patronage were far-reaching, their concerns about positioning themselves advantageously in the court's patronage system shaped their intellectual production.

At the same time, it is not the case that Brahmin intellectual pursuits were simply a reflection of the court's agenda and of their desire to excel within it. Rather, these sectarian groups had their own agenda, which alliances with the court could help implement. The empire's expansion opened up potential new locations for the establishment of sectarian institutions and, correspondingly, for the spread of the sect's ideas and practices. As mentioned above, the emphasis on debate and polemics among Brahmin Vedānta sects in this period strongly suggests that these groups were looking to convert others to their systems of thought. This means that, while the Vijayanagara court's patronage practices engendered a more bounded sense of sectarian identity and increased sectarian competition for courtly resources, it also provided new social frameworks for philosophical dialogue, intellectual exchange, and religious conversion. These processes shaped both a shared religious arena and distinct sectarian identities.

## SECTARIAN COMPETITION AT THE SIXTEENTH-CENTURY COURT

Some scholars have argued that the sixteenth century witnessed a renewed interest in the Sringeri *maṭha*'s historical prominence at the early imperial court.[56] While the aforementioned scholarly theories regarding the role of the Sringeri Smārtas at the fourteenth-century Vijayanagara court are based to some extent on fourteenth-century sources, that many of the legendary accounts likely date from the sixteenth century is significant.[57] The oldest records of the legendary accounts of the empire's founding appear in the travel narrative of the Portuguese horse trader Fernão Nunes, whose account was likely written sometime in the 1530s but based on a visit to the city from an earlier decade during Kṛṣṇadevarāya's rule. It is this account, summarized above in the Nilakanta Sastri quote, that depicts the Saṅgama brothers' breaking of all political ties with Delhi and the founding of a new empire, subsequent to a dramatic encounter with Vidyāraṇya near Hampi.[58] Subrahmanyam has argued that Nunes's version distills narratives that would have been circulated in regional languages and later recorded in their various forms in the Mackenzie manuscripts.[59] However, while such stories were not likely invented by a visitor to the city, their existence prior to the sixteenth century is not supported by any hard evidence.

Writing in 1929, Henry Heras, a European Jesuit priest and epigrapher living in India, argued that the sixteenth-century head of the Sringeri *matha*, Rāmacandra Bhāratī (r. 1508?–1560),[60] forged copper plate inscriptions that recapitulated the above narrative in a manner that overstates Vidyāraṇya's and, by extension, Sringeri's influence, at the fourteenth-century Vijayanagara court.[61] The inscriptions that Heras identifies as spurious recount the legends of Vijayanagara's founding along the lines of what Nunes repeats in his account, except in a longer and more detailed form. These inscriptions also rename the city of Vijayanagara "Vidyānagara" or "City of Knowledge," linking Vidyāraṇya ("Forest of Knowledge") more directly to the empire's founding.[62] In Heras's estimation, Rāmacandra Bhāratī was reacting to the shift in royal patronage practices away from Virūpākṣa and Śaivism and toward the Vaiṣṇava deities Viṭṭhala and Veṅkaṭeśvara. That Rāmacandra Bhāratī's tenure as head of the Sringeri *matha* coincided with Vyāsatīrtha's time at the Vijayanagara court is for our purposes significant:

> Hence it may be concluded that the ascetics of the Śringeri math fabricated the story of Vidyāraṇya as the founder of the city and Empire of Vijayanagara, in the beginning of the XVIth century. And it seems most probably that the fabrication of the whole story and the falsification of a great number, if not of all the spurious grants above referred to, was perpetrated during the rule of Rāmachandra Bhāratī, who directed the Śringeri math from 1508 to 1560.[63]

Heras exhibits considerable bias against Hindu religious leaders in his work,[64] and his use of the terms "falsification" and "fabrication" to refer to the story of Vidyāraṇya's role overstates his case. Indeed, such terminology seems to credit Rāmacandra Bhāratī with completely inventing Vidyāraṇya's significance at the fourteenth-century Saṅgama court. Yet elsewhere, Heras cites as evidence of this fabrication the fact that Rāmacandra Bhāratī recalls an earlier gift of land by Saṅgama king Harihara to Vidyāśaṅkara (also known as Vidyātīrtha), one of Vidyāraṇya's *maṭhādhipati* predecessors at Sringeri. Rāmacandra Bhāratī does this in an inscription in which he is regifting this land. Heras maintains that this reminder of early Saṅgama patronage of the Sringeri *matha* "shows the wish of the Jagad-guru to show the early relations between the math and the Emperors of Vijayanagara. This was perhaps the first step in the campaign of falsification."[65] But falsification is not the same as highlighting the earlier prominence of his *matha* to the court.[66]

Heras's view has penetrated Vijayanagara studies to a significant extent, even the work of those who ostensibly repudiate it. Kulke points out that many studies of Vijayanagara tacitly accept Heras's argument by ignoring those inscriptions that speak of this meeting between Vidyāraṇya and the Saṅgamas at the Virūpākṣa temple.[67] Certainly, the legends of Vidyāraṇya's role as presented in the copper plates cited by Heras oversimplify things and, in doing so, contradict other parts of the inscriptional record. Vidyāraṇya was not the head of the *matha* until at least 1376. Furthermore, the founding of the empire seems to have been a gradual process, as power was transferred from the Hoysaḷas to the Saṅgamas sometime between 1346 and 1368.[68] It does not seem to have been an event that took place all at once, based on a single inspirational meeting.

Heras also seems to be correct that the status of Śaiva institutions, including the most prominent ones such as the Virūpākṣa *mandir,* affiliated with the Sringeri Smārta *matha,* was changing even in the early sixteenth century. At the time of his coronation, Kṛṣṇadevarāya made his very first construction effort in the capital city by adding a *maṇḍapa* (a covered porch) and a *gopuram* (a tower above an entryway) to the Virūpākṣa temple.[69] He continued to patronize Smārta monasteries throughout his reign.[70] Furthermore, as Verghese has demonstrated, when this king built the first Kṛṣṇa temple in the capital city in 1515, to house the Udayagiri Bālakṛṣṇa icon that he captured after his victorious conquest there, he seems to have sought the protection and blessings of Virūpākṣa for what was to be a new cult in the city. He had an image of a nobleman (possibly himself) worshiping a Śivaliṅgam prominently displayed in the porch outside the shrine's inner sanctum. It is situated just opposite a similar image of a nobleman worshipping Bālakṛṣṇa's image. Verghese argues that Kṛṣṇadevarāya asserted "through these two reliefs, that despite his patronage of Kṛishṇa and the promotion of this cult in the capital, he had no intention of relinquishing his links with Virūpākṣha."[71] The fact that Kṛṣṇadevarāya trod lightly around the issue of introducing a Kṛṣṇa cult into the city implies not only that this was a shift in devotional orientation on the part of the court in the early sixteenth century but that that shift might have been considered problematic by Smārta Śaiva religious leaders.

Yet even if Heras is correct about the sixteenth-century Sringeri pontiff Rāmacandra Bhāratī's role in "falsifying" the historical record in the form of forged copper plate inscriptions, it seems better to interpret this act as an embellishment of Sringeri's role in the early empire, rather than a complete invention. Rāmacandra Bhāratī may have been trying to remind everyone of his *matha*'s importance, an importance that is substantiated by many fourteenth-century records but that must have been waning at this time. Insofar as Rāmacandra Bhāratī's actions reflected sectarian competition for royal patronage, they attest to the vagaries of Vijayanagara patronage as well as to the value sectarian groups placed on receiving it. As such, his actions problematize Vijayanagara's vaunted ecumenism. Despite Kṛṣṇadevarāya's efforts to avoid the appearance of favoritism, sects were concerned about losing their standing. This reflects the reality that shifts in royal patronage privileged some groups over others.

Even more intriguing, perhaps, Rāmacandra Bhāratī's actions imply that historically verifiable claims of privilege affected sixteenth-century courtly standing.

As such, they hint at the role that historical consciousness played in shaping sectarian identity in this period. Like the biographies of sectarian leaders discussed in the previous chapter, inscriptions were understood to be powerful documents that could establish a given sect's long-standing sociopolitical prominence. This prominence, in addition to conferring various worldly benefits, might have been understood to validate that sect's intellectual activities and doctrinal positions. Because sectarian concerns about maintaining sociopolitical prominence were linked, inextricably, to the doctrinal and philosophical teachings of that sect, it should not be surprising that doctrinal disputes between such institutions became more pronounced as they also vied for courtly funding. Moreover, these doctrinal disputes, like the historical justification of claims to courtly privilege, also came to bear the imprint of historical thinking in their presentation of opponents' ideas.

## *JĪVANMUKTI* OR "LIBERATION WHILE LIVING"

To judge from Vyāsatīrtha's life story and his own writings, the Sringeri Advaitins' long-standing prominence at the Vijayanagara court made them a force to contend with. Of the two intellectual traditions that Vyāsatīrtha identifies as principal rivals, Advaita Vedānta is the one with which he takes greater issue. This is in keeping with Dvaita Vedānta as conceived by its thirteenth-century founder, Madhva (1238–1317), who was a realist and, therefore, espoused a pluralist ontology in which difference was posited as fundamental to being. In stark contrast to the nondualist Vedānta of Śaṅkara (c. eighth century), embraced by the Smārta Brahmins of Sringeri, in which reality is singular and all experience of difference is illusory, Madhva described reality in terms of a fundamental five-fold difference (*pañcabheda*) between the following ontological units: 1. God and souls, 2. souls and matter, 3. God and matter, 4. one soul and another, and 5. one form of matter and another. The form of difference with which the sect was primarily preoccupied was that between the individual human soul trapped in *saṃsāra* (the cycle of rebirth) and the ultimate reality of Brahman, whom Madhva identified with the Hindu god Viṣṇu.

Because of the stark differences between Advaita's idealistic monism and Dvaita's realistic pluralism, anti-Advaita arguments in Mādhva Vedānta have been part and parcel of the tradition from its inception. As such, they predate the founding of the Vijayanagara Empire. This means that Vyāsatīrtha's anti-Advaita polemics cannot be linked entirely to competition over courtly resources and prestige. Vyāsatīrtha was always operating within an established intellectual tradition that played a central role in shaping his arguments. Moreover, insofar as sectarian groups sought out royal patronage, they did so largely to spread their teachings. To a great extent, the teachings themselves were the focus of the sectarian institution's existence and, as such, were not servants to courtly patronage.

It is also true, in a much more general and obvious way, that philosophical arguments need not be linked to sociopolitical or economic concerns. Arguments may be made against other arguments simply because they are good arguments that need to be reckoned with in order for a philosopher or theologian to make his point. The best example of this, perhaps, is that Buddhist arguments continue to appear in Hindu polemical literature long after Buddhism ceased to exist in India. Thus, one could argue that Vyāsatīrtha's critical engagement with Advaita philosophy was simply a matter of constructing the most conceptually rigorous support for his own system of thought by trouncing its staunchest intellectual opponent.

But there is a definite historical and comparative consciousness evident in Vyāsatīrtha's polemical writings against Advaita that may reflect his sociopolitical circumstances. McCrea has discussed Vyāsatīrtha's historicism in terms of the Dvaitin's polemics on *śravanavidhi* or the injunction to listen to the Veda and the relationship of that injunction to the other important Vedānta injunctions, namely thinking about ("*manana*") and meditating upon ("*nididhyāsana*") the *Upaniṣads*.[72] McCrea demonstrates that Vyāsatīrtha's discussion of the relative importance of these injunctions in Advaita Vedānta presents conflicting perspectives internal to that tradition in historical order. As we shall see, Vyāsatīrtha makes a similar presentation of Advaita arguments supporting the concept of *jīvanmukti*. By referring to each of these arguments in rough chronological order as they were articulated by successive generations of Advaitins, who were responding to and enhancing the arguments of their predecessors, Vyāsatīrtha maps how this Advaita concept evolved. This map reveals both developments and fissures within the Advaita Vedānta intellectual community.

Such a historical approach to the Brahmin intellectual tradition contrasts somewhat with Dvaita's established view of the history of ideas. In Madhva's *Anuvyākhyāna* 2.2, v. 549, a minicommentary on his own commentary on foundational Vedānta scriptures, the *Brahma Sūtras*, Madhva expresses the idea that all currents of thought are, like streams of water, beginningless.[73] In this view, saying that Śaṅkara is the founder of the Advaita system or that Madhva is the founder of Dvaita is incorrect; they each merely gave voice, at particular moments in time, to doctrines that have always been true. This antihistoricist attitude is articulated widely in the Sanskrit literary tradition, especially regarding the Veda. As Pollock and others[74] have argued, the presentation of the Veda as beginningless and authorless is a means of safeguarding that tradition's authority by placing it beyond the vagaries of time and personality. That Vyāsatīrtha does not reject Madhva's notion that the *darśana*s, or philosophical viewpoints, are eternal in an explicit way, therefore, is not surprising. Yet the goal of his intellectual project, which is to thoroughly critique various basic Advaita concepts, arguably requires providing historical overviews of those concepts. At the same time, the period's increased emphasis on sects' historical positioning with respect to the court, evident in the potentially falsified inscriptions of Rāmacandra Bhāratī, may have influenced Vyāsatīrtha's mode of philosophical argument to make it more historical. As we have seen, sectarian communities in this period were concerned about documenting the history of their institutions, institutions within which the sect's ideas and philosophy were formulated. Thus, arguing for the cogency of a sect's philosophical arguments seems to have become intertwined with arguments supporting that sect's historical sociopolitical importance.

The sociopolitical implications of Vyāsatīrtha's critique of Advaita are particularly evident in a section of the fourth book of his *Nyāyāmṛta* ("*The Nectar of Logic*") called "*Jīvanmuktibhaṅga,*" in which he takes to task the Advaita doctrine of *jīvanmukti*. By regarding many of their monastic heads as having achieved this state, Smārta Advaitins implicitly claimed a particularly authoritative spiritual status for their religious leaders. In a paradoxical way, the sect extended its worldly influence through the presumed liberation of their leader from this world.[75] Śaṅkara (c. eighth century) and especially Vimuktātman (c. tenth–eleventh century) each argued for the necessity of a qualified teacher to achieve *mokṣa* and strongly implied that the most qualified teacher would be one who is in the state of *mokṣa* himself.[76] We should not then find it surprising that, as proponents of the Advaita tradition became organized into monastic institutions, leading teachers in these communities came to be regarded as *jīvanmuktas*.

Vyāsatīrtha's arguments against the Advaitins' doctrine of *jīvanmukti* are particularly interesting because his criticisms aim to show the superior suitability of this Advaita concept to Dvaita or "dualist" Vedānta. Indeed, in this section of the *Nyāyāmṛta*, Vyāsatīrtha equates the historically Advaita term *jīvanmukti* with Madhva's doctrine of *aparokṣajñāna* or "direct and immediate knowledge [of Brahman]."[77] As noted above, Vidyāraṇya, the fourteenth-century head of the Smārta *maṭha* and reputed inspirer of the founding of the empire, wrote a treatise on *jīvanmukti* called the *Jīvanmuktiviveka* or *The Examination of the Doctrine of Liberation while Living*. Vyāsatīrtha does not directly engage this text, despite his clear familiarity with much of the Advaita literature on this doctrine. But like the author of *Jīvanmuktiviveka*, Vyāsatīrtha also criticizes the Viśiṣṭādvaita form of Vedānta advocated by the Śrīvaiṣṇavas. While he does not address Viśiṣṭādvaita to any great extent in this section of the *Nyāyāmṛta* (as he will later on in this text, discussed in chapter 5 of this book), Vyāsatīrtha's statements on *jīvanmukti* here can be read as articulating a third alternative for understanding the stages of attaining liberation. Vyāsatīrtha intends this alternative to upstage both Advaita Vedānta, whose idealist monism is fundamentally incompatible with its own concept of liberation while alive, and Viśiṣṭādvaita Vedānta, which rejects the possibility of *jīvanmukti* altogether. In Vyāsatīrtha's formulation, *jīvanmukti* is most compatible with Dvaita's realism and in his system, therefore, does this socially and politically attractive doctrine find a home.

Indeed, if *jīvanmukti* made sense for the social life of Advaita doctrines, it was a challenge to defend philosophically, given Advaita's monist ontology and idealist epistemology, wherein difference of any kind is an illusion rooted in ignorance. Vyāsatīrtha exploits these difficulties in this section of his *Nyāyāmṛta*.[78] His presentation goes in rough chronological order, charting the emergence of various Advaita efforts to defend this doctrine against external criticism. But in organizing his presentation this way, Vyāsatīrtha also highlights debates over *jīvanmukti* internal to the Advaita tradition. His anti-Advaita polemics successfully take advantage of these internal disputes.

In Vyāsatīrtha's view,[79] the Advaitin's biggest difficulty is explaining how embodiment on the part of an enlightened being can continue if the content of that enlightenment exposes both the fundamental oneness of all being as well as the illusory nature of one's corporeal and spiritual individuality. Aware of this difficulty, Advaitin thinkers gradually developed two principal ways to address this problem. Vyāsatīrtha attacks them both.

The older theory that Vyāsatīrtha discusses is that of the *saṃskāra* or the notion that the products of ignorance are "impressions" that will continue for a while even after ignorance itself has been destroyed. It was Maṇḍana Miśra (fl. 690 CE), a rough contemporary of Śaṅkara, who first used the idea of *saṃskāra* to differentiate between *prārabdha karma,* or karma that is in the act of bearing fruit and will continue to do so after liberating knowledge has been acquired, and *avidyā* or ignorance, which ceases to exist.[80] According to Maṇḍana Miśra, the *prārabdha karma* will manifest itself postenlightenment for only a very brief time.[81] But it leaves a *saṃskāra* or an impression that is weaker than the karma itself but which explains why the enlightened being continues to bear witness to a world he knows is illusory. Vyāsatīrtha briefly summarizes this Advaita theory as follows:

> [The Advaitin] says, "The one who is liberated while embodied is he who has his ignorance destroyed through knowledge of true reality and yet who still sees the manifestation of the body, [the material world, etc.]. And the body, [material world, etc.] do not cease to exist immediately upon the destruction of ignorance through knowledge of true reality. [This is] because the continuation of that [body, material world, etc.] is due to the *saṃskāra* of ignorance, which is like the trembling produced by fear [of a snake that one subsequently realizes is a rope] and like a potter's wheel that continues to spin [even after the potter has stopped spinning it].[82]

The analogies of the potter's wheel and the rope misapprehended as a snake are found not only in Maṇḍana Miśra's *Brahmasiddhi* but also Śaṅkara's commentary on *Brahma Sūtra* 4.1.15.[83] They became stock Advaita analogies for the nature of the *saṃskāra*'s existence and its relationship to the ignorance that has been destroyed on the part of the *jīvanmukta*. But opponents met these analogies with the objection that if a *saṃskāra* is truly analogous to either of these examples, it must have either an action (as in the case of the potter's wheel) or a cognition (as in the case of a rope) as its cause. Neither *prārabdha karma* nor ignorance can be regarded as either an action or a cognition. Furthermore, in the case of ignorance, it no longer exists because it has been destroyed by liberating knowledge. And in the case of *prārabdha karma*, even Maṇḍana Miśra himself acknowledges that its continued "existence" is necessarily brief because it, too, arises from ignorance, which has been destroyed. Thus, identifying the cause of the *saṃskāra* remains problematic.

As Vyāsatīrtha then points out, the thirteenth-century Advaitin Prakāśātman dealt with this issue by using yet another analogy, in which the *saṃskāra* left by ignorance is likened to the smell of a flower that lingers in a box that once contained the flower. In the same way, according to Prakāśātman, even after ignorance has been destroyed, the *saṃskāra* of ignorance lingers on. Through this analogy, Prakāśātman attempted to maintain that there was neither relationship of material nor efficient causality between ignorance and the *saṃskāra;* rather the relationship was one of invariable concomitance between the *destruction* of ignorance and the *saṃskāra*. Furthermore, because the *saṃskāra* is not a material product, its eventual demise will not produce any further products. In other words, once the lingering *saṃskāra* (like the removed flower's smell) ceases to exist, the *jivanmukta* will achieve final liberation.[84]

But, as Vyāsatīrtha points out in his further synopsis of Prakāśātman's views, the Advaitin still needed to explain where the *saṃskāra* was located. Invoking established objections to this aspect of the *saṃskāra* theory, Vyāsatīrtha maintains that clearly the *saṃskāra* cannot be located in ignorance because, according to Advaita, ignorance has been destroyed in the state of *jīvanmukti*. Vyāsatīrtha reminds us that Prakāśātman was aware of this objection and, for that reason, maintained that the *saṃskāra* must be located in the pure self, which is in fact the only truly existing reality in Advaita ontology:[85] "Like ignorance, [the *saṃskāra's*] locus is the pure self. [The *saṃskāra* therefore] need not depend upon ignorance for its locus."[86] Of course, the question remained regarding how the pure self would then rid itself of this *saṃskāra*. Again resorting to Prakāśātman's efforts to explain this, Vyāsatīrtha reminds us of that thinker's claim that it is through some kind of ongoing realization of the true nature of reality that one eventually achieves total liberation from embodiment: "The *saṃskāra* ceases [to exist] through the repeated realization of the nature of reality."[87]

Having presented his synopsized chronological overview of the evolution of the *saṃskāra* theory of *jīvanmukti* within Advaita, along with the system's responses to various well-known objections, Vyāsatīrtha analyzes and refutes this theory. As is typical of Vyāsatīrtha's presentation in the *Nyāyāmṛta*, he employs a reductio ad absurdum technique, in which the opponent's faulty premises are taken to their equally faulty but logically unavoidable conclusions. Simultaneously, Vyāsatīrtha contrasts Advaita's idealist epistemology with Dvaita's realism and shows his system to great advantage. Vyāsatīrtha begins by arguing against the notion that a *saṃskāra* can be produced in the absence of a material cause:

> Now we say that as far as the *saṃskāra* [theory of *jīvanmukti*] goes, that is untenable. Because ignorance would have to continue as a cause for each of the following: 1. the *saṃskāra*, 2. the body, etc., and 3. the *prārabdha karma* [or the karma that is currently being worked off and] that is the cause of [the body, etc.]. All of these are positive products [i.e., produced by material causes] and superimposed realities [onto the ultimate singular reality of Brahman.][88]

Vyāsatīrtha is arguing that because all of these things, which the Advaitins themselves see as continuing in the state of *jīvanmukti,* are positive products and superimposed realities, they must have an actual cause. It is illegitimate, in his view, to claim that the *saṃskāra* produced by a mistaken cognition of reality, along the lines of misapprehending a rope for a snake, is real but its immediate cause is not *ajñāna* or ignorance.[89] In Dvaita thought, for the *saṃskāra* to be real, it must have a material cause and that cause would be the mistaken cognition. When a mistaken cognition occurs in Dvaita, an actual misapprehension has taken place, and thus it might produce some actual results. But in Advaita, that mistaken cognition itself is unreal, and thus, you cannot have a real *saṃskāra* produced from it.

Vyāsatīrtha also argues against Prakāśātman's idea that the state of *jīvanmukti* is temporary and will eventually come to an end after repeated incidents of awareness of reality's true nature as nondual. Here, Vyāsatīrtha maintains that, given the singular nature of reality in Advaita, arguing that repeated knowledge of it will reveal new information makes no sense. If ignorance alone was what obstructed insight into the true nature of reality and if ignorance has been removed, there should be the experience of complete liberation and not the halfway measure that is *jīvanmukti.* Furthermore, if the *saṃskāra* is not the same as ignorance, which has been destroyed, and if ignorance was what was blocking full insight into the nature of reality as nondual, the *saṃskāra* cannot now be identified as the factor obstructing complete knowledge of reality:

> Furthermore, it is not the case that the cessation of superimposed realities, which did not take place upon the initial realization of the true nature of reality would occur with subsequent knowledge [of that same reality]. [This is because] even though there is on-going perception [of that reality], [such perception] has no additional content. And because of the fact that, since the cover called "ignorance" no longer exists, there should then be instantaneous manifestation of the highest bliss for the *jīvanmukta.* You yourself have said that the *saṃskāra* is not a cover [obscuring knowledge of reality.][90]

Vyāsatīrtha also rejects the Advaitin's argument that, even though intellectually one may be aware that plural reality is an illusion superimposed onto the singular reality of Brahman, one may still perceive that plural reality because there is some lingering defect in one's cognition. The analogy used for this in Advaita thought, dating back to both Śaṅkara and Maṇḍana Miśra and invoked by many subsequent Advaitins, is that of looking at the moon while applying some pressure to one's eyelid with one's finger, thereby creating the illusion of two moons. Just as one knows intellectually there is only one moon and yet sees two, one may know that plural reality is false and yet still perceive its existence. Vyāsatīrtha concedes that the pressure applied to one's eyelid in the example is not destroyed by the knowledge that there is only one moon; indeed, such pressure may continue to cause the illusion of two moons to coexist with the knowledge that there is only one. However, Vyāsatīrtha also argues that, according to Advaita, once knowledge of Brahman has been attained, all external factors and defects of cognition must cease to exist because they have been revealed to be unreal. Thus, there can be no factor to explain the ongoing cognition of reality as plural once that reality has been revealed to be singular.[91]

Having vanquished to his satisfaction the *saṃskāra* theory as an attempt to explain how *jīvanmukti* is possible in a nondualist view of reality, Vyāsatīrtha then tackles a second theory that emerged within Advaita thought. Again, by tracing the various Advitain attempts to retain this sociopolitically powerful doctrine of *jīvanmukti,* Vyāsatīrtha points out disputes internal to that tradition. The second theory that Advaitins such as Sarvajñātman (c. ninth–tenth century) and Vimuktātman (c. tenth–eleventh century) offered to explain the state of *jīvanmukti* in their system was to argue that there was a *leśa* or a portion of ignorance that remained even after one realizes Brahman's nondual and featureless nature. This portion temporarily obstructs complete liberation on the part of the *jīvanmukta.* Vyāsatīrtha finds this idea an equally unacceptable means of explaining how an individual who has grasped the truth of reality's nondual nature continues to experience plurality:

> And as for the notion that [the world, body, etc. persist in *jīvanmukti*] because there is a *leśa,* a portion [of ignorance that remains], that too is untenable because ignorance is without parts. For the same reason, it also will not work to say that ignorance remains for some time as according to the analogy of the burnt cloth because you cannot apply the analogy of the burnt cloth to that which is without parts.[92]

Advaitins often used the burnt cloth analogy to explain the state of *jīvanmukti.* The burnt cloth, while destroyed by fire and subject to imminent disappearance, retains its basic outline and remains visible for some time. But Vyāsatīrtha contests the validity of this analogy on the grounds that ignorance in Advaita thought is not like a cloth; it is both inultimate (and therefore nonreal) and without parts.

Indeed, Vyāsatīrtha goes on to say that the *leśa* theory is also defective "because whatever persists by virtue of the fact that it is not destroyed by knowledge must be considered as ultimately real."[93] In other words, the *leśa* of ignorance, because it is not destroyed upon realization of the truth of nondualism would itself have to be an ultimate reality and, clearly, this is something the Advaitin would not accept.

Aware of these difficulties with the *leśa* concept, some Advaitin thinkers such as Citsukha (thirteenth century) modified the *leśa*'s definition, presenting it as a "form" of ignorance rather than as a part.[94] Vyāsatīrtha paraphrases his understanding of this view as follows:

> The *leśa* is to be thought of as an *ākāra* or a "form." According to *śruti* statements such as "*indromāyābhir...*" etc.,[95] ignorance has many forms [and thus,] even though there has been the cessation of the form [of ignorance] that causes the mistaken cognition that the material world is absolutely real, the form [of ignorance] that causes the appearance of the body, etc. continues. And there is the continuation [of the appearance of the body, etc.] even though the knowledge of true reality, which has the capacity to obstruct it, is present because *prārabdha karma* [karma that is in the process of being worked off] acts as an obstructor of that knowledge. [ ... ] The continuation of the form, despite the non-existence of the form-holder is legitimate because it is like the *jāti* or class that continues even if the individual members [of that *jāti*] no longer exist.[96]

Vyāsatīrtha's criticism of the *leśa* theory offers three basic alternatives to conceptualizing the *leśa* as a form of ignorance and then proceeds to show the conceptual flaws inherent in each:

> In case [the *leśa* is thought of as an *ākāra,* a form of ignorance], is the *ākāra* of the nature of a peculiar power [of ignorance?] Or is it a specific modification [of ignorance] like an earring that is made of gold [is a modification of gold]? Or is it an additional individual instance of ignorance? [i.e., you have destroyed one manifestation of ignorance, only to have it replaced by a completely new manifestation of ignorance.][97]

Vyāsatīrtha then argues that "it is neither the first nor the second option [i.e., that the *ākāra* of ignorance is a peculiar power or a modified form of ignorance] because if either of those things acts as a material cause of the mistaken cognition of the body, etc. then [you must allow that] there is the continued existence of ignorance [which is supposed to have been destroyed.]"[98] The idea here is that to describe the *leśa* in either of these ways does nothing to circumvent the basic difficulty that ignorance, according to Advaita, has been destroyed in the state of *jīvanmukti*. In this sense, the *saṃskāra* theory works a bit better because the Advaitin can claim that the *saṃskāra* is different from ignorance and persists even after ignorance is destroyed. The conception of *leśa* as a form of ignorance presumes ignorance's abiding existence. But this cannot be the case because, as Vyāsatīrtha says, "In terms of either of [these ways of understanding the *leśa*], which is different from the *ātman* and which is vulnerable to being destroyed by knowledge [of reality as non-dual] and which [must be regarded] either as ignorance itself or as a product of ignorance, it is not legitimate for the *leśa* to continue if ignorance has truly ceased to exist."[99]

Vyāsatīrtha further argues that the *leśa* can be viewed neither as a property of ignorance nor as a modified form of ignorance. If it were the former, the *leśa* could not then act as a material cause and if it were the latter, it is not clear how a form of a nonexistent thing could continue to exist: "In the case of viewing the *leśa* as a property of ignorance, it cannot be a material cause [of the cognition of the body, etc. in *jīvanmukti*] and it is also not legitimate for a form of something to continue in the absence of the form's possessor."[100]

Vyāsatīrtha also rejects the third option, wherein the *leśa* is considered to be an additional instance of ignorance that replaces the one that has been destroyed, "because it is not suitable within a perspective which says that ignorance is singular."[101] He also argues against the idea that there can be multiple instances of that singular ignorance, an idea implicit in Citsukha's argument that the *leśa* of ignorance may temporarily disappear for the *jīvanmukta* in states of meditation, on the following grounds:

> Even from the point of view of difference [within ignorance], is it the case that, after that previous ignorance, there is another type of ignorance that has additional objects of the senses? Or not? It's not the former because, in the case of a *nirviśeṣa* or attributeless reality, it is not proper to say that [ignorance has additional content]. But it is also not the latter view [that whatever was the content of the previous form of ignorance is going to be the same as this form] because, in an earlier chapter of the *Nyāyāmṛta*, the falsity of the following idea was established: "even when there is only one object of knowledge, there can be as many false understandings of it as there can be insights into it."[102]

Continuing with the theme that the *leśa* of ignorance might be conceptualized as something that manifests itself in discrete multiple instances over time, Vyāsatīrtha goes on to state that the Advaitins cannot maintain that an initial insight into reality as nondual occurs but full insight into it as nondual occurs later because the content of the insight cannot possibly have changed: "And it is not legitimate to say that ignorance is caused by a mistaken cognition of reality's true nature even in the state of *jīvanmukti* because it is not legitimate to argue that, even though previously there was complete knowledge of the object, the final apprehension of [reality's nature] occurs later."[103]

Finally, Vyāsatīrtha argues against the idea that *prārabdha karma*, or karma that is in the process of being worked off by the *jīvanmukta*, can be used to explain the state of *jīvanmukti* because its relationship to the *leśa* doctrine is one of mutual dependence. By invoking *prārabdha karma*, Citsukha is attempting to explain the persistence of the *leśa* of ignorance with reference to an individual's karma, but he is also relying on the abiding existence of the *leśa* as a form of ignorance to account for the continued experience of karma on the part of the *jīvanmukta*.[104]

Having criticized to his satisfaction and in historical order the two possible explanations for the continued experience of embodiment and plurality on the part of the *jīvanmukta,* Vyāsatīrtha comes out and declares that *jīvanmukti* is simply not an acceptable doctrine within Advaita thought. However, he also argues that *jīvanmukti* is perfectly consistent with Dvaita:

> Therefore, in the opponent's system of thought, because everything is the product of illusion and because illusion is destroyed by knowledge, *jīvanmukti* is not possible. But for us, in the case of the individual who has achieved *aparokṣajñāna* or direct and immediate knowledge of God, *jīvanmukti* is the continuation of *saṃsāra* due to the working off of *prārabdha karma,* absent the grace of God that is bestowed on the liberated one whose goal was [achieving that grace], because devotion to Brahman has not yet reached its highest peak which would enable one to obtain the highest bliss of which one is capable. But when [God's] grace does transpire, *mukti* has the nature of the complete cessation of suffering and the manifestation of bliss of a higher or lower caliber, depending upon one's innate nature.[105]

In fact, the founder of Mādhva Vedānta, Madhva, did not typically use the term *jīvanmukti* to describe his two-stage view of *mokṣa.* Instead, Madhva used the term, cited by Vyāsatīrtha in the preceding quote, *aparokṣajñāna,* which translates to "direct and immediate knowledge" of God or the ultimate reality. However, as both Daniel Sheridan and Roque Mesquita have argued, Madhva's *aparokṣajñāna* idea presents liberation as a two-stage process, beginning in embodied *saṃsāric* existence, when insight into the divine-human relationship is gained, devotion is practiced, and God's grace is incurred, resulting in a direct and immediate vision of God's multifaceted nature. Because of *prārabdha karma,* the jīva remains in *saṃsāra* until this already manifesting karma is spent, after which final liberation from saṃsāric existence is brought about through God's grace when the soul is released and achieves final and irreversible liberation from rebirth.[106] B. N. K. Sharma also describes Madhva's notion of *aparokṣajñāna* as "the fulfillment and culmination of all the *sādhanas*" and as "the penultimate state of final release."[107]

Thus, liberation in Dvaita Vedānta always was a two-stage process, and Madhva's *aparokṣajñāna* or "the direct and immediate knowledge of God is functionally equivalent to Advaita Vedānta's teaching of *jīvanmukti*."[108] Yet while Madhva may have occasionally made this equation himself,[109] Vyāsatīrtha's *Nyāyāmṛta* advanced the cause of treating the terms *aparokṣajñāna* and *jīvanmukti* interchangeably. In doing so, he attested to the dominance of Advaita categories in his context. Simultaneously, what Vyāsatīrtha did, if not with complete finality, then at least with an impressive display of virtuosity, was to problematize the use of the term *jīvanmukti* in Advaita Vedānta, so as to lay exclusive claim to it on the part of the Dvaita system.

He did this by highlighting all those aspects of Dvaita thought that make it the polar opposite of Advaita: its realism, its hierarchical relationship between the soul and Brahman, its belief that Brahman is qualified by all known attributes, and its emphasis on devotionalism and grace as the essential means to *mokṣa*. It is in Dvaita rather than Advaita thought that the doctrine of *jīvanmukti* can have its proper home. In this manner, Vyāsatīrtha coopted a sociopolitically significant doctrine away from a rival school and marshaled it to his sectarian cause.

This cooptation was helpful in establishing not only the conceptual superiority of Dvaita over Advaita but also its social superiority. Vyāsatīrtha's arguments in favor of *jīvanmukti* in Dvaita and against its possibility in Advaita imply that Mādhva renunciants could or perhaps had achieved a special state that was not conceptually possible within Advaita thought. Furthermore, Vyāsatīrtha's arguments implicitly posited Dvaita as superior to Viśiṣṭādvaita, which simply rejects altogether the possibility of liberation while alive.

## CONCLUSION

Sources from sixteenth-century Vijayanagara attest to the complex links between sociopolitical realities and the articulation of Brahmin sectarian identities, in which philosophical disputes played a key role. The period's intense sectarian polemics, its doxographic mapping of alternative systems of thought, and the renewed interest among Smārta leaders in establishing Vidyāraṇya's historic role in the empire's founding all indicate that a desire to establish strong ties to the court profoundly influenced Brahmin intellectual activity. Furthermore, the court's favoring of Vedic and Vedāntin *maṭhas* over other types of religious institutions and its gradual but ultimately pronounced shift in patronage away from Śaivism and toward Vaiṣṇavism over the course of the sixteenth century imply that royal patronage could be influenced by how Brahmin sectarian groups articulated their identities.

While recent scholarship on the empire emphasizes the "ecumenical" nature of Vijayanagara patronage and while there is evidence that ecumenical patron par excellence Kṛṣṇadevarāya was careful to be evenhanded, royal giving to religious and intellectual groups was certainly not unselective or infinite. Moreover, this selectivity was influenced by a variety of considerations, many of which were outside the control of religious elites. In response to this selectivity—both its predictability and its vagaries—Brahmin sectarian leaders were galvanized to pursue a variety of creative enterprises that influenced philosophical argumentation in important ways. As we have seen, this argumentation demonstrates an increased attentiveness to the history of ideas within rival intellectual traditions. This attentiveness in part reflects the processes of institutionalization that many Vedānta intellectual communities were undergoing in this period. Those communities that were organized into *maṭhas* were more readily linked to the political institutions of the court and the religious institutions of the temple; historical documentation of their existence helped to assert their claims to entitlements to a range of sociopolitical benefits. However, it was not just the desire to establish links to these established social and political institutions that impelled a historical approach to philosophical literature on the part of a *maṭhādhipati* like Vyāsatīrtha. Attentiveness to the history of a rival tradition's arguments often served to reveal the weaknesses of that tradition's ideas; the tradition's internal disputes could be mined to supply the best arguments against it. Precisely for this reason, the polemical literature of the period does not exhibit a simple "us-them" dynamic. There was a coopting of ideas and strategies that resulted in some interesting overlaps and a conceptual repositioning of the sects with respect to each another.

Thus, just as the relationship between royal and religious domains should not be oversimplified, that between different sectarian groups needs to be nuanced. Vyāsatīrtha's criticisms of Advaita Vedānta exhibit his command of a rich heritage of Vedānta argumentation and his development of that argumentation in subtle ways that are pertinent to his circumstances. His knowledge of Advaita positions exhibits a simultaneously historical and doxographic program that is part of a larger polemical agenda. It is ironic perhaps that his emphasis on doctrinal differences actually blurs some of the boundaries between the two sects. Through coopting his intellectual rivals' terminology, Vyāsatīrtha makes a case for Dvaita's unique doctrinal relevance even as he reveals, perhaps inadvertently, that the boundaries between opposing doctrinal traditions could be porous.[110]

That Vyāsatīrtha in some sense triumphed over not just Advaita Vedānta doctrines but Smārta religious institutions may be evident in speculations that he, and not the fourteenth-century Sringeri Advaitin, Vidyāraṇya, is the subject of a painting on the ceiling of the *mahāraṅgamaṇḍapa* or an elaborate covered pavilion on the Virūpākṣa temple's premises. This structure was installed by Kṛṣṇadevarāya in 1510, as one of his earliest construction projects. However, the painting is not contemporary with the king. As Dallapiccola has argued, it was likely added in the nineteenth century, when interest in the site was renewed and the temple was refurbished and reopened.[111]

Many scholars of Vijayanagara art and architecture, as well as of the empire's literary and religious traditions, have assumed that this painting depicts Vidyāraṇya (fig. 1).[112] However, Mādhvas have long held that it is in fact a portrait of Vyāsatīrtha, and there is some evidence to support this.[113] Elements of the central religious mendicant's entourage such as the green flags, the camel, and the drum are still today accoutrements of the *maṭhādhipati*s of those monasteries established by Vyāsatīrtha. Furthermore, these institutions consider these emblems to have been gifts bestowed upon Vyāsatīrtha during the reign of Sāḷuva Narasiṃha in return for Vyāsatīrtha's having filled in for several disgraced priests at Tirupati, who had allegedly stolen temple jewels.[114] That Sāḷuva Narasiṃha possessed these items is

FIGURE 1. Painting of an ascetic on the ceiling of the Virūpākṣa temple's *mahāraṅgamaṇḍapa*. (Photo by Anila Verghese)

attested to in the *Sāḷuvābhyudaya,* a biography of this king.[115] While the historical record connecting Sāḷuva Narasiṃha to Vyāsatīrtha is tenuous, it is nevertheless possible that these elements were widely recognizable aspects of Vyāsatīrtha's iconography prior to the commission of the painting in the Virūpākṣa *mandir*'s *mahāraṅgamaṇḍapa.* A local grandee from the nineteenth century may have been acting on such information, Vyāsatīrtha's reputation as Kṛṣṇadevarāya's guru, and popular legends such as the *kuhuyoga.*

If this image is, in fact, Vyāsatīrtha, his apotheosis in an institution historically affiliated with Sringeri Smārta Advaitins attests to his crossover status as the empire's *guardian saint* (to use Venkoba Rao and Verghese's term) as much as to his particular triumph over Advaita Vedānta in his polemics. That Vyāsatīrtha's image could be inserted into a historically Smārta and Śaiva institution would, if true, attest to the fact that he transcended his sectarian identity and became a generic and highly venerated figure, whose appeal cut across sectarian lines. This is certainly how he is viewed by many in Karnataka today.

This might seem ironic given how central his sectarian identity is to his anti-Advaita polemics and, by extension, to his fame. However, Vyāsatīrtha did transcend his sectarian identity in large part because of his borrowing from, mimicking, and working with other sects; this consolidated his alliances with them in a manner that would lead, ironically but also somewhat inevitably, to a blurring of some boundaries between these intellectual communities. This aspect of his philosophical argumentation becomes apparent only if we are willing to think about the full range of his interaction with the court and with other sects that were active there. While Vijayanagara patronage propelled a process of institutionalization that cultivated sectarian boundaries, these boundaries were also continually renegotiated through ongoing interactions, interactions that were themselves facilitated by Vijayanagara patronage. To understand further the specifics of Vyāsatīrtha's role in these negotiations, let us now examine his material, social, and ritual exchanges with the Śrīvaiṣṇavas.

4

## Allies or Rivals?

*Vyāsatīrtha's Material, Social, and Ritual Interactions
with the Śrīvaiṣṇavas*

In his polemical works, Vyāsatīrtha also identifies the Śrīvaiṣṇavas as intellectual rivals. This movement had affiliated with religious institutions in the Tamil country as early as the tenth century and, from the fourteenth century on, enjoyed a growing institutional presence in southern Andhra. Doctrinally, Śrīvaiṣṇavism encompassed both a popular vernacular piety and a more rarified Sanskrit tradition of Vedānta intellectualism. It flourished at the sixteenth-century Vijayanagara court, and this presented both opportunities and challenges to Vyāsatīrtha and the Mādhvas.

Compared with the documentation of Vyāsatīrtha's relations with the Advaitin Smārtas, which consists primarily of his polemics against them, the documentation of his relations with the Śrīvaiṣṇavas is more multifaceted. This is due to the fact that Mādhvas and Śrīvaiṣṇavas have a lot in common and, therefore, a more complicated relationship. Doctrinally, both Mādhvas and Śrīvaiṣṇavas identify Brahman with Viṣṇu and conceptualize the ultimate reality as possessing attributes. Both communities believe that liberation from the cycle of rebirth (*saṃsāra*) requires some acknowledgment of Viṣṇu's supremacy over the individual human soul. Both sects assert the actual existence of the physical world and the reality of *saṃsāra*. Finally, both argue that souls retain some distinct identity in the state of *mokṣa* rather than losing all individuality as in Śaṅkara's Advaita.

These doctrinal similarities had practical implications in that both Mādhvas and Śrīvaiṣṇavas worshipped in temples dedicated to Viṣṇu's various forms. Moreover, they worshipped these forms according to Pāñcarātra ritual practices, albeit with important sectarian inflections. While it seems that during the sixteenth century, these two groups shared several prominent, royally patronized religious spaces and collaborated on the general format of the ritual proceedings there, evidence suggests the eventual dominance of Śrīvaiṣṇavas in temple life at the sixteenth-century Vijayanagara court.[1] There is also evidence that Vyāsatīrtha worked to gain a firmer foothold for Mādhva Brahmins in these shrines. Thus, much like his relationship with the Advaitin Smārtas, Vyāsatīrtha was in competition with the Śrīvaiṣṇavas for royal attention. This competition manifested itself most clearly in a detailed doctrinal critique of the Śrīvaiṣṇavas' form of Vedānta, Viśiṣṭādvaita, to be examined in the next chapter.

However, when we study the full range of Vyāsatīrtha's interactions with the Śrīvaiṣṇavas, there are many indications that Vyāsatīrtha sought to improve his sect's standing at court precisely by forming an effective functional alliance with this alternative Vaiṣṇava group. He facilitated this alliance, which was rooted in their shared Vaiṣṇavism and which greatly benefited each sect, largely through material exchanges that had both practical and honorific implications. Vyāsatīrtha donated land, cash, and other provisions to Śrīvaiṣṇava-dominated temples in ways that increased this sect's ritual largesse and, by extension, its social and religious prestige. But such gifts, which typically involved perpetual reenactment of specific rituals, also promoted Mādhva Brahminism's long-term visibility in certain regions. Publicly displayed inscriptions documenting these arrangements increased Vyāsatīrtha's fame while the arrangements themselves often created long-standing economic relationships between Mādhva Brahmins and various local constituencies. Because these constituencies included agriculturalists, suppliers, and craftspeople, Vyāsatīrtha's gifts to Śrīvaiṣṇava-dominated institutions implicated a broad swath of South Indian society.

The alliance Vyāsatīrtha forged with the Śrīvaiṣṇavas through gifts to Śrīvaiṣṇava-dominated temples also spread the institutional network of Mādhva Brahminism into Tamil- and Telugu-speaking regions. As we saw in chapter 2, these regions were increasingly the focus of Vijayanagara statecraft owing to a variety of economic and military factors. Rebelliousness in these areas among local chieftains and even, occasionally, on the part of the empire's own heavily militarized *nāyaka*s, or overlords, restricted the empire's access to valuable overseas trade routes and productive weaving communities along the Coromandel coast. In the wake of military reconquests of these rebellious areas, Kṛṣṇadevarāya often lavishly patronized prominent local temples in an effort to integrate these regions more effectively into the empire (see map 4 and its discussion in chapter 2). It seems that Śrīvaiṣṇava institutions in particular benefited from this system. This may have had to do, in part, with the initiative of Śrīvaiṣṇava leaders who, as A. Rao's recent work has demonstrated, sought to establish fruitful connections with the Vijayanagara court through their theologization of the *Rāmāyaṇa* and their related identification of the Vijayanagara king with the Hindu epic's divine protagonist, Rāma.[2] Furthermore, Śrīvaiṣṇava emphasis on vernacular traditions and extensive proselytization efforts throughout the Tamil country also may have improved this group's courtly standing. Thus, by participating in Śrīvaiṣṇava religious projects, Vyāsatīrtha secured his sect's place in the orbit of the court's attention and consolidated his relationship with Vijayanagara royals.

For its part, Kṛṣṇadevarāya's court actively supported this alliance between Mādhvas and Śrīvaiṣṇavas, even as it occasionally fostered competition between these two sects. An alliance between these two Vaiṣṇava groups was good for the court because it brought together different regional and linguistic traditions of Viṣṇu worship under the auspices of large temple complexes that attracted diverse pilgrims. Insofar as royal donations to temples were a means of forging connections with various constituents of the empire, the more variegated and inclusive the temple, the better for royal outreach.

At the same time, Vyāsatīrtha's material exchanges with the Śrīvaiṣṇavas were also motivated by competition, and the court's role in this intersectarian relationship was sometimes that of arbiter. It was always the case that large South Indian temples dedicated to Viṣṇu catered to a variety of Vaiṣṇava publics. In this sense, they were pluralistic spaces that were united in a shared, somewhat open-ended Vaiṣṇava identity that predated Vyāsatīrtha's initiatives to forge a Mādhva-Śrīvaiṣṇava alliance.[3] This shared Vaiṣṇava identity transcended sectarian divisions in many ways, but in other ways, it reinforced them. Indeed, some of the temples that I call "Śrīvaiṣṇava-dominated" got that way only through a concerted effort on the Śrīvaiṣṇavas' part. Often, they "held" these spaces through arrangements that, of necessity, satisfied the requirements of other groups, who had equal, and often older, claims to the temple's management. Issues of control would sometimes arise and there is evidence that the Vijayanagara court occasionally mediated intersectarian or intrasectarian disputes.[4]

Yet while the Vijayanagara court may have used its patronage to negotiate tensions between factions at temples, it also seems on occasion to have stirred them up in an effort to rein in the local power of particular sectarian organizations and leaders. Inscriptions of the *śīlaśāsana* variety, wherein sectarian leaders make donations to temples on their own initiative, indicate that these leaders commanded considerable resources and could use them in ways that promoted their own local authority. As we saw in chapter 2, this authority may have competed with that of the state. In some instances, it seems that Kṛṣṇadevarāya used intersectarian or intrasectarian rivalries to quash this competition. Some of the court's gifts to Vyāsatīrtha at Śrīvaiṣṇava-dominated institutions may have served this purpose.

Thus, even if royal patronage in general conformed to certain patterns, each gift had its own implications that reflected a variety of local, regional, and imperial interests. Vyāsatīrtha's efforts to forge an intersectarian alliance with the Śrīvaiṣṇavas, through material exchanges that carried ritual, social, and honorific implications, are historically significant precisely for this reason. They simultaneously illuminate what constituted a shared Vaiṣṇavism between Mādhvas and Śrīvaiṣṇavas and what boundaries persisted between them. Moreover, they shed light on the context within which these processes of defining relative sectarian identity took place. Yet while Vyāsatīrtha's interactions with Śrīvaiṣṇavas reveal certain patterns, the understanding of which enhances our general sense of this period, they also reflect the dynamic responses of individual agents to historic contingencies. Such responses also played their part in the shaping of sectarian identities.

## MĀDHVAS AND ŚRĪVAIṢṆAVAS AT THE IMPERIAL CAPITAL

Recent scholarship on religion in sixteenth-century Vijayanagara argues that, as Smārta Advaita influence and Śaivism were on the wane, beginning with the reign of Sāḷuva Narasiṃha and continuing through the subsequent rulers of the Tuḷuva dynasty, Śrīvaiṣṇavism rose to a position of prominence in almost direct correspondence.[5] It is true that, beginning during the reign of Kṛṣṇadevarāya, Virūpākṣa's status as the royal court's favored deity was gradually compromised—first by the addition of Viṭṭhala (a form of Viṣṇu) as a witness to the arrangements recorded in various inscriptions and ultimately by the elimination of Virūpākṣa from these records during the reign of Rāmarāya, Sadāśiva's regent.[6] Correspondingly, the main temple to Viṭṭhala in the capital city of Vijayanagara became the hub of religious activity in the early sixteenth century. Many new pavilions (*maṇḍapas*), towered gateways (*gopurams*), colonnades, and subsidiary shrines were built within the temple grounds while monasteries, related temples, feeding houses, and streets for conducting processional festivals were constructed around it (see map 5).

For example, in 1513, Kṛṣṇadevarāya's two queens arranged for large towered gateways, visible from a distance, to be constructed in the outer walls of the Viṭṭhala temple. In 1516–17, Kṛṣṇadevarāya celebrated the recapture of territories lost to the Gajapati kingdom in the northeast by constructing a hundred-pillared hall on the Viṭṭhala temple grounds. According to Verghese, the pillars in this hall are significant because they attest to the Viṭṭhala temple's affiliation with the Śrīvaiṣṇavas; many of them are inscribed with *nāmams* or sectarian marks associated with the northern and southern factions of this sect, later known as Vaṭakalai and Teṅkalai, respectively.[7] From the period after Kṛṣṇadevarāya's reign but during the lifetime of Vyāsatīrtha, another inscription documents the installation of images of the Ālvārs or Śrīvaiṣṇava saints inside the Viṭṭhala temple.[8] Later in the sixteenth century, under the successive reigns of Acyutarāya and Rāmarāya (Sadāśiva's regent), new freestanding temples to Rāmānuja and the Ālvārs were built around the Viṭṭhala temple, attesting to the expansion of Śrīvaiṣṇava dominance in this region of the city.[9]

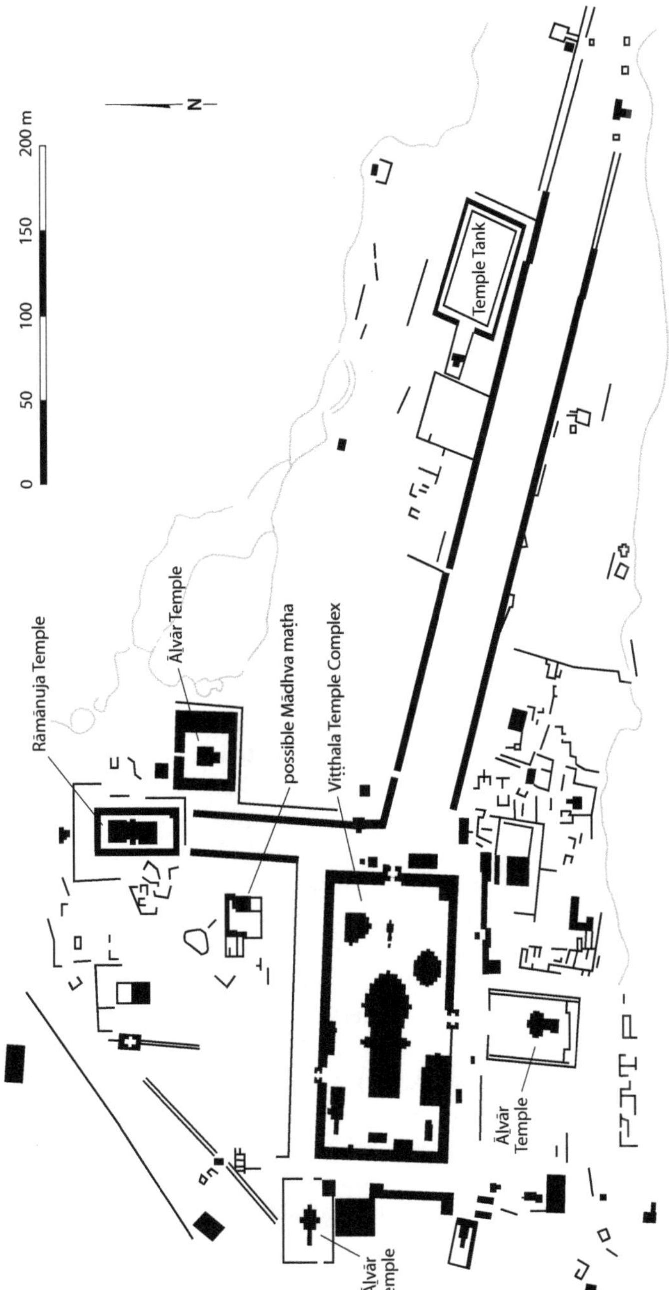


MAP 5. Viṭṭhalapura.

Not all of these developments were royally funded nor were all explicitly Śrīvaiṣṇava. A variety of Vaiṣṇava constituents representing various labor and linguistic communities made contributions to the temple, a fact that is suggested by the languages of the inscriptions. While the majority of the royal grants are in Kannada, one by Kṛṣṇadevarāya is recorded in the empire's three main languages, Kannada, Telugu, and Tamil.[10] In addition to the Tamil-speaking Śrīvaiṣṇava elites, such as merchants who installed various Āḻvār statues and made donations to support their worship, local boatmen, who ran the ferry service across the Tungabhadra river, which was vital to the capital's functioning, also donated shares of their earnings to support temple worship.[11] These diverse nonroyal donors were motivated in part by their personal devotion but also, perhaps, by a desire either to acknowledge or pursue close ties to the court. This is not surprising, given the variety of social, economic, and political networks that were forged through donations to these royally funded temples. Indeed, sectarian leaders themselves made donations to such temples precisely to implicate their communities in such developments.

Strong evidence exists that in the early sixteenth century the Mādhvas had a *matha* in Viṭṭhalapura[12] (see map 5), and in 1513, a royal edict from Kṛṣṇadevarāya granted Vyāsatīrtha three shares of the temple's food offerings.[13] Images of Viṭṭhala are found on the tombs of two Mādhva leaders, including that of Vyāsatīrtha (see fig. 2), located in the capital city; one of these is not far from the Viṭṭhala temple.[14]

Furthermore, there is evidence linking important members of the Haridāsakūṭa, or Mādhva-affiliated devotees of Viṣṇu famous for their devotional songs in Kannada, to the Viṭṭhala temple in the imperial capital. Both Purandaradāsa and Kanakadāsa, who are believed to have been Vyāsatīrtha's disciples, are supposed to have lived and worshipped there, while other members of the community made pilgrimages to the temple.[15] This implies a broad Mādhva-associated constituency was at the temple. Finally, in 1532, during Acyutarāya's reign, Vyāsatīrtha donated an icon of Yogavarada-Narasiṃha to the Viṭṭhala temple,[16] indicating that he sustained his interactions with this temple for a lengthy period (see Viṭṭhala temple floor plan). His donation of this particular icon may have been his way of underscoring his close ties to the court, which placed images of Narasiṃha at the capital's gateways to serve a protective function. The yogic component of the icon that Vyāsatīrtha donated to the Viṭṭhala temple links the more martial nature of this *avatāra* of Viṣṇu to his ascetic side, a side that Vyāsatīrtha, a *saṃnyāsin*, would want to play up. Indeed, sectarian leaders' installation of icons of Viṣṇu's various forms at large, royally funded temples served both to integrate different Vaiṣṇava communities into a single devotional body and gave prominence—by implying a royal seal of approval—to a particular sect's conception of the deity.[17]

Thus, Mādhvas and Śrīvaiṣṇavas were clearly in the habit of sharing sacred spaces. Yet because of the presence of both Mādhva and Śrīvaiṣṇava imagery in the

FIGURE 2. Vyāsatīrtha's *bṛndāvana*, side with Viṭṭhala image.

Viṭṭhala temple, there is some debate in the scholarly literature over which sect controlled it.[18] This debate reflects the ambiguity in this period of Mādhva-Śrīvaiṣṇava relations, which were simultaneously competitive and collaborative. There is strong epigraphic and monumental evidence that ultimately the Śrīvaiṣṇavas came to control the Viṭṭhala temple, as they did many of the other Vaiṣṇava shrines in the capital city. According to Verghese's review of the temple's inscriptions, the Śrīvaiṣṇavas seem to have dominated at the Viṭṭhala temple.[19] However, the dating of these inscriptions indicates that this dominance of Śrīvaiṣṇava festivals and ceremonies did not occur explicitly until after Kṛṣṇadevarāya's reign and that it proliferated after the death of Vyāsatīrtha.[20] Thus, Śrīvaiṣṇava dominance cannot be definitively asserted for the period of Kṛṣṇadevarāya's rule. For this period, all that can be said is that both sects used the temple and made contributions to it.

Verghese also theorizes that the Śrīvaiṣṇavas dominated the new Bālakṛṣṇa temple, built by Kṛṣṇadevarāya in the capital's "sacred quarter" in 1515, to celebrate his conquest of Udayagiri and his triumphant return to Vijayanagara with an icon of the infant Kṛṣṇa taken from that fort (see map 6 for location of Kṛṣṇa temple). Mādhvas have long claimed a special role in that now defunct temple by virtue of the fact that Kṛṣṇa in his infant form is commonly worshipped by Mādhvas.

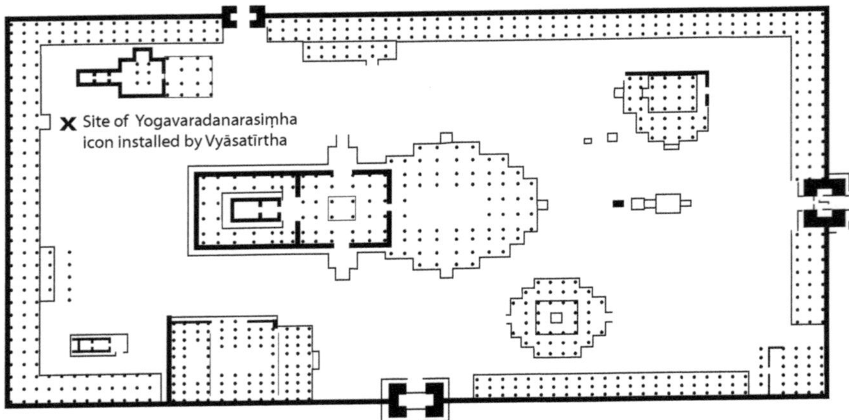


Floor plan of the Viṭṭhala temple.

Furthermore, Vyāsatīrtha is well known to have composed a devotional song in Kannada to this deity upon its arrival in the capital city. Finally, in two lengthy inscriptions, which together document the single most lavish donation to any temple made by Kṛṣṇadevarāya, thirty-seven Brahmins, mentioned by name, are appointed to conduct various temple tasks.[21] The Mādhvas have traditionally held that two of these are Mādhva names, Rāmaṇṇācārya and Mulbagal Timmaṇṇācārya, which indicates that Mādhva Brahmins played an active role in the temple's ritual program. Verghese, however, disputes this and argues that the iconography in the temple, in the form of inscribed Śrīvaiṣṇava *nāmam*s and Āḻvār statues, attests to its association with Śrīvaiṣṇavism. In her estimation, while Mādhvas certainly used the temple, they did not control it and a Śrīvaiṣṇava ritual program would have prevailed there.[22] However, while it does seem that Śrīvaiṣṇavas dominated the temple after the reign of Kṛṣṇadevarāya, there is no clear evidence of this during Vyāsatīrtha's lifetime. In fact, it may be that Kṛṣṇadevarāya mentions the Brahmins individually for the precise reason that they were handpicked from the two different sects, Mādhva and Śrīvaiṣṇava, to manage the temple. Indeed, Mulbagal was a major Mādhva institutional center at that time; it is where Vyāsatīrtha himself spent several years studying under the Mādhva guru Śrīpādarāja.

In contrast to both the Viṭṭhala and the Kṛṣṇa temples, another significant Vaiṣṇava temple, the Rāmacandra temple, was located in the royal center amid the living quarters of the king and other nobles. According to Verghese, this temple, which accommodated only the priests and the royal family, was likely designed exclusively for royal use.[23] Yet even though this was a private temple, it was definitely linked to the public religiosity of the empire. In fact, Fritz, Michell,

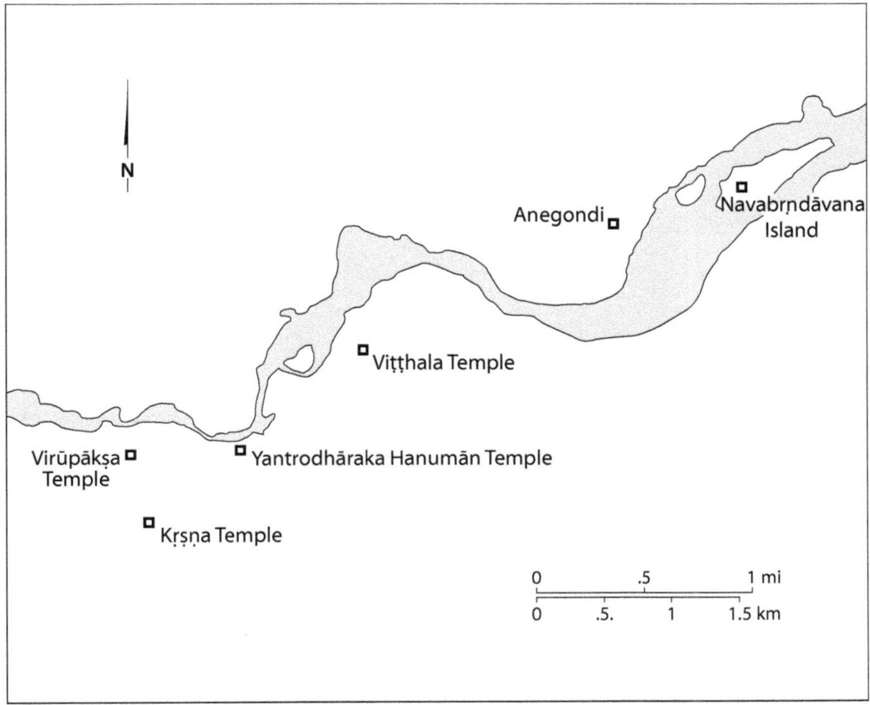


MAP 6. Mādhva sites in the imperial capital.

and M. S. Nagaraja Rao have mapped axial systems and circumambulatory routes to demonstrate that the entire capital city was oriented around this temple at the royal center.[24] Citing this evidence, A. Rao argues that this orientation had the effect of "transforming the geography of the city itself into an emblem of the identification between king and god."[25]

The Rāmacandra cult was particularly important because of the role it played in the Mahānavamī festival. During this festival, the Vijayanagara king and the deity Rāma, in his triumphant return to Ayodhyā as described at the end of the Rāmāyaṇa, were identified ritually: "On a central platform in front of the Rāmacandra temple the king identified himself with Rāma, granted honours and reviewed the army in an ostentatious exercise of military and political power."[26] A. Rao maintains that the Śrīvaiṣṇavas played an active role in promoting the Rāma cult, in ways that enhanced their status at court. As he puts it, "The connection between Śrīvaiṣṇavas and Rāma worship was not an insignificant one but rather the result of a strategic partnership between Vijayanagara kings and members of the Śrīvaiṣṇava order."[27]

FIGURE 3. Yantrodhāraka Hanumān icon.
(Photo by Anila Verghese)

While there is no similar evidence to support any Mādhva affiliation with this temple, it seems significant that, as discussed in chapter 2, Vyāsatīrtha took Rāmacandra as the tutelary deity of his *maṭhas*. This would suggest, that, much like the Śrīvaiṣṇava leaders, Vyāsatīrtha sought to emphasize his sect's affiliations with the epic in a manner that was beneficial to his sect. Indeed, there is evidence that Vyāsatīrtha and his Mādhva contemporaries at Vijayanagara participated in this Śrīvaiṣṇava project of developing a cult at Hampi of Rāmāyaṇa figures, particularly the deity Hanumān. Reverence for Hanumān as an incarnation of the wind god Vāyu had been a significant feature of Mādhva Brahminism since the sect's beginning, when Madhva proclaimed himself the third *avatāra* of Vāyu, after Hanumān and Bhīma. That the region of the Vijayanagara capital had long been associated with Hanumān's residence in the monkey kingdom of Kishkinda was a significant advantage to Vyāsatīrtha for establishing a connection between Dvaita Vedānta and local religious associations. While Vyāsatīrtha may not have installed the 732 icons of Hanumān in the capital city as the *Vyāsa Vijaya* credits him with doing,[28] he is firmly associated with establishing a Mādhva Hanumān shrine, wherein the icon bears distinctive Mādhva imagery (see fig. 3).

The deity in this temple, which is located on the banks of the Tungabhadra (see map 6), is called the Yantroddhāraka Hanumān and sits in meditation inside

FIGURE 4. Vyāsatīrtha's *bṛndāvana*, front.

two intersecting triangles.[29] This temple remains an active one, wherein Mādhva Brahmins conduct the rites.

Furthermore, on Vyāsatīrtha's tomb, located on Navabṛndāvana Island in the Tungabhadra River, an image of Rāma-Sītā-Lakṣmaṇa and Hanumān faces outward into the remains of the *maṇḍapa* that is in front of the tomb (figs. 4 and 5). Across

FIGURE 5. Vyāsatīrtha's *bṛndāvana*, close-up of front.

from this *maṇḍapa* is a small Hanumān temple, which is tended today by Mādhva priests. The Hanumān image is distinctly Mādhva—the deity is seated in a lotus pose and holding a book on his lap—although it does not seem that this temple dates to the sixteenth century. Finally, there is a sixteenth-century image of Caturbhuja Hanumān, or "Four-Armed Hanumān"—facing the tomb of Vyāsatīrtha's sectarian colleague and contemporary, Raghunandana, and located along the banks of the Tungabhadra River—between the Virūpākṣa and the Viṭṭhala temple complexes. This image depicts Hanumān holding, respectively, a conch shell, a discus, a mace, and finally a book in each one of his four hands. Again, it is primarily the book that identifies this icon as distinctly Mādhva. Thus, Mādhvas in the Vijayanagara capital at the time of Vyāsatīrtha participated actively in the theologization of the Rāmāyaṇa project initiated (and, it would seem, dominated) by the Śrīvaiṣṇavas. By linking traditional Mādhva motifs with courtly emblems and associations and by working with their Śrīvaiṣṇava rivals in pursuits that were of clear benefit to the court, Vyāsatīrtha and the Mādhvas promoted their own sect's visibility.

Therefore, while I would agree with Verghese and A. Rao that Tuḷuva Vaiṣṇavism seems to have been largely synonymous with Śrīvaiṣṇavism, (particularly post-Kṛṣṇadevarāya), I would also argue that Vyāsatīrtha actually deserves some of the credit for this. Vyāsatīrtha's interactions with this group likely abetted Śrīvaiṣṇavism's distinctive success, even as these interactions also extended Mādhva Brahminism's influence both at court and in society at large. By involving his sect in various ways with Śrīvaiṣṇava projects in the empire's capital, Vyāsatīrtha helped to articulate a generic, multifaceted, transsectarian, and transregional Vaiṣṇavism that simultaneously made Mādhva gurus, devotional songs, iconography, and institutions better known. Because this generic Vaiṣṇavism had great potential to bring together different Vaiṣṇava linguistic, devotional, ritual, and labor communities under the auspices of large temple complexes, it was particularly attractive to the court, which used temple patronage partly as a form of outreach to different constituents of Vijayanagara society. Insofar as temples with both Mādhva and Śrīvaiṣṇava icons and activities broadened their appeal among different Vaiṣṇava publics, an alliance between these sects attracted royal favor. Because royal gifts were often intended expressly for redistribution among other sectors of society, those sects that enjoyed royal support thereby increased their popular following.

## BEYOND THE IMPERIAL CAPITAL: VYĀSATĪRTHA'S RELATIONS WITH ŚRĪVAIṢṆAVAS AT KANCHIPURAM AND TIRUPATI

### *Kanchipuram*

That Vyāsatīrtha's cultivated alliance with the Śrīvaiṣṇavas was important to his stature at Kṛṣṇadevarāya's court is evident in the fact that the first inscriptional reference to Vyāsatīrtha involves the Śrīvaiṣṇava-dominated Varadarāja temple in Kanchi. A Tamil inscription of the *rāyaśāsana* or "royal edict" genre, dated August 13, 1511, and carved onto the base of the east wall of the Aruḷāḷa-Perumāḷ temple (also known as the Varadarāja temple), documents Vyāsatīrtha's gift of the produce from the village of Pulompakkam in Vadapanadu to this temple. The inscription states that Vyāsatīrtha had received this village as a gift from Kṛṣṇadevarāya and stipulates that the produce from the village be used to conduct worship to the deity on the occasion of Āvaṇi or the annual event in which Brahmins change their sacred thread. The inscription also records the fact that Vyāsatīrtha augmented rituals associated with the commencement of major festivals by arranging for a vehicle throne to be supplied "for the god to relax in during the midday on the occasion of the flag-hoisting ceremony."[30] Flag-hoisting ceremonies typically initiated lengthier festival periods that were associated with royal patronage, as it was often a royal right to raise and lower the temple flag. Thus, the arrangements recorded in this 1511 inscription suggest that the connections of Vyāsatīrtha and the Mādhva sect to Kṛṣṇadevarāya's court were now to be displayed rather prominently at the Varadarāja temple.

As mentioned in chapter 2, Somanātha's biography claims that Vyāsatīrtha spent his early years as a *saṃnyāsin* studying in Kanchi, after his guru, Brahmaṇyatīrtha, had died. According to Somanātha's portrait, Vyāsatīrtha's studies at Kanchi were broad based; he only procured a second Mādhva guru when he left Kanchi for Mulbagal and began studying under Śrīpādarāja. Vyāsatīrtha's first recorded donation to the temple in Kanchi may attest to his personal affinity for that deity, as well as the ties to the temple's authorities that he established during his early career. While this gift was clearly facilitated by the royal court and while the format and rhetoric of the royal edict type of inscription can convey the impression that the arrangements made in a given inscription were being imposed by the king on the various agents involved, Vyāsatīrtha's own preferences may be evident in some of the gift's specifics. For instance, Āvaṇi was a particularly important holiday for South Indian Brahmins. Moreover, as Appadurai has argued, the court's role in such arrangements was often more arbitrative, with the court giving its seal of approval to arrangements that had already been made between the parties in question. Thus, royal edicts in which Kṛṣṇadevarāya gave Vyāsatīrtha valuable resources to regift to others may tell us more about Vyāsatīrtha's preferences or initiative than the king's.

However, it is also true that Kanchi was a significant location for Kṛṣṇadevarāya, who likely had his own multifaceted reasons for having Vyāsatīrtha bestow this wealth on the temple at this particular time. Inscriptional records at Kanchi and elsewhere attest to Kṛṣṇadevarāya's frequent visits to this temple and his patronage of it. Kanchi is one of the places typically listed in the *prasasti* portion of royal inscriptions as evidence of Kṛṣṇadevarāya's lavish support of various Hindu institutions.[31] While Kṛṣṇadevarāya's devotional motivations played a role in Kanchi's importance, the long-standing resistance to Vijayanagara rule on the part of the region's chieftains was also significant. Kṛṣṇadevarāya's August 1511 gift to the Varadarāja temple by way of the Mādhva sectarian leader Vyāsatīrtha seems to have been linked to Kanchi's rebellious history.

This is substantiated by an inscription at another important Vaiṣṇava shrine, the Śrī Veṅkaṭeśvara temple at Tirupati. This inscription, carved into the western section of the temple's second *prakāra* (outer wall) and dated April 7, 1511, records the fact that Appa Piḷḷai, Kṛṣṇadevarāya's general in the region around Kanchi and in Kongunadu, made a grant of the village of Virakampanallur to the Śrī Veṅkaṭeśvara temple in Tirumala. The inscription specifies that Appa Piḷḷai's gift was intended for the merit of Kṛṣṇadevarāya.[32] Tirupati historian Viraraghavacharya points out that Kṛṣṇadevarāya had recently succeeded, after years of failure on the part of his predecessor Vīra Narasiṃharāya (Kṛṣṇadevarāya's older brother), in bringing the rebellious Śambuvarāya chieftains to submission in the region around Kanchi.[33] Thus, Appa Piḷḷai's donations to the Tirupati temple for his ruler's merit seem to have been intended to commemorate this significant military victory.

When, four months later, Kṛṣṇadevarāya authorized Vyāsatīrtha to regift the produce of a village to the Kanchi temple for the purposes of expanding the temple's ritual largesse, he was seemingly implementing his typical economic plan for recently conquered (or reconquered) areas. By funneling donations through sectarian leaders to prominent temples in such areas, Kṛṣṇadevarāya appeared to develop the local economy and to link that apparent development symbolically to the state.[34] In this manner, he hoped to procure a certain measure of political stability and loyalty to Vijayanagara rule.[35]

While this clarifies the general rationale behind Kṛṣṇadevarāya's 1511 donation to the Kanchi temple, it does not explain why Kṛṣṇadevarāya chose a Mādhva sectarian leader as the intermediary. Why not simply make the donation directly to the temple itself or rely on a local Śrīvaiṣṇava leader to implement it? Certainly, Kṛṣṇadevarāya's use of Vyāsatīrtha as the intermediary in part attests to Vyāsatīrtha's early prominence at Kṛṣṇadevarāya's court and substantiates Mādhva claims regarding their leader's importance. While the resources benefited the temple, the Śrīvaiṣṇava community who controlled it, and members of the local population, the honor that the king bestowed on the Mādhvas by having Vyāsatīrtha enact the gift helped to spread Mādhvaism into Tamil-speaking regions. Indeed, Mādhvas did eventually establish *maṭha*s near this temple in Kanchi that continue to function today.[36] The connections that Vyāsatīrtha forged between Mādhva sectarian institutions and historically Śrīvaiṣṇava ones—connections that were facilitated in large part by Vijayanagara patronage—are a critical component of Vyāsatīrtha's historical legacy for the Mādhva sect. It may be that this royal edict reflected the court's approval of Vyāsatīrtha's initiative in pursuing a Mādhva-Śrīvaiṣṇava alliance.

At the same time, however, the gift seems to highlight that the Śrīvaiṣṇava Tamils were of greater use to Vijayanagara statecraft than the primarily Kannadiga Mādhvas, who, by virtue of their historical location in territory more firmly under Vijayanagara control, could not assist as directly in shoring up the empire's territorial holdings.[37] As mentioned above, weaver communities and overseas trade routes situated along the Coromandel coast were increasingly important to the Vijayanagara economy; the rebellious local chieftains and heavily militarized—but sometimes rogue—imperial *nāyaka*s in Tamil country could restrict Vijayanagara access to these valuable entities. These regions therefore demanded constant Vijayanagara attention. By bestowing resources on Vyāsatīrtha and having him donate them to the Śrīvaiṣṇava-dominated temple at Kanchi, the court at once expanded its general support of Vaiṣṇavism while still privileging the form of Vaiṣṇavism that had greater, and more multifaceted, value to the court. Vyāsatīrtha's awareness of the increased importance of the Tamil region and Śrīvaiṣṇavism is what likely prompted his pursuit of an alliance with this community.

From the court's perspective, giving the gift this way implicated two sects in the royal agenda for the price of one. In keeping with conventional understandings of the court's reputed "ecumenism," two-stage gifts of this type enabled the court to maximize its interaction with religious groups who could help to implement its economic and sociopolitical policies in the broadest way possible. The Vaiṣṇava alliance that Vyāsatīrtha sought to establish between Mādhvas and Śrīvaiṣṇavas was appealing to the Vijayanagara court for this very reason; it enabled them to publicize their support of historically Śrīvaiṣṇava-dominated institutions in the Tamil regions that were increasingly important to the empire's stability. At the same time, the alliance encompassed other linguistic, devotional, and doctrinal communities over whom the Mādhva *maṭhas* held greater sway. In this way, the court's two-stage gift to the temple at Kanchi helped to articulate a big tent Vaiṣṇavism that encompassed a variety of regional, linguistic, and devotional publics.

Thus, by collaborating with the Śrīvaiṣṇavas and implementing royal gifts to Śrīvaiṣṇava-dominated institutions, Vyāsatīrtha successfully implicated his sect in the Śrīvaiṣṇavas' rise. In doing so, he did not seek to merge Mādhvaism with Śrīvaiṣṇavism. Indeed, the distinction between the two sects was Vyāsatīrtha's motivation for collaborating with the Śrīvaiṣṇavas: he sought to spread Mādhva Brahminism into new Tamil and, as we shall soon see, Telugu, regions precisely by establishing Mādhva footholds at important Śrīvaiṣṇava shrines. In fact, when we follow the historical arc of this alliance, we see that the court sometimes favored Vyāsatīrtha and the Mādhvas over the Śrīvaiṣṇavas and played the two groups off each other, even as it supported their collaboration.

### Tirupati-Tirumala

Vyāsatīrtha's efforts to spread Mādhvaism into new areas through an alliance with the Śrīvaiṣṇavas that would appeal to the Vijayanagara court are most vividly displayed at the Śrī Veṅkaṭekśvara religious complex in Tirupati-Tirumala in modern-day Andhra Pradesh. The importance of this temple complex to Vijayanagara rule seems to have begun just prior to the short-lived Sāḷuva dynasty, which originated in Chandragiri, about sixteen kilometers south of Tirupati-Tirumala (see map 1). That Sāḷuva Narasiṃha, a general in Emperor Virūpākṣarāya's army, who had been made governor of this region, was able to usurp the authority of the last king of the Saṅgama dynasty and establish the short-lived "Sāḷuva" one attests to how much military power had been placed in his hands. This, in turn, attests to the strategic significance of the Tirupati region to the empire.

As mentioned in chapter 2, the establishment of strong relationships with the local community in southern Andhra enabled Vijayanagara kings to monitor the empire's rebellious northern Tamil holdings and remain within striking distance of Kalinga, a contested area for the empire's duration. Sāḷuva Narasiṃha built alliances in this region by funneling the means for economic developments through the Tirupati temples, the facilitation of which was left largely in the hands of Śrīvaiṣṇava officials, particularly Śrīvaiṣṇavas of the emerging southern/Tamil-oriented faction. Sāḷuva Narasiṃha coordinated the worship programs at the Śrī Veṅkateśvara *mandir* and Śrī Govindarājasvāmi temple, located, respectively, at the top and bottom of the hill, by making simultaneous donations to both; these were then often recorded in the same inscription. Together with his Śrīvaiṣṇava representative at the temple, Kantāṭai Rāmānuja Aiyaṅkār, Sāḷuva Narasiṃha established a Rāmānujakūṭa, or a place for feeding non-Brahmin pilgrims, named for a famous Śrīvaiṣṇava saint. Attendance at the recitation of the Tamil *Prabandham,* or devotional hymns dedicated to Viṣṇu, on the birth star days of the Śrīvaiṣṇava Āḻvārs at ancillary shrines dedicated to them[38] became open to non-Brahmins during Sāḷuva Narasiṃha's reign. Thus, Sāḷuva Narasiṃha's patronage of these temples at Tirupati simultaneously increased the temples' importance and consolidated certain forms of Śrīvaiṣṇava control over them.[39]

Like his predecessor Sāḷuva Narasiṃha, Kṛṣṇadevarāya also generously patronized the Śrī Veṅkateśvara temple complex at Tirupati. Kṛṣṇadevarāya, who explicitly linked his successful rule to his devotion to Lord Veṅkateśvara, made seven separate visits to the temple—more than he made to any other outside the empire's capital—to celebrate important events. His ultimately triumphant 1513–1514 campaign to recapture the fort of Udayagiri, in the region of Kalinga, from the Gajapati Empire, was celebrated by a lavish set of donations to the Veṅkateśvara *mandir* during that time.[40] Like Sāḷuva Narasiṃha, he also seems to have implemented some important changes at the temple.

For example, three inscriptions from the Tirupati-Tirumala temple complex attest to the fact that on January 12, 1524, Kṛṣṇadevarāya gave Vyāsatīrtha three house sites on which to construct two *maṭhas.* As mentioned in chapter 2, two of these sites are located on top of the hill in Tirumala, near the Śrī Venakateśvara *mandir.*[41] The third site is at the hill's bottom, in the town of Tirupati, near the ritually related Govindarājasvāmi temple. Two of the three inscriptions attesting to Kṛṣṇadevarāya's gift were placed on plaques outside the monasteries that Vyāsatīrtha built, while the third was inscribed on a wall surrounding the Śrī Veṅkateśvara *mandir* itself. All three inscriptions state that the house sites had been confiscated by Kṛṣṇadevarāya's predecessor, Sāḷuva Narasiṃha, from the temple's *arcakas* because they had stolen temple jewels.

That this same event was recorded in Tamil, on the same day in three separate locations, attests to its significance, as does the prominence given to it in the Mādhva biographical tradition surrounding Vyāsatīrtha. By giving Vyāsatīrtha this land, Kṛṣṇadevarāya inserted Mādhva Brahmins, who had no previous official role at Tirupati, into the affairs of one of the most important redistributive centers of wealth and honors in the Vijayanagara Empire. The fact that the *arcakas'* thievery is mentioned each time implies that Kṛṣṇadevarāya felt the need to justify his gift to Vyāsatīrtha. This is likely because it upset the temples' established power structure.

It is not entirely clear, however, whom Kṛṣṇadevarāya was punishing by giving these confiscated house sites to Vyāsatīrtha. The *arcakas* arguably represented an older pre-Śrīvaiṣṇava association of the temple with the Vaikhānasa tradition. The Vaikhānasa priests' standing at the temple by this period is somewhat ambiguous.[42] The rituals performed on the *mūlamūrti,* or central image in the main shrine, continued to be observed according to Vaikhānasa practices, thereby attesting to their entrenched significance for the management of the temple. The dominance of Śrīvaiṣṇavas at this temple complex began during the fourteenth century, after the invasion of Madurai by the breakaway sultanate from Delhi, when there was a large influx of Tamils into this Telugu-speaking region.[43] Over time, this Śrīvaiṣṇava presence at the temples amplified; it was manifested in several construction projects, including shrines to Rāmānuja and the Āḻvārs and a Rāmānujakūṭa, or resting house, for Śrīvaiṣṇava pilgrims. Liturgical additions, such as the recitation of the Tamil *Prabandham* on specified occasions at ancillary shrines and the celebration of various lavish public festivals involving processional icons of the temple deities, at the temple complex also promoted Śrīvaiṣṇavism. These festivals followed the Pāñcarātra ritual rules favored by the Śrīvaiṣṇavas and often involved large offerings of cooked food.

Yet despite this increasing Śrīvaiṣṇava presence, the temples at Tirupati and Tirumala remained pluralistic Vaiṣṇava spaces. As stated above, the *mūlamūrti* in the Śrī Venkaṭeśvara *mandir* continued to be worshipped according to Vaikhānasa traditions rather than Pāñcarātra ones and, according to Viraraghavacharya, cooked food was never allowed into the temple's main shrine.[44] Furthermore, while the Śrīvaiṣṇava overlay on the temple was quite pronounced by the time of Kṛṣṇadevarāya, with the emerging "southern" or "Teṅkalai" faction's sensibility dominating the proceedings, the temple's abiding pluralism was formally recognized in the composition of the *sthānattār.* This administrative body acted as the trustee of gifts donated to the temple, oversaw what was to be offered, and made certain that the donor's share of the offerings was distributed according to his or her stipulations. These trustees did not exercise absolute control over the temple nor did they impose unilateral decisions upon it, but by overseeing the donations they played a leading role in the temple's management. Since these donations came from various sources, the *sthānattār* were responsible for maintaining the temple's pluralism, even though the board itself seems to have consisted largely of Śrīvaiṣṇavas. According to inscriptions, this body emerged toward the end of the fourteenth century and, in Viraraghavacharya's view, became formalized in 1390, in an inscription referring to proportionally allocated stipends (*nirvāha*) that the *sthānattār* were to receive according to the following stipulations:[45]

Four shares for Tirupati Śrīvaiṣṇavas;

Three shares for Tiruchanur Sabhaiyār, who were members of Brahmin assemblies in villages of the surrounding area;

One share for the Nampimār, who were the temple's ritual officiants or priests;

Two shares for the Kōyil Kēḷkum Jīyars or Śrīvaiṣṇava sectarian ascetic leaders responsible for inspecting the articles to be offered to the deity;[46] and

Two shares for the Kōyil Kaṇakku or temple accountant.[47]

The *sthānattār's* inclusion of both Tirupati residents and leaders from surrounding villages suggests that the temple was of vital importance to the whole region, which both explains and is explained by royal patronage. Furthermore, the board's composition demonstrates the dominance of Śrīvaiṣṇavas in the running of the temple and perhaps the continued authority of the pre-Śrīvaiṣṇava Vaikhānasa tradition in the inclusion of the temple *arcakas/nampimār* on the board. Thus, the formalization of the *sthānattār* attests at once to the temple's abiding diversity and to the prominent role played by those with a Śrīvaiṣṇava orientation. It also implies the necessity of having a system in place, precisely to manage this diversity and avoid conflict between different interest groups.[48]

When Kṛṣṇadevarāya took away house sites belonging to the temple's *arcakas* to give to Vyāsatīrtha for the construction of Mādhva *maṭhas*, he was perhaps trying to avoid alienating the Śrīvaiṣṇava component of the temples' management too directly while still making a significant change in the temple's power structure. Of course, Vyāsatīrtha and the Mādhvas did not obtain a place on the temple board and all of the arrangements brokered in these inscriptions were done explicitly at the Śrīvaiṣṇavas' approval and protection.[49] However, it does seem that Kṛṣṇadevarāya felt compelled to justify this addition to temple affairs by referencing an earlier crime committed against the temple by less prominent—but still important—members of the temple community.

Some Mādhva scholars have argued that Vyāsatīrtha received this gift from Kṛṣṇadevarāya as a reward for the twelve-year period during Sāḷuva rule, when Vyāsatīrtha was placed in charge of conducting the temple rituals to the *mūlamūrti*. According to Venkoba Rao (1926), the *Vyāsa Vijaya* maintains that Vyāsatīrtha first went to Tirupati during the reign of Sāḷuva Narasiṃha, who had just punished these priests for their theft; since there were no sons of appropriate age to perform the daily *pūjās*, Vyāsatīrtha filled in for a period of several years. According to the *Vyāsa Vijaya*, Vyāsatīrtha did so by conducting rituals according to Madhva's *Tantrasārasaṅgraha*, a ritual manual written by Madhva at the community's founding in the thirteenth century. In this view, by giving Vyāsatīrtha these house sites roughly thirty years later, Kṛṣṇadevarāya was rewarding him for his earlier service to the temple during a period of crisis.

There are no inscriptions that locate Vyāsatīrtha in Tirupati-Tirumala prior to the period of Kṛṣṇadevarāya's rule, however, so the notion that Vyāsatīrtha served as the temple *arcaka* during Sāḷuva Narasiṃha's reign is uncorroborated. Furthermore, the inscriptions from Sāḷuva Narasiṃha's time do not mention this theft at all. What the biographies may be reflecting in their portrayal of events at Tirupati is Vyāsatīrtha's lengthy collaboration with the Śrīvaiṣṇavas at many of their most prominent shrines, such as those in Kanchi and in the imperial capital.[50] The *Vyāsa Vijaya*'s claim that Vyāsatīrtha conducted rituals at Tirupati according to Madhva's manual could also be a reference to the tension present at Tirupati between the Śrīvaiṣṇavas' more lavish Pāñcarātra traditions and the sparer ritual traditions of their Vaikhānasa predecessors.

That Vyāsatīrtha himself was more in line with the Śrīvaiṣṇavas' ritual style, but with distinctive Mādhva inflections, could signify that Kṛṣṇadevarāya's insertion of the Mādhvas into the ritual program at Tirupati actually promoted Śrīvaiṣṇava ritual practices over Vaikhānasa ones. Kṛṣṇadevarāya may also have just been extending some of his apparent efforts at Vaiṣṇava temples in the capital city, such as the Viṭṭhala *mandir*, to address different constituencies within his empire simultaneously. The temple complex at Tirupati-Tirumala now had Telugu, Tamil, and Kannada publics, and the inscriptional records come to reflect this.[51] By fusing such groups into a shared temple culture, Kṛṣṇadevarāya likely sought to articulate a cosmopolitan and yet distinctly Vijayanagara Vaiṣṇavism.

However, there is also evidence that Kṛṣṇadevarāya's gesture here was one of control over sectarian entities and a response, not only to Śrīvaiṣṇava dominance in the region, but also to infighting between different factions of that sect. Indeed, Kṛṣṇadevarāya's gift of these confiscated house sites to Vyāsatīrtha may be read as an attempt to stir up conflict between emerging factions within the Śrīvaiṣṇava community. What later came to be known as the "Vaṭakalai," or "northern," and more Sanskritic branch and the Teṅkalai, or southern, and more Tamil-oriented branch seem to have coexisted at Tirupati during Sāḷuva Narasiṃha's reign. Appadurai and Viraraghavacharya, however, both maintain that a hardening of divisions between these two groups took place precisely during the period under discussion.[52] The central issues were the recitation of the Tamil *Prabandham* and the associated inclusion of non-Brahmins in the proceedings versus the recitation of the Veda by Brahmins only. Both Appadurai and Viraraghavacharya cite Tirupati temple inscriptions, between 1520 and 1528, that document gifts to the temple from the northern faction that explicitly excluded *Prabandham* reciters from any share.[53]

By inserting the Mādhvas into the mix at Tirupati, Kṛṣṇadevarāya, in contrast to his predecessor Sāḷuva Narasiṃha, may have been expressing a preference for Vedic recitation over Tamil *Prabandham*. It is certainly possible to infer that Vyāsatīrtha had a preference for the northern, Sanskritic branch of Śrīvaiṣṇavism. As will be demonstrated in the next chapter, Vyāsatīrtha assumed this group's preferred approach to obtaining *mokṣa* was superior to that of the southern faction. His partiality is also evident in Vyāsatīrtha's independent gifts to the temple, documented in inscriptions of the *śīlaśāsana* variety, to be discussed below. However, when it comes to Kṛṣṇadevarāya's motivations, I think it is more likely that he saw an opportunity in the Śrīvaiṣṇavas' infighting to destabilize their increasing power in the region. Adding an additional sectarian entity, the Mādhvas, into the mix at Tirupati reminded the Śrīvaiṣṇavas that their control over this prominent shrine was not absolute.

Whatever the (likely, multifaceted) motivations behind Kṛṣṇadevarāya's gift to Vyāsatīrtha of these confiscated sites, the gesture amounted to direct and significant royal patronage of Mādhvaism within the context of a historically Śrīvaiṣṇava-dominated shrine. It resulted in the permanent installation at the temples of an additional sectarian presence. As such, this royal gift was quite different from the one that Kṛṣṇadevarāya bestowed upon Vyāsatīrtha at Kanchi thirteen years earlier, wherein he empowered Vyāsatīrtha to donate land and ritual paraphernalia to the temple in ways that affiliated the Mādhva sect with the temple's ritual activities but which did not explicitly establish any Mādhva institutions there. Furthermore, in the royal edict carved into the second outer wall of the Śrī Veṅkaṭeśvara *mandir*, the longest and most detailed,[54] Kṛṣṇadevarāya also granted the Śrī Veṅkaṭeśvara temple the tax proceeds collected during the Puraṭṭāsi Brahmotsava at Tirumala, along with the proceeds of several villages in the "inner" and "outer" divisions of Tirupati. These grants were for the purpose of making offerings to the deity. It is significant that Kṛṣṇadevarāya then arranged for the donor's share of this *prasād*, which would normally have been returned to himself, to be conducted to Vyāsatīrtha's *maṭha* for the *maṭha*'s use in perpetuity (i.e., "as long as the moon and the sun shine").[55] According to Viraraghavacharya's calculations, this *prasād* amounted to enough food to feed two hundred people, who, he presumes, were the residents of Vyāsatīrtha's *maṭha*.[56]

Subsequent to receiving the gift of house sites from Kṛṣṇadevarāya and constructing his two monasteries, Vyāsatīrtha took steps to promote an active role for Mādhvas in temple affairs. An inscription in the Śrī Veṅkaṭeśvara temple[57] says that on November 8, 1524, Vyāsatīrtha constructed *maṇḍapa*s in front of the *maṭha*s at both the top and bottom of the hill. He also arranged that, for 96 days of the eight Brahmotsava festivals that were taking place each year, the processional icon of the deity from the Śrī Veṅkaṭeśvara temple at the hilltop would be brought to the *maṇḍapa* in front of his *maṭha* and worshipped there, with the *prasād* being distributed there as well. Vyāsatīrtha also arranged for other offerings to be made on other festival days so that, for the annual festival cycle in Tirumala, *prasād* would be distributed in front of Vyāsatīrtha's *maṭha* on 222 festival days. Meanwhile the same inscription indicates that Vyāsatīrtha made a similar set of donations to the Govindarājasvāmi temple down the hill in Tirupati, with the *prasād* being distributed on the festival calendar at the *maṇḍapa* in front of his second *maṭha* located there.

But if Vyāsatīrtha's gifts were intended to promote Mādhva Brahminism at Tirupati-Tirumala, they also reflect his ongoing efforts to build an alliance with the Śrīvaiṣṇavas. For example, many of his more lavish donations coincided with the period of the *Adhyayanotsava* or "Festival of Recitation," a prominent Śrīvaiṣṇava festival during which not only Vedic hymns but the Tamil *Prabandham* were recited. Viraraghavacharya notes that Vyāsatīrtha clearly wanted to respect established practice at the temple by coordinating one of his gifts to coincide with this important Śrīvaiṣṇava festival.[58] Yet he also notes that Vyāsatīrtha did not give any part of the donor's share of the *prasād* to the *Prabandham* reciters as was typical of many other donors who contributed to the *Adhyayanotsava*.[59] Again, this may have reflected Vyāsatīrtha's preference for the northern, more Sanskritic and Vedic-oriented form of Śrīvaiṣṇavism, even as he was careful not to alienate members of the other faction.

The same inscription also documents the fact that Vyāsatīrtha made a sizeable donation in the form of fourteen thousand coins to the temple treasury, with the stipulation that the money "be spent for the excavation of tanks and channels in the temple villages" and that the produce derived therefrom be used to supply a long list of articles to be offered on various days to the deity.[60] At the two *maṇḍapa*s in front of his *maṭha*s, Vyāsatīrtha arranged for a lavish amount of additional produce and prepared foods to be distributed on a daily basis.[61] Yet while such gestures undoubtedly increased the Mādhvas' prominence in the region, they did so in large part by benefiting other local groups. Vyāsatīrtha's arrangements to irrigate land and to supply produce and other items, such as lamps and oil, to the temples created long-standing economic links between the temple, Vyāsatīrtha's *maṭha*s, and various local artisans and labor groups such as basket weavers, torch bearers, and fuel suppliers. Simultaneously, Vyāsatīrtha's largesse forged new relations with the Śrīvaiṣṇavas.

Indeed, the November 1524 inscription notes that Vyāsatīrtha donated a village and several hamlets to the temple, again for the purposes of procuring various food and other elements to be offered to the deity eight times daily. It also states that temple servants and temple cooks were to be given their due portions. The *sthānattār* also received a share of these offerings: "After deducting the portion for these servants the remaining portion shall be distributed among the 12 nirvāham of the *sthānattār* and the 4½ vagai equally. The remaining appam shall be set apart for distribution at the early distribution hour."[62] Thus, Vyāsatīrtha's gifts to the temple in part went to the temple servants and suppliers involved in rendering them as well as to the temple management, whose stipends ("nirvāha") were enlarged by these gifts. Finally, shares of Vyāsatīrtha's donations were also distributed as *prasād* to the general population while some were returned to Vyāsatīrtha's *matha*.[63]

A separate inscription dated April 2, 1528,[64] indicates that Vyāsatīrtha made an additional set of donations to the Govindarājasvāmi temple down the hill in Tirupati, where his second monastery and *mandapa* were located. Here, Vyāsatīrtha's donation to the temple of a village authorizes the *sthānattār* to collect sixty gold coins, the annual income of the village (and the first to be recorded in a Tirupati inscription),[65] to cover the cost of various items from the temple store to be given to the deity on Vyāsatīrtha's behalf. The sixty coins also will cover the cost of the labor of various temple servants. Monetary gifts of this type, which were bestowed upon a variety of laborers and suppliers, broadened the web of Vijayangara's increasingly cash-based economy and enabled new modes of status acquisition, social mobility, and the exercise of power among recipients. Other offerings included noncomestibles as well as ten meals to be supplied daily. In this case, Vyāsatīrtha received the typical quarter share of the offering, but the inscription notes that the "remaining *prasādam* we shall set apart for distribution at the time of early *sandhi*." This arrangement implies that Vyāsatīrtha's gift here actually increased Śrīvaiṣṇava ritual largesse because the distribution of the *prasād* does not seem to have been officially linked to Vyāsatīrtha's *matha*; rather, it was folded into the general distribution and thereby linked more clearly to the temple's Śrīvaiṣṇava leadership. Furthermore, the gift involved the purchase of goods from the temple stores, in addition to goods that Vyāsatīrtha had donated. By enriching the temple's cash coffers, Vyāsatīrtha increased the temple leadership's discretionary power in the region.

Thus, Vyāsatīrtha's gifts to the Śrīvaiṣṇavas at Tirupati acknowledged their established dominance there while simultaneously promoting Mādhvaism in this new and politically significant region. His efforts to reshape the local economy through lavish donations to the temples reflected the court's agenda. Indeed, his patronage, which emphasized cash infusions into the temple's coffers as well as food redistribution that was a direct result of irrigation schemes, bore a distinctive Vijayanagara imprimatur. But Vyāsatīrtha's patronage also attests to just how wealthy and powerful *mathādhipatis* in sixteenth-century Vijayanagara could become. Vyāsatīrtha seems to have commanded a variety of considerable resources and was able to distribute them in ways that increased his sect's prominence. He even seems to have been able to initiate and fund large-scale public works projects, such as irrigation schemes, independent of Kṛṣṇadevarāya's authority. Clearly, Vyāsatīrtha had his own power to exercise, power that, in some instances, may have competed with that of the state.

## AN INTERSECTARIAN *AGRAHĀRA*?

While Kṛṣṇadevarāya's gift to Vyāsatīrtha of these house sites likely disrupted established power structures at the temple and forced Śrīvaiṣṇavas to cede some of their dominance at these temples to the Mādhvas, the manner in which Vyāsatīrtha redistributed his wealth paved the way for mutually beneficial intersectarian relations. Such dynamics are also evident in a land endowment near the modern-day Andhra-Karnataka border that was given by Kṛṣṇadevarāya to Vyāsatīrtha in 1526 (see Vyāsasamudra on map 3).[66] This gift is recorded on a Sanskrit copper plate inscription, referred to in *Epigraphia Indica* vol. 31 as the *Kamalapur Plates of Krishnadevaraya*. As noted in chapter 2, this inscription documents Kṛṣṇadevarāya's gift to Vyāsatīrtha of the village of Bettakonda, together with several lesser hamlets, located today in the district of Chittoor, in which Tirupati is also located.[67] The inscription indicates that the village was popularly known as "Vyāsasamudra," in reference to a large tank that Vyāsatīrtha had earlier constructed in the area. It may be that the November 1524 Tirupati inscription cited above, in which Vyāsatīrtha arranged for the excavation of tanks and channels in the temple villages for the purpose of producing more goods to be donated to the deity, refers to what was to become "Vyāsasamudra."[68] The 1526 Kamalapur copper plates indicate that Kṛṣṇadevarāya gave this land to Vyāsatīrtha as a reward for his having developed it. However, as was discussed in chapter 2, the inscription also documents the fact that the village will now be called Kṛṣṇarāyapura, after the king.[69] This suggests that, although Kṛṣṇadevarāya was rewarding Vyāsatīrtha for his work to irrigate the area, thereby promoting a specific version of economic well-being that linked the region culturally to the state, he was also reminding Vyāsatīrtha that the latter's wealth was largely dependent on the king's generosity. This inscription thereby attests to the court's anxiety about investing too much wealth in *maṭhādhipati*s, whose local influence could eclipse that of the king.

The endowment documented in the Kamalapur Plates is also significant for what it reveals about Vyāsatīrtha's work to forge mutually beneficial relations with the Śrīvaiṣṇavas, by establishing an *agrahāra* or Brahmin settlement "to be enjoyed in succession by students and their students as long as there are the moon and the stars."[70] According to the inscription, Vyāsatīrtha subdivided the land grant among 308 individual Brahmins, each of whom is identified by name, father's name, *gotra,* and the portion of the Veda that he can recite. The number of *vṛtti*s or "shares" allocated to each recipient varied, presumably based upon the recipient's intellectual accomplishments or other status markers.

The use of land to establish a Brahmin settlement is arguably an anachronism. Appadurai has argued that "starting from about AD 1350, and during the next three centuries of Vijayanagara rule, there was a serious decline in the status of *brahmadēya*s [land gifts to Brahmins for settlement purposes] and a concomitant growth and expansion of temples in South India."[71] It does seem that, relative to earlier periods in South Indian history, the Vijayanagara Empire was notable for the fact that most gifts to Brahmins were through their association with temples and *mathas*. The latter institution had eclipsed the *agrahāra* as the center for Brahminical learning. However, it was also the case that some of the land grants, discussed in chapter 2, that Vyāsatīrtha received from the court were likely intended as Brahmin settlements; several make no explicit reference to *mathas* being built. But even these *agrahāras* were often linked in one way or another to *mathas* and temples. Indeed, a close reading of the Kamalapur plates indicates that Vyāsatīrtha's redistribution of this land was intimately related to events at the Tirupati-Tirumala temple complex.

While it is impossible to state definitively the sectarian affiliation of the 308 donees, a high proportion of recipients seem to have had an established association with either Tirupati-Tirumala or Ahobila, two major centers of Śrīvaiṣṇava religious activity. Ahobila was and is the location of an important Śrīvaiṣṇava *matha* that was situated in the region of Andhra along the Vijayanagara Empire's perennially contested northern border (see maps 3 and 4). Of the 308 donees mentioned, 37 are named "Tirumala" or some variant thereof, while 23 are identified as sons of a Tirumala; 3 individuals fall into both categories, that is, are named Tirumala and are sons of a Tirumala. Indeed Tirumala is the most common name in the inscription, with roughly 20 percent of the total number of recipients either having that name or having a father with that name. In addition, of the 308 mentioned, 10 are named "Ahobala" while 6 are sons of an Ahobala. Three of the recipients are named "Veṅkaṭa," after the deity at Tirupati, while 4 are "Perumaḷ," a common Tamil epithet for the deity. Adding these names to the 57 who are either Tirumala or sons of a Tirumala brings the total percentage of recipients who seem to have had an established affiliation with a major Śrīvaiṣṇava religious center to 26.

While we must be cautious about presuming that place or deity names indicate sectarian affiliation, the numbers are striking. It is possible that these were Mādhva Brahmins, who took the name Tirumala in deference to the deity installed there. While there is not much evidence of an alliance between Mādhvas and Śrīvaiṣṇavas prior to Vyāsatīrtha, who seems to have been responsible for establishing it, Mādhvas may have worshipped in Śrīvaiṣṇava shrines prior to this period. Indeed, if Somanātha's biography is accurate, Vyāsatīrtha himself went to Kanchi to study after his first guru died and before he left for the established Mādhva *matha* at Mulbagal. His Mulbagal guru, Śrīpādarāja, then urged him to take up residence at Chandragiri, sixteen kilometers south of the Tirupati-Tirumala temple complex. Perhaps this was a well-worn path, despite the lack of evidence of any Mādhva presence at Tirupati prior to Vyāsatīrtha's receipt of the house sites in 1524.

A second possible way of reading these names is that these were Śrīvaiṣṇava converts to Mādhvaism. As discussed in previous chapters, conversion from one school of Brahminical Vedānta thought (and related ritual practices) to another did not necessarily require the radical rejection of one's former identity and affiliations. However, as will be demonstrated in the next chapter, significant doctrinal and ritual differences did persist between Mādhvas and Śrīvaiṣṇavas, despite their collaboration at large temples; Vyāsatīrtha was not only conscious of these differences, he emphasized them in his polemical writings. Vyāsatīrtha likely addressed these polemical writings not only to his own followers but also to the Śrīvaiṣṇavas, in an effort to convince them of the unique correctness of Mādhva Vedānta. It is therefore possible that Vyāsatīrtha established this *agrahāra* to welcome new Śrīvaiṣṇava, and perhaps even Smārta, members who had been so convinced to his community.[72]

But given what we know about Mādhva-Śrīvaiṣṇava relations in this period, that is, that they were both collaborative and competitive, it is also plausible that Vyāsatīrtha was establishing a different kind of Brahminical space, in which sectarian divisions would be less significant. In this scenario, Vyāsatīrtha was giving land shares to Brahmins who would remain Śrīvaiṣṇava in orientation. However, the purpose of Vyāsatīrtha's gift was to encourage the two sectarian communities to develop their working relationship. Kṛṣṇadevarāya's 1524 gift of confiscated house sites enabled Vyāsatīrtha to make a significant inroad into the Śrīvaiṣṇava-controlled temples at Tirupati. This may have required him to smooth things over by giving some land back to important community members in order to inaugurate a new era of religious collaboration with this locally prominent group. Indeed, the emphasis the inscription places on the Vedic recitation skills of the recipients may indicate that Vyāsatīrtha was privileging Vedic religiosity precisely to override those sectarian divisions among the recipients that were based on Vedānta ideology and guru-śiṣya lineages.

The Vedic orientation of Vyāsatīrtha's gift also may have consolidated a special relationship between Mādhvas and the more Sanskritic, Vedic branch of Śrīvaiṣṇavism, later called the Vaṭakalais or "Northerners." In establishing a multisectarian *agrahāra* in nearby territory that emphasized traditional Vedic learning, Vyāsatīrtha may have been advocating for Vedic recitation at the Tirupati temples and consolidating an alliance with the emerging Vaṭakalai branch of the Śrīvaiṣṇava school. As mentioned above, the place name "Ahobila," featured in the names of many of the recipients of shares in the *agarahāra,* was a center for the more Sanskritic/Veda-oriented form of Śrīvaiṣṇavism.

A final interesting feature of the 1526 Kamalapur copper plate inscriptions is that Vyāsatīrtha gave land shares in the *agrahāra* to the three sons of the prominent Viṭṭhala worshipper and Kannada devotional singer Purandaradāsa. While Vyāsatīrtha may have been trying to highlight the vernacular side of Mādhvaism in this gift and, thereby, cultivate popular awareness of the tradition's teachings, it is important to note that Purandaradāsa was a Brahmin, as many members of the Haridāsakūṭa seem to have been. This inscription makes that status very clear by describing Purandaradāsa's sons' Vedic education and by mentioning the fact that they were "twice-born."[73] Thus, Vyāsatīrtha's inclusion of Purandaradāsa's sons in the *agrahāra* may have been an attempt to highlight the Mādhva sect's inclusion of vernacular, popular, and accessible forms of devotion but still link those forms very clearly to the Vedic Brahminical power structure. Such a gesture may have simultaneously aligned Vyāsatīrtha with the Veda-oriented Vaṭakalai Śrīvaiṣṇavas and showcased to the court the Mādhva sect's lack of factionalism between its own Sanskrit and vernacular traditions.[74]

Even if Vyāsatīrtha's inclusion of Purandaradāsa's sons in the allocation of shares in the *agrahāra* was not a way of taking sides in the Śrīvaiṣṇavas' intrasectarian rivalry, it is of historical significance. By installing the sons of one of the most prominent Viṭṭhala worshippers of that time in the region of Andhra, Vyāsatīrtha imported a new Vaiṣṇava cult. Not only did the Viṭṭhala cult have a distinctively Mādhva heritage but Viṭṭhala was also one of Kṛṣṇadevarāya's favored deities. The worship of Viṭṭhala at the capital became increasingly important for the Tuḷuvas, with Viṭṭhala eventually replacing the Śaiva deity, Virūpākṣa, as the divine signatory of all royal inscriptions. Because Viṭṭhala was significant at home and Veṅkaṭeśvara abroad, synchronizing the worship of these two Vaiṣṇava deities made sense.[75] Vyāsatīrtha's gift to Purandaradāsa's sons likely helped to bring this about.

Thus, we should read Vyāsatīrtha's founding of the *agrahāra* in light of both his activities at Tirupati and his relations with the Vijayanagara court. Vyāsatīrtha played a pivotal role in the implementation of several features of the king's agenda in southern Andhra. By investing in regions associated with the Tirupati temple complex and by infusing the temple coffers there with significant amounts of cash, he helped to forge new economic and social relations between different labor communities in the region. These new relations reflected the values, aspirations, and functional apparatus of Kṛṣṇadevarāya's rule and thereby linked this region to the state in a variety of symbolic and practical ways. Furthermore, by helping to import the cult of Viṭṭhala into southern Andhra, Vyāsatīrtha established a cultural link between religious practices at the capital and in Tirupati. Finally, by sharing his wealth with the Śrīvaiṣṇavas, he demonstrated his willingness to work with his sectarian rivals when the king required it. But all of these benefits to the king were also beneficial to Vyāsatīrtha and Mādhvaism, which now spread into new regions and had obtained a firm foothold in the most important Vaiṣṇava shrine in South India. Thus, by reallocating material wealth to forge a working relationship with the Śrīvaiṣṇavas, Vyāsatīrtha gained greater prominence for his sect.

## CONCLUSION

An overview of Vyāsatīrtha's material exchanges with the Śrīvaiṣṇavas indicates that he collaborated with this group to mutual benefit. The Tuḷuva dynasty's favoring of the Śrīvaiṣṇavas was due to several factors, some of which were beyond Vyāsatīrtha's control and others of which he could use to implicate Mādhva Brahmins. The southern Śrīvaiṣṇava faction's support of various forms of non-Brahmin participation in religious festivals, its use of Tamil in temple liturgy, and its proselytization efforts across caste lines were distinct features of this Śrīvaiṣṇava community that enjoyed a broad appeal. It was partly this appeal that seems to have initially attracted Vijayanagara patronage. While some of these Śrīvaiṣṇava activities were sect specific, others could be augmented by Mādhva collaboration. These included the Śrīvaiṣṇava theologization of the Rāmāyaṇa, which established an isomorphic relationship between Rāma and the Vijayanagara king and cultivated the popular worship of various Rāmāyaṇa deities associated with the region around the imperial capital. Still other, more incidental factors for lavish Vijayanagara support of Śrīvaiṣṇavism included the serendipitous location of these Śrīvaiṣṇava shrines in a region that was becoming of increasing strategic significance for the Vijayanagara Empire. Here, Vyāsatīrtha could offer little by way of competition, but he could use his collaboration with the Śrīvaiṣṇavas and with the court to spread awareness of Mādhvaism into Tamil- and Telugu-speaking regions through donations to historically Śrīvaiṣṇava-dominated temples there.

Thus, Vyāsatīrtha deserves credit for the deft manner in which he responded to historical realities in ways that benefited his sect. By consolidating relations with the Śrīvaiṣṇavas through donations to their temples and by possibly including them in Brahmin settlements he formed, Vyāsatīrtha at once increased Śrīvaiṣṇavism's prestige and publicized various features of his own community. He also helped to fuse various regional forms of Vaiṣṇava worship at large temple complexes into a big tent Vaiṣṇavism that was attractive to Vijayanagara patrons for its ability to reach out to a variety of publics. In these ways, Vyāsatīrtha's donative acts—both those that were by royal decree and those that he undertook independently—consolidated Vyāsatīrtha's relations with the Vijayanagara court.

Perhaps because of his cultivation of stronger ties between the two sectarian communities, Vyāsatīrtha is typically praised in inscriptions of both the *rāyaśāsana* and *śilaśāsana* type as "Vaiṣṇava-āgama-siddhānta-sthāpana" or "the establisher of the correct philosophical position among traditions of Viṣṇu worship."[76] This title, on the one hand, could be emphasizing Vyāsatīrtha's sectarian identity by implying that Mādhva *siddhānta* in particular is the correct philosophical form of Vaiṣṇavism. On the other hand, it could also be praising Vyāsatīrtha for establishing a more generic Vaiṣṇava position, rooted in philosophy (*siddhānta*) and tradition (*āgama*) but common to all Vaiṣṇavas.[77] In this sense, he was the establisher of Vaiṣṇavism, both philosophically, through his polemical texts, and practically, through his multifaceted religious collaboration with other Vaiṣṇava groups. Read in this way, this moniker may highlight the role that Vyāsatīrtha's alliance with the

FIGURE 6. Navabṛndāvana.

Śrīvaiṣṇavas played in the eventual exclusion of Śaiva Smārtas from royal patronage over the course of the Tuḷuva dynasty.

In fact, carvings on Vyāsatīrtha's tomb, located on an island in the Tungabhadra River, approximately three kilometers downriver from the Viṭṭhala temple and approximately half a kilometer to the northeast of the royal village of Anegondi,[78] seem to attest to Vyāsatīrtha's role as a Vaiṣṇava synthesizer of various forms of Viṣṇu worship (see map 6). This island is known locally as "Navabṛndāvana," for the nine Mādhva saints whose tombs, including Vyāsatīrtha's, are located there (see fig. 6). These shrines, called either "*bṛndāvanas*" or "*samādhis*" by Mādhvas, are understood to house the mortal remains of these saints, who are thought to have entered into *samādhi* or a sustained meditative state. Although these saints are understood to have transcended this world, their advanced spiritual aptitude enables their abiding presence in the shrines, making the shrines a focus of pilgrimage and veneration. Vyāsatīrtha's *bṛndāvana*, which is situated in the middle of the eight other tombs of prominent Mādhva saints, is the most elaborately decorated. It is distinctive today for the partial remains of the *maṇḍapa* still in front of it and is encircled at its base by a ring of linked elephants and at its top by carved tulasi leaves that also resemble a crown (see fig. 4 for the clearest depiction of this;

FIGURE 7. Vyāsatīrtha's *bṛndāvana*, side with Narasiṃha image and side with Bāla-Kṛṣṇa image.

actual tulasi plants grow out of the top of all nine of the shrines).[79] Vyāsatīrtha's *bṛndāvana* is also directly across from a small Hanumān shrine, still in worship.

On the four faces of Vyāsatīrtha's *bṛndāvana* are different depictions of Viṣṇu's forms. The front of the shrine depicts Rāma, seated with Sītā and flanked by Lakṣmaṇa on the right side and a small, kneeling Hanumān next to a standing figure on the left.

That standing figure, whose hands are folded in the *añjali mudrā* indicating devotion, is an elite male devotee but not an ascetic. His headdress suggests that he is a nobleman, possibly the king, underscoring again the entombed *maṭhādhipati's* royal connections (see figs.4 and 5 above).[80]

The next side, if one proceeds clockwise around the square-shaped tomb, has an image of Viṭṭhala (see fig. 2 above), followed by an image of Narasiṃha and, finally, by an image of Kṛṣṇa in his infant form (see figs. 7–9).

As we have seen, Mādhvas under Vyāsatīrtha's direction were associated with shrines dedicated to all of these forms of Viṣṇu. Their appearance together on Vyāsatīrtha's *bṛndāvana* is distinct, as such extensive imagery is not found on the other *samādhi* shrines on the island. In addition to highlighting Vyāsatīrtha's historical prominence among Mādhva leaders, this imagery also suggests that one of

FIGURE 8. Vyāsatīrtha's *bṛndāvana*, side with Narasiṃha image.

Vyāsatīrtha's main legacies for the Mādhva sect was his role in unifying different forms of Vaiṣṇavism, even as he also advocated for his system's supremacy.[81]

Vyāsatīrtha's reputation as both the architect of a trans-sectarian Vaiṣṇava alliance and as the arbiter of correct Vaiṣṇava Vedānta thought is also evident in how Vyāsatīrtha is remembered by subsequent generations of Vaiṣṇava groups. Hawley's research on the concept of the four *sampradāya*s in the Vallabhite community indicates that Vyāsatīrtha plays an important role in how this North Indian Vaiṣṇava sect understands both its own lineage and the relationship between different Vaiṣṇava groups. While the composition date and authorship are uncertain, a text called the *Sampradāyapradīpa* or *The Lamp of the [Vaiṣṇava] Tradition*, written by a Vallabhite community member, "represents itself as having been composed in Brindāvan in . . . 1553 or possibly 1554 C.E." and forges a connection between the Vallabha or Puṣṭimārga Sampradāya and that of Vyāsatīrtha/Madhva.[82] At one point in the narrative, Vallabha travels south to Vijayanagara or, as the text calls it, "Vidyānagar."[83] When Vallabha arrives, a debate between the Māyāvādīs and the Tattvavādīs is taking place before King Kṛṣṇadevarāya.[84] The Māyāvādīs are just about to win when Vallabha reverses the course of the debate by throwing out a challenge and establishing Vallabha's form of Vedānta, *Śuddhādvaita,* as supreme. Not only is Vallabha subsequently

FIGURE 9. Vyāsatīrtha's *bṛndāvana*, side with Bāla-Kṛṣṇa image.

honored by Kṛṣṇadevarāya with a *kanakābhiṣeka*, or a showering with gold, and with the offering of the king's throne but Vyāsatīrtha, who had been presiding over the debate "beseeches the younger man [Vallabha] to replace him on the sāmpradāyik throne, and thereby effectively to accept a spiritual coronation that will parallel the physical one the monarch has just promised."[85]

Vallabha ultimately refuses to take up Vyāsatīrtha's mantle because the form of Vaiṣṇavism that Vyāsatīrtha espouses is distinct from the true lineage that Vallabha is meant to inherit. As Hawley puts it, the text presents the formulations of Vaiṣṇavism offered by Madhva, Rāmānuja, and Nimbāditya (Nimbārka) as "ineffective against Śaṃkara and the Māyāvādīs."[86] Thus, while the text establishes a connection between the different *sampradāya*s of Vaiṣṇavism, it does so in a hierarchical way that privileges Vallabha's system. But the roles played by Vijayanagara, Kṛṣṇadevarāya, and Vyāsatīrtha in the story are intriguing. Even though Vyāsatīrtha is portrayed as deferring to Vallabha's authority, his entitlement to choose a successor implies that Vyāsatīrtha was, until the advent of Vallabha, the arbiter of Vaiṣṇavism. His is not the most correct or truest Vaiṣṇavism but it is, in some way, connected to Vaiṣṇavism's other forms.[87]

This text of course reflects the concerns of a somewhat later time, place, and sect. Vyāsatīrtha may have been selected to play such a crucial role in this story because he made Mādhvaism famous in the north.[88] Moreover, he did this in large part through his royal associations. Yet Vyāsatīrtha could also have been selected in this narrative, which at once unifies and hierarchically orders the four different *sampradāya*s, because he was one of the original and most prominent unifiers, the establisher of a shared tradition of Vaiṣṇava philosophy and practice, the "Vaiṣṇava-āgama-siddhānta-sthāpana." He brought together Mādhvas and Śrīvaiṣṇavas in what seems to have been a newly close and intricate way and highlighted the potential benefits of intersectarian Vaiṣṇava collaboration. At the same time, he also used some of the Vaiṣṇava sects' inherent similarities and shared features so as to establish his own particular sect's system more widely and firmly.

Vyāsatīrtha's collaboration with the Śrīvaiṣṇavas also indicates that the sectarian leader's role in sixteenth-century South Indian society was not set in stone. An effective *maṭhādhipati* had to respond creatively to situations as they unfolded and be willing to collaborate with his rivals if the circumstances, such as increasing royal attention, warranted it. Vyāsatīrtha's material exchanges with the Śrīvaiṣṇavas show his ingenious responsiveness to historic contingencies even as they also reveal what was less malleable and more constrictive about his context. For example, as we have seen, Vyāsatīrtha sometimes took advantage of the open-ended pluralism of Vaiṣṇava temples to establish sectarian institutions and practices on temple grounds. That this enabled a clearer affiliation between specific and bounded sectarian religious institutions and the more pluralistic temple's ritual affairs is somewhat ironic. Furthermore, there were aspects of Vyāsatīrtha's doctrinal positions that were nonnegotiable, precisely because they distinguished his tradition from that of the Śrīvaiṣṇavas. Thus, to understand better the role of doctrinal differences in Mādhva-Śrīvaiṣṇava relations in this period, we now turn to Vyāsatīrtha's polemics against the Śrīvaiṣṇavas' form of Vedānta, Viśiṣṭādvaita or "qualified nondualism."

# 5

# The Social Life of Vedānta Philosophy

## *Vyāsatīrtha's Polemics against Viśiṣṭādvaita Vedānta*

While material exchanges of royally gifted land and collaborative ritual enterprises at prominent temples indicate there was a blossoming alliance between Mādhvas and Śrīvaiṣṇavas during Vijayanagara rule, significant doctrinal divisions also persisted between these two groups. Vyāsatīrtha was not only aware of these divisions, he emphasized them in his polemical writings. Despite the fact that Vyāsatīrtha forged a productive working relationship with the Śrīvaiṣṇavas, he was also the first Mādhva intellectual to criticize the doctrines of their qualified nondualist ("Viśiṣṭādvaita") Vedānta in any detail. This indicates that he saw the Śrīvaiṣṇavas not as teammates but as rivals. However, a common refrain in Vyāsatīrtha's polemics against the Śrīvaiṣṇavas is that many of their own basic premises logically conduce to certain key Mādhva (or Dvaita) Vedānta doctrines rather than to Viśiṣṭādvaita Vedānta's faulty conclusions.[1]

This chapter will focus on Vyāsatīrtha's complex polemics against Viśiṣṭādvaita's conception of *mokṣa* or liberation from the cycle of rebirth. The final section of Vyāsatīrtha's *Nyāyāmṛta,* entitled "The Defense of a Hierarchical Ordering of Brahmā and [Other Souls] Even in the State of Mokṣa," argues in favor of an eternal hierarchy of souls in the state of *mokṣa* and against the Śrīvaiṣṇava view that souls experience *paramasāmya* or "absolute parity" in the liberated state. As I argued in chapter 3, sectarian doctrinal debates were always in part about establishing or defending a given sect's placement in its social world. Counterintuitive though it may seem, this was particularly true of Vedānta sects' debates about their ultimate goal, *mokṣa.* Different Vedānta systems answered shared philosophical questions in ways that were inextricably linked to social reality. These questions included who could pursue liberation from worldly existence, what means were acceptable, and what the experience would be like.

For instance, in Advaita Vedānta, only high-caste males were considered eligible for *mokṣa* precisely because *mokṣa* required certain knowledge that could be attained only through the study of Vedic texts. This study was off limits to low-caste people and all women. In contrast, in keeping with its general efforts to proselytize across caste lines, Viśiṣṭādvaita Vedānta offered two paths to *mokṣa*, one of which was restricted to elite males because it required Vedic study (*bhakti*); the other required only mental surrender to God (*prapatti*) and was therefore open to all. Mādhva or Dvaita Vedānta posited a third way, in which more people could pursue *mokṣa* than in Advaita Vedānta but wherein worldly hierarchies would remain in place in the liberated state. Dvaita argued that one's worldly identity reflected one's innate nature and thereby determined both the means by which one could pursue *mokṣa* and the stratified experience of *mokṣa* itself.[2] Thus, each of these Vedānta systems considered the human being's existential situation in terms that took into account worldly identity, meaning that Vedānta arguments about *mokṣa* were always informed by social context. The role of context in shaping these arguments was further amplified by the fact that each of these Vedānta systems defined its understanding of *mokṣa* in ways that responded to the teachings of its intellectual predecessors and opponents. Furthermore, as we shall see, Vyāsatīrtha's criticisms of Viśiṣṭādvaita views of *mokṣa* reflected his on-the-ground interactions with the Śrīvaiṣṇavas as well as his desire to locate his sect's understanding of this goal advantageously within the broader Vedānta landscape.

In terms of the latter objective, Vyāsatīrtha's discussion of popular notions about how to liberate oneself from *saṃsāra*, such as through death in a holy city,[3] or through *dveṣabhakti*, that is, devotion in the form of hatred of God,[4] indicates that he was attempting to write the definitive chapter on *mokṣa* and to demonstrate how that concept is best expressed in Madhva's teachings. His style of argument follows a pattern that attempts to be exhaustive: Whether he is pointing out an opponent's flawed reasoning or making a constructive argument defending his own view, Vyāsatīrtha typically quotes different strata of the Brahminical Vedānta canon. But he also often includes texts that encompass more popular sensibilities and, finally, adds a standalone reasoned argument. He usually starts by quoting *śruti* texts, or passages from revealed Vedic literature, considered universally authoritative by the elite, twice-born males who alone had access to it. Then he quotes from *smṛti* texts, literally "remembered" traditions. In theory, these texts have grown up around the Veda in order to illuminate its complex meanings. But the category of *smṛti* also encompasses a range of religious material, not all of which can be traced to the Veda and which often reflects various forms of Brahminical engagement with alternative, popular, and sometimes quite localized religious sensibilities.

(One of the more controversial features of Madhva's system of Vedānta was his reliance on less well-known or widely accepted *smṛti* material to interpret *śruti* texts. As will be discussed below, Vyāsatīrtha adhered closely to Madhva's teachings on this.) Vyāsatīrtha then typically quotes the *Brahma Sūtras* (also called the "*Vedānta Sūtras*") or the collection of aphoristic statements designed to encapsulate the teachings of the last portion of the Veda, the *Upaniṣads*. It is these Vedic texts in particular that deal with issues central to all Vedānta thought, including the nature of the *ātman* (the self), the nature of Brahman (the ultimate reality), and the relationship between the two. Finally, Vyāsatīrtha provides a *tarka* or reasoned argument. Thus, in terms of both style and content, Vyāsatīrtha presents his views in this chapter as an all-encompassing doxography of *mokṣa* within the Hindu tradition. Not surprisingly, this presentation positions Vyāsatīrtha's sectarian viewpoint at the top of what is meant to be the full list of competing alternatives. However, he also returns repeatedly in his discussion to specific Viśiṣṭādvaita arguments. In doing so, he highlights the doctrinal similarities and differences between Mādhvas and Śrīvaiṣṇavas in ways that complicate our understanding of their quotidian interactions.

One of the unifying features of Dvaita's and Viśiṣṭādvaita's respective conceptions of liberation from rebirth is that the experience retains some important elements of worldly reality, rendering it more pleasurable. This was distinct from Advaita Vedānta, wherein liberation consisted of a total loss of individual identity as one realized one's absolute oneness with the ultimate reality, Brahman. This realization was understood in Advaita to expose all worldly differences and limiting qualifications as illusory. In contrast, in both Dvaita and Viśiṣṭādvaita thought, souls retain their individuality and even, to some extent, their physicality in the state of *mokṣa*,[5] precisely so that they may experience some type of eternal bliss. But the mechanics of how this bliss transpires differ significantly between the two traditions. In Dvaita's case, souls do not merge into the ultimate reality of Brahman (identified with Viṣṇu) because they remain fundamentally distinct from and inferior to Him. But they do experience a kind of blissful proximity to Viṣṇu, as suits their innate capacity or *yogyatā*, which is a key concept in Dvaita philosophy. In Viśiṣṭādvaita, souls do experience a kind of blissful merger with Viṣṇu but simultaneously retain some separateness and individuality by virtue of the *śeṣin-śeṣa* doctrine. According to this doctrine, souls are subsidiary parts (*śeṣas*) to Viṣṇu's great whole (*śeṣin*); the souls in Viśiṣṭādvaita are like the body of God and thus are not completely identical with His perfect, transcendent nature. Souls exist to serve the Lord in the same way that the body exists to serve the soul.

Perhaps the most critical difference between Viśiṣṭādvaita and Dvaita conceptions of *mokṣa* is the extent to which worldly hierarchies are retained in the liberated state. As mentioned above, Viśiṣṭādvaita argues for *paramasāmya* or the "ultimate parity" of souls in *mokṣa*, regardless of what means or *sādhana* a given aspirant to liberation (*mumukṣu*) has used to achieve this state. In this view, a given soul's physical or social status or his or her mental aptitude prior to liberation has no impact on the state of liberation. In fact, as mentioned above, Viśiṣṭādvaita distinguished itself from Advaita Vedānta by extending access to *mokṣa* to non-elites and granting that not all aspirants needed to be twice borns schooled in Vedic doctrine and ritual. Instead, they could practice *prapatti* or complete surrender to God as an alternative—and, in some Śrīvaiṣṇava assessments, a preferable—means to *mokṣa* than "bhakti" or "devotion," which required ritual activities rooted in Vedic learning and was therefore only for male elites. In contrast, Dvaita maintained that souls would be hierarchically arranged in *mokṣa*, in part because their innate differences would determine the method, or the type of *sādhana*, they would use to attain liberation. Vyāsatīrtha argues in this chapter of the *Nyāyāmṛta* that, because not all *sādhana*s are equally demanding, they will not all conduce to the same experience of *mokṣa*. In this sense, innate spiritual hierarchies that exist among souls and inform the social status of different individuals in *saṃsāra* are retained in Dvaita's view of liberation from rebirth.[6]

Much of the *Nyāyāmṛta*'s final section is devoted to pointing out the inevitable logical inconsistencies that Viśiṣṭādvaita incurs by adhering to this *paramasāmya* doctrine while maintaining the individuality of liberated souls and the distinct methods for achieving liberation (*sādhana*s) available to them. In particular, Vyāsatīrtha emphasizes the fact that Viśiṣṭādvaita's commitment to the souls' eternal individuality is meaningless in the absence of different—and stratified—experiences of *mokṣa*. Furthermore, the system's own distinction between *bhakti* and *prapatti* as means to *mokṣa* suitable to different aspirants of relative capacity and social standing strongly implies innate and eternal *qualitative* differences between souls. Such a view conduces more logically to Dvaita conclusions supporting a hierarchy of souls within *mokṣa*.

By pointing out that those who performed *bhakti* and its attendant ritual obligations were utilizing a more difficult method for achieving *mokṣa* than *prapatti* and, therefore, should be rewarded with a superior form of *mokṣa*, Vyāsatīrtha may have been accentuating a rift that was already opening within the Śrīvaiṣṇava community. The intrasectarian debate that was emerging at that time between the respective Śrīvaiṣṇava advocates of *bhakti* and *prapatti* did not imply radical division within the community; it was only in the seventeenth century that actual subsects emerged.[7] Nevertheless, Śrīvaiṣṇava contingents at different locations articulated arguments regarding the relative merits of *bhakti* and *prapatti*. And these arguments were linked to a larger discussion about authoritative texts, the use of Sanskrit or Tamil in liturgy, and the appropriate role of non-Brahmins in temple proceedings. Because the suitability of certain *sādhana*s to certain aspirants was often indexed to caste status within Viśiṣṭādvaita, Vyāsatīrtha's arguments about the superiority of *bhakti* to *prapatti* highlighted both doctrinal and social tensions within the early sixteenth-century Śrīvaiṣṇava community. As we saw in chapter 4, Viraraghavacharya and Appadurai find evidence of a hardening of divisions between those Śrīvaiṣṇavas who supported the recitation of the Tamil *Prabandham* and those who supported Vedic recitation in the donative inscriptions at the Tirupati temple complex. This is exactly contemporary with Vyāsatīrtha's receipt of land for building *maṭhas* and *maṇḍapas* at this complex.

Vyāsatīrtha's argument that the *bhakti* method is superior to *prapatti* and therefore ought to lead to superior forms of *mokṣa* suggests that he was courting certain Śrīvaiṣṇava elites, either to win them over to the Mādhva fold or to consolidate some special alliance with them at shared temples. But his discussion of Śrīvaiṣṇava views of *mokṣa* in the *Nyāyāmṛta* also seeks to broaden the appeal of Dvaita theories of *mokṣa* beyond the parameters of the Śrīvaiṣṇava community. While Vyāsatīrtha's arguments about hierarchical means leading to hierarchical ends in *mokṣa* advocate the eternality of elite privilege, they also open up access to *mokṣa* to a wide array of *mumukṣus*. By taking on a wide array of possible means to *mokṣa*, from those of a particular sect (e.g., the Advaita view that knowledge alone is the means to *mokṣa*) to those that are more broadly embraced (e.g., death in a holy city), Vyāsatīrtha indirectly engages the issue of who has access to this goal.[8] By not denying the validity of readily accessible *sādhanas* for achieving *mokṣa*, such as death in Prayāg or hatred of God as a form of *bhakti*, Vyāsatīrtha maintains fairly broad access. This is somewhat surprising given that Madhva taught that souls were predestined to achieve certain soteriological ends, with not all being eligible for the state of *mokṣa*. Some souls, Madhva argued, were predestined to remain forever in *saṃsāra* while others were predestined for eternal hell. It is potentially significant that Vyāsatīrtha does not raise or address this doctrine at all in this chapter, despite his quoting some of the very passages from the sacred canon that Madhva used to justify it. Indeed, in this chapter, Vyāsatīrtha cites many of Madhva's "unknown *śrutis*" and untraceable quotes from known *smṛtis*, sources that are unique for their explicit mention of the doctrine of hierarchy in *mokṣa*. Thus, while his personal commitment to Dvaita Vedānta as taught by Madhva is clear, Vyāsatīrtha also presents Dvaita arguments in a manner that reflects the broader audiences he sought to engage in his specific context.

## HIERARCHY AS FUNDAMENTAL TO REALITY

The doctrine of a *mokṣatāratamya* or hierarchy of souls in *mokṣa* is one of the most controversial doctrines in Dvaita philosophy. But Vyāsatīrtha argues, in his final section of the *Nyāyāmṛta*, that an eternal gradation of souls is not only in keeping with Viśiṣṭādvaita views of reality but necessary to any theistic system that also takes our worldly experiences seriously. As in his treatment of Advaita Vedānta's doctrine of *jīvanmukti*, discussed in chapter 3, Vyāsatīrtha uses a reductio ad absurdum technique to point out the contradiction in the Śrīvaiṣṇava position that liberated souls are equal while other forms of hierarchy, necessary to Śrīvaiṣṇava theism, persist. He begins by identifying the two broadest possible implications to the Śrīvaiṣṇavas' rejection of the notion of *tāratamya* or hierarchy in *mokṣa:*

> Is your position that there is no hierarchy between the liberated soul (*jīva*) and God? Or is it that there is no such hierarchy among the liberated souls? It cannot be the former, that is, that there is no hierarchy between the liberated souls and God, because in your own system there already is such a hierarchy by virtue of the fact that one is all pervasive, and the other is atomic, one has the status of being a *śeṣin* and the other has the status of being a *śeṣa,* one is independent, and the other is dependent, etc. And it would not be suitable for the world if there were multiple Īśvaras/Gods [which would be the case if there were no hierarchy between God and the *jīvas*].[9]

Vyāsatīrtha thereby dismisses the first possibility—that there is no hierarchical relationship between God and individual human souls—on the grounds that Viśiṣṭādvaita describes God in a way that emphasizes His superiority to the *jīvas.* Having established that Viśiṣṭādvaitins must acknowledge that hierarchy is fundamental to their own understanding of the God-soul relationship, Vyāsatīrtha moves on to discuss the second possible way of construing Viśiṣṭādvaita's rejection of hierarchy in *mokṣa,* that is, that there is no gradation among the individual liberated souls:

> It is not the second option either because, even in your system of thought, there is Lakṣmī, who is a *tattva* or a fundamental principle in reality and who is of the nature of a *śeṣin* to the *jīvas,* that is, the *jīvas* are subsidiary parts to Her whole, and because there is also superiority to [the *jīvas*] of other *jīvas* such as Viṣvaksena, etc., by virtue of their being *niyāmakas* or controllers.[10]

Here, Vyāsatīrtha is alluding to those works, such as the *Gadyas* and the *Nitya-grantha,* attributed to foundational Viśiṣṭādvaita thinker Rāmānuja, that deal with ritual. These texts call for a subordinate kind of reverence for deities other than Viṣṇu, who possess specific cosmic powers, including the goddesses Śrī, Bhūmi, and Nīla and some of the celestial ministers, especially Ananta and Viṣvaksena.[11] Similar practices are present in Mādhva ritual, where there is an acknowledged hierarchy of deities, who are supposed to be honored in accordance with their particular role in reality. In fact, the hierarchy of *jīvas* in Dvaita extends downward from the divine to the human realm. Vyāsatīrtha is apparently implying that in Śrīvaiṣṇava practice, if not in theory, there is a hierarchy of deities; therefore, why would there not also be a corresponding hierarchy of liberated souls in the state of *mokṣa?*

Stratified reverence for a hierarchy of deities implies that spiritual identities are somewhat fixed. This seems to contrast with the more fluid sense of identity that underlies the basic logic of the karma and rebirth theory. However, the Mādhvas are not wrong when they argue that portions of the Hindu sacred canon juxtapose this fluidity of identity with a more fixed vision of the cosmos as consisting of layers of stratified beings who possess innate spiritual aptitudes. For instance, there is a long tradition within the Hindu sacred texts of positing different types of celestial beings who are superior to humans yet lower than gods (e.g., the Gandharvas), as well as certain kinds of humans who have special cognitive abilities (e.g., the ancient *ṛṣis*). Thus, in addition to arguing on logical grounds that theism requires hierarchy, Vyāsatīrtha cites those *Upaniṣads* and Vedic mantras that refer both explicitly and implicitly to eternal hierarchical arrangements among different kinds of beings. Some of these passages also support the idea that degrees of bliss exist in *mokṣa* and that these degrees are indexed to the souls' hierarchical status. For instance, *Taittarīya Upaniṣad* 2.8.1 (often referred to as the Ānanda or "Bliss" *śruti* in Dvaita) differentiates degrees of bliss among different types of beings as follows: "Next follows an analysis of bliss. . . . A single measure of bliss that human Gandharvas enjoy—and also a man versed in the Vedas and free from desires—is a hundred times greater than human bliss."[12] Vyāsatīrtha also quotes the *Bṛhadāraṇyaka Upaniṣad* (4.3.33), which allots degrees of bliss to different kinds of deities and men: "A hundred measures of bliss enjoyed by gods-by-rites equal a single measure of bliss enjoyed by gods-by-birth—and, one might add, by those who are learned in the Vedas and who are not crooked or lustful."[13]

Vyāsatīrtha thereby maintains that, not only does a hierarchical arrangement of *jīva*s make reasonable sense in a theistic conception of reality, the sacred texts also endorse this view.[14] Furthermore, because Viśiṣṭādvaita Vedānta posits a hierarchical relationship not only between Viṣṇu and all other reality but among Viṣṇu's closest divine assistants, it also must acknowledge the foundational role hierarchy plays in structuring reality. Finally, Vyāsatīrtha maintains that if divine beings such as Lakṣmī, Nīla, and Viṣvaksena can be simultaneously inferior to Viṣṇu, superior to human souls, and hierarchically ordered among themselves, this tells us something important about the nature of individual identity.

Indeed, in addition to arguing that theism requires a hierarchical ordering of reality, Vyāsatīrtha also maintains that any system that advocates the eternal individuality of souls must also advocate their hierarchical arrangement. Recapitulating Madhva's arguments, Vyāsatīrtha maintains that individuality requires hierarchy because, if no two souls are alike, they must have moral and intellectual differences that will position them in relative terms to each other. If we do not allow that we are innately different and therefore innately predisposed to certain behaviors, experiences, and insights, we will always be asking ourselves on what grounds a being like Brahmā, for example, is superior. In other words, not allowing for innate spiritual hierarchies as part of the *jīva*s' eternally distinct natures sets up a *regressus ad infinitum* when it comes to explaining self-evident hierarchies in capacity among different beings:

> The hierarchical ordering [of souls within] *mokṣa* is established through reasoned arguments such as the following: The superiority of Caturmukha Brahmā above others is without any cause, seen or unseen, that can be proven to be an independent cause without there being an infinite regress, [wherein we are] always searching for another cause [as a means of explaining it]. Therefore, the cause [of Caturmukha Brahmā's superiority in *mokṣa*] must be his beginningless and innate capacity that is part of his very nature.[15]

In light of these hierarchical implications for the *jīvas'* eternal individuality in Dvaita thought, Vyāsatīrtha takes issue with Viśiṣṭādvaita's attempts to retain liberated souls' eternal individuality while insisting on their ultimate parity (*paramasāmya*). In marked distinction from Advaita, or nondualist Vedānta, Viśiṣṭādvaita stipulates that liberated *jīvas* retain some individuality in the state of *mokṣa* and argues that, in the absence of such individuality, liberation is not much of an experience at all. However, the Viśiṣṭādvaitins also sought to describe the *jīvas* in such a way as to erase any real differences between them in order to leave the conceptual door open to their ultimate parity in the liberated state. In Viśiṣṭādvaita thought, the *jīvas* are individualized and atomic yet identical; any difference in their experience is due to external features like karma and not due to their innate natures.[16] In keeping with their commitment to the *paramasāmya* doctrine, Viśiṣṭādvaitins argue that such circumstantial differences are erased in the state of *mokṣa*. To Vyāsatīrtha's way of thinking, this makes no sense; if something is spatially and numerically distinct from other things, then it must have its own individual nature (*svarūpa*) and, as such, will be prone to certain kinds of experiences. This would hold true even in *mokṣa*:

> And even if any discrepancy among the individual states of happiness in the *jīvas* is not brought about by their being individually enumerated and atomic in dimension, there is such discrepancy brought about by the fact that they have their own innate natures, *svarūpas*, as when the different degrees of sweetness in water and nectar produce different degrees of enjoyment.[17]

Vyāsatīrtha is arguing that it is not conceptually possible to concede that something is distinct, spatially and numerically, while also arguing, as Viśiṣṭādvaita attempts to do, that these features do not make the *jīvas* essentially different from each other. The mere fact that each *jīva* is individual and atomic requires that it have some kind of essence unto itself. Having such an essential identity, it must have some fundamental nature that is distinct unto it. This nature must also affect the kind of experiences it has, including its experience of liberation from rebirth.

Vyāsatīrtha also argues that we cannot view the *jīvas* as identical but distinct units making up an ontological category. Rather, in contrast to Viśiṣṭādvaita,

Vyāsatīrtha argues that the *jīvas* are individual entities located within a given category. Their status as members of said category cannot possibly reveal all there is to know about them. Moreover, because the *jīvas'* innate natures are precisely what created hierarchy among them in *saṃsāra,* that hierarchy will be sustained in *mokṣa* because the *jīvas'* individuality is therein sustained.[18] Bondage does not create hierarchy nor is hierarchy exclusively a feature of bondage. Rather, hierarchy is an unavoidable outcome of the fundamental individuality of *jīvas.* This individuality not only persists in liberation but, in some sense, is fully manifest there. For this very reason, the cessation of bondage will not eliminate hierarchy:

> The cessation of bondage in material reality [*prakṛti*] is a state also marked by hierarchical arrangement [of the *jīvas*] because [these *jīvas*] are each [individually] the locus of this cessation of bondage from a particular class [or category of being]. Thus, the cessation of bondage from *prakṛti* is akin to the cessation of bondage from a chain gang.[19]

The idea is that the condition of liberated *jīvas* is similar to that of individuals freed from a chain gang. Just because the prisoners were once all part of the same category of "criminal" does not mean they are prevented from being individuals upon liberation. Even when they were bound in shackles, they were individuals who shared a single common feature, that is, the state of being bound. In the same way, the *jīvas* bound in *saṃsāra* are individuals who happen to share the state of bondage. Once they are liberated from that state, their individuality is not erased. Because this individuality is constituted by innate abilities that are distinct to a given *jīva,* this individuality sustains hierarchy in both bondage and liberation.

An obvious objection to Dvaita's hierarchical view of *mokṣa* is, if worldly limitations remain in the form of gradation in *mokṣa, mokṣa* is hardly worth pursuing. The principal worldly limitation that the goal of *mokṣa* is intended to surmount is that of impermanence, the worst attribute of the cycle of rebirth (*saṃsāra*). By insisting that many *saṃsāric* features of one's identity are retained in *mokṣa,* Dvaita implies that *mokṣa,* too, is impermanent. Vyāsatīrtha responds to this objection in a manner that specifically highlights Viśiṣṭādvaita's views by saying that Viśiṣṭādvaita, too, holds that in *mokṣa,* Brahman remains superior to the other liberated beings (*muktas*). Therefore, Viśiṣṭādvaitins cannot argue that hierarchy cannot coexist with eternality. Otherwise, they would have to argue against both Brahman's superiority to the *muktas* as well as the individual *muktas'* gradation:

> Based on the strength of *śruti* and other [authoritative statements], the state of being eternal is appropriate [for *mokṣa*] even if [*mokṣa* encompasses] the state of [Īśvara's] being superior while the [souls] are inferior to Īśvara and, similarly, [if there is the state of gradation] among the various liberated souls. Otherwise, the bliss of the deity Brahmā would also be noneternal because it too is pervaded by the state of noneternality by virtue of being superior [to that of other *muktas*].[20]

By invoking the deity Brahmā's status, Vyāsatīrtha once again reminds the Viśiṣṭādvaitins that they, like the Mādhvas, believe in a further stratification of the deities in the state of *mokṣa* above the ordinary liberated souls. It is not simply Viṣṇu who is superior to liberated human souls. Other high-ranking deities with a special relationship to Viṣṇu are also given a prominent place in *mokṣa* in Viśiṣṭādvaita thought. Thus, Vyāsatīrtha maintains that hierarchy as a feature of *mokṣa* is already embraced by that system and needs only to be recognized as obtaining among the liberated human *jīvas* by the Śrīvaiṣṇavas.

Vyāsatīrtha also confronts a second objection to Dvaita's theory of a hierarchically ordered state of liberation, which is that hierarchy in *mokṣa* would create jealousy and other forms of suffering that are conceptually incompatible with the liberated state. He attempts to turn this issue on its head by pointing out that jealousy is just as likely to occur if more righteous beings see inferior souls, who did not try as hard to achieve *mokṣa,* becoming comparable to them in that state:

> Nor [does hierarchy in *mokṣa*] conduce to hatred, envy, etc., because of the following statements:
>
> Through so many rebirths, [certain souls] have lost all their sins. Only then shall there be a direct knowledge of Hari. Thus, [having lost those defects], how can they still be prone to hatred, envy, etc.? And if hatred and envy, etc. are allowed to exist [in liberation] why wouldn't those things exist even if [the liberated beings] were equal to one another? Indeed, those refined beings, having seen others become equal to them, would be full of hatred, envy, etc.[21]

Vyāsatīrtha thereby maintains that, as a realist and theistic system of thought, Viśiṣṭādvaita must acknowledge that hierarchy is fundamental to reality. In doing so, he highlights the conceptual overlap of Dvaita and Viśiṣṭādvaita, even as he argues for Dvaita's superiority. This manner of presenting the doctrinal relationship between these two forms of Vedānta echoes Vyāsatīrtha's competitive collaboration with the Śrīvaiṣṇavas at royally funded shrines.

## HIERARCHICAL MEANS (SĀDHANAS) LEAD TO HIERARCHICAL ENDS (SĀDHYAS)

Vyāsatīrtha's most incisive criticisms of Viśiṣṭādvaita reasoning on the parity of souls in *mokṣa* occur in his discussion of *sādhanas* (the means to *mokṣa*) and the role they play in hierarchically ordering the individual soul's experience of liberation. Vyāsatīrtha maintains that, if the *sādhanas* or means to *mokṣa* are different—with some being more arduous and also, perhaps, more wholesome than others—then there must also be difference in the *sādhya*, the goal achieved through these different means.[22] The idea that there are different means to *mokṣa* is both a generic one that is referred to in different places in Hindu sacred literature and one that is specific to the Viśiṣṭādvaita tradition, which opened up access to the goal of *mokṣa* to śūdras and other nonelites with the *sādhana* of *prapatti,* or total surrender to God. *Prapatti,* unlike the other valid Viśiṣṭādvaita *sādhana, bhakti,* required no Vedic knowledge or rituals. For this reason, it was considered an appropriate means to *mokṣa* for those who lacked the *adhikāra* or mandate to study the Veda and carry out its enjoined activities.

Because one of the main goals of his intellectual project is to map competing perspectives on certain shared beliefs (and, simultaneously, to situate his sect's position advantageously on that map), Vyāsatīrtha begins his discussion on this topic by identifying the broad range of *sādhanas* that seem to be endorsed by a variety of authoritative texts and popular traditions. In doing so, Vyāsatīrtha acknowledges that there are many possible ways to attain *mokṣa.* But in Vyāsatīrtha's view, this variety of means to *mokṣa* supports a hierarchy of ends within *mokṣa:*

> Liberation [must be hierarchical] because there is agreement that the happiness enjoyed by liberated beings is stratified since the means of attaining this goal of *mokṣa* are stratified. From the perspective that "the means to *mokṣa* are either death in Prayāg, hatred of God, or knowledge and righteous action together," there is [clearly] dissimilarity between performing one's duties of *varṇa* [caste] and *āśrama* [stage of life] versus dying in Prayāg [or one of the other easier means].[23]

What Vyāsatīrtha is arguing above is that hatred of God or the simple act of dying in a particular place is clearly nowhere near as difficult as spending one's lifetime fulfilling a variety of social and ritual obligations or studying and meditating on transcendental truths in order to achieve *mokṣa.* Thus, if we are to accept that tradition endorses this variety of clearly unequal means, we must also adhere to a variety of ends in *mokṣa* rather than advocating for an identical experience of *mokṣa* for all liberated individuals.

As further evidence that the Hindu tradition collectively endorses a hierarchy of means to *mokṣa,* Vyāsatīrtha quotes a variety of sacred texts, mostly *purāṇas,* that support the view that there is a correlation between the *sādhana* one uses to achieve *mokṣa* and the quality of *mokṣa* one achieves. The following example from the *Bhāgavata Purāṇa* indicates that some *mumukṣus* worship God for the fulfillment of a personal desire and others do it out of pure devotion. Both will incur results. However, the pure devotion of the desireless *mumukṣu* is superior to the one whose devotion is tainted with personal interest:

> He who in prayers is seeking to attain [something] is not a [true] servant [i.e., a devotee]. Instead, he is a merchant. He is truly a servant and he is truly a master, when the two are of sympathetic qualities, without desiring anything from the other. But the best of the *mumukṣus* is the one who, with single-minded *bhakti,* is not desirous of liberation.[24]

Vyāsatīrtha goes on to clarify that such *smṛti* statements imply that there are gradations in the practice of *bhakti* and in the pursuit of *mokṣa*. Thus, why should there not also be gradations in the goal of *mokṣa* achieved through those different forms of *bhakti?*

> [There is gradation of souls in *mokṣa*] because of *smṛti* statements like this, indicating the superiority of the devotion of the one not desiring liberation to that of the one who is; and because such superiority [of devotion] is also widely observed in the world; and because it has been stated that superior forms of *bhakti* conduce to superior forms of liberation while lesser forms of *bhakti* conduce to lesser forms of liberation in such *smṛti* statements as [*Bhāgavata Purāṇa* 7.10.4], "There is more arduous devotion to reach that goal."[25]

To similar ends, Vyāsatīrtha also quotes passages from the *Bhagavadgītā* that he believes attest to a hierarchy of spiritual practice that results in a hierarchy of spiritual experiences in *mokṣa*. With these quotes, Vyāsatīrtha seems to remind the reader of conventional Indian social hierarchies involving both caste and gender. Because Brahminical Hinduism typically restricted types of religious activity on the basis of individuals' placement within these social hierarchies, Vyāsatīrtha argues that these hierarchies suggest a widespread belief in relative innate capacities on the part of different types of individuals to perform the various *sādhanas*:

> And [the idea that there is a hierarchy in *mokṣa* that reflects the hierarchy of *sādhanas*] is well established by the word *api*, meaning "even," in the following statement: "But those who are ignorant, having heard [the truth] from others [who are more knowledgeable], [and who] therefore worship [Brahman], *even* they cross over death, intent upon what they hear."[26] And this [idea is expressed] even more strongly here [in this *Gītā* passage], where it says "women, vaiśyas, likewise *even* śūdras, they go beyond, how much more so is this true for pure Brahmins?"[27]

Having thereby attempted to locate Dvaita's view of *mokṣa* as stratified, in part on the basis of the means by which one pursues it, within the shared sacred Hindu canon,[28] Vyāsatīrtha homes in on an emerging dispute within the Viśiṣṭādvaita tradition over the correct means to *mokṣa*. Vyāsatīrtha maintains that Viśiṣṭādvaita draws important distinctions between different *sādhanas* or means to *mokṣa;* indeed, he talks at some length about the difference between *bhakti* and *prapatti* in Viśiṣṭādvaita. As stated above, the discussion within Śrīvaiṣṇavism during Vyāsatīrtha's lifetime about these two *sādhanas* did not imply rejecting one in favor of the other. Nor did it reflect hard and fast divisions within the community. However, as work by Mumme, Raman, and others has shown, different groups of Śrīvaiṣṇavas did tend to emphasize one method over the other. These groups also tended to advocate different ritual styles in the temples and the privileging of certain kinds of texts to inform doctrine. Moreover, while the two groups coexisted at various temples, one group tended to dominate the proceedings and there were occasional struggles for control. This is evident, as we have seen, at Tirupati during Vyāsatīrtha's lifetime.

Throughout this section of the *Nyāyāmṛta*, Vyāsatīrtha presumes the superiority of *bhakti* over *prapatti*, indicating his affinity for the more Sanskritic[29] branch of Śrīvaiṣṇavism that was associated with centers in Kanchi and Ahobila and which later came to be identified as the Vaṭakalai or northern school. Indeed, his audience for this aspect of his critique of Viśiṣṭādvaita seems to be this northern, Kanchi-based branch, with which Vyāsatīrtha himself had direct familiarity and members of which he may have been trying to convert to his system. If scholars are correct that no real dispute over these issues existed during Vyāsatīrtha's lifetime and acrimony regarding the superiority of *bhakti* over *prapatti* did not emerge until the seventeenth century, then Vyāsatīrtha may have been actively driving a wedge between advocates of the relative merits of each. But this rift may also have been opening on its own, and Vyāsatīrtha's arguments may have served only to widen it.

Vyāsatīrtha maintains that if Viśiṣṭādvaitins believe there are in fact two different paths to *mokṣa*, they must, on the basis of which path has been taken, also advocate distinctive and hierarchical experiences of *mokṣa* itself. Vyāsatīrtha makes it clear that in his view the *bhakti* path is more arduous than the *prapatti* one because it requires the agent to perform certain tasks repeatedly:

> And [there is hierarchy in *mokṣa*] because there is difference between the two causes of *mokṣa* distinguished by your school as separate: 1. constant meditation or *bhakti* and 2. absolute surrender or *prapatti*. In accordance with the nature of each path, [*bhakti*] is accompanied by actions [enjoined in the Śāstras] that need to be performed repeatedly while [*prapatti*] is not accompanied by such actions and [therefore] need not be repeatedly performed.[30]

In Vyāsatīrtha's view, because one path is more demanding than the other, the two paths ought not to lead to exactly the same goal, despite Śrīvaiṣṇava assurances that they do. Indeed, the Śrīvaiṣṇavas' attempt to justify the greater difficulty of *bhakti* compared with *prapatti* was to argue that the practitioner of the latter, the *prapanna*, had greater faith and thus merited an equal experience of *mokṣa* to that of the *bhakta* (the practitioner of *bhakti*). But Vyāsatīrtha rejects this on the grounds that *bhakti*'s very nature demands intense devotion:

> And it cannot be argued, as has been postulated, that even if one of the two means [i.e., *bhakti*] is greater than the other [i.e., *prapatti*], there would still be parity [in the obtained result, *mokṣa*] owing to the greatness of faith [of the one practicing *prapatti*] versus the relative smallness of faith [of the *bhakta*]. Because of the fact that, as much as *bhakti* requires repetition, there is that much greater faith in the practice of such repeated *bhakti* than in [the practice of] *prapatti*, which does not require repetition.[31]

Vyāsatīrtha thereby argues against the notion the two *sādhana*s are equal on the grounds that, even though *bhakti* is more arduous than *prapatti, prapatti* requires greater faith. He points out that equalizing the two means to *mokṣa* in such a manner, so as to protect the notion that the experience of *mokṣa* is the same for all, contains the flaw of mutual dependence.[32]

Vyāsatīrtha also argues that the Viśiṣṭādvaitin cannot maintain there is difference in the means but still parity in the result because this would contradict the system's own views of the Vedas and of God. The idea that the Vedas impose more difficult techniques for achieving *mokṣa* on some individuals than others, without any corresponding difference in outcome, seems extremely unfair. And it is difficult to comprehend a deity who would allow this:

> And if there were difference in the means but parity in the result, then there would be unacceptable statements in the Vedas that enjoin more difficult *sādhana*s [for those pursuing *bhakti* as opposed to *prapatti*] as well as unfairness and other bad qualities in Īśvara Himself, the grantor of *mokṣa*.[33]

Here Vyāsatīrtha is arguing that, because Viśiṣṭādvaita allows people to achieve *mokṣa* through surrendering to God (Īśvara), thereby incurring His grace even if they have not performed all the actions enjoined in the Vedas, the system is unfair. Such unfairness can be conceptually overcome by the idea, advanced in Dvaita, that the experience of *mokṣa* will not be the same for all. In this manner, Vyāsatīrtha shows that there is greater unfairness in Viśiṣṭādvaita's claim that some *mumukṣus* must work harder than others to achieve the same goal. Hierarchy in *mokṣa* is fairer than parity.

Most strikingly, perhaps, Vyāsatīrtha argues that the Viśiṣṭādvaitins must believe there are differences in capacity among the individual *mumukṣus*, those desirous of liberation, precisely because Viśiṣṭādvaita argues for different paths to *mokṣa* and acknowledges that individuals follow those paths in different ways. Vyāsatīrtha maintains this strongly implies that individual *mumukṣus* have innate abilities. It is with regard to this idea that Vyāsatīrtha is most closely arguing for the conceptual overlap between the two rival systems, Dvaita and Viśiṣṭādvaita, of Vedānta thought:

> And you cannot say there is no discrepancy in the results as when a *nityakarma* action [an obligatory action enjoined to be performed regularly] is performed in a very capable or a less capable manner merely because [the performer] is very capable or not so capable by virtue of his [relative] status as a god, a human being, etc. Therefore what ought to be asserted is that the knowledge acquired by a less capable person is a means to a liberation that is suitable to himself by virtue of his individualized perfection [of the practice of the *sādhana*], just like *kāmyakarma*s or ritual actions motivated by a desire for certain results and performed by lame, blind, and other people [who are less capable of performing such rituals perfectly] are [still] *sādhana*s or means for their desired ends, regardless of their imperfections.[34]

Here, Vyāsatīrtha is arguing that Viśiṣṭādvaita wrongly equates the perfection of *mokṣa* with equality within *mokṣa*. Instead, Vyāsatīrtha argues, the perfection of *mokṣa* should be thought of as each individual's achieving an experience of liberation that is individually suited to him and reflective of the manner in which he has gone about achieving it. Thus, Vyāsatīrtha argues that if there is a difference of methods for achieving the goal of *mokṣa* and if this difference implies that not only some *sādhanas* but also some aspirants are superior to others, then why wouldn't there be a hierarchy within the goal itself?

> Therefore, the following idea is refuted: that even though there may be a difference between *bhakti* and *prapatti* by virtue of a distinction in capability [on the part of the *mumukṣu*], there is equality in the result achieved. Likewise, [it is refuted] because it is not indicated in *śruti*. And, as an independent theory, it goes too far. Therefore, because there is a hierarchy of methods [for achieving *mokṣa*], there is hierarchy within *mokṣa*.[35]

## THE *STHITAPRAJÑA'S* ONGOING EFFORTS

In addition to exposing the conceptual difficulties in Viśiṣṭādvaita Vedānta's distinction between *bhakti* and *prapatti,* Vyāsatīrtha also takes to task, in the final section of the *Nyāyāmṛta,* the Viśiṣṭādvaita concept of the *sthitaprajña.* According to Viśiṣṭādvaita Vedānta, even the *sthitaprajña,* or the one who has achieved some kind of liberating insight into Brahman yet who is still embodied and living in this world, needs to continue performing dharmic actions, such as Vedic rituals. While Viśiṣṭādvaita does not endorse the idea of *jīvanmukti* or liberation while a person is alive, it does acknowledge that some individuals achieve an insight into the nature of reality (*aparokṣajñāna*) that results in liberation at the point of death, after this individual's residual karma has been spent. Such a person is known as the "*sthitaprajña*" or "one having firm wisdom."[36] According to Rāmānuja, the *sthitaprajña* still needs to perform dharmic action because such action helps to process bad karma that is ripening. Given the *sthitaprajña*'s insight, all other karma will disappear and no new karma can be acquired. But, as Andrew Fort points out, "[Rāmānuja] also states in ŚB iv.1.16 that performance of ritual actions like the *agnihotra* must continue even after knowing *brahman*; these actions are means causing knowledge to arise and repetition of them further perfects knowledge by clarifying the mind (*antaḥkaraṇa*). This seems to suggest, contra Śaṅkara, that degrees of knowledge are possible and that one might 'fall back' from knowledge without the constant support of ritual activity."[37] But such an understanding conflicts somewhat with the view that the *sthitaprajña* is one who has already achieved liberating insight and is merely trying to work off the bad karma that is continuing to bear problematic fruit.

Vyāsatīrtha exploits this apparent contradiction within Viśiṣṭādvaita thought so as to advocate for hierarchical experiences of *mokṣa.* Because the *sthitaprajña*—like the *jīvanmukta* in Advaita Vedānta—represents Śrīvaiṣṇavism's ideal practitioner, it is not surprising that Vyāsatīrtha takes the concept to task. In general, his tactic here is to maintain that, if Viśiṣṭādvaita is going to argue ongoing work is required for the *sthitaprajña,* such work ought to result in something of benefit once he achieves *mokṣa.* Rather than constructing an ironclad argument in support of his own view in this section, Vyāsatīrtha engages mainly in the *prasaṅga* type of argument, wherein he points out the various problems with the Viśiṣṭādvaita stance on the *sthitaprajña.* Indeed, in this section, Vyāsatīrtha examines Viśiṣṭādvaita's various possible justifications for requiring these ongoing efforts on the part of the *sthitaprajña* and finds all of them to be either logically deficient or scripturally unsupported. In some instances, Vyāsatīrtha seems so intent on criticizing the implications of Viśiṣṭādvaita's view that he ends up providing radically different and even opposing arguments against this Viśiṣṭādvaita doctrine. For instance, Vyāsatīrtha claims at one point that Viśiṣṭādvaita is wrong to require ongoing ritual efforts for the *sthitaprajña* because the sacred texts say it is unnecessary to do so. In contradiction of this, he shortly thereafter argues that Viśiṣṭādvaita has not taken the *sthitaprajña*'s obligation to perform these rites seriously enough in light of statements in the sacred texts supporting the gravity of certain types of ritual performance. However, Vyāsatīrtha does eventually return to his main point, which is that the only way for this Viśiṣṭādvaita doctrine to make sense is for the Viśiṣṭādvaitins to embrace the Dvaita view: that is, any additional knowledge acquired by the *sthitaprajña* through his ongoing efforts must result in an increase in the form of bliss he will experience in the liberated state.

Vyāsatīrtha begins his critique by pointing out that the Viśiṣṭādvaita doctrine, according to which the *sthitaprajña*s must continue to perform Vedic rituals and other dharmic duties, depending upon their station, contradicts the sacred texts:

> Is it the case that *sthitaprajña*s, such as Śuka and other sages, whether they be *aparokṣajñānin*s, *bhakta*s, or *prapanna*s, have nothing else to do for the sake of *mokṣa,* such as meditating on Brahman or performing obligatory rites (*nityakarmas*)? This seems to be indicated in *śruti* statements such as (*Chāndogya Upaniṣad* 6.14.2) which says, "I shall remain here only so long as I shall not be released (from ignorance). Then I shall reach perfection."[38] And in the *smṛti* statement (*Gītā* 3.17), which asserts, "But when a man finds delight within himself and feels inner joy and pure contentment in himself, there is nothing more to be done."[39]

Not only do the sacred texts reject this doctrine, the doctrine itself defies, according to Vyāsatīrtha. This is because the very status of the *sthitaprajña* is of one who has already achieved the insight necessary for liberation:

> It has not been established that such activities [are suitable] for such a being [*sthitaprajña*]. Rather, it is only for the ignorant still seeking [liberating] knowledge that [such undertakings] would be helpful, either as a means of inquiry, for the destruction of bad karma, or for the removal of impediments.[40]

Vyāsatīrtha also points out that Viśiṣṭādvaitins cannot maintain that ritual activities, even obligatory rites, cause the *sthitaprajña*'s release from *saṃsāra* because this perspective would amount to Viśiṣṭādvaita's endorsement of the *karmajñānasamuccaya* doctrine—the view that knowledge and ritual activities are equally involved in the attainment of *mokṣa*.[41] Furthermore, Vyāsatīrtha argues that advocating the efficacy of ritual as a means to *mokṣa* is problematic because there are so many enjoined rituals of different duration and difficulty that adopting such a view would require acknowledging hierarchical results in *mokṣa*: "And because you would also have to allow for a variety of experiences of *mokṣa* because of the variety of ritual activities [some of which are much easier than others]."[42]

Vyāsatīrtha also observes that the Viśiṣṭādvaitins, in advocating that the performance of the *nityakarmas* (obligatory rites) leads to superior knowledge on the part of the *sthitaprajña*, contradict the widely held view that the *nityakarmas* produce no positive results at all. This is precisely because they are, by definition, obligatory and, therefore, only conduce to demerits if left unperformed:

> And because the view [that the *sthitaprajña* needs to keep performing these activities] is contradicted by *śruti* statements indicating that nothing else needs to be done by him for the sake of *mokṣa*. And these activities cannot be undertaken for any other goal precisely because they are "nitya" activities, that is, obligatory, and [not performing them] produces [only] a negative effect for the *aparokṣajñānin*.[43]

arguments Vyāsatīrtha makes against the Viśiṣṭādvaita view that the *sthi-* must continue to perform the *nityakarmas*, even though the reasons for re unclear, include the idea that such ritual obligations cannot be un- serve some more general, abstract end, such as setting an example for ply following God's command. Nor can they be understood to incur from God for the *mumukṣu* so long as Viśiṣṭādvaita adheres to the view of *mokṣa*:

> actions to be undertaken for the sake of setting a good example for use God has commanded it because neither of these would constitute Nor can you argue that [the *sthitaprajña*] performs these activities for love because you have established that such love, which is the cause chieved only through *bhakti*, etc. Nor can you argue that [he per- ake of [achieving] a *superior form* of God's love because such an pointless in the absence of any superior experience in *mokṣa*.[44]

in to the sacred texts and points out that the *sthitaprajña* *nityakarmas* in imitation of God's *līlā* or "play" in light statements about these obligatory rituals. He argues rform these acts "for the sake of imitating God's *līlā* uotes indicate [in a very serious manner] that the *aparokṣajñānin must* perform *nityakarma*s [and thus, it cannot be that they do so simply out of a playful spirit]."[45] He then quotes passages to that effect, such as Gītā 9.34: "The one who does all action for my sake, for whom I am paramount, devoted to me, freed from attachment, keep me in your mind and devotion, sacrifice to me, bow to me, discipline your self toward me, and you will reach me."[46] Such verses imply that ongoing efforts, even on the part of one who has reached the necessary spiritual state to achieve *mokṣa* upon death, are significant and not optional or playful actions.

Vyāsatīrtha's argument in this section is that the Viśiṣṭādvaitins do not want to let the *sthitaprajña* off the hook for ritual and devotional activities enjoined by the sacred texts, although they do not clarify how these activities serve any goal that is not already served by *bhakti* or *prapatti*. In order to make such ongoing efforts purposeful, Vyāsatīrtha maintains that any additional efforts undertaken by the *sthitaprajña*—efforts that are, in fact, required by Viśiṣṭādvaita doctrine on the grounds that they help to maintain the *sthitaprajña*'s insight and are part of leading the life of a *mumukṣu*—must be understood to give the observant *sthitaprajña* tangible benefits in the form of a superior experience of *mokṣa*. Because he is mainly concerned with pointing out the flaws in the Viśiṣṭādvaita view, Vyāsatīrtha's arguments here are not developed to the same meticulous degree as elsewhere. This section is similar to the rest of the chapter, however, in attempting to show that the basic premises of Viśiṣṭādvaita thought conduce more naturally to Dvaita conclusions.

## THE SACRED CANON'S CONCORDANCE ENDORSES HIERARCHY

Eventually, Vyāsatīrtha turns his attention to those *śruti* statements that refer explicitly to the existence of *paramasāmya* or parity of blissful experiences in *mokṣa* so that he might offer an alternative reading. He does this by problematizing some of the implications of such statements, both logically and in light of other statements in authoritative literature. As elsewhere, Vyāsatīrtha's focus remains on Viśiṣṭādvaita and that system's concordance of various statements on *mokṣa* in the authoritative texts. But while criticizing Viśiṣṭādvaita's *samanvaya* (concordance), Vyāsatīrtha also advances a distinctively Mādhva approach to textual interpretation—one that equates statements in *śruti* with statements in selected *purāṇas* and that reads the sacred texts in light of other means of knowledge (*pramāṇa*s) such as perception. Finally, Vyāsatīrtha also quotes many passages from Madhva's "unknown *śruti*s," or sources that Madhva was accused of fabricating by other Vedāntin exegetes. This accusation may have been made as early as the fourteenth century by Viśiṣṭādvaita philosopher Vedānta Deśika in his *Śatadūṣaṇī*; Madhva is explicitly criticized for this in the late sixteenth century by the Advaitin Appayya Dīkṣita.[47] Siauve's study of Madhva's presentation of the doctrine of spiritual hierarchy in his *Anuvyākhyāna*, a brief commentary on the *Brahma Sūtras*, argues that this doctrine is mentioned explicitly only in untraceable quotes in Madhva's writings.[48] Vyāsatīrtha's use of these quotes, which seems heavier in this chapter than in the rest of the *Nyāyāmṛta* (supporting Siauve's argument), demonstrates that his intellectual practices are defined in large part by his sectarian commitments.

Vyāsatīrtha begins his analysis of the Hindu canon's concordance with the logical argument that Vedic statements that speak of *paramasāmya*, if taken literally, create an untenable view of the relationship between Brahman and human souls. As we have seen, this relationship is preserved as hierarchical not only in Dvaita but also in Viśiṣṭādvaita. In Dvaita, arguments in favor of this hierarchy often apply analogies from perceptual experience to the sacred texts:

> There are *śruti* statements that speak of the "ultimate parity" and that is because there is parity in the sense that the fullness of bliss of the being, whose desires are fulfilled and who is without suffering, is according to his individual capacity, as [we may speak of] a stream and an ocean [both being "full"—and, in that sense, "the same"—without the quantity of water being the same.][49]

Vyāsatīrtha goes on to maintain that such *śruti* statements are qualified by *smṛti* statements indicating that the highest bliss is differentiated. This arguably represents a distinctive Mādhva approach to reading *śruti* texts, according to which certain *smṛti* sources are considered to be on par with the Veda:

> [Those *śruti* statements that refer to the ultimate parity of souls cannot be taken literally] because there is a *smṛti* text that says "the highest bliss is differentiated based on an individual mark [in the *jīva*] while the absence of pain is common [to all liberated souls]." Otherwise, would it not be the case that the liberated souls would be like Īśvara and capable of creating, maintaining, and destroying the world?[50]

Here, Vyāsatīrtha is not only advocating reading *śruti* statements in light of the broader authoritative tradition as defined by Madhva,[51] he is also pointing out that a literal interpretation of the *paramasāmya śruti*s contradicts Viśiṣṭādvaita's understandings of both the ātman-Brahman relationship and the proper way to interpret the *Brahma Sūtras*, particularly *sūtra* 1.4.19: "And such an interpretation of the *sūtra* '*jagadvyāpāravarjam*' is forbidden even by you, [because] even your concordance of the text [links the words from the *sūtra* '*bhogamātra*'] with the [words from this *sūtra*] '*jagadvyāpāra*.'"[52]

What Vyāsatīrtha is referring to here is the fact that Rāmānuja's Bhāṣya on *Brahma Sūtra* 1.4.17 "*jagadvyāpāravarjam*," which supports the idea that Brahman alone is master of the cosmic processes of creation, maintenance, and destruction, syntactically connects this *sūtra* to *sūtra* 4.4.21, "*bhogamātrasāmyaliṅgāc ca.*" This latter *sūtra* implies that there is a mark of similarity between Brahman's enjoyment and that of souls in liberation. Vyāsatīrtha allows that it might be possible to infer a similarity between types of enjoyment experienced by the liberated soul and Brahman from this latter *sūtra,* on the basis of a reading of the term *sāmyaliṅga,* literally "similar mark." However, he maintains that both the word *mātra,* used in a restrictive sense of "only," and Rāmānuja's syntactical connection to *sūtra* 1.4.17 create significant nuance for such a reading. Because of this syntactical connection, forged by Rāmānuja, the term *mātra* in *sūtra* 4.4.21 means that the *jīva* is similar to Brahman *only* in terms of enjoyment in liberation and not in terms of any of Brahman's other powers. Thus, the *jīva* is dissimilar to Brahman in its inability to create, maintain, or destroy the world. As Vyāsatīrtha points out, interpreting *sūtra* 1.4.17 differently would require that "even the liberated souls must be thought of as independent realities," an idea that would contradict both Dvaita and Viśiṣṭādvaita views of God.[53]

Vyāsatīrtha also discusses Upaniṣadic and *Brahma Sūtra* references to the liberated soul's status as a *satyakāma* or "one who has his desires fulfilled" in *mokṣa.* There is an implicit contradiction in equating *mokṣa* with such a state while limiting the capabilities of the *mukta* or liberated soul so that they are distinct from those of Brahman: "The state of being a *satyakāma* is appropriate [to the *mukta*] because of the absence of desire, even if [the *mukta*'s] bliss is inferior to that of the One who has emitted, etc., the world."[54] To support such an understanding of the *satyakāma*'s situation, Vyāsatīrtha quotes a passage from the *Varāha Purāṇa* that supports the idea that the fulfillment of bliss is always relative to one's innate capacities. Using a *purāṇa* to interpret *śruti* statements, again, is an exegetical tactic advanced by Madhva that met with some controversy.[55] Furthermore, this particular *Varāha Purāṇa* quote is, according to Mesquita, one of Madhva's untraceable citations: "In the *Varāha Purāṇa* it says, 'When he has attained his own highest bliss, there shall be no desires for the liberated one, along the lines of emitting the world, pervading it, etc. But he will fulfill all other desires.'"[56]

Thus, in his arguments regarding the concordance of sacred literature's support of a hierarchy of souls in *mokṣa,* Vyāsatīrtha again demonstrates not only a thorough familiarity with his Viśiṣṭādvaitin opponents' *samanvaya* of the sacred canon but a commitment to Dvaita's more distinctive interpretative practices. But even if this latter feature makes Vyāsatīrtha's arguments here more vulnerable to criticism, his point is that many features of Viśiṣṭādvaita's reading of the canon actually conduce to a concordance that is more in line with that of Dvaita. In this manner, Vyāsatīrtha uses Madhva's distinctive exegetical tactics against Viśiṣṭādvaita precisely to make the case that these interpretive practices ought to be more widely embraced by other Vedāntins.

## CONCLUSION

Vyāsatīrtha's doctrinal polemics against Viśiṣṭādvaita understandings of *mokṣa* in his final section of the *Nyāyāmṛta* indicate that his court-sponsored collaboration with the Śrīvaiṣṇavas at large temple complexes throughout the empire did not erase the intellectual boundaries between these communities. While the pluralism of these religious spaces helped forge a shared Vaiṣṇavism that cut across sectarian lines, those lines—determined largely by doctrinal commitments and intellectual practices—remained in place. Vyāsatīrtha's use of quotes from sources that are deemed "unknown" by those outside Mādhva tradition, to justify the very Dvaita arguments most susceptible to criticism, reflects the magnitude of Vyāsatīrtha's sectarian commitments. This is equally true of his adherence to the exegetical practice of interpreting authoritative *śruti* statements in light of these other sources.

However, it is also true that, in some important ways, Vyāsatīrtha's arguments in the final section of his *Nyāyāmṛta* reflect his ongoing collaboration with the Śrīvaiṣṇavas at royally patronized temples. His arguments against Viśiṣṭādvaita do not display outright rejection of this sect's views so much as they highlight the superior suitability of Dvaita conclusions to Viśiṣṭādvaita premises. In arguing thus, Vyāsatīrtha emphasizes the fact that his system's teachings are implicit in Viśiṣṭādvaita teachings and therefore, for the sake of consistency, ought to be acknowledged as valid by the Śrīvaiṣṇavas. In his critique of the Śrīvaiṣṇavas, he is arguing that they must accept the Dvaita view on *mokṣa* as more consistent with their own basic premises or, at least, with the basic premises of the northern, Sanskritic form of Śrīvaiṣṇavism that seems to have been taking a distinctive shape during this period. Vyāsatīrtha thereby emphasizes, to some extent, what the two sects have in common, even as he demonstrates his system's superiority.

Furthermore, Vyāsatīrtha's emphasis on *sādhana* as one of the main justifications of hierarchy within *mokṣa* represents a repackaging of Madhva's view that is pertinent to his particular circumstances. By arguing that Viśiṣṭādvaita's positing of two different means to mokṣa—*bhakti* and *prapatti*—is conceptually incompatible with that system's commitment to *paramasāmya,* Vyāsatīrtha seems to be emphasizing an emerging rift within the Śrīvaiṣṇava community. Whether he does this to win over high-caste converts from Śrīvaiṣṇavism to Mādhvaism, precisely by reasserting the eternal significance of caste privilege and promising them a better form of *mokṣa* than that of the generally lower-caste *prapanna*s, is not clear. An alternative explanation is that he may have been seeking to forge a particular alliance with the *bhakti*- and Sanskrit-oriented faction of Śrīvaiṣṇavism that would later be called the Vaṭakalai or northern school. (Indeed, we encountered some evidence of this in chapter 4, in Vyāsatīrtha's founding of a possible intersectarian *agrahāra,* wherein he donated many shares to seemingly Vaṭakalai Śrīvaiṣṇavas.) Vyāsatīrtha may even have been pursuing both goals simultaneously. Whatever his reasons, Vyāsatīrtha's detailed criticisms of the Viśiṣṭādvaita position on *mokṣa* reflect his awareness, not only of that system's philosophical fault lines, but also of its social ones. Insofar as doctrinal coherence made for a stronger, more unified sectarian leadership, pointing out doctrinal incoherence, particularly that which exposed social rifts within a sectarian community, was of sociopolitical value.

Further evidence that Vyāsatīrtha's arguments were shaped by his environment consists of his avoidance, in his discussion of *mokṣa* in Dvaita, of some of the implications of Madhva's doctrine of the predestination of souls. While Madhva was explicit in saying that not all souls were eligible for *mokṣa* because some were innately qualified only for hell or eternal *saṃsāra,* Vyāsatīrtha does not discuss this in this chapter. If anything, Vyāsatīrtha's presentation on *mokṣa* in this chapter implies that many people are eligible for *mokṣa* because there is such a variety of possible *sādhana*s for achieving it. These include what we might label "readily accessible" options such as either death in the holy city of Prayag or the *bhakti* of hatred, wherein an enemy of God is actually deemed a devout devotee because of the intensity of his or her feelings toward the divine. They also include the more elite Vedānta *sādhana*s put forward by Advaita and Viśiṣṭādvaita. While Vyāsatīrtha does not explicitly state that all of these approaches result in *mokṣa* and should be viewed as successful *sādhana*s, his argument about hierarchy (*tāratamya*) in *mokṣa* in some ways depends upon the notion that all of these *sādhana*s have merit. He is trying to show that, because tradition endorses a variety of means to *mokṣa*—and clearly not all are equally taxing—the more challenging *sādhana*s must conduce to a form of *mokṣa* that is superior to the form one gets by, for example, merely dying in a holy city.

If Vyāsatīrtha was in fact trying to present a form of Dvaita Vedānta that was, on the one hand, more internally consistent than Viśiṣṭādvaita but, on the other hand, less unforgiving than Madhva's formulation (with its stringent predestination that put *mokṣa* permanently out of reach for some), does this imply that he was trying to promote Dvaita doctrines among a wider public? It might seem so, given Vyāsatīrtha's cultivation of links with Kannada *bhakta*s and his efforts, discussed in chapter 4, to promote Mādhva ritual practices at large and popular temples.[57] However, to judge purely from Vyāsatīrtha's textual presentation, the audience for his philosophical arguments is other Brahmin elites, who were knowledgeable about the Sanskrit textual tradition and its related intellectual practices. Yet his positioning of Dvaita as both more elitist and more flexible in his philosophical texts did have some social implications, in terms of his relationships not only with the Śrīvaiṣṇava leadership but also with the Vijayanagara court.

Indeed, Vyāsatīrtha's efforts to forge a kind of doctrinal alliance with one faction of the Śrīvaiṣṇava leadership while making Dvaita Vedānta seem less rigid in its soteriological outlook may reflect the specific Vaiṣṇava leanings of Kṛṣṇadevarāya. That Kṛṣṇadevarāya strove to reach a variety of publics within the context of religious spaces is documented in multilingual temple inscriptions referring to economic privileges conferred by him upon a range of social agents: for example, *maṭhādhipatis*, merchants, ferrymen, and weavers.[58] Yet Kṛṣṇadevarāya's patronage activities at Tirupati arguably represent a shift away from the Sāḷuva dynasty's support of more mixed-caste initiatives and leadership at that temple complex. In giving land to Vyāsatīrtha to construct two *maṭhas* at Tirupati-Tirumala, Kṛṣṇadevarāya may have been doing more than reining in an increasingly factionalized Śrīvaiṣṇava leadership; he may have been advocating for a more Brahmin- and Veda-centered ritual order there. As we have seen in chapter 2, Kṛṣṇadevarāya relied heavily upon Brahmins to play a variety of roles in his statecraft and conferred upon them privileged political positions. Thus, Vyāsatīrtha's hierarchical yet somewhat open-ended arguments about *mokṣa* may parallel Kṛṣṇadevarāya's efforts to extend courtly privileges to a variety of agents while maintaining—and enhancing—established elite privilege.

Indeed, Kṛṣṇadevarāya's reshuffling of normative Brahminical roles may have converged uneasily, for some constituents, with certain Śrīvaiṣṇava challenges to the exclusivity of Brahmin authority at temples. Upward economic mobility in the early sixteenth century brought with it changes in social status for many traditional labor communities.[59] This upward mobility in turn reflected the dramatic transformations that were taking place in South Indian society during this period. By the sixteenth century, the Vijayanagara Empire stood at the center of a global economic network that attracted many different types of people, not only to the subcontinent, but to the Vijayanagara capital specifically. This increased ethnic and religious diversity encouraged new explorations of identity.[60] The expansion of trade networks and the increase in migration characteristic of the period also occasioned the advent of significant new technologies in the subcontinent. Firearms and horses were much sought-after items, a fact that both reflected and contributed to the period's increased militarism. New polities, such as the Portuguese state of Goa, were established and fairly regular upheaval and conflict took place among the older states of the Deccan Plateau. The period's intense warfare provided new opportunities for individuals and groups to prove themselves politically useful and, as such, enabled certain types of social mobility.[61] But it also generated reasonable anxieties about violence, the allocation of resources, and the maintenance of stability, concerns that likely stimulated not only actual social maneuvering but active reflection upon it. Finally, Vijayanagara's increasingly cash-based economy wrought significant shifts in local social values, changing people's relationships to land and older forms of wealth while providing new opportunities for status acquisition and the assertion of influence.

We have seen in earlier chapters that many of these broad social, economic, and political transformations were either wrought or managed by Hindu sectarian leaders in their capacity as courtly agents in the empire's different regions. Some of these sectarian leaders, like Vyāsatīrtha, were also traditional intellectuals who therefore occupied both established and emerging positions of power. That some of these thinkers sought clarity on the issue of identity is not at all surprising given their own shifting social status.[62] One could argue that Vyāsatīrtha's version of such clarity involved making *mokṣa* more accessible to a variety of individuals while ordering that experience hierarchically so as to eternalize worldly privilege.

While many of these interpretative possibilities remain no more than that, reading Vyāsatīrtha's polemics against Viśiṣṭādvaita views of *mokṣa* nevertheless highlights the influence that social realities had over the articulation of philosophical arguments. Yet his polemics also indicate that doctrinal commitments mattered very much to the leadership of sectarian communities; such commitments provided a framework for sectarian identity that was often nonnegotiable. To borrow Clayton's arguments about "defensible differences" providing the good fences that make good neighbors,[63] Vyāsatīrtha's philosophical arguments against Viśiṣṭādvaita served to define the boundaries between the Mādhvas and Śrīvaiṣṇavas in a way that enabled them to share common ground without conflict. Vyāsatīrtha's polemics against Viśiṣṭādvaita allowed the two sects to collaborate comfortably at royally patronized temples, precisely by defining in great detail their ideological differences. In doing so, Vyāsatīrtha's incisive anti-Viśiṣṭādvaita polemics removed the threat that such collaboration might otherwise have posed to the two sects' core identities, even as his arguments also revealed the two sects' shared assumptions.

Thus, while Vyāsatīrtha cooperated with the Śrīvaiṣṇavas at large, royally funded temple complexes and while his arguments reflect this cooperation, they also attest to his abiding commitment to Mādhva Vedānta. Reading his activities at Tirupati and elsewhere in light of these arguments shows that he was not looking to merge Dvaita and Viśiṣṭādvaita or Mādhvas and Śrīvaiṣṇavas into a single Vaiṣṇava Vedānta system. Rather, his collaboration—ritual, material, social, and even intellectual—with the Śrīvaiṣṇavas was in the interest of promoting his distinctive sect, a social formation rooted largely in doctrinal commitments.

# 6

# Hindu, Ecumenical, Sectarian

## *Religion and the Vijayanagara Court*

At the outset of this book, I stated that Vijayanagara patronage of religious institutions was selective and flexible and responded in creative ways to the particular circumstances of specific locations. Nevertheless, our detailed study of Vyāsatīrtha's relationship with the court enables us to generalize about how and why Vijayanagara rulers patronized certain religious institutions and about the impact this patronage had, not only on particular sects, but on South Indian society more broadly.

While Vijayanagara patronage of religious institutions was generally evenhanded, Vijayanagara royals consistently privileged Brahmin sectarian institutions, particularly *mathas*, with a Vedānta focus. This began with the fourteenth-century Saṅgama dynasty's patronage of the Smārta Advaita community at Sringeri and continued through the sixteenth-century Tuḷuvas' increasing support of Mādhva and Śrīvaiṣṇava institutions. While the reasons for the empire's Vedāntin and Brahminical preferences remain debatable, the court clearly relied on these institutions to implement many features of its statecraft. As I argued in chapter 2, *mathas* replicated the court's power and authority in far-flung locations in both symbolic and practical ways. In a manner similar to but often more efficient than that of Hindu temples, *mathas* deployed royal patronage for economic and agrarian development. They thereby integrated recently conquered and rebellious territories more firmly into the empire.

Of course, not all *mathas* functioned in exactly the same way, and their diverse roles within their respective religious and intellectual communities likely affected the kinds of tasks they could perform for the state. For some religious communities, such as the Śrīvaiṣṇavas, *mathas* were but one of several organizational units;

the leaders of *maṭhas* in this community often shared religious authority with elite householders.[1] Furthermore, *maṭhas* within a given sectarian community could compete with one another in ways that impinged upon the monasteries' relative power. Finally, *maṭhas* and their leaders had to respond to local circumstances in ways that often required negotiation. Particularly in strategically significant areas with large, royally patronized temple complexes, *maṭhas* brokered power-sharing arrangements with various local constituents. These arrangements explicitly acknowledged the claims of different interest groups and, in doing so, restricted *maṭhas'* agency.

Yet precisely because of their innately complex roles in South Indian society, *maṭhas*—and their leaders—came to wield much local political and economic power. This was true even though *maṭhas* typically housed ascetics who were pursuing nonworldly religious goals. This apparent contradiction may be explained by the royal notion that detached individuals made ideal courtly agents. At the same time, as sources examined in chapters 2 and 4 reveal, *maṭhas* receiving royal support could become alternative seats of power that competed in certain ways with the court's authority. Both because of their potential royal connections and their self-perpetuating authority, *maṭhas* proliferated as a form of religious institution even among those communities, such as the Vīraśaivas, who were not receiving royal support. Thus, Vijayanagara patronage of religious institutions fostered a generic institutionalization process that implicated a variety of South Indian Hindu communities while encouraging religious diversity.

Indeed, although *maṭhas* receiving royal patronage were often engaged in a shared project that promoted intersectarian collaboration of various kinds, Vijayanagara patronage also formalized and advanced Hindu sectarianism. As I have argued in chapter 2, the *maṭha's* status as a sectarian institution is evident in both its daily functioning and its intellectual production. Internally, *maṭhas'* use of instructional manuals to govern many aspects of daily life for full-time residents and their documentation of intellectual lineages in *guru-paramparā* texts demarcated the boundaries between intellectual and religious communities. Externally, the increasing affiliation of *maṭhas* with temples, and the replication of temple practices at freestanding *maṭhas*, linked these monastic communities in highly public ways with popular devotional and ritual practices. The literary production, which included polemics against rival systems of thought and biographies of sectarian leaders, of many sixteenth-century Brahmin *maṭhas* may have addressed a specialized audience. But *maṭhas'* efforts to promote their sectarian distinctiveness among a wider public are evident in their cultivation of *samādhi* shrine worship, their installation of icons and *maṇḍapas* at existing temple complexes, and their selective affiliation with popular vernacular devotional movements.

Despite the court's clear patronage preference for a specific type of religious institution–the Brahmin Vedānta *maṭha*–Vijayanagara royals remained fairly noncommittal when it came to personal religious affiliation.² Unlike the kings of Sanderson's "Śaiva Age"—which he dates from the fifth to the thirteenth centuries and which will be discussed in more detail below—Vijayanagara royals did not routinely or publicly take gurus. They patronized a variety of not only distinct but competing sectarian communities. As we know, Vijayanagara patronage, although granted predominantly to Hindu institutions, was also occasionally extended to Jain and Muslim communities.³ But the court's noncommittal religious stance was not completely neutral or indifferent. For instance, as we saw in chapter 4, the court's deliberate cultivation of a transsectarian Vaiṣṇava alliance between Mādhvas and Śrīvaiṣṇavas manipulated some significant divisions between and within these respective communities. Moreover, as noted in chapter 3, this alliance threatened the Advaitin Smārtas, who attempted to advocate for their entitlement to royal patronage in the sixteenth century, using inscriptions attesting to their prominence at the fourteenth-century court.

The motivations behind the Vijayanagara court's selective yet noncommittal patronage of a variety of Brahminical, Vedānta *maṭha*s were often politically strategic. For example, as discussed in chapters 2 and 4, the court's support for Śrīvaiṣṇava institutions was motivated to a significant extent by concerns about heavily militarized chieftains and overlords (*nāyaka*s) in the regions of both southern Andhra and northern Tamilnadu, as well as by concerns about the Gajapati rulers' designs on prominent forts in the border zone between the two kingdoms. As Ajay Rao has demonstrated, the Śrīvaiṣṇavas actively pursued close ties to the court through a variety of intellectual, literary, and ritual activities that supported courtly endeavors.⁴ Furthermore, the Śrīvaiṣṇavas' popular vernacular and often mixed-caste devotionalism, together with their established tradition of Vedānta intellectualism, enabled this community to appeal simultaneously to different social groups. This in turn enabled the Tuḷuva court to work with the Śrīvaiṣṇava leadership to forge relationships with a variety of constituents in regions of strategic significance to the empire.

Most important to our purposes, the royal shift toward Vaiṣṇavism, which began during the Sāḷuva dynasty and accelerated during the Tuḷuva, encompassed within it a new prominence for Mādhva Brahminism. Much of the credit for this goes to Vyāsatīrtha, whose deft management of his relationships with both the court and other sectarian groups—as well as his intellectual virtuosity—established Mādhva Vedānta as a major social and intellectual force. Vyāsatīrtha's success as a sectarian leader is reflected in large part in his procurement of land from the Vijayanagara court to establish Mādhva institutions such as *maṭha*s and *agrahāra*s in new locations. Several of these locations were already Śrīvaiṣṇava in orientation; Vyāsatīrtha did the court's bidding by collaborating with this alternative Vaiṣṇava group to establish a transregional and transsectarian Vaiṣṇavism that was of high political utility. Manifested primarily in temples in the multilingual zone at the empire's core, where Tamil, Telugu, and Kannada intersected, this big tent Vaiṣṇavism enabled the court to showcase its generous temple patronage, which was deeply entangled with its military activities, to a variety of publics.

Not only did these Vaiṣṇava megatemples, created through royal patronage, expand Vijayanagara outreach, they also articulated a distinctive Vijayanagara cosmopolitanism. These spaces were de facto multilingual and devotionally pluralistic but unified in an overarching religious purpose and integrated into a shared economic and social network. However, precisely because pluralism was not an accidental reality at these megatemples but one that had been orchestrated by Vijayanagara patronage, they were also highly sectarian spaces. Sects—typically represented by *maṭha*s on the premises of these temples—could collaborate with one another and benefit from increased ritual largesse before an expanded and diverse audience. But precisely through these collaborative activities, sects could also promote their distinctive doctrines and practices. Vyāsatīrtha was particularly adept at such promotion, which took the form of added ritual activities, new architectural structures for *prasād* distribution, the installation of icons associated with his *maṭha*s, and possible collaboration with vernacular devotional movements at these large temple complexes.

As we have seen, Vyāsatīrtha was also adept at doctrinal debate, the more elite and intellectual form of sectarian promotion. His polemical texts against alternative forms of Vedānta exhibit a nuanced understanding of those systems that is highly attuned to their internal debates and their historical evolution. His thorough parsing of the various arguments of his Vedāntin rivals exposes a multitude of logical inconsistencies while also providing a doxography of key Vedānta concepts. Through his incisive polemics and his historical doxography, Vyāsatīrtha successfully located Dvaita Vedānta more advantageously in the philosophical landscape and stimulated significant responses from his Vedāntin rivals. Moreover, Vyāsatīrtha's reframing of some key Mādhva doctrines, such as his reformulation of *aparokṣajñāna* as *jīvanmukti* and his emphasis on *sādhana* or the soul's agency in the pursuit of *mokṣa*, reflect a coopting of successful doctrinal positions from other communities to benefit his sectarian cause. However, this coopting also reflects his dialogic context and the intersectarian negotiations that were taking place as a direct result of Vijayanagara patronage of Brahmin Vedānta communities. Indeed, while the word *polemics* implies outright opposition, these polemics also involved significant intellectual borrowing and exchange. In this way, the competitive collaboration between sects that Vijayanagara patronage inspired in ritual and material exchanges at temples also manifested itself in Vyāsatīrtha's philosophical arguments.

Indeed a key, if obvious, point of this book has been that intellectual practices and religious doctrines do not unfold in a sociopolitical vacuum. In making this point, however, I want to stress that one of the things we understand better by contextualizing Vyāsatīrtha's arguments against alternative forms of Vedānta is the specifics of the arguments themselves. A decontextualized reading of Vyāsatīrtha's polemics against rival Vedānta systems—one that ignores his on-the-ground interactions with these groups—risks overlooking some of the subtle areas of intellectual overlap that Vyāsatīrtha himself identifies. Speaking of religious claims and their contestation, Clayton has argued that "'reasons' are always reasons for someone; they become persuasive when they are regarded as 'good reasons' by some audience."[5] In other words, even the most abstract philosophical arguments make their fullest sense only when the context in which they are put forward is understood. This is true not just for arguments that are aiming to be more cogent than valid, to borrow Griffiths's distinction,[6] but even for arguments that are trying to be logically airtight. It is therefore only through a historically informed reading of Vyāsatīrtha's polemics that we can fully clarify his philosophical positions and better understand how those philosophical positions shaped his community's actions in the world.

For some readers, my historic contextualization of Vyāsatīrtha's philosophical and religious discourse may remain intellectually problematic. Such contextualization runs the risk of not taking the ideas seriously enough on their own terms, thereby compromising the integrity of both rationality and belief as independent, closed systems. Certainly if they are not done carefully, historical studies of religious philosophy can reduce belief systems and philosophical ideas to shadowy reflections of social and political reality or, worse yet, to utilitarian strategies for worldly gain. At the same time, I suspect that for other readers, the philosophical and doctrinal component of Vyāsatīrtha's life story will remain largely irrelevant to their understanding, not only of the role of religion in this period, but even of Vyāsatīrtha's particular significance. Such a reader might argue that, while it is important to know that Vyāsatīrtha was engaged in doctrinal disputes with his sectarian rivals, one does not need to know the precise details of those arguments. Because few of Vyāsatīrtha's own contemporaries would have been familiar with those details, knowing them does little to enhance our understanding of the period. In this view, Vyāsatīrtha's roles as a state agent, an economic stimulator, a public works patron, and a temple donor teach us far more about religion's functionality, its social value, and its historic significance than the precise nuances of Vyāsatīrtha's polemics ever could.

But while this book could have been written without a study of Vyāsatīrtha's philosophical works, that omission would have made for a strange testament to Vyāsatīrtha's life and his own understanding of what he was doing and why. The rationale behind his activities and those of his followers was deeply embedded in a particular reading of the sacred corpus and a particular understanding of its form. Moreover, his actions were prompted by concern about the human individual's existential situation, the need for correct devotion to God, and the quest for right knowledge. Other, more evanescent concerns about land, influence, and the spread of Mādhva institutions were important, mainly insofar as they enabled meaningful reflection on the former issues.

Even more significant, perhaps, Vyāsatīrtha's responses to timeless religious and existential questions *do* tell us how religion functioned as a lived reality in early sixteenth-century South India. This reality unfolded in a particular time and place and under a specific set of circumstances, even as it engaged timeless canonical teachings and spoke in the language of eternal truth. As demonstrated in chapter 3, Vyāsatīrtha's arguments gained a hearing in large part because of his activities as a state agent and his implementation of the court's agenda. However, we have also seen how his role in implementing that agenda was inextricably linked to the shoring up of his own constituency, a constituency that was connected by the doctrinal and intellectual as much as it was by the ritual, social, and political. The manner in which Vyāsatīrtha made his arguments against rival Vedānta systems not only reflected and influenced his negotiations with other sectarian groups, it also shaped, to a significant extent, his own following. The intellectual fame he achieved was partly due to his sociopolitical prominence. Yet it was also due to the incisiveness of his arguments and the magnitude of his engagement with alternative Vedānta traditions. Indeed, the extensive and diverse philosophical responses that Vyāsatīrtha's works elicited from his intellectual opponents confirmed Vyāsatīrtha's intellectual virtuosity. In doing so, these responses reinforced the Mādhva sect's worldly stature. As a result, Vyāsatīrtha's philosophical works have profoundly influenced the geographic scope, material resources, social functioning, and self-understanding of the Mādhva community in South India, and they continue to do so even today.

By being attentive to these sometimes abstruse and demanding arguments, we do learn something significant about how religion, as a complex social and intellectual system, operated both within and upon its milieu. Rather than reducing the kind of religious questioning and philosophical argumentation that we encounter in Vyāsatīrtha's works to a reflection of something else that is putatively more "real" (e.g., politics, economics, or military strategy), reading religious and philosophical texts as constitutive features of their historical context helps to preserve religion's integrity and illuminate its role more brightly in our analysis of the past.

Just as we can only understand Vyāsatīrtha's life story by examining his philosophical and religious arguments, and just as those arguments make their fullest sense when we read them as part of the historical record, we can only understand Vijayanagara patronage of religious and monastic institutions if we take the literature produced by those institutions seriously. This is true not only of biographies of sectarian leaders and doxographies of various religious and intellectual systems but of polemical and philosophical texts as well. It is not my contention that arcane doctrinal disputes between Brahmin sects espousing different views of Vedānta canonical literature determined royal behavior in any direct way—for example, how royals patronized religious institutions. Sectarian leaders, however, undeniably did use polemics and debate as key means of articulating their identity. Insofar as such debate had an impact on intersectarian alliances and rivalries, it also affected royal giving. These rivalries and alliances played a direct role in temple management. They therefore had implications for the redistribution of royal wealth and for sectarian institutions' efficacy as funnels of patronage into strategically significant locales. Thus, the implementation of the court's agenda, insofar as it depended upon sectarian leaders, also depended to some extent on their relations with one another. These relations were enacted not only through religious rituals and temple management but also through doctrinal debates. In this admittedly indirect way, religious doctrines implicated the Vijayanagara state and its policies. That the court was aware of this is evident in the rhetoric of royal inscriptions discussed in chapters 2 and 4, in which religious leaders are praised for their doctrinal commitments, spiritual endeavors, and intellectual acumen.

Thus, while I would not argue that religious ideology was fundamental to politics or served as a primary impetus to royal behavior, I would also be quite wary of the view that religion played no role whatsoever in Vijayanagara statecraft. Certainly, there was no state religion under Vijayanagara rule, if what we mean by that is a religion imposed by the state on its citizens. In fact, even the extent to which Vijayanagara royals embraced a particular religious ideology is unclear. But, as the work of Fritz, Michell and M. S. Nagaraja Rao; Verghese; Eaton and Wagoner; Ajay Rao; and others has shown,[7] the pageantry of the Vijayanagara state—displays of its power in the abstract—depended upon religious symbols to a significant extent. Because those symbols were selected from a range of possible options, royal use of particular religious iconography to make claims about the state's authority privileged certain forms of religious expression over others. This, in turn, privileged the sociopolitical position of certain religious institutions throughout the empire's holdings.[8]

Indeed, this book has demonstrated that the empire's reliance on religious institutions and their leaders was not merely in the interest of asserting or legitimating Vijayanagara rule in a symbolic way. Rather, as we have seen, Vijayanagara royals' religious patronage played a critical role in shaping the various practical mechanisms that enabled the empire to function. When sectarian institutions irrigated land and arranged for village produce to be dispatched to (sometimes quite remote) temples, when they filled temple coffers with cash and distributed donations of *prasād* to various publics, and when they commissioned goods and services for conducting elaborate festivals and celebrations, they shaped a variety of social, political, economic, and logistical networks. These networks, in turn, facilitated the circulation of goods and services throughout the empire's various regions and promoted different forms of discretionary power among a range of local agents. Such structures had a significant impact on people's daily lives, including the kinds of crops they planted, the food they ate, the ways in which they maneuvered through space, how they organized themselves into groups, and the manner in which they paid their taxes. In short, these networks structured South Indian peoples' material and social worlds and their degree of influence upon and status within them.

Sectarian leaders like Vyāsatīrtha played a large role in the shaping of these everyday realities for many people, and their ability to do so was a direct result of Vijayanagara patronage. Thus, the state did use "religion" both as a set of symbols designed to make certain abstract claims and as a practical means of constructing and imposing the state's quotidian apparatus. Of course, as we know from Morrison's work, this apparatus functioned quite differently and with varying degrees of success in different imperial regions.[9] But that variability, too, was often managed by sectarian monastic leaders.[10]

Most important, perhaps, I would argue that Vijayanagara patronage of religious institutions in the early sixteenth century actively encouraged new ways of thinking about religious identity. It is here that Vijayanagara patronage most clearly distinguished itself from earlier Indian polities in ways that reflected the many transformations that were taking place in South Indian society during this period. In recent years, scholars have posited that the period of early modernity in India was inaugurated in the sixteenth century.[11] While the phrase "early modern" is a highly ambiguous one,[12] most scholars of South Asia would agree that some of the changes taking place in South Indian society at this time were unprecedented. As the Vijayanagara Empire took center stage in an emerging global economy, not only did new ways of life come into being, but new ways of thinking about identity also emerged. Increased migration to and within South India, the advent of new technologies, expanding militarism, the infusion of cash into a rapidly changing economy, and growing ethnic and religious diversity all contributed to reformulations of social identity. Royally patronized religious institutions played a significant role in these reformulations. Religious intellectuals actively engaged questions of what was different and what was shared between sectarian groups while the court used its patronage to encourage these conversations. By relocating Brahmin Vedānta *maṭha*s to shared temple environments, Kṛṣṇadevarāya's court promoted intersectarian collaboration at large and popular temples in ways that facilitated doctrinal exchange and religious synthesis, even as it also occasioned the inscribing of sectarian boundaries. That the sixteenth-century court had something at stake in these maneuvers is suggested in its active efforts to create a distinctive Vijayanagara cosmopolitanism that integrated different regions and constituencies of the empire into a shared religious culture at certain strategically located temples. It is also evident in the court's selective use of religious iconography that showcased the empire's diversity while also privileging specific religious articulations.[13]

Further evidence that Vijayanagara royals were aware of and actively reflected upon religious and ethnic differences can be seen in their self-referential use of the phrase "sultans among Hindu kings." This proclamation of identity, found in inscriptions as early as the fourteenth-century Saṅgama dynasty, casts the Vijayanagara state in terms that are relative to other South Asian polities. This label sought to establish a connection between the Vijayanagara Empire and the northern sultanates, which dominated much of the Indian subcontinent at that time. But while this connection attests to the existence of a shared cultural and political sphere that cut across religious and ethnic distinctions between Vijayanagara and the sultanates, it also asserts the Vijayanagara court's distinctive identity in an increasingly Turkish, Persianized, and Islamic political environment. In a similar way, the Vijayanagara court's increasing reliance on sectarian leaders of *mathas* to implement many features of its statecraft bore a close resemblance to the Deccan sultanates' use of Sufi shrines to similar ends. The Vijayanagara court's reliance on *matha*s, however, was arguably a "Hindu" version of this practice, inflected in ways that helped forge a distinctive imperial religious identity for the empire.

To be sure, ethnic and religious diversity were facts of life in the Indian subcontinent for centuries before the advent of Vijayanagara rule. Finbar Flood's work on cultural encounters between ethnically, linguistically, and religiously diverse elites in the regions of what is now Afghanistan, Pakistan, and North India from the ninth to the thirteenth centuries shows how confrontation with various forms of difference came to configure South Asian identities in that period. Moreover, Talbot has argued, in her studies of the Telangana and Andhra Pradesh regions between the eleventh and seventeenth centuries, that all instances of identity-formation are responses to broader social change. These responses often involve a deliberate and selective engagement with the past in order to confront the complex realities of the present. She therefore maintains that there is no great rupture between premodern and modern mechanisms of identity formation.[14]

Talbot is certainly correct that thinking about difference and identity was not something that Vijayanagara royals or religious elites invented. Some of the strategies deployed by Vijayanagara agents to construct their own histories in ways that would improve their status in the present, such as their use of inscriptions to make certain claims, were very similar to what obtained, for example, under Kākatīya rule (c. 1175–1324).[15] Moreover, sixteenth-century Vijayanagara responses to changing conditions reflect an inheritance of deeply rooted symbolic and practical structures. One could argue, in fact, that the empire's ecumenical tolerance of a diversity of religious institutions and its concurrent privileging of certain religious formations was in line with a lengthy tradition of Indian rulers that extends all the way back to the third century BCE's Buddhist emperor Aśoka. Aśoka, like many Indian rulers after him, accepted the de facto state of religious pluralism within his empire and did not seek to restrict it. He speaks explicitly, in his widely distributed rock edicts, about the need to respect the views of all sects, even as these edicts also promote awareness of the Buddha's *dhamma*.[16]

Other pre-Vijayanagara Indian texts that discuss royal attitudes toward religious diversity display a similar mindset. For example, the ninth-century Sanskrit play *Āgamaḍambara* or "Much Ado about Religion," composed by the Nyāya intellectual and royal advisor Bhaṭṭa Jayanta, in Kashmir, focuses explicitly on the issue of religious diversity. In this text, the actual king of Kashmir, Śaṅkaravarman, seeks advice from logicians and Vedic exegetes on how much tolerance ought to be extended to the "Black Blanket Observance," a group that seems to have engaged in deviant sexual behaviors as a form of religious rite. The king seeks to suppress this practice "because he kn[ows] that it [i]s unprecedented, but he d[oes] not suppress the religions of Jains and others in the same way."[17] The basis of the king's general tolerance is that religions that are widely practiced but pose no threat to the social order ought to be respected.

This pragmatic tolerance, in which nonthreatening religions are allowed to continue even though other religious formations and intellectual commitments are considered superior, seems to have been a shared feature of Śaṅkaravarman's and Kṛṣṇadevarāya's respective reigns. However, we can also find differences. One such difference may have been in the two kings' practical interactions with temples. In his *Rājataraṅgiṇī*, Kalhana, the twelfth-century chronicler of Kashmir's kings, has unflattering things to say about Śaṅkaravarman's treatment of religious institutions. Kalhana describes Śaṅkaravarman as having stripped temples of their wealth in the interest of funding his wars.[18] If Kalhana's description is accurate, Śaṅkaravarman seems also to have had a rather antagonistic relationship with temple leadership. This is quite different from Kṛṣṇadevarāya's reliance on tax revenue to fund his wars and his expansion of temple wealth and of the power of temple leadership in the wake of his military conquests. Clearly, under Śaṅkaravarman, tolerance of religious diversity and interest in questions of religious correctness did not translate into lavish patronage of religious institutions or collaboration with religious leaders to achieve certain social, political, or economic ends.

In contrast, Sears's study of Kalachuri patronage of the monastic institutions of the Mattamayūra sect of Śaiva Siddhānta at the turn of the first millennium in North India reveals many similarities between the complex dynamics of royal-religious interaction in this period and under later Vijayanagara rule. Sears shows that in the Kalachuri kingdoms, the Mattamayūra monasteries played many practical roles, such as helping to develop urban centers, roads, and trade networks. Moreover, just as *maṭhādhipati*s receiving Vijayanagara patronage came to play a variety of roles in Vijayanagara society and advocated for themselves and their sects in diverse ways, so, too, according to Sears, were Mattamayūra monks able to expand their social influence significantly through their royal connections.[19] But Sears's research also reveals important contrasts between royal-religious interactions under Kalachuri versus Vijayanagara rule. She argues that Kalachuri kings took Mattamayūra ascetics as *rājaguru*s, who not only consecrated the king's rule but initiated the king into the Śaiva Siddhānta order. This made the king "the head of the social order established by caste and religious discipline"[20] or, as Sanderson has put it, "imbued [the king] with the numinous power of Śivahood in the exercise of his sovereignty."[21] In these ways, Kalachuri royals apparently displayed an affinity for the doctrines and practices of the Mattamayūra sect and used that affinity to define the social order more explicitly than what obtained under Kṛṣṇadevarāya's rule. As we have noted, the association of Vijayanagara kings with *rājaguru*s is not firmly established in the historical record; in Kṛṣṇadevarāya's case this ambiguity is borne out by ongoing competing sectarian claims over who held this position. Furthermore, Vijayanagara royals, especially Kṛṣṇadevarāya, encouraged forms of religious collaboration that deemphasized the doctrinal supremacy of any particular group. It is partly for these reasons that I have characterized the influence of religious doctrine on royal practice at Kṛṣṇadevarāya's court as having been "indirect."

Sears's research does not consider the Kalachuris' relationship to the other religious traditions that must have coexisted with the Mattamayūras. For such a discussion, we may turn to Sanderson, who argues that royal support for Śaivism throughout the subcontinent between the fifth and thirteenth centuries (a period Sanderson labels the Śaiva age) did not mean that royals refused to tolerate or even actively support other forms of religious practice. However, this royal affinity for Śaivism did exercise a homogenizing influence on other religious traditions, including Buddhism and Jainism. These traditions, Sanderson argues, eventually adopted many of the ritualistic, conceptual, and institutional trappings of court-endorsed Śaivism.[22] We have noted that in a similar way, under Vijayanagara rule, many religious communities came to pattern their institutional structure along the lines of those Brahmin Vedānta *maṭha*s that were receiving royal patronage. However, Sanderson's description of the religious homogeneity that resulted from royal support for Śaivism implies that this was largely due to religious agents' efforts to remake themselves in an image that was appealing to royalty. In contrast, I would argue that Vijayanagara royals like Kṛṣṇadevarāya used their patronage, in part, to stimulate reconsiderations of religious diversity on the part of religious elites. In doing so, Vijayanagara royals actively encouraged not only certain forms of religious behavior but certain types of intellectual reflection thereupon. Moreover, Kṛṣṇadevarāya's manner of supporting religious institutions and his proclamations of this support in the *praśasti* portion of his inscriptions endorsed a particular type of religious diversity as emblematic of the empire itself. This endorsement implicated a variety of royal and religious practical endeavors and contributed to the simultaneous creation of a shared religious sensibility and significant sectarian divisions.

Thus, Vijayanagara royals drew upon a deep well of Indian traditions of tolerance and inclusivism that nevertheless privileged specific religious formations.

This is quite different from European states in the same period, which, for the most part, would have to await the Enlightenment to recognize the political value of religious tolerance. Yet while in some ways, these enlightened Indian attitudes toward religious diversity functioned as cultural *doxa* and were very much taken for granted, in other ways, the precise mechanisms by which these attitudes were implemented were deliberately constructed. Moreover, this construction took place under particular historical circumstances that were highly contingent.

My concern for this particularity and contingency is why I have focused here on individual agents confronting specific circumstances over the course of a thirty-year period of South Indian history. This might make my analysis seem too micro—and too elite—to be about anything so expansive and complex as religious identity in early modern South India. In the details of individual lives and communities operating under specific, unfolding circumstances, however, is precisely where we see how larger categories were created, sustained, and transformed over time. By extension, this book's focus on the ideas and activities of individual royal and religious agents locates those agents in their social environments fairly precisely. It thereby maps the contours of their influence in ways that give that influence its due, while acknowledging the inherent interpretive limitations of a study of elite behavior.

An analysis of Vyāsatīrtha's relations with his sectarian rivals and with the royal court demonstrates that the sectarian leader's status in sixteenth-century Vijayanagara society could not be taken for granted. The *maṭhādhipati*'s success—and by extension the success of the sect he represented—depended in large part on his management of complex and often-conflicted relationships. In his relations with the court, the *maṭhādhipati* sought to showcase all the intellectual, ritual, and charitable virtues of himself and his community at the expense of his rivals, in hopes of increasing the royal patronage his sect would receive. However, he also had to do the king's bidding with the material resources he was given and make sure he neither eclipsed his royal patron's fame nor allowed partisan differences to interfere with the court's economic agenda as enacted through gifts to religious institutions. Indeed, in managing his relations with sectarian rivals, the *maṭhādhipati* had to be careful to clarify what made his sect superior without alienating potential allies in the receipt and management of royal patronage. The successful sectarian leader could not allow doctrinal disputes to get in the way of mutually beneficial intersectarian collaboration. But he also needed to advocate for the doctrines that were at the heart of his own sect's identity and were often the principal motivation behind his activities.

Thus, for all its reputation as an ecumenical polity, the sixteenth-century Vijayanagara court was sectarian insofar as it contributed to the significant wealth and prestige of particular *maṭhas* and *maṭhādhipati*s, whose causes were greatly advanced through these gifts. The royal court's granting of significant local power to monastic institutions directly supported their sectarian projects by expanding their networks into new territories and creating fresh opportunities to engage with new audiences. Kṛṣṇadevarāya's patronage of different Hindu monastic communities was ecumenical mainly in the sense that it was religiously noncommittal and benefited a variety of sectarian organizations. Moreover, the empire was sectarian in the sense that its manipulative pluralism fostered an increased sense of sectarian boundaries and competition among religious elites over royal resources. Shifts in patronage practices reflected this, privileging some groups over others and creating competition that had a significant impact on intersectarian relations at various practical and intellectual levels.

But the sixteenth-century Vijayanagara Empire was also Hindu insofar as it helped to articulate a unified religious identity that was bound up with a specific cultural and economic way of life. Through its patronage activities, the sixteenth-century Vijayanagara court actively provided contexts within which shared religious identities were enacted, and it did so, not against, but in awareness of non-Hindu religious others. Its cultivation of a cosmopolitan, transregional form of temple worship strove for a particular version of inclusivism, one that privileged specific religious articulations. In doing so, the Vijayanagara Empire distinguished itself from other religious and political formations of sixteenth-century South Asia. It put a particular form of transregional and transsectarian Hindu identity into practice.

## 1. HINDU SECTARIANISM AND THE CITY OF VICTORY

1. While European and Middle Eastern migration to India in this period was largely voluntary, most Africans arrived in the subcontinent as military slaves, serving in some of the Deccan sultanates. However, military slavery as practiced in India did not confer a lifelong state of bondage. Many Africans in the subcontinent eventually experienced social mobility, with some acquiring their own military and political power and others hiring themselves out as paid laborers, including as soldiers to different armies. Thus, it was the quest for economic opportunities that often drew former African slaves to Vijayanagara, in much the same way that it drew Europeans and Middle Easterners. For discussions of Africans in Indian history, see Eaton (2005, ch. 5) and Chatterjee and Eaton (2006).

2. Carla Sinopoli (2000, 370) estimates that the population of the Vijayanagara capital in 1500 was 250,000. This made it one of the largest cities in the world at that time. According to John Haywood (2011, 116), the capital had 480,000 people by 1530, making it second only to Beijing in terms of population. Europe's population, which had been decimated by the Black Death in the fourteenth century, began to increase to numbers approaching those in India only in the late sixteenth century. Delhi's population seems to have peaked at just under 300,000 in the early fourteenth century, but it never rebounded from the effects of raids that took place from the end of that period until the reign of Shah Jahan (1628–58). Vijayanagara was thus the largest city in India for most of the capital's history. See Irfan Habib (2011, 125–26) for a fuller discussion. Anila Verghese's work (1995) on the art and architectural remains in the city documents the sculptural depiction of ethnic diversity, conveyed primarily through distinctive clothing styles, on many of the capital's sixteen hundred remaining structures. Textual sources in a variety of languages documenting this diversity will be discussed below.

3. This perspective can be found in the work of Krishnaswami Aiyanagar (1921), B. A. Saletore (1934), and K. A. Nilakanta Sastri ([1955] 1994). Vijayanagara kings also had

ongoing military clashes with "Hindu" kings, such as the Gajapatis ruling in Orissa, and with Hindu chieftains throughout the South, a fact downplayed in some of this older scholarship. It should be noted that these pioneering works in the field, despite their biases, have provided a significant basis on which further study has been built.

4. For example, Burton Stein (1999) and Catherine B. Asher and Cynthia Talbot (2006). The Vijayanagara Empire was ruled by three successive dynasties, the Saṅgama (c. 1346–1485), the Sāḷuva (1485–1505), and the Tuḷuva (1505–65). Most royal patronage of Jainism took place in the first dynasty or the Saṅgama period: for example, an inscription of Bukka II documents a grant to a Jain *basadi*; in 1424, Devarāya II granted a village to another Jain *basadi*; and in 1426, Devarāya II funded the construction of the Pārśvanātha Caityālaya in the Vijayanagara capital (see Verghese 1995, 121, for citations to the relevant inscriptions). Christianity did not establish a strong presence in Vijayanagara, but in the sixteenth century, Portuguese envoys, soldiers, and masons seem to have resided there on a temporary basis. The fifteenth-century court of Devarāya II extended its support for and protection of Muslim mosques and tombs, so much so that "Ahmad Kahn dedicated the mosque that he constructed for the merit of his patron, Devarāya II" (Verghese 1995, 128; she cites *SII*, vol. 9, pt. 2, no. 447 as her evidence).

5. The work of Anila Verghese (esp. 1995, 2000) on the capital's religious monuments is attentive to this privileging as is recent research by Ajay Rao (2015).

6. The term *Smārta* derives from the term *smṛti* referring to the "remembered" religious literature and related practices of Hinduism. But because the *smṛti* corpus is so vast, defining Smārtas in reference to it is not terribly precise. Originally, *Smārta* seems to have connoted those Brahmins whose religious sympathies lay with purāṇic literature and with the devotional cults to deities described therein (see G. Flood 1996, 113, for a brief discussion). Smārta Brahmins apparently fused these purāṇic devotional cults with a Vedic sensibility. In the region and time frame under discussion in this book, however, I am using Smārta a bit more narrowly to refer to those Brahmins affiliated with Śaṅkara's Advaita Vedānta and, in the case of the Sringeri Smārtas active at the Vijayanagara court, with Śaivism. These Smārtas effected a rapprochement between Vedic Hinduism, the Purāṇas, devotion to Śiva, and Advaita Vedānta philosophy.

7. Madhva is credited with founding eight *maṭhas* or monasteries in Udupi, the most famous of which contains the Kṛṣṇa icon that Madhva received, reportedly through miraculous means, and which he personally installed and worshipped. These eight *maṭhas* are laid out in a square formation at the city center; the Kṛṣṇa *maṭha*, which functions largely as a temple and has a public worship area and large facilities for feeding pilgrims, draws significant numbers of visitors annually from throughout India. While there are no inscriptional records dating these *maṭhas* to Madhva's period, the eight *maṭhas* were certainly in existence by the fifteenth century (see *SII* 1932, nos. 295ff.). The late sixteenth-century Mādhva philosopher and saint Vādirāja is credited with putting into place the current system (known as *paryāya*) of biennial rotation among the *maṭhas* for managing the worship of the deity Kṛṣṇa. See Vasudeva Rao (2002) for a historical overview and ethnographic study of the Mādhva *maṭhas* in Udupi.

8. Lawrence McCrea (2015) documents the lack of engagement with Dvaita views on the part of other Sanskrit intellectuals prior to the sixteenth century. A few tombs of

Mādhva sectarian leaders located near the Vijayanagara capital and dating to the mid-fourteenth century attest to a fledgling Mādhva presence in the early days of the empire. However, beginning during Vyāsatīrtha's lifetime, Mādhva architectural forms and institutional networks proliferated at the capital and throughout the empire. Concurrently, criticism of Dvaita doctrines by proponents of other Hindu systems of thought also proliferated throughout the subcontinent.

9. See Michael Williams (2011) for a discussion of these tactics in Vyāsatīrtha's *Nyāyāmṛta* and Elaine Fisher (2013) for a discussion of how these tactics influenced early modern South Indian intellectualism more generally.

10. McCrea (2015) argues that Vyāsatīrtha engaged in a new type of doxographic writing that did not merely summarize the ideas of various systems of thought but also traced the evolution over time of certain ideas and arguments within his opponents' systems. It is largely through this historicism, McCrea maintains, that Vyāsatīrtha was able to criticize his intellectual rivals most effectively. McCrea also points out that this "historical turn" within Mādhva doxography may not have originated with Vyāsatīrtha; his fifteenth-century Mādhva predecessor Viṣṇudāsācārya made similar attempts. But Vyāsatīrtha practiced it to a far more sweeping and thorough degree. He thereby inspired the production of similar historical doxographic texts among rival traditions (e.g., Appaya Dīkṣita's late sixteenth-century *Śāstrasiddhāntaleśasaṃgraha*).

11. McCrea's (2015) work focuses primarily on Vyāsatīrtha's criticisms of Advaita Vedānta. This is true of most scholarship on Vyāsatīrtha whose treatment of Viśiṣṭādvaita or qualified nondualism, advanced by the Śrīvaiṣṇavas, has received far less scholarly attention.

12. Eaton (2005, 88–89) summarizes these military engagements as follows:

The string began in 1509, when at Koilkonda, sixty miles southwest of Hyderabad, Krishna Raya defeated the last remnant of Bahmani power, Sultan Mahmud, along with Yusuf 'Adil Shah of Bijapur, who was killed in the engagement. Soon thereafter the king turned south and seized Penukonda, Śrirangapattan, and Śivasamudram from the chiefs of the powerful Ummattur family. In 1513, turning to the southern Andhra coast, he reconquered the great fort of Udayagiri, which had fallen into the hands of the Gajapati kings of Orissa. Two years later his armies seized from the Gajapatis the fort of Kondavidu in the Krishna delta. In 1517 he took Vijayavada and Kondapalli, also in the Krishna delta, and then Rajahmundry, up the coast in the Godavari delta. In 1520, with the help of Portuguese mercenary musketeers, he reconquered the rich Raichur region which, lying between the Krishna and Tunga-bhadra rivers, had been perennially contested by his Sangama predecessors and the Bahmani sultans. In 1523 he penetrated further north and seized, but chose not to hold, Gulbarga, the former Bahmani capital and city of Gisu Daraz.

13. See, for example, the respective travel accounts of Nunes and Paes, edited, translated, and discussed in Robert Sewell ([1900] 1995).

14. See Sinopoli (2000, 370) for a discussion of this figure.

15. Wagoner, 1996b, 851.

16. The Protestant Reformation began in this period. Martin Luther composed his *Ninety-Five Theses* calling for reform in the Catholic Church in 1517, and bibles were being

translated into various European vernaculars, contra Church doctrine, in the early 1500s. The reigns of Vijayanagara emperors Kṛṣṇadevarāya (1509–1529) and Acyutarāya (r. 1529–1542), as well as the first part of Rāmarāya's regency, are contemporary with the rule of Henry VIII in England (r. 1509–1547), which marked a major turning point in relationships between European states and the Church. While Henry's official break with papal authority in Rome did not occur until 1534, there were popular stirrings of antipapal sentiment in England during his early rule. His establishment of the Church of England inaugurated a period of intense, and often state-supported, religious strife in Europe.

17. Talbot (1995) and Wagoner (1996b) have also shown that the Vijayanagara Empire mimicked many of the Islamic courtly styles of dress and architecture, revealing the engagements taking place across political, religious, and cultural borders in South Asia. For further discussion of Hindu-Muslim material-cultural encounters in a slightly earlier period, see Finbar Flood (2009), who effectively problematizes how scholars think about cultural and other boundaries.

18. Talbot (1995, 700) argues against older scholarship that assumes the word *Hindu* was a religious designation, maintaining it was largely an ethnic and geographic one. Still, she allows that ethnicity encompassed a variety of features, some of which were religious (720). See also Sinopoli (2000) for an overview of different constituents of identity under Vijayanagara rule.

19. Eaton 1978.

20. Sanderson (2009). While Alexis Sanderson documents the various forms of power that Śaiva-initiated kings conferred on their gurus, he also acknowledges that many such kings continued to patronize other religious institutions. Thus, even in kingdoms where royals made their religious preferences known, a policy of exclusivism did not prevail. However, according to Sanderson, the royal affinity for Śaivism throughout the subcontinent between the fifth and thirteenth centuries, imbued many non-Śaiva and even non-Hindu communities (e.g., Buddhist, Jaina) with Śaiva motifs, practices, and sensibilities. In this way, royal patronage exercised a homogenizing influence over diverse religious institutions. As I will demonstrate, a similar homogenizing dynamic, albeit different in scope and content, obtained under Vijayanagara rule, despite a general royal reticence regarding personal religious affinity.

21. This ambiguity seemingly dates to early Saṅgama-period inscriptions, wherein Kālāmukhas are referred to as "gurus" while Smārta Śaivas at Sringeri received more patronage (see Verghese 1995, 7–8). This ambiguity is also evident in inscriptions of Kṛṣṇadevarāya's era. In a 1516 inscription, published in *EC* 1943, vol. 14, no. 115 (see also the discussion in Verghese 1995, 114), one Śrīvaiṣṇava teacher, Govindarāja, is referred to as "the ācārya of kings" and as "one's own ācārya" (ll. 68–69). The phrase "Govindarājaguru" also appears but, rather than identifying Govinda as the *rājaguru,* it seems to be addressing him as "Guru Govindarāja." Some Mādhva scholars (e.g., B. N. K. Sharma [1961] 1981, 290) have pointed out that there is another inscription in the Viṭṭhala temple in Hampi, in which Vyāsatīrtha is addressed as "Gurugaḷu Vyāsarāyaru" or "Guru Vyāsatīrtha" (*SII* 1986, vol. 4, no. 277). Sharma ([1961] 1981, 290) also points out a text attributed to Kṛṣṇadevarāya, in which Kṛṣṇadevarāya refers to Vyāsatīrtha as his guru. Certainly, the term *guru* was a common honorific title in these inscriptions. (See, for example, Verghese 1995, appendix A, which provides an overview

of all the inscriptions at the capital, one of which is a 1519 grant by Kṛṣṇadevarāya to "Guru Basavadīkṣita.") But I think we must consider Govindarāja's designation as the *ācārya* or "teacher" of kings and as Kṛṣṇadevarāya's own teacher to be significant; it certainly aligns with Kṛṣṇadevarāya's lavish support for Śrīvaiṣṇavaism, which is discussed throughout this book. However, I will also demonstrate that Kṛṣṇadevarāya's Vaiṣṇavism was not limited to the Śrīvaiṣṇava formulation but encompassed within it a significant role for Mādhvas. As I will document in chapter 4, Kṛṣṇadevarāya encouraged the two sects to collaborate. Indeed, this very 1516 inscription documents that Govindarāja was given land in the region of Srirangapatna. In the same year, Kṛṣṇadevarāya also granted several villages in Srirangapatna to Vyāsatīrtha, who established a *maṭha*. This ambiguity in Kṛṣṇadevarāya's relationship to different Vaiṣṇava groups is likely what has led to confusion today about who his *guru* was.

22. Matthew Clark (2006, 221) demonstrates that the Kālāmukha and other Śaiva groups, which did not reference the Vedas but which had earlier enjoyed royal patronage, seem to have lost their courtly support in the Vijayanagara period. Such Śaiva groups may have aligned with or given way to the Smārta-Advaita-Śaiva formation that emerged under Vijayanagara rule and which composed Vedic commentarial traditions that became emblematic of the early Saṅgama court.

23. I discuss various theories in chapter 3.

24. Legendary accounts of the empire's founding credit Vidyāraṇya, the fourteenth-century head of the Advaita Smārta *maṭha* at Sringeri, with inspiring the empire's creation and choosing the location of its capital near a Śaiva pilgrimage site. Inscriptional records attest to the early Saṅgama court's support of not only this monastic community's material well-being but also of its intellectual projects, particularly Sāyaṇa's commentary on the Vedas. While scholars impute different motives to the Vijayanagara court's support of this *maṭha*, the relationship between the Vijayanagara *darbār* and this sectarian monastery remains central to the empire's image. This will be dealt with at some length in chapter 3.

25. Nicholson 2010.

26. For example, in chapter 2 and in the conclusion of his *Premodern Communities and Modern Histories*, Prithvi Datta Chandra Shobhi (2005, 280) juxtaposes the lack of patronage of Vīraśaivism by the Vijayanagara court with that community's burgeoning *maṭhas*, many of which are located in or near the Vijayanagara capital itself, during the period of Vijayanagara rule: "Many Śaiva and Vīraśaiva ascetics had established their *maṭhas* in the city of Vijayanagar, even though state patronage to these *maṭhas* wasn't forthcoming. That fact is amply illustrated by the spectacular absence of any inscriptions or any other royal document making any grants to especially *virakta maṭhas* of Vijayanagar."

27. See Tamara Sears (2014) for an excellent discussion of royal patronage of the Mattamayūra ascetic order at the turn of the first millennium in North India. Of course, from an early date, Buddhist and Jain monasteries, the latter of which experienced a heyday in South India in the eighth–tenth centuries, also enjoyed royal patronage (Pierce Taylor 2014).

28. For an overview of the literature on the problems of defining Hinduism and the related issue of sects, see Laurie Patton n.d.

29. As Fisher (2013, 5) has recently argued, much of this distinction between using the terms *sect* or *religion* to define entities like *Śaivism* and *Vaiṣṇavism*, respectively, is a matter of taxonomical preference.

30. Those scholars (e.g., Venkoba Rao 1926; Sharma 1981; Verghese 1995) who argue that many *maṭha*s were not rigidly sectarian and functioned more along the lines of a university correctly note that a *maṭha*'s sectarian affiliation did not prevent students from other sectarian backgrounds from studying there. Vyāsatīrtha himself seems to have studied for some time at Kanchi, where there was no Mādhva *maṭha*.

31. That *maṭha*s by this time in South Indian history had clear sectarian affiliations is suggested in the instructional manuals, written by members or leaders of these communities, governing many aspects of daily life for full-time monastic residents. Mādhva *maṭha*s followed practices laid out by the community's thirteenth-century founder, Madhva, in texts such as the *Tantrasārasaṅgraha* (on Mādhva forms of ritual practice), the *Sadācārasmṛti* (on daily habits and routines), and the *Yatipraṇavakalpa* (on monastic rules and initiation). The last discusses an oath sworn by the Mādhva monastic initiate never to forsake Viṣṇu and the Vaiṣṇavas, to deem other gods equal to Viṣṇu, or to associate with advocates of monism (Sharma [1961] 1981, 190). Other communities used their own such works, such as Yādava Prakāśa's twelfth-century *Yatidharmasamuccaya*, used by Śrīvaiṣṇava monastics (see Yādava Prakāśa 1995). Many *maṭha*s were constructed during the Vijayanagara period on temple grounds, linking them to specific ritual and devotional practices. Verghese's research on sectarian marks in the temples of the Vijayanagara capital attests to the potency of such emblems to claim religious spaces (1995, 57ff.). Finally, as will be argued in chapter 2, *maṭha*s themselves came to function like temples, further manifesting their specific devotional/ritual affiliations. Thus, while *maṭha*s did offer a variety of public services, such as accommodation for pilgrims and some educational opportunities, many of these were linked to specific sectarian teachings, lifestyles, and obligations.

32. Many contemporary scholars assume that the Śrīvaiṣṇava community is mostly nonmonastic and that the institution of the *maṭha* therefore has not played an important role in that community's history. This is due to the fact that many important Śrīvaiṣṇava leaders, including one of the tradition's leading lights, Vedānta Deśika, were householders with wives and children who never renounced their families to take up *saṃnyāsa*. Certainly, it is not considered necessary to renounce a worldly life to be an *ācārya* in Śrīvaiṣṇavism. However, the Śrīvaiṣṇava community does have a tradition of *maṭha*s with renunciant leaders, and these have played an important role in the community's sociopolitical development. In fact, Vedānta Deśika's disciple Brahmatantra-Svatantrar (c. 1286–1386) founded a *maṭha* in Kanchi in 1359, and this *maṭha* played a leadership role in the maintenance of the Varadarāja temple in that city (see K. V. Raman 1975, 73). The Ahobila *maṭha* has also been of historic importance to the Śrīvaiṣṇava community, especially the Vaṭakalai branch. This will be discussed more in chapter 4.

33. For example, the observation of monastic practice in Vyāsatīrtha's branch of Mādhva *maṭha*s differs somewhat from that of the Udupi *maṭha*s. While Vyāsatīrtha himself was a *bālasaṃnyāsin* (or one who undertook worldly renunciation as a child), the Udupi *maṭha*s are the only ones that today require their initiates to be *bālasaṃnyāsin*s. Members of Vyāsatīrtha's *maṭha*s can be former householders who renounce as adults. Different branches of the Mādhva *maṭha*s also adhere to slightly different versions of the textual tradition of Madhva's works. See Sharma ([1961] 1981, 192–200) for a discussion.

34. Over the course of the sixteenth century, the Tuḷuva dynasty gradually excluded Śaivas from patronage while actively cultivating a shared Vaiṣṇava sensibility among the

Kannadiga Mādhvas and the Tamil and Telugu Śrīvaiṣṇavas. One could therefore argue that the Tuḷuva-cultivated Hinduism of which I speak was primarily a transregional, trans-sectarian, and translinguistic Vaiṣṇavism. However, efforts were made by the early Tuḷuva kings Kṛṣṇadevarāya and Acyutarāya to cultivate both Śaiva and Vaiṣṇava institutions as part of courtly religious culture. In this sense, Vijayanagara religiosity was more generically Hindu. The details of this aspect of my argument will be discussed at length in chapters 3, 4, and 5.

35. These benefits were not experienced uniformly by all social groups, a fact I discuss more in chapter 2.

36. It should be noted that such rejection has always been largely a matter of theory rather than actual practice in the act of converting to Christianity, a religious tradition that would look much more monolithic than it actually does if converts completely severed all of their former religious allegiances. By the same token, Hindu sects would never have undergone any historic growth or diminution if individuals had never changed sectarian identities. Further evidence that Hindu sectarianism not only allowed for but encouraged acts of conversion can be found in Madhva's thirteenth-century handbook on entering the monkhood (*Yatipraṇavakalpa*), wherein initiates undertake an oath of allegiance to cer-tain doctrines and simultaneously swear to avoid other doctrines and their proponents: "Never shall I forswear Viṣṇu and the Vaiṣṇavas. Never shall I deem Viṣṇu to be on a par or identical with the other gods. Never shall I associate with those who hold the doctrine of identity or equality of God and soul" (trans. by Sharma [1961] 1981, 190, who also provides the original Sanskrit).

37. Griffiths's (1999) study of Hindu-Buddhist debates on the existence of God in the eleventh and twelfth centuries maintains that arguments against other systems of thought were principally addressed to the adherents of one's own system. In his view, "Antithesistic argument for Indian Buddhists was principally a tool for elaborating, embroidering, and knitting together the conceptual fabric of their tradition, and only secondarily (if at all), a device for convincing anyone of anything" (520). In Vyāsatīrtha's case, I would agree that a central goal of his arguments against alternative forms of Vedānta was to strengthen the intellectual commitments of his own constituency. However, history shows that intellectual and religious communities arise, grow, change, and even dwindle over time. These pro-cesses, while not determined entirely by doctrinal debate, are informed by it. I therefore maintain that Vyāsatīrtha's polemical arguments were not addressed solely to his own fol-lowers but were intended to increase his following by convincing others of Dvaita Vedānta's correctness.

38. For example, Sharma ([1961] 1981, 1991), Williams (2011), and McCrea (2015).

39. O'Hanlon and Washbrook's 2012 anthology of essays (originally published in 2011 as a special issue of *South Asian History and Culture* vol. 2, no. 2) contains many excel-lent examples of scholarship that contextualize various South Asian religious communities and their literary traditions, as does the 2015 collection (also originally published in 2015 as a special issue of *South Asian History and Culture* vol. 6, no 1), edited by O'Hanlon, Minkowski, and Venkatkrishnan. Many of these essays are cited in this book. When I do so, I reference the page numbers in the edited volumes. Other efforts to historicize Sanskrit authors include the collaborative research project *Sanskrit Knowledge Systems on the Eve of Colonialism,* directed by Sheldon Pollock.

40. Voix 2011. A similar notion regarding the superior moral nature of an ascetic's worldly engagement is also identified in Clémentin-Ojha's 2011 study of Ārya Samāj-ist, Swami Shraddhananda.

41. See Thomas R. Metcalf (1995) for an overview of such materials.

## 2. ROYAL AND RELIGIOUS AUTHORITY IN SIXTEENTH-CENTURY VIJAYANAGARA: A *MAṬHĀDHIPATI* AT KṚṢṆADEVARĀYA'S COURT

1. Sharma (1961) 1981, 290.

2. Verghese 1995, 114.

3. Stein 1999, 102. The subsequent block quote follows almost immediately upon this claim.

4. Stein 1999, 103.

5. Stein 1980, 433.

6. There is strong evidence for *maṭhas* acting as state agents, not just under Vijayanagara rule but in earlier Indian polities. The work of Tamara Sears (2014), Alexis Sanderson (2009), R. N. Misra (1997), and others demonstrates this in various ways, with Sanderson and Misra making particularly strong cases for the functional overlap of *maṭhas* and courts. Citing Misra's 1997 research on nine Śaivasiddhānta *maṭhas* in the Kalachuri kingdom in the ninth and tenth centuries, Clark (2006, 192–93) summarizes their various functions as follows: "The *maṭhas* employed not only artisans and tenant farmers, but also a contingent of law-enforcement officers (*virabhadras* and *vajramuṣṭis*) whose powers of enforcement included mutilation and castration. . . . The *maṭhas* rendered services to the state in various ways, including the garrisoning of war-forces, the provision of elephants, horses and perhaps wealth, the manufacture of armaments for battle, the maintenance of arsenals, training in warfare, and even participation in battle." Sanderson (2009, 261–62) provides specific examples of such warfare participation on the part of monastic leaders/residents. I have not come across any such references from the Vijayanagara period, but there is ample evidence that *maṭhas* were involved in postwar cleanup and the political integration of conquered regions.

7. J. Duncan M. Derrett (1974) shows that not all *maṭhas* were necessarily run or populated by *saṃnyāsins*. However, in the case of Vyāsatīrtha's *maṭhas* (and most Mādhva *maṭhas*), the residents were *saṃnyāsins*. In fact, some were *bālasaṃnyāsins* or individuals who had renounced the world as children and never entered the householder stage; this was true of Vyāsatīrtha. Not all Mādhva monastic communities insist on *bālasaṃnyāsa*; today, former householders may become not only members but heads of Vyāsatīrtha *maṭhas*. Smārta Advaita *maṭhas* were also generally run and populated by *saṃnyāsins*. As mentioned in chapter 1, the Śrīvaiṣṇava community has historically had *maṭhas* run by ascetic leaders, but there has also been a parallel tradition of householder *ācāryas*, who wield significant religious authority.

8. This point will be demonstrated at various places in this book, including the section of this chapter that discusses the inscriptional and monumental records. A summary of some of the evidence for this sectarianism in *maṭhas* was provided in chapter 1. Of course, not all sectarian *maṭhas* performed exactly the same roles in their respective communities.

9. See note 12, chapter 1, and Eaton (2005, 88–89) for an overview of these military engagements.

10. See chapter 1 for an overview of this complexity.

11. There are three printed editions of this text. Two of these are based on one manuscript: Venkoba Rao's (1926) and the more recent one by D. Prahladachar (1993). The third edition is a reprint of Venkoba Rao's (n.d.), edited by K. T. Pandurangi but with additional historical information, such as excerpts from the inscriptional record, provided by Srinivasa Ritti. Rao's 1926 edition provides a lengthy historical introduction that attempts to situate the biography in the broader historical record. Prahladachar's introduction provides a helpful overview of each of the text's chapters.

12. It is this term, *kuladevatā*, and not *rājaguru* or "guru to the king," that is consistently used to describe Vyāsatīrtha throughout the biography.

13. While Verghese (1995, 8) disputes Somanātha's account of Vyāsatīrtha's life in several instances, she does take it for granted that the two men were contemporaries. B. N. K. Sharma ([1961] 1981, 286ff.) also takes it for granted that Somanātha and Vyāsatīrtha were contemporaries.

14. The Sanskrit text in Venkoba Rao's (1926, 83–84) edition states that Somanātha has the text read aloud to Vyāsatīrtha and that Vyāsatīrtha approves it. In an apparent gesture toward verisimilitude, the two readers are identified by name as Kambukaṇṭha and Kalakaṇṭha (see Rao 1926, intro., xlix, for a discussion of this; see Rao's Sanskrit text, 83, for the passage). Vyāsatīrtha is presented at this moment in the text as being seated on his ascetic throne and surrounded by foreign kings, poets, grammarians, logicians, medical men, astronomers, and of course his own disciples.

15. Arguably the sole miraculous occurrence in the *Vyāsayogicarita*'s account of Vyāsatīrtha's life is when he raises the only son of Brahmin parents from the dead after a poisonous snakebite. Other events that are given a miraculous tint in the later biographies are typically located in dreams in the *Vyāsayogicarita*, perhaps to soften their factual claim.

16. Venkoba Rao (1926) points out that there is some ambiguity in the text on this point. While Somanātha seems to take great pains in this final section to demonstrate Vyāsatīrtha's familiarity with Somanātha's biography and while the author does mention Acyutarāya's devotion to Vyāsatīrtha, it is also true that the text states earlier that Acyutarāya had worshipped Vyāsatīrtha in the past (Sanskrit text, 78). This could be interpreted as a reference to Vyāsatīrtha's demise. Rao reconciles these differences by claiming that Somanātha had a first version of the text read aloud to Vyāsatīrtha and then subsequently revised it into its current form after the *maṭhādhipati*'s demise (see Rao's discussion in his introduction, li).

17. Rao, Shulman, and Subrahmanyam 2001, 19ff.

18. Ibid., 21.

19. The term *digvijaya* refers literally to the act of conquest of all directions, but the texts in which such acts are recounted are usually titled *digvijaya*s or simply *vijaya*s. Thus, I here use these terms interchangeably to refer to a particular subgenre of sacred biography that is distinct from the *carita*.

20. Sax (2000, 47–51) provides an overview of all *digvijaya* literature but focuses on those materials involving religious renouncers. While dating these texts is problematic, Sax maintains that the earliest possible date for any of the Śaṅkara *digvijaya*s, which are often considered to be archetypal for the genre, is the thirteenth century. But other authors (Sundaresan 2000; Bader 2000; Clark 2006), who provide a more detailed discussion of these texts' dates, give the earliest possible century as the fourteenth.

21. Nārāyaṇa Paṇḍitācārya is the author of this text. His traditional dates are 1295–1370. I would argue, following Clark (2006, 157), that this text is one of the very oldest *digvijaya* texts for a religious leader, possibly even the prototype. The text has been edited and translated by G. V. Nadgouda and was published in Bangalore by the Poornaprajna Vidyapeetha in 1991.

22. Summarizing other scholarship on this issue, notably that of Jonathan Bader, Clark (2006) argues that Anantānandagiri's *Śaṅkaravijaya* and Cidvilāsa's *Śaṅkaravijayavilāsa* are probably the oldest and date from the sixteenth century. For a list and rough chronology of these various texts, based largely on Bader's research, see Clark (149, esp. n5).

23. The Nepal text is the *Vaṃśāvali of Nepal* (Clark 2006, 156).

24. See Clark (2006, 173). Vidyāraṇya, head of the Sringeri *maṭha*, who played an influential role in the fourteenth-century Vijayanagara court (discussed at some length in chapter 3), is often credited with composing the seminal Śaṅkara *digvijaya*. According to Hacker (1995) and Kulke (2001), the point of Vidyāraṇya's *Śaṅkaradigvijaya* was to demonstrate the pan-Indian popularity of Śaṅkara's thought and, therefore, the importance of those *maṭhas* that promulgated it. However, other scholarly opinion (e.g., Bader 2000; Clark 2006; Lorenzen 1976) assigns this text a much later date, possibly as late as the eighteenth century. Clark points out that neither the Sringeri *maṭha* nor its pan-Indian influence over a network of Śaṅkara *maṭhas* figure all that prominently in this text, despite its attribution to the erstwhile Sringeri *maṭhādhipati*, Vidyāraṇya.

25. Sundaresan (2000) thoroughly problematizes the dates and authorship of most of the Śankara *digvijayas* and links these difficulties to modern (i.e., colonial and postcolonial) disputes among Śaṅkara *maṭhas*.

26. For example, in the *Sumadhvavijaya*, Madhva (ch. 5, v. 29ff.) is able to eat what would seem to be impossibly large quantities of food.

27. Novetzke 2007, 172.

28. According to Novetzke (2007, 174–75), "Both endeavors, the theographic and the historiographic, exist not as oppositional categories but as perceptible shifts in genre. . . . They function together, not in contrast to one another."

29. Sax 2000, 42–46.

30. Ibid., 51.

31. This text and the third biography discussed below have been available to me in incomplete form only through quotes and references to them in the work of Venkoba Rao (1926). Rao supplies some lengthy discussion, as well as several direct quotes, of the two later biographies. However, what I say about each here must be taken as speculative, since I have not had the opportunity to read either text in full.

32. The text presents Vyāsatīrtha as visiting what are fairly stock pilgrimage places in digvijaya literature, with many of them located in North India: "Kāśi, Gayā, Gaṅgā Setu, Badarikāśrama and other places" (see Venkoba Rao 1926, intro., lxxxviii-lxxxix). The *Sumadhvavijaya* presents Madhva as visiting many of the same places.

33. Venkoba Rao 1926, intro., xlviii-lii, lxxii.

34. Venkoba Rao 1926, intro., xlviii; Sharma (1961) 1981, 286.

35. One of the differences, in addition to the role of pilgrimage, between the *Vyāsa Vijaya* and the *Vyāsayogicarita* is that the *Vyāsa Vijaya* elaborates Vyāsatīrtha's role at

Tirupati. This will be discussed further in chapter 4. According to citations from it in Venkoba Rao's (1926, intro., xc) edition of the *Vyāsayogicarita*, the *Vyāsa Vijaya* claims that Vyāsatīrtha was asked by Vijayanagara emperor Sāḷuva Narasiṃha to conduct the worship of Veṅkaṭeśvara in the main Tirupati temple for a period of twelve years because the regular temple *arcaka*s had been put to death for stealing temple jewels. Vyāsatīrtha filled in until one of these priest's sons was of age to take over. In the interim period, Vyāsatīrtha conducted the rituals according to Madhva's *Tantrasārasaṅgraha* manual on worship. There are also references in the *Vyāsa Vijaya* to Vyāsatīrtha conducting his all-India tour in state, that is, with "retainers and with a drum on an elephant" (lxxxix). According to Venkoba Rao (xci), these are honors that Vyāsatīrtha receives only later, after living at the Vijayanagara court in Hampi. The *Vyāsa Vijaya* also tells a story of Vyāsatīrtha's confrontation at Kanchi with Śaivas, who refused to let Vyāsatīrtha enter the temple to Ranganātha on the grounds that Jambukeśvara, a form of Śiva, was also there. Vyāsatīrtha arranged to run throughout the jurisdiction holding his breath. The territory he covered would subsequently belong to Ranganātha and what remained would belong to Jambukeśvara (lxxxix). Animosity regarding sectarian divisions along devotional (as opposed to intellectual) lines seems to have emerged in a slightly later historical period and is likely linked to the shift in the Vijayanagara court's patronage from an ecumenical Śaivism to a more biased Vaiṣṇavism. There are no references to sectarian tensions along devotional lines in the *Vyāsayogicarita,* although different systems of Vedānta thought are certainly described as adversarial.

36. This text, like the *Vyāsa Vijaya,* has been available to me only through quotes found throughout Venkoba Rao's edition of the *Vyāsayogicarita.* Prahladachar (1993, iv) mentions this text in passing but does not discuss its contents at much length. However, Prahladachar does identify some ways in which the *Vyāsayogicarita* differs from "the tradition['s]" version of Vyāsatīrtha's life (xvii). What Prahladachar likely means by "the tradition" is both the story of Vyāsatīrtha's life as told in the *Vyāsa Vijaya* and the version told by the brief poem encapsulating the main points of Vyāsatīrtha's life composed by the early twentieth-century Mādhva *maṭhādhipati* Śrī Vidyāratnākaratīrtha.

37. Recently, there was a Mādhva effort afoot to locate and identify all 732 of these icons. Due to the organizer's unexpected death, the effort has been suspended. The link (www. vyasasamudra.org) to the website documenting these efforts is now broken.

38. If the *Vyāsa Vijaya* has had undue influence on Mādhva conceptions of Vyāsatīrtha, Somanātha's text has had an equally imbalanced influence on scholars' (including this one's) understanding of the religious leader's life. This is evident in the fact that Somanātha's text has been published three times, while the other two have never been published. That the text is readily accessible perpetuates its scholarly impact.

39. There are references to Vyāsatīrtha's sectarian identity framed in terms of his intellectual, Vedāntin identity, as opposed to his Vaiṣṇava devotional one. These references occur in the sections on debates with Advaitins, discussed below. See also Venkoba Rao's Sanskrit text (1926, 69) for a reference to Vyāsatīrtha's elucidation of "Mādhvamata" or "Mādhva thought." The text also specifically mentions some of Vyāsatīrtha's works such as the *Nyāyāmṛta,* the *Tātparyacandrikā,* and the *Tarkatāṇḍava* (64).

40. An example of the *Vyāsayogicarita*'s attention to veracity is when Vyāsatīrtha receives Somanātha in order to discuss his account (Venkoba Rao 1926, Sanskrit text, 83ff.). In

addition to Novetzke (2007) and Sax (2000), Granoff and Shinohara (1994) and Winand M. Callewaert and Rupert Snell (1994) have done work on religious biographies in South Asia.

41. This procedure is discussed in Venkoba Rao (1926, intro., lxxvi, Sanskrit text, 25).

42. Venkoba Rao 1926, Sanskrit text, 13.

43. *EC* 1905, vol. 9, no. 153. The inscription dates from Śaka year 1445 or 1523 CE. See map 3, where the general location of the gifted villages is labeled "Abbur Maṭha."

44. This portion of the text appears in Venkoba Rao (1926, Sanskrit text, 32); see his introduction (lxxvi-lxxvii) for a discussion.

45. We find versions of this story in Buddhist Jātaka tales and in lives of Jain saints as well as in Hindu *digvijaya* literature. See Clark (2006, 152–53) for some discussion of this.

46. See Venkoba Rao (1926, Sanskrit text, 35–36).

47. It is possible that, due to a famine that occurred in 1475–76, Brahmaṇyatīrtha was deceased by this point (Sharma [1961] 1981, 287).

48. "Krameṇa sanisargagabhīracetās tuṅgataraśṛṅgāliṅgitapayodharān dharādharān anokahanivahavikasitakusumamadhudhārāsaṃpātadāmitadāvadahanāni vanāni madakalakalahaṃsasaṃsadā lolitanalinagalitaparimalaparimalena salalita vyalīkamedasvinīs srotasvinīs cātiśayanṛttakalāmattakāśinīmañjīrajhañjhalitamukharitasaudhaśikharāṇi nagarāṇi āścaryatapaścaryādīpramaṇipeṭikāmaṭhikāś ca vilaṅghya nirantaraniṣevyamāṇān ekadaśaśatamukhaphaṇitimadhurimādharīkṛtasudhair budhaiḥ pratibhaṭaghaṭāḍambara-jambālaravibhiḥ kavibhiḥ prakaṭitatridaśabhuvanapratyādeśaṃ deśam agāhiṣṭa|" (Venkoba Rao 1926, Sanskrit text, 37).

49. In fact, the word *Kanchi* is not used but the description of the icons in the Varadarāja temple indicate the location (Venkoba Rao 1926, Sanskrit text, 37–38).

50. Venkoba Rao 1926, intro., lxxxi; and Sanskrit text, 38.

51. Venkoba Rao 1926, Sanskrit text, 38–39.

52. *ARSIE* 1919, no. 370, repr. in Venkoba Rao n.d., appendix 1 by K. T. Pandurangi. The significance of this gift will be discussed more in chapter 4.

53. Named in Venkoba Rao (1926, Sanskrit text, 39).

54. Venkoba Rao 1926, Sanskrit text, 39–41.

55. See Venkoba Rao (1926, intro., viii-ix) for a discussion of this.

56. "Ato dinavirāmeṇeva khalajanavayovyāmohacūrṇena sarojinyā iva cireṇānidrāṇāyāḥ vaidikācāramandrāyāḥ dinakara iva bhavān pratibodhanakārmaṭhī bhavati| Tatra sarveṣām api dharmāṇāṃ rājā setur iti nyāyena bhavatā sarvadā tadā tadā sthānīstheyuṣā bhavitavyaṃ| Purākila yogino niḥsaṅgā api mahānto dattātreyādayaḥ jagadupakaraṇāya rājanyasabhālaṅkārā babhūvuḥ|" (Venkoba Rao 1926, intro., lxxxiii-lxxxiv; Sanskrit text, 40).

57. "Evam eva bhaktyā sambhāvayantaṃ rahasyenaṃ dharmapadopadeśena pratyaham anugṛhnan..." (Venkoba Rao 1926, intro., lxvii; Sanskrit text, 59).

58. "Vasudhādhipena haṃseneva kamalākaraḥ pratyaham upasevyamānaḥ|" (Venkoba Rao 1926, intro., lxvii; Sanskrit text, 64).

59. "Nṛpanikarais sevyamānaḥ . . . aparimitair yodhaiḥ pariveṣṭyamānaḥ" (Venkoba Rao 1926, intro., xv; Sanskrit text, 56).

60. An *āsana* is a seat and a *mudrā* can refer to a seal used by royals.

61. "Tadanu samaṭham āgāt kṣmādhipena pradiṣṭaṃ, sphaṭikamaṇimayūkhaś śārasopānamārgaṃ|

Vipulakanakavedīvidrumastaṃbharājiṃ, mṛgapatir iva kuñjaṃ medinībhṛdvarasya‖
Tatra vyarājata samastatamonihantā, mudrāsane sa nivasan munisārvabhaumaḥ|
mārtāṇḍabimba iva mārgavaśena mandaṃ, mandākinīpulinamadhyabhuvaṃ praviṣṭaḥ‖
arcayantam imam arghyapūrvayā bhāgadheyapariṇāmam ātmanaḥ|
pārthivas sapadi paryapūjayat pāṇḍusūnur iva bādarāyaṇam‖" (Venkoba Rao 1926,
intro., xvi; Sanskrit text, 58).

62. Despite the fact that Somanātha makes no reference to this event, Venkoba Rao (1926) uses it at length in his introduction to the text and attempts to identify when the event took place by looking at astronomical and epigraphic records. He also refers to how Vyāsatīrtha's other two biographers present this event: "The *Vyāsa Vijaya* speaks of the Kuhuyoga as having occurred after the grant of Vyāsasamudra, but this appears to be a mistake" (intro., clxv). Rao does not supply a quote from the *Vyāsa Vijaya,* but he goes on to say that the third biography by the early twentieth-century Mādhva *maṭhādhipati,* Śrī Vidyāratnākara, presents the Kuhuyoga's date and implications more accurately: "'Sri Vidyaratnakara Swami's statement of the tradition is more in accordance with epigraphical and astronomical evidence'" (clxv).

63. This event is popularly understood to be an explanation for why Vyāsatīrtha is more commonly known as "Vyāsarāya" or "King Vyāsa" even today. But, in fact, "rāya" seems to have been a common epithet for these sectarian leaders during the sixteenth-century, especially in vernacular sources. Vyāsatīrtha is referred to as "Vyāsarāya" in a Kannada inscription in a 1513 inscription in the Viṭṭhala temple in the capital city. His second teacher, Lakṣmīnārāyaṇa, was also called "Śrīpādarāya." For an explanation of why these *maṭhādhipati*s were also "*rāyas,*" see the following section of this chapter on inscriptions.

64. Prahladachar 1993, intro., xi.

65. Inserted into a long sentence documenting various ways in which Vyāsatīrtha is honored at court is the following phrase: "dvīpāntarabhūpālasaṃpreṣitapradhānapuruṣair asakṛtsamarpyamāṇāni bahuvidhopahārapūjanāni ca" (Venkoba Rao 1926, 65). "And [to him] pūjās consisting of manifold offerings were given repeatedly by the great emissaries sent by rulers from other continents."

66. These works would be *Nyāyāmṛta* and *Tātparyacandrikā.* The *Tarkatāṇḍava* or "Dance of Reasoning" is in the service of the polemics of these other two texts, insofar as it discusses proper rules of argumentation.

67. The reasons for Kalinga's importance are the subject of some scholarly debate. In general, all regions with coastal access were valuable to the largely inland empire. Moreover, Vijayanagara's military policy in general emphasized the expansion of its northern borders. However, a recent article by Venkata Raghotam (2013) argues that Kalinga's significance to the Vijayanagara kings was largely symbolic. Because they kept seizing and subsequently losing border forts to Kalinga's Gajapati rulers, retaking these entities and their surrounding regions became a matter of honor.

68. Of the twenty-eight inscriptions documenting Kṛṣṇadevarāya's gifts to the Tirupati temple, six give a lengthy praise of his conquest of Kalinga and his recapture of the Udaya-giri and other forts held by the Gajapati rulers; a few other inscriptions give a briefer account (see *TDI* [1935] 1984, vol. 3, nos. 66–68). See also Verghese (2014) for further analysis of this event and its implications.

69. For an overview of this section of the text, see Prahladachar (1993, intro., x).

70. See Venkoba Rao (1926, intro., xixff, Sanskrit text, 60).

71. "Prāvādukasya paripanthijanasya jetā, yogīśvaro narapatiś ca tathā vadānyaḥ| Anyo-nyam ucchritakṛpārasabhaktibhājau, vyatyastav āsa bhavanāv iva tāv abhūtām||" (Venkoba Rao 1926, intro., xx; Sanskrit text, 62).

72. "Purastād eva bhūbhṛtas tasya muhūrtamātre bahvībhir ativajrapātābhir upari dūṣaṇān avaprakāśapradāyinībhir yuktiparāṃparābhiḥ śataśaḥ khaṇḍayitvā|" (Venkoba Rao 1926, intro., cxliii; Sanskrit text, 70).

73. Indeed, the *Vyāsayogicarita* states that "Śrī Krishnadevarāya vowed to devote every-thing he had to the worship of Śrī Vyāsarāya": "The king wishes to do pūjā to Śrīvyāsabhikṣu with as many material objects as he has, with as much strength as he possesses, to the extent of the many enemies that he has defeated, with as much generosity as may be resorted to in action and speech, with as much accumulated wealth, and with as many qualities and as much glory as he possesses" (Venkoba Rao 1926, intro., lxvi). (Yāvanto viṣayāhṛtā bhujabalaṃ yāvatsapatnā jitā yāvantaś ca vadānyatā karasarojātaśrayā yāvatī| Yāvatyo dhanasaṃpado guṇagaṇo yāvāṃś ca yāvad yaśas tāvat kartum iyeṣa pūjanam asau śrīvyāsabhikṣor nṛpaḥ|| [Sanskrit text, 71].)

74. According to Venkoba Rao's (1926, intro., cxlvii) translation/paraphrase, "The King wishes to bathe you himself in gems today, like the Parijata tree which rains its flowers on the peak of a guardian mountain. By coming to comply with his desire, kindly favour the devotion of him who looks upon every inch of your holy self as a guardian angel." (Svāmin bhavantaṃ svayam adyaratnair ākāṅkṣate bhūramaṇobhiṣektuṃ| kūṭāgrabhāgaṃ kulabhūdharasya prasūnajātair iva pārijātaḥ|| taṃ bhaktipallavitam āgamanotsavena svāmin prasīda bahumantum apārakīrte| puṣpāñjaliḥ pratikalaṃ bhagavannarasya konepi yaḥ kalayate kuladaivabhāvam|| [Venkoba Rao 1926, Sanskrit text, 71].)

75. Venkoba Rao 1926, Sanskrit text, 72. (tatra bhūpaś śaratkāle rājahaṃsam ivāṃbuje| svarṇapīṭhe svayaṃ datte vyāsabhikṣuṃ nyaveśayat||)

76. Venkoba Rao 1926, Sanskrit text, 71. (kṣaṇaṃ vicintya bhaktavatsalatayā karuṇām asṛṃhṛdayaḥ sabhājigamiṣayā maṇibṛsīvarād udasthāt|)

77. Literally, "kṣoṇīsura" or "gods on earth."

78. The Lāṭas would have referred to rulers from the region of what is now the southern coast of Gujarat.

79. That is, rulers of what is now Bengal.

80. I am not sure to whom the text is referring, but it may be local rulers from the region around Delhi who are not the sultanate or the Mughals.

81. "Kṣoṇīsurayatnaviśrāṇitāvaśeṣāṇi tāni rāśiṃ kārayitvā nānādiśāṃ calebhyas samāgatānāṃ kuṇḍalāya, tuṇḍirādhipānāṃ, keyūrāya keralānāṃ, hārāya pārasīkānāṃ, makuṭāya lāṭānāṃ, aṅgulīyakāya kaliṅgānāṃ, kaṅkaṇāya koṅkaṇānāṃ, niṣkāya turuṣkānāṃ, cūḍanāya gauḍānāṃ, taralāya colānāṃ, kāñcīguṇāya pāñcālānāṃ, anyeṣām api bhūbhujāṃ vadānyāgranīs sabhikṣuḥ prādikṣat||" (Venkoba Rao 1926, Sanskrit text, 74).

82. This could be a geographic reference to the Tamil country and not to its Coḷa leaders.

83. For example, in 1513, weaving communities along the Coromandel coast got Kṛṣṇadevarāya to rescind an order taxing their looms. This generosity on the part of the king is mentioned in several inscriptions, attesting to its significance (e.g., Eaton 2005, 86).

84. Because inscriptions were often carved into the walls of architectural structures, this section considers both inscriptional and monumental records together, with the heavier emphasis being on inscriptions. This will be counterbalanced somewhat in later chapters (especially chapter 4) that emphasize monumental remains.

85. Those inscriptions carved into temple walls seem to attest to the public nature of the information and ideology being documented therein. As Alexandra Mack (2011, 154–55) notes, most people were illiterate, so even if these inscriptions were publicly displayed, they would not have been comprehensible. Still, the fact that they were so displayed suggests that they were meant to be well known and talked of (Sears 2014, 46). Those inscriptions carved onto copper plates were less public and tended to be for the religious leaders of the community in question, who were typically the people benefiting most from the arrangements recorded in the inscription. In some instances, copper plates may have been forged by religious groups to make certain claims (see discussion of Heras in chapter 3 of this book). In Vyāsatīrtha's case, copper plate inscriptions are typically in Sanskrit and bear on issues that are slightly different from those carved into temple walls, which are usually in the local vernacular or, if they involve different linguistic communities, in more than one vernacular. But many of the Sanskrit copper plates also have vernacular insertions that typically describe the land/villages involved, implying that the plates could be accessed by locals to explicate certain arrangements.

86. Orr (2000) focuses on female donors in the inscriptional record.

87. Vyāsatīrtha appears in several inscriptions posthumously, attesting to his continued significance. He is mentioned in copper plate grants, found in the Sosale *maṭha*, dating from 1627, 1642, 1703, 1708, 1709, 1712, and 1715 (see *EC* 1976, vol. 5, nos. 109–14, 116).

88. "Inscriptions, just like medieval court literature, are forms of discourse containing representations of the self and the world. As such, the social and political aspirations they embody must be recognized along with the ideology they convey" (Talbot 2001, 15).

89. I discuss legitimation theory in Indian history more critically in chapter 3, where I argue that political and economic motivations, more than a quest for legitimacy, were at the heart of royal interactions with religious groups and leaders. However, legitimacy was part and parcel of the honorific exchanges that did transpire between the Vijayanagara court, sectarian leaders, and temples. The economic developments brought about by royal gifts of material resources to religious institutions facilitated political integration, largely through the development of new transactional networks. These transactional networks were materially based. But such material/economic developments also improved a ruler's standing in the public's eyes or, in other words, gave his incursions into local affairs "legitimacy." Of course, as will be discussed more below, Vijayanagara initiatives did not benefit all residents equally; for some citizens, the empire certainly did not feel the need to justify its actions.

90. As noted above, of the twenty-eight inscriptions documenting Kṛṣṇadevarāya's gifts to the Tirupati temple, six give a lengthy praise of his conquest of Kalinga and his recapture of the Udayagiri and other forts located there, while a few other inscriptions mention it briefly (see *TDI* vol. 3, [1935] 1984, nos. 66–68, 76–81). See also Verghese's (2014) study of the links between the conquest of Kalinga and Kṛṣṇadevarāya's temple benefactions.

91. *EC* 1976, vol. 5, no. 105, and, again, in no. 106. (The translation is based on that of the inscription's editor.) This *praśasti* appears in most of Kṛṣṇadevarāya's longer inscriptions,

albeit in different languages. (Shorter inscriptions, such as those found at the Viṭṭhala temple in the imperial capital, seem to supply a truncated testament to Kṛṣṇadevarāya's greatness [see Filliozat and Filliozat 1988]. In addition, different Indian agencies charged with documenting inscriptions have observed different protocols; some omit those sections, like the *praśasti,* that are redundant with other inscriptions.) Other instances where the above list of sacred sites appears in the *praśasti* include the following: *EC* 1905, vol. 9, nos. 30 and 153; *EC* 1902, vol. 7, pt. 1, no. 85; *ARMAD* 1942, no. 28; *EC* 1943, vol. 14, no. 115; *EI* 1960, vol. 31, no. 21, "Kamalapur Plates of Krishnadevaraya"; *TDI* 1935 (1984), vol. 3, no. 65, *Inscriptions of Krishnaraya's Time.*

92. Sewell's (1995, 329) translation.

93. Mack 2011, 154. See also Stein 1980.

94. While the first two of the place names mentioned in the *praśasti* quoted above are easily recognizable today (Kanchi and Srisailam), the other places are more recognizable under other names: "Sonachala" is Tiruvannamalai, "Kanakasabha" is Cidambaram, and "Venkatadri" is Tirupati. The "others" mentioned above include Kālahasti, Virūpākṣa, Harihara, Ahobila, Sangama, Srirangam, Kumbakonam, Nanditirtha, Nivṛtti, Gokarna, and Ramasetu. As map 4 indicates, some of these sacred sites are either in or near the contested border zone while the bulk are in either the Tamil country or Andhra Pradesh. The *praśasti* portion of the inscriptions does not mention any of the sites in central or western Karnataka that Kṛṣṇadevarāya also routinely patronized. This suggests that the monarch was particularly concerned about his control over the eastern regions of his empire.

95. Mack 2011, 156.

96. The Chikkabbehalli grant of 1516 is located in Srirangapatna taluk (*ARMAD* 1942, no. 28). It is marked on map 3 as "Sosale Maṭha." (In the same year, Kṛṣṇadevarāya also granted the Śrīvaiṣṇava teacher Govindarāja land for establishing an *agrahāra* in the region of Srirangapatna, which may be significant. See chapter 4 of this book for a discussion of the role of Kṛṣṇadevarāya's patronage in Śrīvaiṣṇava-Mādhva material exchanges and collaborations.) One copper plate inscription (*EC* 1976, vol. 5, no. 105) records gifts of land in this same region that were made to Vyāsatīrtha in 1521. The Channapatna copper plate grant of Kṛṣṇadevarāya from 1523 (*EC* 1905, vol. 9, no. 153) records a gift of land to Vyāsatīrtha of his teacher Brāhmāṇyatīrtha's native village (see Abbur Maṭha on map 3) and surrounding areas.

97. I do not intend this phrasing to convey that the recipients of royal land grants "owned" the land in the modern capitalist sense. Others continued to live on and work it and to share in its proceeds, but the recipients did get *sarvamānya* rights to it, meaning that they had dominion over it and that the land's produce (agrarian, mineral, aquatic, etc.) was not taxed by the state.

98. See, for example, *EC* 1976, vol. 5, no. 106, ll. 20–22. This is the modern-day town of Abbur in the Channapatna Taluk.

99. Eaton 2005, 88.

100. Viraraghavacharya (1953) 1954, 2:637. This will be discussed in greater detail in chapter 4.

101. *EC* 1976, vol. 5, no. 106. The village given is Kannerumadugu in the Kanakagiri region, north of the empire's capital (see map 3).

102. B. N. K. Sharma ([1961] 1981, 295) cites a Telugu manuscript from the Madras Government Oriental Manuscript Library, in which a powerful chief in the Uttara Karnataka district bordering the Adil Shahi kingdom, Peddarama of Pippala Gotra, affirms his allegiance to Vyāsatīrtha: "It is now known that Vyāsatīrtha had numerous families owing allegiance to his Mutt in the Uttara-Karnataka areas bordering the Adil Shahi kingdom. Many of these were entrusted with civil and military responsibilities of 'Deshpandes.'" Sharma goes on to note that the local authority of these "Deshpandes" (*despāṇḍes*) continued for centuries in the Uttara-Karnataka region.

103. Leela Prasad cites a case where Kṛṣṇadevarāya makes his expectations of his donees explicit: "The [1515] inscription recording the donation to the [Sringeri] *maṭha* [of a village] notes that Kṛṣṇadevarāya's objective in making the grant 'was threefold, viz. the destruction of his foes, unswerving attachment of his supporters and allies, and increase of his life, health and prosperity'" (B. R. Row, ed. *Selections from the Records of the Śringeri Mutt* [Mysore: Government Branch Press, 1927], qtd. in Prasad 2007, 74).

104. These similarities to the temple are likely what caused the *maṭha* to overshadow, gradually, the *agrahāra* as the main form of royal land grant to Brahmins in the Vijayanagara period. Agrahāras or settlements of Brahmin families in grouped villages often attended the founding of a *maṭha*. This happened in Sringeri, where "in 1346 . . . the first Vijayanagara emperor, Harihara I, founded the first Sringeri agrahara in the immediate vicinity of the maṭha" (Prasad 2007, 44). Some of Vyāsatīrtha's *maṭha*s also seem to have had *agrahāra*s established in their vicinity. This accounts for the "secular" power structure that would evolve in the region of the *maṭha* and was affiliated with both the *maṭha* and the court.

105. Kathleen Morrison (2009) has demonstrated that the empire's emphasis on irrigation privileged elite patterns of food consumption in ways that disadvantaged others, notably dry crop farmers. *Maṭha*s' reshaping of land use in potentially controversial ways is also implicit in an incident from the *Vyāsayogicarita*. Vyāsatīrtha is wandering in the forest and some forest residents are about to attack him. But they are so beguiled by his holy nature that they become his servants, bringing him branches, wood, leaves, and other useful materials for his survival and comfort (Venkoba Rao 1926, intro., cxx; Sanskrit text, 57). Kṛṣṇadevarāya's (2004, v. 257) references (in "Rājanīti" of his *Āmuktamālyada*) to the existence of forest-dwelling hunter-gatherers as irritants to the empire may reflect similar difficulties: "Trying to clean up the forest folk is like trying to wash a mud wall. There's no end to it. No point in getting angry."

106. Of course, in the absence of more specific records we cannot know how evenly such benefits were distributed, and they likely were not. Yet to assume that as elite institutions, *maṭha*s had only exploitative engagement with the local population is probably incorrect.

107. Inscriptional sources confirm that this was the practice at Udupi at least by the fifteenth century. See *SII* 1932, vol. 7, nos. 296ff. Speaking generally of *maṭha*s under Vijayanagara rule, Verghese (1995, 115) asserts the following: "Also, mūrtis of gods and goddesses were installed in the *maṭha*s and regular worship was offered to them, as in the case of the famous Śṛṅgēri *maṭha*, where goddess Śāradā-devī and god Vidyāsaṅkara were worshipped." It should be noted that Michell (1995, 276) argues that the Vidyāśankara temple is likely a mid-sixteenth-century construction.

108. Many *maṭha*s in South India have these *samādhi*s. This is true of the Sringeri Smārta *maṭha* (Prasad 2007, 255n41). The Mādhva *maṭha* in Abbur (where Vyāsatīrtha's

teacher was from) contains Brahmaṇyatīrtha's *samādhi,* often called a *"bṛndāvana"* in Vaiṣṇava communities. The Mādhva *maṭha* in Mulbagal, headed by Śrīpādarāja, another of Vyāsatīrtha's teachers, also houses the latter's *samādhi.* There are eleven Mādhva *samnyāsins* entombed in or very near the Vijayanagara capital. One is Vyāsatīrtha's *samādhi,* on an island in the Tungabhadra River, known as *navabṛndāvana* or "nine *bṛndāvana* (island)" because of the eight other Mādhva saints who are also buried there. While the form of the tombs likely derives from pre-Buddhist stupa-like tumuli, the *samādhi*s also resemble thrones. The carved leaves encircling the top of many Mādhva *samādhi*s are those of the tulasi plant and are indicative of Vaiṣṇava ascetic identity (McLaughlin 2014). But their arrangement also resembles a crown. Images of Rāma, Lakṣmaṇa, and Hanumān installed either on or near many of the *samādhi*s of the Mādhva saints buried in Vijayanagara suggest a long period of multifaceted worship (see ch. 4, figs. 2 and 4–9.).

109. *ARSIE* 1922, no. 710 (trans. in full in Filliozat and Filliozat 1988, 58).

110. Oral traditions surrounding several *maṭha*s in South India date the practice of "holding court" at these *maṭha*s on certain days to key moments of patronage from the Vijayanagara court. At such times, in both the Sringeri Smārta *maṭha* and the Vyāsatīrtha *maṭha* in Sosale, the *maṭhādhipati* wears certain royal emblems and explicitly mimics the *darbār.* On this practice at Sringeri, see Prasad (2007, 68–69); at the Vyāsatīrtha maṭha, see Sharma ([1961] 1981, 290n1).

111. The Śrīvaiṣṇava thinker Yāmunācārya (tenth century) was referred to as "Aḷavantār" ("he who came to rule"), and Rāmānuja (eleventh-twelfth centuries) was referred to as "Uṭaiyavar" (literally "He who has possession" or the "Lord"). In various inscriptions, many Mādhva *samnyāsin*s were also called *Udaiyar/Wodeyar,* a term often applied to royalty. See Sanderson (2009) for other examples.

112. Virūpākṣa functioned as the empire's tutelary or protective deity and his "signature" was consistently found at the bottom of all inscriptions documenting royal grants by the Saṅgama and Sāḷuva dynasties. However, Viṭṭhala gradually started to appear as a signatory deity under the Tuḷuvas and eventually replaced Virūpākṣa in this capacity during Rāmarāya's rule (1542–65). While Virūpākṣa remained the empire's emblematic tutelary deity, Viṭṭhala's temple in the capital received increasing royal attention over the course of the Tuḷuva dynasty, attention that eclipsed that lavished upon Virūpākṣa's shrine. I discuss this in more detail in chapter 4.

113. In one such inscription, shares of the land grant used to found the *maṭha* are set aside "for the Lord of the oblation at the place of the *maṭha*" (*maṭhāvanisutapateḥ*). This seems to be a reference to Rāmacandra, whose protection for the arrangement is then sought (*EC* 1902, vol. 7, pt. 1, Shimoga, no. 85). The gifted village is Gaurapura and the year of the gift was 1527. See map 3.

114. Verghese (1995, 50) surveys the literature on this temple.

115. This term is discussed at much greater length in the conclusion of chapter 4. Inscriptions in which Vyāsatīrtha is referred to in this way include the following: *EC* 1902, vol. 7, no. 85; *TDI* (1935) 1984, vol. 3, nos. 157, 158, 159, and 165; *EC* 1976, vol. 5, nos. 105–6; *ARMAD* 1942, no. 28.

116. As mentioned in note 21 in chapter 1, in *EC* 1943, vol. 14, no. 115, one Śrīvaiṣṇava leader, Govindarāja, is referred to as the *ācārya* of kings and Kṛṣṇadevarāya's own *ācārya.* To counter this piece of inscriptional evidence, Mādhvas often cite another inscription in the Viṭṭhala temple in Hampi, in which Vyāsatīrtha is addressed as "Gurugaḷu Vyāsarāyaru"

or "Guru Vyāsatīrtha." (*SII* 1986, vol. 4, no. 277) But the term *guru* was a common honorific title in these inscriptions. Verghese (1995, appendix A) provides an overview of all the inscriptions at the capital. One is a 1519 grant by Kṛṣṇadevarāya to "Guru Basavadīkṣita."

117. *TDI* (1935) 1984, vol. 3, nos. 157–59.

118. This is also documented in the Mādhva hagiographical traditions surrounding Vyāsatīrtha. According to the *Vyāsa Vijaya,* Vyāsatīrtha started worshiping the main deity according to Madhva's *Tantrasārasaṅgraha* while at Tirupati.

119. This land endowment will be discussed further in chapter 4 under "An Intersectarian Agrahāra?"

120. After indicating the coordinates of the land with reference to neighboring villages and listing off the hamlets included in the gift (ll. 39–57), the inscription discusses the main village's various names as follows: "Kṛṣṇarāyapuraṃ ceti pratināmasamanvitam|| grāmaṃ vyāsasamudrākhyaṃ beṭṭakoṇḍāparāhvayam|." I have come across other instances of Kṛṣṇadevarāya having a village renamed "Kṛṣṇarāyapura" as part of the donation (e.g., *EC* 1976, vol. 5, no. 105, l. 83; and *EC* 1943, vol. 14, no. 115). The scholarly literature on Vijayanagara debates how centralized the state was. This is outside my area of expertise, but it does seem that Kṛṣṇadevarāya's inscriptions recounting his military conquests and his support of various religious institutions, as well as his renaming of villages after himself, imply that he wanted people in far-flung holdings to associate themselves with his reign. See Morrison (2009) and Sinopoli (2000). See also Eaton and Wagoner (2014, 289ff.) for a discussion of how, as a means of conveying his "expansionist intentions," Kṛṣṇadevarāya constructed a new gate, with his emblems prominently displayed, immediately after capturing the fort of Raichur from the Adil Khan of Bijapur.

121. Telugu was not Kṛṣṇadevaraya's mother tongue, a fact that the text itself alludes to when Kṛṣṇadevarāya is commanded by "Āndhra Viṣṇu" in a vision to compose a text in Telugu for His delight.

122. Rao, Shulman, and Subrahmanyam (2004) and Loewy Shacham (2015) believe that it is the work of Kṛṣṇadevarāya.

123. Again, the text's focus on the life story of Yāmunācārya is generally thought to underscore Kṛṣṇadevarāya's Śrīvaiṣṇava leanings.

124. V. N. Rao, Shulman, and Subrahmanyam 2004, 601.

125. Ibid., 603.

126. Ibid., 605.

127. Stein 1980, 411–15.

128. Kṛṣṇadevarāya 2004, Verse 207, (Trans. by V.N. Rao, Shulman, and Subrahmanyam), 613.

129. Ibid., v. 217, pp. 614–15.

130. Ibid., v. 242, 618.


### 3. SECTARIAN RIVALRIES AT AN ECUMENICAL COURT: VYĀSATĪRTHA, ADVAITA VEDĀNTA, AND THE SMĀRTA BRAHMINS

1. See Williams (2011) for a detailed study of the role of *navya-nyāya* in Vyāsatīrtha's works.

2. As McCrea argues (2015), Vyāsatīrtha's detailed identification of all possible Advaita arguments on particular topics as well as counterarguments to Dvaita objections amounts to a mapping of the tradition's historical development. But like many Indian doxographies

of different philosophical systems, this map is polemical in that it helps to locate the Dvaita system advantageously in the broader philosophical landscape. Nicholson (2010, 145) points out that earlier doxographies, such as Mādhava's *Sarvadarśanasaṃgraha* and Haribhadra's *Ṣaḍdarśanasamuccaya*, are ahistorical and present the systems of thought they cover as "completely static." He sees polemic and doxography as distinct and maintains that true doxographies typically do not take the opponents' views to task so much as they try to elucidate them. But he does allow that some types of texts straddle these two genres, for example, the Buddhist Bhāviveka's *Madhyamakahṛdayakārikā* (151).

3. In all, Vyāsatīrtha composed nine works, which include several commentaries on Madhva's works. His three principal works, however, are the *Nyāyāmṛta*, the *Tātparyacandrikā*, and the *Tarkatāṇḍava*. The first two are detailed criticisms of Advaita and Visiṣṭādvaita Vedānta, with the *Tātparyacandrikā* focusing on the systems' respective commentaries on the *Brahma Sūtras*. The third work is indirectly in the service of the same goals as the other two in that it maps out alternative argumentation techniques that support a Dvaita epistemology and metaphysics.

4. As mentioned in chapter 1, further evidence that Hindu sectarianism not only allowed for but encouraged acts of conversion can be found in Madhva's thirteenth-century handbook on entering the monkhood (*Yatipraṇavakalpa*). According to the handbook, initiates undertook an oath of allegiance to certain doctrines and simultaneously swore to avoid other doctrines and their proponents: "Never shall I forswear Viṣṇu and the Vaiṣṇavas. Never shall I deem Viṣṇu to be on a par or identical with the other gods. Never shall I associate with those who hold the doctrine of identity or equality of God and soul" (Sharma [1961] 1981, 190).

5. Another text, *Bhedadhikkara* or *Laying a Curse on Dualism* (c. 1550), written by the South Indian Advaitin Nṛsimhāśrama, is often identified as being anti-Dvaita but, according to McCrea (2015), this text does not engage Madhva's system. However, the same author does engage and criticize Dvaita arguments in his *Advaitadīpikā*. It is not surprising that Mādhva intellectuals in turn responded to their rivals' critiques throughout the sixteenth and seventeenth centuries. Among the more significant of these respondents were Vijayīndratīrtha (1514–95), Vādirājatīrtha (c. 1480–1600), Rāghavendratīrtha (1623–71), Nārāyaṇācārya (c. 1600–60), and Satyanātha Yati (1648–74). See B. N. K. Sharma (1981, pt. 5) for a discussion of some of their works.

6. Gerow 1987, 1990.

7. Somanātha's *Vyāsayogicarita* (ch. 4 in Prahladachar 1993), discusses preparations for one of Vyāsatīrtha's debates, specifying that an uneven number of judges must be selected and a scribe designated to record the arguments. The passage also indicates that the terms of the debate adhere to the rules laid down in the Nyāya philosopher Gaṅgeśopādhyāya's *Tattvacintāmaṇi*. See Prahladachar's (1993) introduction for a discussion and Venkoba Rao's edition (1926, 52ff.) for the Sanskrit passage.

8. Along with this evidence of royal interest in Brahmin intellectual activity is the fact that Indian royals themselves engaged in literary pursuits. In addition to his Telugu text, the *Āmuktamālyada*, discussed in chapter two of this book, Kṛṣṇadevarāya is also credited with composing several works in Sanskrit (the king himself mentions them in the beginning of his *Āmuktamālyada*). Besides writing the five works mentioned there, he is also acknowledged as the author of a play, *Jāmbavatī Pariṇayam*. This is significant mainly because it

is the only one of his Sanskrit works that is still extant. Understanding the arguments of Vyāsatīrtha and his peers required that the audience have a certain intellectual aptitude and knowledge base, but one should not assume there was little public interest in philosophical debate in sixteenth-century South India. Whether or not Vijayanagara kings actually composed all the texts they are credited with, rulers who were literate and thoughtful were clearly seen in a positive light.

9. This shift is discussed more in chapter 4. Between 1354 and 1516, all royal grants documented in the imperial capital were witnessed by Virūpākṣa, a form of Śiva. From 1516 onward, some were witnessed by Virūpākṣa and others by Viṭṭhaleśvara, a form of Viṣṇu. Beginning in 1545, during the regency of Rāmarāya (for Tuḷuva Emperor Sadāśiva), all of the grants were witnessed by Viṭṭhala. See Verghese (1995, appendix A).

10. Of course, it was not always the teachings themselves that people responded to. It could also be the sectarian leader's charisma, local authority, wealth, devotional fervor, displays of asceticism, and so on. But that intellectual prowess, displayed in debate, as well as knowledge of sacred texts were valued attributes is attested to in inscriptions praising sectarian leaders in these terms.

11. Asher and Talbot 2006; Stein 1999; Verghese 1995, 2000.

12. For example, Aiyangar 1921, Saletore 1934, and Nilakanta Sastri (1955) 1994. See also chapter 1, note 3 of this book.

13. Verghese 1995, 3.

14. Clark 2006, 221ff.

15. See Verghese (1995, 115–17) for an overview of *maṭhas* in the Vijayanagara capital. Examples of other sectarian institutions established in the imperial capital would include shrines to deities and deceased gurus as well as guesthouses, feeding stations, and pavilions for *prasād* distribution. Specific examples of how sects used such things to promote their presence in a given area are provided in chapter 4.

16. As I discuss in detail in chapter 4, Vijayanagara royals encouraged a variety of sectarian religious activities (including the construction of ancillary shrines, *maṭhas*, guesthouses, and feeding stations) at several temple sites. These included the Kṛṣṇa and Viṭṭhala temples in the imperial capital, the Śrī Veṅkaṭeśvara and Govindarājasvāmi temples in Tirupati/Tirumala, and the Varadarāja temple in Kanchi.

17. An example of the former attitude can be found in Verghese (1995, 9): "The conscious effort at religious conciliation seen in the Jaina-Vaishnava accord of Bukka I in A.D. 1368 was continued by the later rulers. For, despite their sectarian preferences, the Vijayanagara rulers, on the whole, adopted the deliberate policy of tolerance towards all sects, so as to incorporate them all within the polity." Pollock's (2006) view is discussed in greater detail below.

18. For this insight, I am grateful to Jon Keune and the panel, "The Limits of Royal Patronage," he organized for the Annual Meeting of the American Academy of Religion, Chicago, IL, November 2012.

19. As will be discussed, Kulke (2001, 234) has argued that the *maṭha* came into being around the same time as the empire; the oldest inscriptional reference to an actual *maṭha* at Sringeri is from 1356.

20. "Avyāhataprajñaḥ sāyaṇāmātyaḥ" (Sāyaṇa, *RSBh* 7.3, qtd. in Galewicz 2009, 47).

21. See Galewicz for an overview of these statements: "Other examples of 'self-esteem' are to be found in preambles to RS VII.3, which refers to the author as 'avyāhataprajñaḥ

sāyaṇāmātyaḥ' ('Sāyaṇa, the king's minister and one of unimpeded understanding'), to RS VII.4, where the author is called 'śrutitattvajñaḥ sāyaṇāmātyaḥ' ('Sāyaṇa, the minister knowing the true essence of the Śruti')" (2009, 47).

22.  "An inscription on a copper plate dated 1377 commemorates a gift made by Harihara II in the form of an *agrahāra* land grant named Bukkarāyapura and consisting of fourteen villages in the Hassan district. It mentions the name of Sāyaṇācārya and his son Singana as the first two out of the sixty donees. Another inscription of Harihara, dated to 1378 and commemorating an *agrahāra* named Bonallapura, also mentions Sāyaṇācārya as the first out of thirty-six donees" (Galewicz 2009, 44). Kulke notes that Harihara II refers to himself as "the establisher of the Vedic path" in this 1377 inscription (2001, 238).

23.  For an overview of these legends, see Subrahmanyam (1998).

24.  Vidyāraṇya is often identified with Mādhava, Sāyaṇa's brother, and "Mādhava" is also the name of a minister in the Saṅgama court. Clark (2006) argues, following Kulke, that there are two Mādhavas (the minister and Sāyaṇa's brother) but he also rejects the identification of Mādhava, Sāyaṇa's brother, with Vidyāraṇya. There is ample debate regarding the identity of these early Sringeri Smārta Brahmins, which creates some problems in determining the authorship of important texts.

25.  Between 1354 and 1516, all royal grants documented in the imperial capital were witnessed by Virūpākṣa. See Verghese (1995, appendix A). As mentioned above in note 9 and further discussed in Chapter 4 of this book, the Vaiṣṇava deity Viṭṭhala rose to a position of prominence that in some ways eclipsed that of Virūpākṣa during the Tuḷuva dynasty. But Viṭṭhala never usurped Virūpākṣa's status as tutelary deity.

26.  *Vijayanagara Inscriptions,* vol. 2, no. 526 (cited in Verghese 1995, 119n7).

27.  For the importance of Virūpākṣa's temple to the founding of the Vijayanagara empire, as well as to the historical evolution of the site, see Wagoner (1996a). That the Sringeri *maṭha* became linked to this temple at least symbolically from an early period is evident in the following inscription cited by Kulke, who refers to an inscription from the year 1384 in which "two other brahmin scholars, who were clearly named as disciples (*śiṣya*) of Vidyāraṇya, received land grants from king Harihara II in the presence of god Virūpākṣa at Vijayanagara" (2001, 229–30). He identifies the inscription as "Belugula inscription, lines 41d" (*ARMAD* 1933 [pub. 1936], p. 135).

28.  *ARMAD* 1933 [pub. 1936], pp. 117ff.; *ARSIE* 1961–62, no. 500 (both cited in Verghese 1995, 14n75).

29.  Bukka I's successor (1377–1404).

30.  Belugula inscription of the year 1384 (*ARMAD* 1933 [pub. 1936], p. 134, ll. 29–31, qtd. in Kulke 2001, 229).

31.  According to Kulke, in 1378 "an inscription mentions that Harihara II donated land to Sāyaṇa and to two Brahmin scholars" (2001, 229). He cites *EC,* 1976, vol. 5, no. 256; *ARMAD* 1934 [pub. 1936], p. 116.

32.  For this information, Kulke (2001, 229n59) cites the following source, which I have not been able to locate: R. Narasimhachar, ed., *Archaeological Survey of Mysore, Annual Report: 1906–1909,* vol. 2, *A Study* by S. Settar (Dharwad: Karnatak University, 1976), 64ff.

33.  Belugula inscription (*ARMAD* 1933 [pub. 1936], p. 135, l. 41d, cited in Kulke 2001, 230n62).

34. *ARMAD* 1933, no. 24, cited in Verghese 1995, 14n78.

35. *ARSIE* 1936–37, no. 283, cited in Verghese 1995, 14n79.

36. Kulke 2001, 233–34.

37. Kulke 2001, 234n75. The inscription he cites again is Belugula (*ARMAD* 1933 [pub. 1936], p. 135, l. 25).

38. Nilakanta Sastri (1955) 1994, 238–39.

39. Wagoner (1996b) and Talbot (1995) have shown that the Vijayanagara Empire mimicked many of the Islamic courtly styles of dress and architecture, to establish their authority in a Turkish and Persianized political world.

40. Asher and Talbot 2006; Stein 1999; Verghese 1995, 2000.

41. Pollock goes on to say, "There was no specifically Śaiva or Vaiṣṇava political practice, no specifically Jain political philosophy (as Somadevasūri's political tract shows), no specifically Mahāyāna theory of political power. The disconnect between religion and rule was far more fundamental than contemporary scholarship acknowledges—and far more fundamental than in late medieval and early modern Europe. It is, in short, a serious misreading to claim that for the premodern period 'the essentials of Indian politics can never be grasped without an understanding of religion'" (Pollock 2006, 431, and note 105, citing Guha 1997, 47).

42. Hacker 1995, 28. Kulke also assumes Mādhava to be the author.

43. Vidyashankar Sundaresan (2000) outlines the contours of this dispute and effectively problematizes the authorship of this text.

44. "Sringeri's claim that its *maṭha* was founded by Śaṅkara and that afterwards Śaṅkara established in the course of his *digvijaya* three other *advaita maṭhas* at the cardinal points of India, put Sringeri at the centre of a new religious network covering India as a whole. Thus Sringeri's "Śaṅkara tradition" provided a further legitimation to Vijayanagara's claim to be the centre of the new orthodoxy" (Kulke 2001, 238).

45. Galewicz (2009, 75) notes the following:

> It can be surmised that in addition to local agents of political power, a number of important centres of authority must have remained in the hands of priestly (mostly, though not only brahminical) elites and collective bodies presiding over big temples and other religious and educational institutions like maṭhas, some of them constituting not only religious but also economic core institutions of the hinterland. This plurality of centers of authority is what should be taken into account while explaining the early Vijayanagara rulers' need for a unifying ideological principle that could appeal to most of them. A royal initiative presented as a commentary on the whole of the Veda could by principle serve that purpose.

In this view, the Sringeri *maṭha* created unity through its religious and scholarly activities, which enabled more efficient rule. While I agree that *maṭhas* were both religious and economic centers of authority and that the court's bestowal of wealth on them was an efficient means of promoting certain types of economic development, I am not clear on how the very abstract and elite unity articulated in a Vedic commentary would have benefited the state in any direct way.

46. "The monastic traditions that developed at Śṛṅgeri and Kāñcīpuram, as represented in the works that we have at our disposal from the hand of the early known (as opposed to

hagiographically presented) pontiffs, were essentially and distinctly orthodox. As has been indicated, they were essentially Śaiva, yet, in accord with Brahminical tradition, Smārta orthodoxy was demonstrated by their acknowledgement of the Veda as the ultimate source of knowledge.... After the fourteenth century the influence and estates of the Kālāmukha and Mattamayūra orders significantly declined, their role to a significant extent being eclipsed by the new and heavily patronized Smārta Advaita *maṭhas*" (Clark 2006, 221).

47. See Chandra Shobhi (2005, ch. 2 and conclusion) on how, despite receiving no patronage from the court, the Vīraśaiva *maṭhas* burgeoned under Vijayanagara rule.

48. It is also hinted at in inscriptions referred to in the *kaḍita*s or record books of the *maṭha* (cited in Kulke 2001, 232), which say that the Sringeri Smārtas destroyed Buddhists and Jains.

49. Authority is not the same as orthodoxy. The Veda, by virtue of nonelites' limited access to it and Brahmins' distinctive role as its preservers, was certainly a symbol of the former and, for Vaidika Brahmins, an arbiter of the latter. However, other Brahmins may have identified other works more closely with orthodoxy.

50. This work is typically attributed to the Mādhava often identified as Sāyaṇa's brother. But there is evidence that it was composed by a younger contemporary of Mādhava and Sāyaṇa named Cannibhaṭṭa. Cannibhaṭṭa's father, Sahajasarvajña Viṣṇu Bhaṭṭopādhyaya, was Sāyaṇa and Mādhava's teacher (see Thakur 1961, qtd. in Clark 2006, 209–210n114).

51. Wilhelm Halbfass 1988, 353.

52. Ibid., 351.

53. See [Mādhava?] (1914), 273.

54. "If we can place anything about the [*Jīvanmuktiviveka*] in time and space and consider Vidyāraṇya's motives beyond teaching his own Advaitin followers, I think his deliberate cultural politics was to promote Advaita among sectarian Śrīvaiṣṇava laypeople in these newly controlled territories and defend the idea of liberation-in-life against the Śrīvaiṣṇava theologians" (Goodding 2002, 19).

55. Goodding 2002; Hacker 1995. On North Indian Hindu responses to Islamic political power manifested in doxographies and other forms of Brahmin intellectual output, see also Nicholson (2010).

56. Heras (1929); Verghese (1995); A. Rao (2014); Stoker (2011).

57. See Wagoner (2000) for a helpful overview of the available sources on the empire's founding and for a discussion of how a particular amalgamation of the themes in these sources came to influence modern scholarship on the empire.

58. Nunes's chronicle has been translated in full by Robert Sewell. See Nunes ([1900] 1995).

59. Subrahmanyam 1998.

60. A. K. Shastry (2009) supplies a different date for Rāmacandra Bhārati of 1517–1560.

61. Heras cites inscriptions, one from the Kolar district that explicitly places Vidyāraṇya at the Virūpākṣa temple prior to the founding of the City of Victory there. The inscription recounts the story of Harihara, who had been out hunting across the river from Anegondi, when he saw that his dog had been bitten by a hare: "And seeing the god Virūpākṣa along with the goddess Pampā he did obeisance to them; and drawing near, paid respect to Vidyāraṇya, the yati in that temple, and informed him of the above very curious circumstance" (Heras 1929, 2). Vidyāraṇya responds by telling the king that the place is special and that he ought

to make a city "named Vidyā" there. A similar inscription from Nellore also indicates that Vidyāraṇya is already being associated with the Virūpākṣa and Pampā temples. This inscription also includes Vidyāraṇya's instructions advising the king to found a city there and call it Vidyānagara (Heras 1929, 3). Those inscriptions referred to earlier in this chapter, which do attest to an important connection between the Saṅgama court and the Sringeri Smārta community, do not mention this legend in any way, a fact noted by Heras (4).

62. If a Portuguese horse trader visiting the city between 1509 and 1520 was aware of stories recounting Vidyāraṇya's role in the founding of the empire, then Vyāsatīrtha would certainly have been aware of them, as well as of Rāmacandra Bhāratī's use of them. We know that Vyāsatīrtha spent much time at the Vijayanagara capital. His presence is implied in inscriptions, wherein Vijayanagara royals bestowed land grants on him that were witnessed by deities at temples in the capital (e.g., two inscriptions from the Viṭṭhala temple dated 1513 and 1532, the latter of which documents an icon Vyāsatīrtha installed at that temple, and four inscriptions witnessed by Virūpākṣa, dated 1516, 1521, 1523, and 1527). Vyāsatīrtha is buried, together with eight other Mādhva saints, on an island in the Tungabhadra River a short boat ride from the capital. (See map 6 and figs. 2 and 4–9 in ch. 4.) Vyāsatīrtha is also credited with founding a small but still active Hanumān temple on the banks of the Tungabhadra River near the city's sacred center, and there are remains of what seems to have been a Mādhva *matha* in the Viṭṭhalapura section of the city. Most of these monuments are discussed in chapter 4 of this book.

63. Heras 1929, 34.

64. For example, see the following quote: "Such religious ascetics and recluses psychologically are persons often inclined to fabricate such fables. Their knowledge of what they call absolute reality, acquired only by their practice of asceticism, inclines them to place all other things, whether existing or not existing, whether true or false, on the same level of relative reality. Hence the fabrication of a story which one might derive some profit from—provided no harm should result from the concoction to a third person—is always attractive to such religious recluses" (Heras 1929, 34).

65. Heras 1929, 34–35.

66. Heras himself seems to acknowledge the Sringeri *matha*'s fourteenth-century prominence at court, even as he maintains that Rāmacandra Bhāratī was completely fabricating this history: "In fact, there is an inscription of the year 1513, in the Chikmagalur Taluka, recording a grant made by Śrī-Rāmachandra Bhāratīswāmi of the village of 'Kūduaḷḷi, belonging to us, in the Melepāḷu of Vasudhāre-Sīme, which Harihara-Mahāraya when he was protecting the kingdom in peace, granted to our Śringeri math as an offering to Vidyāśankara' [*EC*, 5, cm. 88].' This Vidyāśaṅkara is the famous Vidyātīrtha, one of the predecessors of Vidyāraṇya as head of the Sringeri math. The inscription shows the wish of the Jagad-guru, to show the early relations between the math and the Emperors of Vijayanagara. This was perhaps the first step in this campaign of falsification; the second was to be the story of Vidyāraṇya as the founder of the capital of the Empire" (Heras 1929, 34–35).

67. Kulke 2001, 212–14.

68. Ibid., 220.

69. Verghese 2000, 77.

70. In 1515, Kṛṣṇadevarāya issued several land grants to the Sringeri *matha* leadership for the performance of certain rituals in their affiliated temples in Sringeri. See Shastry

(2009, 73–75) for the original text of the inscriptions as well as Prasad (2007, 74) for a discussion. According to Verghese (1995, 149), Kṛṣṇadevarāya also gave grants of villages to the Śankarācārya *maṭha* at Kanchi in 1529.

71. Verghese 1995, 56.

72. McCrea 2015. See also Venkatkrishnan (2011) for a discussion of historicism in Vedāntin intellectual debates.

73. "Darśanānāṃ pravṛttatvān manda āśankate punaḥ| anādikālato vṛttāḥ samayāḥ hi pravāhataḥ" (Madhva 1989, 100). (The fool doubts that [the *darśanas*] are streams that flow in [real] time in a continuous way from time that is beginningless, because [he is confused] by the fact that the different *darśanas* are proclaimed [by specific individuals].)

74. Pollock (1989); Clooney (1987); and Halbfass (1990) also address this issue in terms of the Veda's *anāditva, apauruṣeyatva,* and *svataḥ prāmāṇya.*

75. It may be that Smārta Advaitins did not make a conscious decision to view their leaders in this way, so as to achieve specific worldly ends. However, the doctrine of *jīvanmukti* helped to qualify gurus to teach about the experience to others and thereby establish their religious authority. As Patricia Mumme (1996, 263) notes, Śankara himself says as much: "Commenting on *Chāndogya Upaniṣad* 6.14.2, Śankara states that one of the reasons a state of living liberation must be affirmed is the need for authoritative *gurus* and teachers. His point is compelling: if there is no one who has attained liberation in this life, then who would be qualified to act as a guru, teacher, or example worthy of emulation for those who are still bound? The various traditions that aim at liberation would be reduced to the blind leading the blind." She also notes, "Jīvanmukti is a doctrinal concept whose practical importance is in authorizing founding teachers and *gurus*" (263). Andrew O. Fort (1998, 164–71) documents the fact that many recent Jagadgurus of the Sringeri and other Śankara *maṭhas* are revered by their disciples for having achieved this state.

76. Fort (1998, 56) paraphrases Vimuktātman's arguments on this issue as follows: "[Vimuktātman] says, following *Gītā* IV. 34, that the wise teacher realizes the truth and truth-knowers (*tattva-darśin*) alone teach the highest knowledge. If the body fell immediately after knowledge, there could be no teacher, thus no reaching *vidyā,* thus no liberation— which again shows that the knower's body remains for a while."

77. Much of the scholarly literature on Dvaita credits Vyāsatīrtha with introducing the use of this term in Dvaita. (e.g., Sheridan 1996; Sharma 1991, n. 7, 440). However, Roque Mesquita's (2007, 9ff.) recent work on this concept maintains that Madhva himself was amenable to this term and utilized it on occasion. Mesquita's evidence for this consists primarily of two quotations in Madhva's works from unknown sources that Mesquita believes Madhva authored himself. Mesquita's analysis of Madhva's commentary on these quotes as well as Madhva's discussion of liberation are persuasive in showing that Madhva made some equation between his two-stage view of *mokṣa* and Advaita Vedānta's *jīvanmukti* concept. However, based on Mesquita's discussion, my own assessment is that Madhva did not use the term *jīvanmukti* frequently and generally preferred to present his theory of *mokṣa* in terminology that would not be confused with that of Advaita.

78. Vyāsatīrtha's presentation in this text assumes a lot of knowledge on the part of his audience of his opponents' doctrines, which he often explains very cursorily prior to refuting. This partly reflects the dialogic context in which this text was produced.

79. It is important to note that Vyāsatīrtha often treats his particular interpretation of his opponents' positions. His opponents, for more than a century, articulated counterarguments, some of which pointed out Vyāsatīrtha's misrepresentation of their ideas. However, as mentioned above, the fact that Vyāsatīrtha's polemics elicited such a protracted and detailed response from his intellectual rivals attests to the cogency of his critique.

80. Fort 1998, 47ff.

81. Ibid., 48.

82. "Yac cocyate tattvasākṣāt kāreṇa naṣṭāvidyo 'nuvṛttadehādipratibhāsaś ca jīvanmuktaḥ| na ca tattvajñānād avidyānāśe sadyaḥ śarīrādinivarteteti vācyam| cakrabhramaṇavad bhayakampādiccāvidyāsaṃskārād api tadanuvṛtteḥ|" (Vyāsatīrtha 1996, vol. 3, 695).

83. Fort 1998, 47ff.

84. Vyāsatīrtha summarizes his understanding of these aspects of Prakāśātman's argument as follows: "And it is not the case that a *saṃskāra* is only made by an action or a cognition, because of the example of the smell of a flower lingering in the box even after the flower itself has been removed. And because of the following inference: 'The destruction which is under dispute is [the destruction of ignorance which], like the destruction of knowledge, is invariably concomitant with a *saṃskāra* because this is the nature of destruction, except in the case of the destruction of a *saṃskāra* [in which case there is no invariable concomitance with another *saṃskāra*]'" (Vyāsatīrtha 1996, vol. 3, 695). (na ca kriyājñānayor eva saṃskāraḥ, niḥsāritapuṣpāyāṃ tatpuṭikāyāṃ puṣpavāsanādarśanāt| vimato nāśaḥ saṃskāravyāptaḥ, saṃskāranāśānyatve sati nāśatvāt, jñānanāśavad ity anumānāc ca|.) This last line demonstrates Prakāśātman's care to maintain that the destruction of an impression will not invariably give rise to another impression precisely because this would mean that the achievement of final liberation would never take place. Vyāsatīrtha's paraphrase of Prakāśātman's argument goes on to say, "A *saṃskāra* is an effect that is without a material cause just like that destruction [is without a material cause]" (Vyāsatīrtha 1996, vol. 3, 695). (saṃskāraḥ kāryo 'pi dhvaṃsa iva nirupādānaḥ|.)

85. According to Fort's (1998) analysis of Prakāśātman's *Pañcapadika-vivaraṇa,* a commentary on Padmapāda's *Pañcapadika,* Prakāśātman argues that both the *saṃskāra* and ignorance are based on the self, "which is why *saṃskāra*s can continue even without the presence of *avidyā.*" He goes on to say Bharatītīrtha's subcommentary on the *Pañcapadika-vivaraṇa,* the *Vivaraṇa-prameya-saṅgraha,* "agrees that pure consciousness is the locus of both, and adds that *saṃskāras* need no material cause, since such a cause is necessary only for existent things (not mere traces of ignorance)" (61).

86. "Avidyeva ca śuddhātmāśrita iti nāvidyāpekṣaḥ|" (Vyāsatīrtha, vol. 3, 695).

87. "Saṃskāranivṛttiś cāvṛttāt tattvasākṣātkārāt|" (Vyāsatīrtha 1996, vol. 3, 695). According to Fort (1998, 61), this idea is implicit in Prakāśātman's *Pañcapadika-vivaraṇa:* "*Saṃskāra* cessation (and consequent body dropping) happens gradually but inevitably due to the remembrance (anusamdhana) of knowledge of the real (*tattva-jñāna*). Bharatītīrtha adds that after such knowledge, living liberation with a remnant of ignorance continues until *prārabdha karma* is destroyed."

88. "Atra brūmaḥ na tāvat saṃskārapakṣo yuktaḥ| bhāvakāryamadhyastaṃ saṃskāraṃ dehādikaṃ taddhetuprārabdhakarmādikaṃ ca pratyupādānatvenājñānānuvṛtty āpātāt|" (Vyāsatīrtha 1996, vol. 3, 695).

89. "Sarpādibhramasaṃskāras tu satyo na tv ajñānopādānakaḥ|" (Vyāsatīrtha 1996, vol. 3, 695–96).

90. "Pūrvasākṣātkārānivṛttasyādhyastasya tadanadhikaviṣayeṇāvṛttenāpy attareṇa jñānena nivṛttyadarśanāc ca| jīvanmuktasyāvidyāvaraṇābhāvena tadā niratiśayānandasphūrtyāpātāc ca| saṃskāras tu nāvaraṇam iti tvayaivoktam|" (Vyāsatīrtha 1996, vol. 3, 696).

91. "The following view has been rejected, namely, 'that [the state of *jīvanmukti*] is like when you accept something contrary to known reality because there is some defect [in cognition] as in the example of seeing two moons [when you apply pressure to your eyelid with your finger] even though you know that there is only one moon.' In this case [of *jīvanmukti*], [unlike] in that [example], there is no defect that is not removed by true knowledge of reality." (Etena tattve jñāte 'pi dvicandrādivaddoṣād bādhitānuvṛttir iti nirastam, tatrevātra tattvajñānānivartyadoṣābhāvāt" [Vyāsatīrtha 1996, vol. 3, 696].)

92. "Leśapakṣe 'pi na tāval leśo 'vayavaḥ, ajñānasya niravayavatvāt| etenāvidyaiva dagdhapaṭanyāyena kiṃcit kālaṃ tiṣṭhatīti nirastam| niravayave dagdhapaṭanyāyāsambhavāt|" (Vyāsatīrtha 1996, vol. 3, 696).

93. "Anuvṛttasya jñānānivartyatvena sattvāpātāc ca|" (Vyāsatīrtha 1996, vol. 3, 696).

94. Fort 1998, 62ff.

95. This is the *pratīka* for *Ṛgveda* 6.47.18c (Indro māyābhiḥ pururūpa īyate), which is quoted in *Bṛhadāraṇyaka Upaniṣad* 2.5.19c. It implies that *māyā* or illusion is plural. Citsukha cites this text in his *Tattvapradīpikā* at the close of his discussion of *ākāra* and *jīvanmukti* (Fort 1998, 63).

96. "Atha mataṃ leśo nāmākāraḥ| indro māyābhir ityādiśrutyā avidyāyā anekākāratvena prapañce paramārthasattvādibhramahetvākāranivṛttāv api dehādyaparokṣapratibhāsa-hetvākāro 'nuvartate| virodhini tattvajñāne saty api tadanuvṛttiś cārabdhakarmabhir jñānapratibandhāt| karmānuvṛttiś ca taddhetvajñānaleśānuvṛtteḥ| [ . . . ] ākārinivṛttāv apy ākārasyānuvṛttir vyaktinivṛttāv api jāter iva yukteti|" (Vyāsatīrtha 1996, vol. 3, 696).

97. "Tatrākāro jātiśaktyādirūpo dharmo vā? Svarṇasya kuṇḍalādir ivāvasthā viśeṣo vā? Ajñānavyaktyantaraṃ vā?" (Vyāsatīrtha 1996, vol. 3, 696).

98. "Nādyadvitīyau, tayor dehādibhramopādānatve 'vidyātvāpātāt|" (Vyāsatīrtha 1996, vol. 3, 696).

99. "Ātmānyatvena jñānanivartyatvena ca tayor avidyātatkāryayor anyataratvāvaśyambhāvenājñāne nivṛtte sthityayogāc ca|" (Vyāsatīrtha 1996, vol. 3, 696).

100. "Dharme upādānatvasyāvasthāyāṃ cāvasthāvantaṃ vinā sthiter ayogāc ca|" (Vyāsatīrtha 1996, vol. 3, 696).

101. "Na tṛtīyaḥ, ajñānaikyapakṣe tad ayogāt|" (Vyāsatīrtha 1996, vol. 3, 696).

102. "Tadbhedapakṣe 'pi vyaktyantaraṃ pūrvājñānād adhikaviṣayam? Na vā? Nādyaḥ, nirviśeṣe tadayogāt|

Nāntyaḥ, ekasminn api viṣaye yāvanti jñānāni tāvanty ajñānānīti matasya pratikarmavyavasthābhaṅge dūṣitatvāt|" (Vyāsatīrtha 1996, vol. 3, 696).

103. "Caramasākṣātkārānyūnaviṣayasākṣātkārasya pūrvam api satve paścād iva jīvanmuktāv api tadajñānahetukādhyāsāyogāc ca|" (Vyāsatīrtha 1996, vol. 3, 696–97).

104. "If you establish the *leśa*'s existence with reference to the continued working off of karma and yet you also establish the continuation [of karma] with reference to the existence of the *leśa* as something that obstructs complete knowledge, there would be the flaw of

mutual dependence" (Vyāsatīrtha 1996, vol. 3, 697). (Sthite leśe karmānuvṛttis tadanuvṛttau ca jñānasya pratibandhena leśasthitir ity anyonyāśrayāc ca|.) For a discussion of Citsukha's position here, see Fort (1998, 64).

105. "Tasmāt paramate mohakāryatvād akhilasya ca|
jñānena mohanāśāc ca jīvanmuktir na yujyate||
Asmākam tu aparokṣajñānino 'pi svayogyaparamānandahetuparamakāṣṭhāpanna-bhaktyabhāve tatsādhyasya mocakasyeśvaraprasādasyābhāvena prārabdhakarmaṇā saṃsārānuvṛttyā jīvanmuktiḥ| bhāve tu prasādasyāpi bhāvena niḥśeṣaduḥkhanivṛttiviśiṣṭa-svatonīcoccabhāvāpannasvarūpānandāvirbhāvarūpāmuktir yukteti||" (Vyāsatīrtha 1996, vol. 3, 697).

106. Sheridan 1996; Mesquita 2007, 9ff.

107. Sharma 1991, 426.

108. Sheridan 1996, 91.

109. See note 77 above, which explains my response to Mesquita's position (outlined in 2007, 9ff.) on this issue.

110. For more on this irony, see Fisher (2013, 6ff.), who applies to seventeenth-century Hindu sectarianism, Luhmann's use of the cell/organism analogy to explain the interaction of different social groups and their systems of meaning.

111. "It is probable that some local patron commissioned the paintings when the temple started functioning again, at the beginning of the nineteenth century. The nineteenth century spelled a period of prosperity and unprecedented stability for both the local ruling families and the merchant community, and it would be not surprising if the patron of the Virupaksha Temple paintings was either a local grandee or a wealthy merchant" (Dallapiccola 2011, 280).

112. Galewicz (2009) puts two copies of this image in the front of his book on Sāyaṇa's commentary "in the service of empire" as an emblem of the links between the Vijayanagara *darbār* and the Sringeri *maṭha*.

113. K. G. Gopala Krishna Rao, personal communication, January 8, 2012.

114. See Venkoba Rao's introduction to his edition of the *Vyāsayogicarita* for his efforts to verify this (1926, cviii and cxxx–cxxxi). The putative theft of the jewels is discussed more in Chapter 4 of this book.

115. Sharma 1981, 290n1.


## 4. ALLIES OR RIVALS? VYĀSATĪRTHA'S MATERIAL, SOCIAL, AND RITUAL INTERACTIONS WITH THE ŚRĪVAIṢṆAVAS

1. Verghese 1995, 63–66; A. Rao 2015, ch. 4.

2. A. Rao 2015, ch. 4.

3. T. K. T. Viraraghavacharya (1953–54) amply documents this pluralism as well as various conflicts and negotiations between different constituents over the course of the history of the large Vaiṣṇava temple complex at Tirupati-Tirumala.

4. For more specific information on the court's arbitrative role, see Arjun Appadurai 1981, 68.

5. According to Verghese (2000, 104), the growth in the cult of Viṭṭhala was at direct expense, in terms of royal patronage, to the cult of Virūpākṣa.

6. Between 1354 and 1516, all royal grants documented in the imperial capital were witnessed by Virūpākṣa. From 1516 onward, some were witnessed by Virūpākṣa and others by Viṭṭhaleśvara. Beginning in 1545, during the regency of Rāmarāya (for Sadāśiva), all of the grants were witnessed by Viṭṭhala. See Verghese (1995, appendix A), for a list and summary of the inscriptions. As mentioned in note 25 of chapter 3, Virūpākṣa apparently remained the empire's tutelary or protective deity for the empire's duration, but Viṭṭhaleśvara increasingly became a "signatory" deity on royal grants and his shrine at the capital received more attention.

7. As will be discussed in greater detail in this chapter and in chapter 5, the divisions between these two factions did not become formalized until a later period, but they do seem to have been emerging during Vyāsatīrtha's lifetime.

8. Verghese (1995, 79) discusses this 1534 inscription (*SII* 1941, vol. 9, pt. 2, no. 566) as do Filliozat and Filliozat (1988, 60). The inscription states that images of thirteen Ālvārs, including one preceptor, were installed in a special shrine within the Viṭṭhala temple and the donor of the images was a sandalwood merchant. None of the statues are in situ today.

9. See Verghese (1995, ch. 5) for an overview of construction efforts in Viṭṭhalapura in the sixteenth century.

10. For example, *SII* 1941, vol. 9, pt. 2, no. 502, Kannada; *SII* 1988, vol. 16, no. 56, Telugu; *ARIE for 1922–25* 1986, vol. 6, 711–13, Tamil (all trans. in Filliozat and Filliozat 1988, 51). The inscription recording Vyāsatīrtha's donation of an icon of Yogavaradanarasiṃha to the temple is in Sanskrit (*ARIE for 1922–25* 1986, no. 710, trans. in Filliozat and Filliozat 1988, 58).

11. According to an inscription, on May 30, 1531, a ferryman gave to the Viṭṭhala temple the revenue of the seven points of ferry service on the river. As Filliozat and Filliozat (1988, 55) point out, we know from a 1526 inscription in this temple that there were eight total points on the ferry, implying perhaps that the boatman kept the earnings made at that one point while donating the rest. This 1526 inscription is a royal decree by Kṛṣṇadevarāya proclaiming that tax revenues would be used to subsidize this ferry service for Vijayanagara residents. Verghese (2000, ch. 19) provides a helpful discussion of the likely importance of this community of boatmen (which was possibly organized into a guild) to the capital's functioning. It appears that these ferries were the only means of crossing the river in the early sixteenth century; Domingo Paes's 1520 travel narrative describes these boats in some detail and claims they are the only method used to cross the river (Paes [1900] 1995). Verghese (2000, 306–7) theorizes that the pylons of the ruined stone bridge, still visible in the river today near the city's sacred center, were likely an earlier, Saṅgama-dynasty attempt to provide an alternative method of crossing. This proved infelicitous in times of war and was therefore discontinued. Verghese also discusses a later inscription from 1556, in which three hundred such boatmen of Anegondi (the "royal village" directly across the Tungabhadra from the capital) act in unison to make a significant donation to a Śaiva temple. Finally, the boatmen's potentially high status is suggested, not only by their appearance in the 1526 royal inscription and their ability to make notable temple donations, but also by their appearance in sculptural reliefs found on slabs near one ferry gateway at Anegondi.

12. Verghese and Dieter Eigner (1998) have identified a *maṭha* with likely Mādhva affiliation in Viṭṭhalapura, although there is no explicit reference to Vyāsatīrtha. The only extant inscription from the largely destroyed structure does not mention Vyāsatīrtha. Filliozat and Filliozat also theorize that this Viṭṭhalapura building may be a Mādhva maṭha and draw attention to a carving on a pillar of a religious teacher standing before a lectern. They also

cite the inscribed name, "Śrī Surendra Vodeyaru," found on the floor of the gallery near the structure's northern entrance and hypothesize that this may be the Mādhva teacher Surendra (1988, 19), who would have been a contemporary *maṭhādhipati* to Vyāsatīrtha. Indeed, according to Sharma ([1961] 1981, 208), this Surendratīrtha and Vyāsatīrtha shared a student, Vijayīndratīrtha, and both men died in the same year (1539). Filliozat and Filliozat (1988, 24) also report another piece of evidence of the existence of a Mādhva *maṭha* in Viṭṭhalapura, namely, two copper plate inscriptions from Nanjanagudu, which they cite as appearing in "Ep Carn III 113–4, p. 203 sq." (Unfortunately, their text does not supply a full bibliographic reference or a date for the inscription.) According to Filliozat and Filliozat, these copper plates document donations of villages to Surendratīrtha of the Mādhva sect and state that this arrangement was consecrated "in a maṭha situated at the southern gate of Vijaya Viṭṭhala, at the time of the ablution of Rāma, in the presence of Rāma Viṭṭhala" (24). Filliozat and Filliozat note the interesting fusion of Rāma and Viṭṭhala, a fusion that is also found in the carvings of two Mādhva tombs located in Vijayanagara. These are discussed below.

13. *ARSIE* 1922, no. 710 (cited in Verghese 1995, 67n84; trans. in Filliozat and Filliozat 1988, 52).

14. There is a tomb or *samādhi* shrine of Vyāsatīrtha's fellow Mādhva ascetic and slightly older contemporary, Raghunandana (d. 1533), just downriver from the Viṭṭhala temple, which has a Viṭṭhala image carved into one side of it. (The religious significance of these *samādhi* shrines in the Mādhva community is discussed in the conclusion of this chapter.) Raghunandana's tomb has images of Rāma, Veṇugopāl, Viṭṭhala, and Mādhava on each of its four sides. See Verghese (1995, 54, 134, 267) for a description of this shrine and again, page 267, for its location on a map of the area. Vyāsatīrtha's *samādhi* shrine, to be discussed later in this chapter, also has prominent carvings of Viṭṭhala and Rāma.

15. As Verghese (1995, 60) points out, "Of the eighteen prominent Haridāsas, eleven have Viṭhala appended to their names for their *mudrika* (nom de plume)," suggesting that Viṭṭhala worship was a prominent feature of popular Mādhvaism. However, the extent to which these Haridāsas were explicitly affiliated with Mādhva institutions and their Brahmin leadership requires much further study, as does the influence of distinctly Mādhva teachings and sensibilities on the Haridāsa movement. As will be discussed below (under the heading "An Intersectarian Agrahāra?"), we can connect the Haridāsa singer, Purandaradāsa, who was a Brahmin, to Vyāsatīrtha, in an inscriptional record. Furthermore, as mentioned briefly in chapter 2, one of Vyāsatīrtha's gurus, Śrīpādarāja, who was *maṭhādhipati* at the Mādhva monastery in Mulbagal, was also famous for his devotional songs in Kannada. However, the connections between Vyāsatīrtha and Kanakadāsa, a śūdra devotee who composed Vaiṣṇava devotional songs in Kannada that remain very popular, are largely anecdotal. These anecdotes, which are difficult to date, suggest that historically there has been conflict over lower caste participation in Mādhva institutions, such as *maṭhas* and temples. See William J. Jackson (1998, 165–70) for a brief discussion of this feature of the legends of Kanakadāsa's life. For recent studies of the complex links between Brahminical Hinduism and various strands of the bhakti movement in the early modern period, see Jon Milton Keune (2011, 2015), Novetzke (2008, 2012), and Venkatkrishnan (2015).

16. Verghese (1995, 59ff.) discusses this. See also Filliozat and Filliozat (1988, 58).

17. Vijayanagara royals certainly used icons of deities to convey, not only their religious affiliations, but also their power and authority in a given region. One of the best examples,

discussed by Eaton and Wagoner (2014), is Kṛṣṇadevarāya's insertion of Rāmāyaṇa-themed reliefs into the gateways at the Raichur fort after his conquest of it in 1520. Images of Rāma, Lakṣmaṇa, and Hanumān are found in several of the gateways, juxtaposed with panels depicting the king himself, in what Eaton and Wagoner have called a "deliberate conflation" (308). By aligning their own iconography with that of Vijayanagara royals, sectarian leaders, too, could make political claims.

18. Filliozat and Filliozat(1988, 47) maintain that certain sculptures in the temple reflect the influence of Purandaradāsa's music. It is true that the Mādhvas have a longer history of Viṭṭhala worship than Śrīvaiṣṇavas, who seem to have been introduced to it at Hampi. However, Verghese (1995, 65ff.) counters this evidence with the fact that the Śrīvaiṣṇavas have left a much more extended monumental and inscriptional mark on the Viṭṭhalapura region of the capital. Temples dedicated to the Āḷvārs, Rāmānuja, and Śrīvaiṣṇava feeding houses and sectarian marks inscribed in Viṭṭhala temple pillars all would indicate the eventual Śrīvaiṣṇava dominance in this temple complex.

19. "A survey of the inscriptions also shows that, as far as we have evidence, the festivals and ceremonies in the temple were according to Śrī-Vaishṇava practices. We have no inscriptional data of Mādhva festivals and rituals being conducted there" (Verghese 1995, 66). Another significant Vaiṣṇava temple, the Rāmacandra temple, which was located in the royal center amid the living quarters of the king and other nobles and which is well known for its relief carvings of scenes from the Rāmāyaṇa, also seems to have been affiliated with the Śrīvaiṣṇavas. *Nāmam*s (sectarian marks) of the northern faction of the sect predominate there. There is no similar evidence to support any Mādhva affiliation. But, as discussed in chapter 2, Vyāsatīrtha took Rāmacandra as the tutelary deity of his *maṭha*s.

20. The installation of the images of Āḷvārs by one Tippisetti happened on July 22, 1534 (Filliozat and Filliozat 1988, 60). In 1543, there is further mention of the Rāmānujakūṭa, or the feeding house for Śrīvaiṣṇava pilgrims, and various lavish donations made to benefit it as well as rituals being performed in the Āḷvār shrines (68–70).

21. *SII* 1986, vol. 4, nos. 254 and 255.

22. Verghese 1995, 58–59.

23. Verghese 1995, 47.

24. Fritz, Michell, and Rao 1984, 149.

25. A. Rao 2015, 106.

26. Ibid., 100.

27. Speaking of additional Rāma temples constructed after the one dedicated to Rāmacandra in the royal center, A. Rao (2015, 106) writes,

> I would like to point out that the surrounding points—the Tuṅgabhadrā River, Mātaṅga Hill, and Mālyavanta Hill—gained special prominence in the fifteenth and sixteenth centuries as Śrīvaiṣṇava temples, heightening the mythic associations of these sites dating to pre-Vijayanagara times. Śrīvaiṣṇavas, therefore, would have been agents in the construction of the landscape of the Vijayanagara capital into a virtual theophany of Rāma. The mapping of the identification of Rāma and the Vijayanagara king with the layout of the city was not, therefore, a mere synchronic fact of the Vijayanagara world but rather the result of a collaborative project on the part of both royal and Śrīvaiṣṇava agents.

28. See Venkoba Rao's (1926, intro., xiv) discussion of this passage from the *Vyāsa Vijaya,* which he quotes at length in his edition of the *Śrīvyāsayogicaritam.*

29. Philip Lutgendorf (2007, 71) describes the icon as having "his knees braced with a cloth band such as is sometimes used by *yogis* to help support themselves" and goes on to note that "such a band is a normal feature of images of Yoga-Narasimha (a meditating image of the man-lion avatara of Vishnu, also popular among Madhvas." While I do not see that band here on the Yantrodhāraka Hanumān icon, Lutgendorf is correct that Hanumān and Yoga-Narasimha share an iconographic affinity that was likely accentuated by the Mādhvas. As already mentioned, it was a Narasimha icon of this type that Vyāsatīrtha donated to the Viṭṭhala temple.

30. The reprint of Venkoba Rao's (n.d., appendix 1, 213–14) edition of Somanātha's *Vyāsayogicarita* includes this inscription, which it states originally appeared in "*ARSIE,* 1919 B., no. 370." The English summary of the inscription supplied here is that of Srinivasa Ritti (appendix 1, 213).

31. This *praśasti* passage, translated in full in chapter 2, appears in most of Kṛṣṇadevarāya's inscriptions: "Going round and round Kanchi, Srisailam, Sonachala, Kanakasabha, Venkatadri and other places, often and in various temples and holy places, for his well-being in the present and future, did he again and again bestow in accordance with the śāstras, various great gifts like man's weight in gold, together with the other grants associated with such gifts." See also map 4 for the location of these sites.

32. *TDI,* Inscriptions of Krishnarāya's Time, vol. 3, no. 18.

33. "Considered in chronological order the first officer to make an endowment during Krishnadevarāya's reign was a general of the army, named Appa Piḷḷai son of Karavaṭṭippuli āḷvār and a resident of Uttaramērur (Mahipāla Kulakālachchēri). He had made three endowments previously during the reign of Krishna Deva's elder brother Vira-Narasimha . . . The last endowment was specially meant for the merit and welfare of Vira-Narasingaraya Maharaya. It has to be remembered here that Vira Narasingaraya had great difficulty in putting down revolts and rebellions, particularly around Kānchi and in Kongu nādu. Appa Piḷḷai was the general in charge, at any rate of the country around Kānchi. He may therefore have considered it desirable to express his loyalty to his sovereign in this manner." (Viraraghavacharya 1954, 2:637)

Viraraghavacharya then goes on to explain the grant Appa Piḷḷai made in 1511 on behalf of Kṛṣṇadevarāya, after the general and the king successfully brought those Kanchi kings under submission.

34. As noted in chapter 2, Morrison (2009) argues that sixteenth-century Vijayanagara royal initiatives to irrigate temple lands and thereby promote certain forms of agrarian production throughout the empire were actually unsustainable in many regions and privileged elite patterns of food consumption at the expense of other more easily generated crops. There were certainly symbolic resonances to imposing these royal tastes on conquered areas. But they also had practical implications. The expansion of rice cultivation to meet elite demand both decreased subsistence farming in targeted areas and increased the monetization of the Vijayanagara economy. The latter development brought varying degrees of cost and benefit to different segments of Vijayanagara society.

35. As Appadurai (1981, 73) puts it,

Specifically, it is argued that in the sociopolitical context of the period from 1350 to 1700 sectarian leaders were crucial intermediaries for the introduction, extension, and institutionalization of warrior control over constituencies and regions that might otherwise have proved refractory. This intermediary role of sectarian leaders, which rendered control by conquest into appropriate (and thus stable) rule, was effected primarily in, and through, sectarian control of the redistributive capacities of the temples. Thus sectarian leaders permitted Telugu warriors to render their military expansion culturally appropriate by "gifting" activity and its main product, temple honor.

Again, see Morrison (2009) for a more nuanced view of this redistribution and some of its imbalances and contradictions.

36. According to K. V. Raman's (1975, 137) history of the Varadarājasvāmi temple in Kanchi, there was a *maṭha* called "Veda *maṭha*," which "specialized in the teaching of the Vedas" and was "probably patronized by the Mādhvas who were also Vaishnavas but not followers of Rāmānuja." Today there is another Mādhva *maṭha* in Kanchi affiliated with the Mādhva guru Raghavendra. The historical origins of these *maṭhas* merit further exploration.

37. As discussed in chapter 2, Kṛṣṇadevarāya did give Vyāsatīrtha land grants in the Mādhva stronghold region between Mysore and Bangalore, in the wake of conquering some important forts there. He also donated land to Govindarāja, a Śrīvaiṣṇava ācārya who is identified in a 1516 inscription as "the teacher of kings," in this region, indicating that Kṛṣṇadevarāya's cultivation of a Mādhva-Śrīvaiṣṇava alliance also occasionally played out in Karnataka territory.

38. According to Viraraghavacharya (1954, 1:232ff.), this practice had begun in 1360.

39. Viraraghavacharya (1954, 1:232ff.) discusses many of these changes, which he takes up in greater depth in chapter 16 of volume 2. Appadurai (1981, 94) also discusses these changes at length, emphasizing the increased role given to non-Brahmins at the temple during Sāḷuva Narasiṃha's period:

> Sāḷuva Narasiṃha linked himself to the redistributive cycle of the Tirupati Temple and publicly established his patronage of non-Brahmin worshippers there. He did this by allocating taxes from some villages for some food offerings to the deity. He allocated the "donor's share" of the *prasātam* to the Rāmānujakūṭam that he established at Tirupati, which was to be managed by Rāmānuja Aiyaṅkār. In this case, the Rāmānujakūṭam managed by Rāmānuja Aiyaṅkār was for the benefit of non-Brahmin Śrī Vaisnavas, a group of whom were his disciples. It was the non-Brahmin constituency that benefited from the "donor's share" of the prasātam created by Sāḷuva Narasimha's endowment. Between AD 1456 and 1473, Rāmānuja Aiyaṅkār was the intermediary between this non-Brahmin constituency and the sanctified products of royal endowments, as well as endowments by other land controllers.

Appadurai also claims that Rāmānuja Aiyaṅkār gave these non-Brahmins some "important roles in temple worship and thus in temple honors" (94). Narayanan (2007, 250) agrees that the Tirupati-Tirumala temples reallocated wealth and honors in ways that increased social mobility among various castes. However, see Lester (1994) for an alternative perspective.

40. *TDI* (1935) 1984, vol. 3, nos. 70–81.

41. *TDI* (1935) 1984, vol. 3, nos. 157–59.

42. Viraraghavacharya (1953, 1:525) maintains that these Vaikhānasa Arcakas were Telugu speakers, "who never gave up their old customs and their adherence to the

Chandramanapanchangam." Yet he also writes, "It must be admitted that the Tamil speaking Tirumalai Nambi went to Tirumalai to co-operate with the Vaikhānasas in rehabilitating that place of worship and not to effect any radical changes."

43. Verghese (1995, 69) maintains that, although this region eventually became Telugu-speaking, it was in the northern reaches of Tamil country during the Vijayanagara period. As evidence of the dominance of Tamil speakers in this region, she cites the Tirupati-Tirumala inscriptions, most of which are in Tamil. This contradicts Viraraghavacharya's assessment (see above note 42) that Tamil speakers flooded the region only after the Madurai invasion and that their active role in the temples at Tirupati is what explains the dominance of Tamil in the inscriptions. I think it likely that this region in the border zone between Tamil and Telugu country had strong representation of speakers of both languages in the Vijayanagara period but that the Tamil Śrīvaiṣṇava influence at the Tirupati temples explains the heavy use of Tamil in the inscriptions.

44. "The Periyal Perumal (Mula Murti) has not at any time even to this day admitted inside the Kulaśēkharappaḍi into His sanctum any cooked food besides the four nāḷi of rice provided in 966 A.D. Fruits, flowers, and camphor harathis are the only exceptions. All food offerings, however costly they may be, have to be kept outside the Kulaśēkharappaḍi. They are all considered as Kāmyārtha offerings and therefore inferior" (Viraraghavacharya 1953, 1:523).

45. Cited in Viraraghavacharya (1953, 1:539): "A staff of competent accountants was set up in the temple and we found in 1379–80 that the Tiruninra-ur udaiyan made his debut. Ten years later in 1390 the Sthanattar as a self-constituted body came to view. Their composition is revealed in the same inscription No. 187 . . . [wherein] is found a scheme of distribution of the quarter share of the prasadams due to the donor of the gift."

46. Jīyars were often affiliated with monastic institutions and thus, their position on the temple board at Tirupati-Tirumala suggests that Śrīvaiṣṇava *mathas* had a hand in running the temple.

47. Viraraghavacharya 1953, 1:539.

48. Appadurai (1981, 47) explains temple pluralism at the Śrī Pārthasārati temple and the way different claims are managed as follows:

What holds these various "servants" together is not a simple hierarchy of functions, no single pyramid of authority, but rather 1. their shared orientation to, and dependence on, the sovereignty of the deity they serve and 2. the sheer logic of functional interdependence, without which the ritual process would break down. Even the managerial roles, such as that of trustee and the *amīnā,* are not conceived to be superordinate in any clear hierarchical way. They are authoritative only insofar as they do not disturb any one of the shares that they must orchestrate to keep the moral and economic cycle of temple ritual going. This should not imply, however, that the temple is an ill-disciplined collection of independent agents. Particular chains of command do exist, as well as particular norms that govern these chains. But these norms, which vary from temple to temple, are legitimated by a shared idea of the past, of hallowed convention, which is based on a fragile consensus. Thus changes in the social and political environment of the temple tend to fragment this delicate consensus fairly easily.

49. All of the inscriptions documenting these arrangements end with the phrase "May the Śrīvaiṣṇavas protect this (arrangement)."

50. Somanātha makes no such claim and does not mention the theft incident either. He does, however, maintain that Vyāsatīrtha visited Tirupati during the rule of Sāḷuva Narasiṃha, at whose court in Chandragiri he remained for several years.

51. Royal inscriptions were often recorded at this complex in several languages, notably Tamil, Telugu, Kannada, and, on occasion, Sanskrit (e.g., *TDI* [1935] 1984, vol. 3, nos. 31–87). However, there are also nonroyal inscriptions at this complex that are in Kannada (e.g., vol. 3, no. 91) and Telugu (vol. 3, nos. 92–95).

52. Appadurai (1981, 96–97); Viraraghavacharya (1954, 2:1055–57).

53. Appadurai (1981, 96–97); *TDI* (1935) 1984, vol. 3, nos. 143, 173, 178; Viraraghavacharya (1954, 2:1055–57).

54. TDI (1935) 1984, vol. 3, no. 159.

55. The actual prasād itself is described as follows: "15½ prasādams, 2 akkāli-maṇḍai, 26 appam, 26 atirasam, 1¼ palam of chandanam, 75 areca nuts and 150 betel leaves" (Viraraghavacharya 1954, 2:657; see also *TDI* [1935] 1984, vol. 3, no. 159).

56. "It was from the offerings made out of the income from these sources that the quarter share of the prasadams became due to the Emperor and it was this quarter share that was transferred to Vyasa Tirtha Sri Pada Udaiyar to be used in his Matham, obviously for feeding his Sishyas, although not specially so stated in the inscription" (Viraraghavacharya 1954, 2:658).

57. TDI (1935) 1984, vol. 3, no. 165.

58. Viraraghavacharya 1954, 2:659.

59. Viraraghavacharya (1954, 2:1054): "The noteworthy point about these offerings is that no portion of the donor's share was distributed to the Sri Vaishnavas, not to speak of those reciting the Prabandhams. . . . This shows that although Srī Pāda Udaiyar [i.e., Vyāsatīrtha] respected all festivals celebrated in the Temples, he did not countenance the Prabandham recital to any extent." This strong statement regarding Vyāsatīrtha's antipathy toward the *Prabandham* contradicts Viraraghavacharya's earlier analysis (2: 659).

60. All quotes from the *Tirupati Devasthanam Inscriptions* (1984, vols. 2 and 3) are the translations of Subrahmanya Sastry and Vijayaraghavacharya, respectively.

61. The inscription specifies that on top of the hill, 222 rice cakes each will be offered to Śrī Veṅkaṭeśvara and the processional deity. It then stipulates the exact amounts of the ingredients to be used in the preparation of these cakes as follows: 22 vaṭṭi plus 4 marakkāl of rice, 666 nāḷi of ghee, 22,200 palam of sugar, and 27 nāḷi of pepper. It also states that 222 palam of chandanam, 11,110 areca nuts, and 22,200 betel leaves will be offered daily at the Mādhva *maṭha's maṇḍapam*. At the bottom of the hill, 132 rice cakes (consisting of 13 vaṭṭi plus 4 marakkāl of rice, 396 nāḷi of ghee, 13,200 palam of sugar, and 16 nāḷi plus 1 uri of pepper) along with 132 palam of chandanam, 6,600 areca nuts, and 13,200 betel leaves will be distributed at the second Mādhva *maṭha's maṇḍapam*. The inscription also requests the daily preparation of eight meals consisting of 8 measures of rice; 1 āḷākku of ghee; 1 uri of green gram, salt, pepper, vegetables, and curds; 1 palam of chandanam; 20 areca nuts; and 40 betel leaves to be presented daily to Govindarājasvāmi. If Viraraghavacharya is correct that the amount of *prasād* described in inscription number 159 (*TDI* [1935] 1984, vol. 3) would feed approximately two hundred people living in Vyāsatīrtha's *maṭhas*, the amounts

here would feed far more. This attests to the extent that Vyāsatīrtha's arrangements amplified the ritual programs at this temple complex.

62. *TDI* (1935) 1984, vol. 3, no. 165.

63. "Further, we are empowered to receive the 6 prasādam out of the 8 sandhi (tiruppōnakam) offered to Śrī Govindarājan and as we have granted to you 4 prasādam daily for free distribution, these 4 prasādam shall be conducted to your maṭham. The remaining 2 prasādam we shall receive as our share."

64. *TDI* (1935) 1984, vol. 3, no. 175.

65. Viraraghavachyarya (1954, 2:660) claims that this is the oldest record in the Tirupati Devasthānam inscriptions of a village's annual cash worth. The increasing use of cash in sixteenth-century Vijayanagara society contributed to a new social dynamism that implicated religious institutions and ideology, as will be discussed more in chapters 5 and 6.

66. The inscription's editor identifies the village's district as Chittoor based upon the village's tank that Vyāsatīrtha had constructed; it is identified on map 3. Called "Vyāsasamudra," it still exists as a regional landmark and was recently the focus of a now defunct Mādhva renovation effort, which had been documented at the now broken link www.vyasasamudra.org.

67. Bettakonda is about 128 kilometers due west of Tirupati.

68. Lest the distance of 128 kilometers between the village of Bettakonda and Tirupati seem too great for there to have been any meaningful practical connection between them, it should be noted that many Vijayanagara-era inscriptions suggest that the distances between those villages whose produce was donated to support temple worship and the temples themselves could be quite significant. More research needs to be done to map these distances in order to illuminate the manner in which goods and services circulated and, thus, the precise contours of economic and social networks in this period.

69. After indicating the coordinates of the land with reference to neighboring villages and listing off the hamlets included in the gift, the inscription discusses the main village's various names as follows: "Kṛṣṇarāyapuraṃ ceti pratināmasamanvitam‖ grāmaṃ vyāsasamudrākhyaṃ beṭṭakoṇḍāparāhvayam|" (*EI* 1960, vol. 31, no. 21)

70. "Śiṣyapraśiṣyasambhogyaṃ kramād ā candratārakam" (*EI* 1960, vol. 31, no. 21, l. 63ff.). The word *agrahāra* is not used in the inscription nor is there an explicit statement regarding settlement of people. Many villages given to Brahmins did not involve relocation to those villages; the gift of villages could confer upon Brahmins discretionary use of the village's wealth from a distance. Indeed, several of the other Tirupati inscriptions cited above conform to this type of gift. However, the format of the Kamalapur plate inscriptions, particularly their reference to the Vedic education of generations of students, implies that it is to be a Brahmin settlement with the traditional Vedic educational focus.

71. Appadurai 1981, 64.

72. In fact, a few potentially Śaiva-Smārta recipients, with names such as Śṛṅgeri Lingabhaṭṭa, Basava Bhaṭṭa, and Virūpākṣa, are mentioned; such names total eight. The editor of the inscription finds it striking that Vyāsatīrtha "included scholars of every persuasion among the shareholders of the endowment" (*EI* 1960, vol. 31, no. 21, "Kamalapur Plates of Krishnadevaraya," 139).

73. Purandaradāsa's sons are here identified as Laksmaṇadāsa (*EI* 1960, vol. 31, no. 21, "Kamalapur Plates of Krishnadevaraya," l. 269), Hebaṇadāsa (l. 271), and Madhvapadāsa (l. 426).

74. As mentioned in note 15, the extent to which these Haridāsa singers were explicitly affiliated with Mādhva institutions and their Brahmin leadership requires much further study, as does the influence of distinctly Mādhva teachings and sensibilities on the Haridāsa movement.

75. See Verghese (1995, 61) for a refutation of the theory that the Viṭṭhala cult in Tirumala-Tirupati predated the Viṭṭhala cult at the Vijayanagara capital in Hampi. On the basis of the monumental evidence, she argues that the cult moved in the opposite direction.

76. Inscriptions in which Vyāsatīrtha is referred to in this way include the following: *EC* 1902, vol. 7, no. 85; TDI (1935) 1984, vol. 3, nos. 157, 158, 159, 165; *EC* 1976, vol. 5, nos. 105–6; and *ARMAD* 1942, no. 28.

77. The term *siddhānta* is a compound consisting of two words: "siddha" or "accomplished" and "anta," meaning "end" or "aim." When these meanings are taken together, the term connotes "the established position," or the correct viewpoint arrived at through systematic inquiry and reasoned argument.

78. Anegondi, located across the river from the Vijayanagara capital, seems to have been the ancestral home of powerful chieftains in the area for several generations prior to the empire's founding and to have served, therefore, as an important administrative center. It also seems to have attracted scholars, intellectuals, and religious mendicants and leaders, who took up residence in the town over the centuries and left their architectural mark on it. Subsequent to the sacking of the Vijayanagara capital in 1565 and the unraveling of the empire, members of the royal family retreated to the river's other side and took up residence there. See Natalie Tobert (2000) for a fascinating ethnohistoric interpretation of Anegondi's royal, religious, and domestic architecture down to the present day.

79. Older photographs of the island, for example, the insert in Sharma ([1961] 1981), indicate that *maṇḍapa*s were once placed in front of each *samādhi* shrine. That these tombs were considered sacred and served as a focus of worship as early as the mid-sixteenth century is attested to by Mādhva philosopher-saint Vādirāja's pilgrimage text, the *Tīrthaprabandha,* which describes this island as a *tīrtha.* During his time, there were only eight Mādhva saints' shrines on the island.

The Tulasi plant is deified by Vaiṣṇavas, who believe Tulasi to be an incarnation of Viṣṇu's consort, Lakṣmī. The Kannada term *bṛndāvana* or Sanskrit *vṛndāvana* (Hindi *vṛndāvan/bṛndāvan*) can mean a sacred grove of Tulasi plants and is also the name of the North Indian temple town where Kṛṣṇa is believed to have spent significant time.

80. If this depicted devotee is meant to represent the Vijayanagara king, it is likely Acyutarāya, who reigned during the last years of Vyāsatīrtha's life.

81. As mentioned in note 14 of this chapter, there is an additional *samādhi* shrine of Vyāsatīrtha's contemporary and fellow Mādhva leader, Raghunandana (d. 1533), located not on Navabṛndāvana Island but along the Tungabhadra, between Viṭṭhalapura and the Virūpākṣa temple complex. This shrine also has four different forms of Viṣṇu carved into it: Rāma, Veṇugopāl, Viṭṭhala, and Mādhava (Verghese 1995, 54). Clearly, Vyāsatīrtha did not work alone in promoting this collaboration with the Srīvaiṣṇavas nor in consolidating the Mādhva sect's standing at court. He must have had help from other Mādhva leaders, such as Surendratīrtha, another contemporary who seems to have resided at Vijayanagara, according to inscriptions cited in Filliozat and Filliozat (1988, 24). But given the much greater volume of inscriptional and literary records left by and about Vyāsatīrtha, as well as the

response to his writings and activities, we can surmise that his role in this effort was the most significant.

82. Hawley 2012, 31.

83. Ibid, 32.

84. According to Hawley (2012, 32), this term refers specifically to Mādhvas, but it can also refer generically to Vaiṣṇavas because "none of them follows without qualification an illusionist reading of phenomenal existence."

85. Hawley 2012, 32–33.

86. Ibid., 33.

87. As will be developed in the next chapter, the devotional overlap between different Vaiṣṇava communities did not necessarily result in shared religious doctrines. One's Vedāntin identity and one's Vaiṣṇava identity could imply different degrees of affinity and distinction.

88. Madhusūdana Sarasvatī's line-by-line response to Vyāsatīrtha's *Nyāyāmṛta* was composed in Varanasi sometime around 1550.

## 5. THE SOCIAL LIFE OF VEDĀNTA PHILOSOPHY: VYĀSATĪRTHA'S POLEMICS AGAINST VIŚIṢṬĀDVAITA VEDĀNTA

1. In this sense, Vyāsatīrtha's anti-Viśiṣṭādvaita polemics are somewhat different from the anti-Advaita polemics he exhibits in both the *Nyāyāmṛta* and the *Tātparyacandrikā*. A striking feature of Vyāsatīrtha's polemics against Advaita Vedānta and Viśiṣṭādvaita is the different manner in which he addresses the proponents of these two schools. In both his *Nyāyāmṛta* and his *Tātparyacandrikā*, Vyāsatīrtha usually introduces the Advaitins' position with the phrase "pare tu" or "anye tu," meaning "but others say." But he consistently introduces the Viśiṣṭādvaita position with the phrase "kecit tu" or "but some say." This conveys the impression that Advaitins are completely distinct in their understanding of Vedānta, whereas the Viśiṣṭādvaitins and the Dvaitins share some common ground. At the same time, however, Vyāsatīrtha uses similar styles of argument and methods of presentation against both Advaita and Viśiṣṭādvaita. These include the reductio ad absurdum technique; his tendency to historicize his opponents' doctrines while also summarizing them in ways that are suitable to his own purposes; and, finally, his attention to debates internal to his opponents' systems. But in his case against Viśiṣṭādvaita, Vyāsatīrtha tends to use these strategies to argue that Viśiṣṭādvaita premises conduce to Dvaita conclusions.

2. Of note, Dvaita never maintained an exact one-to-one correspondence between one's caste or gender identity and one's experience of *mokṣa*. Like most Hindu thinkers, Dvaitins understood caste and gender to be somewhat fluid, in that they would change over the course of an individual soul's many rebirths. In other words, while one's intellectual and spiritual aptitude could certainly be indexed to one's social identity in Dvaita, such an identity was also viewed as a temporary manifestation of one's karma. Thus, one's caste or gender status did not have the final say on one's capacity for *mokṣa*. However, Dvaita is distinct from other systems of Hindu thought in arguing for the innate capacity of souls to achieve certain soteriological ends (i.e., for the soul's predestination). Thus, there are potentially greater eternal implications to one's caste or gender identity in Dvaita than in other traditions of Hindu thought. See Sarma (2005) for a discussion of some of this complexity in Madhva's writings.

3. The example he resorts to most often is Prayag, not Varanasi, contrary to what one might expect.

4. The *bhakti* of hatred is an idea that is presented in various Purāṇic narratives (as well as in epic episodes that were likely inserted some time during the post-Epic Purāṇic period), wherein enemies of God are revealed, at the moment of their deaths, actually to have been devotees. Examples include Rāvaṇa's death scene in Kamban's Tamil *Rāmāyaṇa* and Pūtana's death in the *Bhāgavata Purāṇa*. Both of these adversaries of the divine are rewarded at death for their single-minded fixation upon the deity, even if that fixation was negative.

5. See Ganeri (2014, 252) for a discussion of this in Rāmānuja's thought. Vyāsatīrtha discusses the soul's ability to choose a body in *mokṣa* in the fourth *pariccheda* of the *Nyāyāmṛta* (Vyāsatīrtha 1996, 3:712–13).

6. Again, souls' spiritual hierarchies and their worldly hierarchical arrangement do not always correspond exactly in Dvaita thought, although some indexing between the two is definitely implied. See note 2 above.

7. Mumme (1988) and S. Raman (2007) both argue this, while acknowledging that important distinctions in emphasis and interpretation between northern and southern factions existed in earlier periods.

8. See Sarma (1997) for an overview of places where Vyāsatīrtha discusses the issue of *adhikāra* in relation to the study of the Vedas and *Brahma Sūtra*s to learn about Brahman, *ātman*, and *mokṣa*. See also Vyāsatīrtha's discussion in the *apaśūdrādhikaraṇam* of his *Tātparyacandrikā* (1.3.9) (Vyāsatīrtha 2000, 2:484ff.) for a discussion of *śūdra*s' *adhikāra* to learn of Brahman's nature from certain *smṛti* literature.

9. "Antye 'pi kiṃ muktajīveśayor atāratamyam? Kiṃ vā muktajīvānām eva? Nādyaḥ, tvan mate 'pi tayor vibhutvānutvaśeṣatvasvātantryapāratantryādinā tāratamyāt| anekeśvarāpattyā jagat pravṛttyayogāc ca|" (Vyāsatīrtha 1996, 3:704).

10. "Na dvitīyaḥ, tvan mate 'pi jīvān prati śeṣiṇo 'pi lakṣmītattvāt tān prati niyāmakād viṣvaksenāditaś cetarajīvānām nikṛṣṭatvāt|" (Vyāsatīrtha 2000, 2:705).

11. Carman 1974, 242.

12. *Upaniṣads* 1996, 181.

13. Ibid., 63.

14. Vyāsatīrtha also quotes more partisan sources than the *Upaniṣads* in his defense of Madhva's doctrine of a hierarchy of souls that persists into the state of liberation. For instance, he also quotes a *śruti* text that is embedded in a *smṛti* text cited by Madhva in his *Viṣṇutattvanirṇaya*: "A *śruti* says that 'beginning with kings and ending with Caturmukha Brahmā, liberated souls in the midst of bliss, [experience] one hundred times all the qualities in that bliss in relative hierarchy [to one another].' Oh, great sage, even among thousands of liberated souls who have accomplished reaching Nārāyaṇa, true tranquility is very rare." (Nṛpādyāḥ śatadhṛtyantā muktigā uttarottaram| sarvair guṇaiḥ śataguṇā modanta iti hi śrutiḥ|| muktānām api siddhānāṃ nārāyaṇaparāyaṇaḥ| sudurlabhaḥ praśāntātmā koṭiśv api mahāmune|| ityādi smṛtibhiḥ [Vyāsatīrtha 1996 3:705].) According to Mesquita (2008, 262), this is one of Madhva's untraceable quotes, which Madhva was criticized for using by other Vedāntin exegetes. For further discussion of this, see this chapter's penultimate section on concordance.

15. "Caturmukhāder itarebhya utkarṣasya dṛṣṭenādṛṣṭena vā āgantukahetunā sādhyatve tatrāpi hetvantarānveṣaṇe 'navasthāpattyā 'nādiyogyatāhaṭhāparaparyāyasvabhāvo hetur vācya ityādiyuktyā ca tāratamyasvabhāvatvāt|" (Vyāsatīrtha 1996, 3:711).

16. Mumme (1998, 63) discusses this view in terms of the fourteenth-century Viśiṣṭādvaitin Vedānta Deśika's interpretation. She maintains that Vedānta Deśika does acknowledge that different souls have different capacities but these are due to karma and are not caused by God's partiality:

> [Vedānta Deśika] also points out that the Lord is not being cruel or partial in granting various degrees of ability and knowledge, in presenting various kinds of sense objects to spark the soul's desire, or in giving permission even to harmful activities. In all these instances, the Lord is acting in accord with the soul's past karma and present effort; thus He maintains his egalitarianism (*sāmya*): "The unequal distribution of limbs, ability, knowledge, desire, etc.; the lack of prevention of harmful activity; and the permission which promotes the arising of sin—since all these are conditioned by differences in previous karma, they do not bring cruelty or partiality to the Lord.

As B. N. K. Sharma (1991, 454) puts it, "Rāmānuja in his theory of selves is inclined to put down the difference among the different classes of souls such as gods and human beings as the outcome of Karma and other Prākṛtic accretions and therefore not touching their essence, which he regards as equal in all, though there is numerical distinction."

17. "Svarūpasukhānāṃ pratyekam ekatvenāṇutvena ca saṃkhyāparimāṇakṛtavaiṣamyābhāve 'pi jalasudhāpānasukhayor iva madhuramudharataratvādivatsvarūpakṛtavaiṣamyaṃ yuktam|" (Vyāsatīrtha 1996, 3:705).

18. Vyāsatīrtha (1996, 3:705) summarizes this view as follows: "The bliss that is of the very nature of the *jīva* (*jīvasvarūpānanda*) is hierarchically arranged relative to the bliss of other *jīva*s, all of whom belong to the same category by virtue of the fact that they share the state of having a bliss that depends upon another (i.e., Brahman, who is the sole independent reality). This is because of the fact that the bliss of the *jīva* [in liberation] is similar to its bliss in the worldly realm [which is hierarchically arranged]." (Jīvasvarūpānandaḥ paratantrānandatvasākṣād vyāpyadharmeṇa sajātīyānandapratiyogikatāratamyavān, jīvānandatvāt, tadīyavaiṣayikānandavat|)

19. "Prakṛtibandhanivṛttiḥ, svasajātīyabandhanivṛttyāśrayapratiyogikatāratamyavanniṣṭhā, bandhanivṛttitvāt, nigaḍabandhanivṛttivad ityādy anumānaiś ca virodhāc ca|" (Vyāsatīrtha 1996, 3:705)

20. "Sātiśayatve 'pi nityatvaṃ ceśvarād apakṛṣṭatva iva muktāntareṇa sāmya iva ca śrutyādibalād yuktam| anyathotkarṣasyāpy anityatvavyāptyā brahmānando 'py anityaḥ syāt|" (Vyāsatīrtha 1996, 3:711).

21. Na ca dveṣerṣyādiprasaṅgaḥ:

> Niḥśeṣagatadoṣāṇāṃ bahubhir janmabhiḥ punaḥ|
> Syād āparokṣyam hi harer dveṣerṣyādi tataḥ kutaḥ||
> Bhaveyur yadi cerṣyādyāḥ sameṣvapi kuto na te|
> Tapyamānāḥ samān dṛṣṭvā dveṣerṣyādiyutā api||
> Dṛśyante bahavo loke doṣā evātra kāraṇam|
> Yadi nirdoṣa[tāta]taivātra kimādhikyena dūṣyate|| ity ukteḥ| (Vyāsatīrtha 1996, 3:711).

I have not translated this passage in full above; it continues along the following lines: "Many faults are evident in this world; if faultlessness alone is the cause [of *mokṣa*], how much more will our current reality become corrupted [if liberated beings were to have these feelings]?" It is a quote that I have, so far, been unable to trace, but I suspect it is from the fifteenth-century Mādhva Viṣṇudāsācārya, whom Vyāsatīrtha sometimes quotes and frequently paraphrases.

22. As will be discussed below, Vyāsatīrtha uses the examples of death in Prayāg as a very easy means to *mokṣa* and hatred of God as a form of *bhakti* as a somewhat unwholesome one.

23. "Api ca "muktasukhaṃ parasparaṃ tāratamyavat, parasparaṃ tāratamyavat-sādhanasādhyatvāt sammatavat|" na cāsiddhiḥ muktiḥ prayāgamaraṇabhagavad-dveṣabhaktyādinā jñānakarmasamuccayena vā sādhyeti mate prayāgamaraṇādīnāṃ varṇāśramakarmaṇāṃ ca viṣamatvāt|" (Vyāsatīrtha 1996, 3:707).

24. "Yasta āśiṣa āśāste na sa bhṛtyaḥ sa vai vaṇik|
sa vai bhṛtyaḥ sa vai svāmī guṇalubdhau na kāmukau||
mumukṣor amumukṣus tu varo hy ekāntabhaktimān|" (*Bhāgavata Purāṇa* 7.10.4) (Vyāsatīrtha 1996, 3:707).

25. The *smṛti* quote is from chapter 3 of the *Bhāgavata Purāṇa*, the section where the sage Kapila addresses his parents on devotion: "Ityādismṛtyā mumukṣubhaktād amumukṣor nirupādhikabhaktasyādhikyokteś ca| tatrādhikyasya lokarītisiddhatvāc ca| bhaktiḥ siddher garīyasītyādismṛtyā 'lpabhaktisādhyamuktito 'dhikamuktihetubhakter ādhikyokteś ca|" (Vyāsatīrtha 1996, 3:707).

26. *Bhagavadgītā* 13.25. Following is Barbara Stoler Miller's (*Bhagavadgītā* 1986, 118) (more elegant) translation: "Others, despite their ignorance, revere what they hear from other men; they too cross beyond death, intent on what they hear."

27. *Bhagavadgītā* 9.32–33. Miller's (*Bhagavadgītā* 1986, 87) translation: "If they rely on me, Arjuna, even women, commoners, people of low rank, even men born in the womb of evil reach the highest way. How easy is it then for holy priests and devoted royal sages?"

Anye tv evam ajānantaḥ śrutvānyebhya upāsate|
Te 'pi cātitaranty eva mṛtyuṃ śrutiparāyaṇāḥ|
ity atrāpi śabdena, striyo vaiśyās tathā śūdrās te 'pi yānti parāṃ gatim| kiṃ punar brāhmaṇāḥ puṇyā ity atra kaimutyena sādhanatāratamyena sādhye tatpratīteś ca| (Vyāsatīrtha 1996, 3:708).

28. Vyāsatīrtha (1996, 3:708) also quotes passages from the *Brahma Purāṇa* and the *Mahābhārata* to make his point and reminds us that these texts only support what the *Taittarīya Upaniṣad*, quoted at the outset of his chapter, has said about states of bliss in liberation:

And because it is stated in the *Brahma Purāṇa*, with regard to the goal [of *mokṣa*] as being [shaped by] a hierarchy of methods: "And they obtain the best goal through the highest means" and [a similar idea is expressed] in the *Mokṣadharma* [section of the *Mahābhārata*], where it says "your knowledge is better so your departure is better." Thus, Brahmā and other beings are learned in that very order as has been stated in the *Ānanda Śruti*. (*Ānanda Śruti* is Madhva's name for the *Taittarīya* Upaniṣad.)

(Sādhanasyottamatvena sādhyaṃ cottamam āpnuyuḥ|" iti brāhme, "adhikaṃ tava vijñānam adhikā ca gatis tava| brahmādayaḥ kramenaiva yathānandaśrutau śrutāḥ" iti mokṣadharme ca sādhanatāratamyena sādhye taduktes ca|)

29. Raman (2007: 13ff.) has argued that this characterization of the division within the Śrīvaiṣṇava community as one between Sanskrit and Tamil is inaccurate and ignores the existence of an ample literature in Maṇipravālam that fused the two languages. When I refer to the "Sanskritic" branch or faction, I am referring, narrowly, to those Śrīvaiṣṇavas who advocated Vedic recitation in temple liturgy as opposed to the Tamil *Prabandham*. This was in dispute, at "megatemples" like Tirupati, during Vyāsatīrtha's lifetime as was discussed in chapter 4.

30. "Tvadrītyā pratyekaṃ mokṣahetvor nirantaracintābharanyāsarūpayor bhaktiprapattayoḥ svarūpataḥ karmāpekṣānapekṣābhyām āvṛttyānāvṛttibhyāṃ ca viṣamatvāc ca|" (Vyāsatīrtha 1996, 3:708).

31. "Na ca tayor uktarītyādhikālpatve 'pi viśvāsālpatvādhikyābhyāṃ sāmyam iti vācyam| viśvāsasyāvartanīyāyāṃ bhaktāv eva yāvad āvṛttyapekṣitatvenānāvartanīyaprapattito 'dhikatvāt|" (Vyāsatīrtha 1996, 3:708).

32. Vyāsatīrtha (1996 3:708) states, "And if, for the sake of establishing parity in the sādhanas or the means to *mokṣa*, you imagine that there is greater faith in the practice of *prapatti* [than in the practice of *bhakti*] so that there is parity in the result [of the two kinds of practice], your argument will contain the flaw of mutual dependence." (Yadi ca phalasāmyena sādhanasāmyārthaṃ prapattāv adhikaviśvāsaḥ kalpyeta, tarhy anyonyāśrayaḥ|.)

33. "Sādhanavaiṣamye 'pi sādhyasāmye cādhikavidhātryāḥ śruter anupādeyatvaṃ phaladātur īśvarasya vaiṣamyādikaṃ ca syāt|" (Vyāsatīrtha (1996, 3:708).

34. "Na ca devamanuṣyādīnāṃ tatra śaktyaśaktimātreṇa śaktāśaktānuṣṭhita nityakarmaṇa iva na phalavaiṣamyam iti vācyam| aśaktārjitasya jñānasyāndhapaṅgvādikṛtakāmyakarmaṇa iva vikalatvena kāmyamokṣasādhanatvāyogena tatsādhanatvāya svocitamuktiphalam pratyavikalatāyā vaktavyatvāt|" (Vyāsatīrtha (1996 3:708).

35. "Etena bhaktiprapattyor viṣamatve 'pi śaktāśaktaviṣayatvāt phalasāmyam iti nirastam, tathā 'śravaṇāt| kalpane cātiprasaṅgāt| tasmāt sādhanatāratamyān muktitāratamyam|" (Vyāsatīrtha (1996 3:708).

36. Translation in Fort (1998, 100).

37. Fort 1998, 79.

38. *Chāndogya Upaniṣad* 6.14.2, dialogue between Uddālakka and Śvetaketu in the section on the need for a teacher.

39. "Kiṃ ca "tasya tāvad eva ciraṃ yāvan na vimokṣye 'tha sampatsyata" ityādi śrutyā "tasya kāryam na vidyata" ityādismṛtyā ca yasya sthitaprajñasya mokṣāya kartavyāntarābhāva uktas tasyāparokṣajñānino bhaktasya prapannasya vā śukāder nityādikarmabrahmadhyānādikam" (Vyāsatīrtha 1996, 3:709). The quote from the *Bhagavadgītā* is Miller's translation (1986).

40. "Ca na tāvad ajñasyaiva vividiṣādidvārā vā pāpakṣayādidvārā vā, pratyavāyaparihāradvārā vā jñānādeḥ sannipatyāṅgam, tasya siddhatvāt|" (Vyāsatīrtha 1996, 3:709).

41. Vyāsatīrtha (1996, 3:709) writes, "Nor can you argue that such activities help bring about the result [of *mokṣa* for the *sthitaprajña*]. Because that would force you to adopt the

position that karma and *jñāna* are equally important for the attainment of *mokṣa*." (Nāpi phalopakāryaṅgam, muktau jñānakarmaṇoḥ samuccayāpātāt|) For a discussion of the role of rituals in the Śrīvaiṣṇava ascetic *mumukṣu*'s life, see Yādava Prakāśa's (1995, 37) *Yatidharmasamuccaya*, 1.22–25.

42. "Karmaṇāṃ vicitratvena mokṣavaicitryāpātāc ca|" (Vyāsatīrtha 1996, 3:709).

43. "Mokṣāya kartavyānatarābhāvaparoktaśrutyādivirodhāc ca| Nāpi phalāntarārtham, nityatvāt, jñānino 'niṣṭatvāc ca|" (Vyāsatīrtha 1996, 3:709).

44. "Nāpi lokasaṃgrahārtham īśvarājñāpālanārthaṃ vā, tayor api svato 'phalatvāt| nāpīśvaraprītyartham, bhaktyādinaiva mokṣahetuprīteḥ siddheḥ| nāpi tatprītyatiśayārtham, phalātiśayābhāve tasya pāribhāṣikatvāpātāt, tadvaiyarthyāc ca|" (Vyāsatīrtha 1996, 3:709).

45. Nāpīśvaravallīlārtham,  ācāryād  vidyām  avāpyaitam  ātmānam  abhigamya śānto  bhaved  dānto  bhavet  paśyann  apīmam  ātmānaṃ  kuryāt  karmāvicārayann ityādināparokṣajñāninaḥ,

> Matkarmakṛn matparamo madbhaktaḥ saṅgavarjitaḥ|
> Manmanā bhava madbhakto madyājī māṃ namaskuru||
> Ityādinā bhaktiprapattimataś ca tadvidhānāt| (Vyāsatīrtha 1996, 3:709)

I have not translated the entire passage above. It continues, "This follows from the textual connection [of certain stories with injunctions to perform certain acts]" (*Brahma Sūtra* 3.4.24) and in places like these two Gītā verses: "[May you become one] whose mind is committed to me, devoted to me, whose rituals are offered to me, may you surrender to me. [Acting only for me, intent on me, free from attachment, hostile to no creature, Arjuna, a man of devotion comes to me]" (*Bhagavadgītā* [11.55] 1986, 109). For Madhva's comments on *Brahma Sūtra* 3.4.24, see B. N. K. Sharma (1986, 3:518): "Sūtra 24 points out that it is only by adopting this threefold standpoint of *adhikaribhedād vyavasthā* that a proper reconciliation can be arrived at between texts that seem to be mandatory in respect of good and bad alike and others that throw the choice open to the doer to do as he pleases."

46. *Bhagavadgītā* 1986, 94.

47. See verse 65 of Vedānta Deśika's *Śatadūṣaṇī*: "There are statements that are not found in any of the agreed upon *śruti* and *smṛti* texts. Some sinful people, in the interests of their own system of thought which conforms to their behaviour, interpolate these statements, claiming to have read them in Purāṇas that are unknown, lost, or whose beginnings and ends are not easily determined. Learned people who are steeped in the study of the available *śruti*s, etc. (*pratyakṣaśrutyādi*) can nowhere ascertain these statements." (Yāni cānyāni vākyāni sampratipannaśrutismṛtiṣv adṛśyamānāni svācārānurūpamataparicaryayā keṣucid aprasiddheṣu vā nāṣṭakośeṣu vānirūpitamūlāgreṣu vā purāṇeṣu prakṣipya paṭhanti pāpiṣṭhāḥ, tāni pratyakṣaśrutyādipariśīlanaśālinīṣu gariṣṭhagoṣṭhīṣu nāvakāśaṃ labhante.) (Qtd. in Mesquita 2000, 27–28; my translation follows Mesquita's.) See also Appayya Dīkṣita's *Madhvatantramukhamardana*, or *Crushing the Face of Madhva's Philosophy*, which claims that Madhva invents fake texts, poses as an *avatāra* of Vāyu, concocts original readings of the Veda, and in the process, transgresses the very boundaries (*maryāda*) of *vaidikatva*, "what is Vedic" (vv. 2–3; qtd. in Mesquita 2000, 30).

48. "Il est de fait qu'aucun des textes sur lesquels repose la hiérarchie des deva ne nous est connu. La multiplicité des références concordantes ne prouve pas l'existence d'une tradition qui ne nous est donnée que par Madhva" (Siauve 1971, 13).

49. "Paramasāmyaśrutis tu duḥkhābhāvasatyakāmatvādinā saraḥsāgarayor iva svayogyānandapūrtyā ca sāmyāt|" (Vyāsatīrtha 1996, 3:710).

50. "Liṅgabhedaḥ parānando duḥkhābhāvaḥ samānatā" iti smṛteḥ| anyathā muktasyeśvaravajjagatsraṣṭṛtvādi kiṃ na syāt|" (Vyāsatīrtha 1996, 3:710).

51. Madhva's (1971) clearest statement on this is in his *Viṣṇutattvavinirṇaya* verse 3, where he quotes a statement reputedly from the *Brahmāṇḍa Purāṇa* to argue for this parity of certain *smṛti* texts with *śruti*: "The right scriptures consist of the four Vedas beginning with the *Ṛgveda*, the *Bhārata*, the whole of the *Pañcarātrāgama*, the original *Rāmāyaṇa*, the *Purāṇa*s corroborating these and all other works that follow these. Texts other than these are bad testimonies and through the latter Janārdana cannot be known."

52. "Tac ca 'jagadvyāpāravarjam' iti sūtre tvayāpi niṣiddham, atra jagadvyāpāraśabda upalakṣaṇārtha iti tavāpi sammatam|" (Vyāsatīrtha 1996, 3:710).

53. "Anyathā muktasya svātantryādy api syāt|" (Vyāsatīrtha 1996, 3:710). He specifically compares the Dvaita and the Viśiṣṭādvaita interpretations of the *Brahma Sūtras* as follows:

In our system, the word "sāmya" or "equivalent/identical" only refers to a general type of "bhoga" or "enjoyment" due to the word "mātra" in the *sūtra*. It does not refer to the specific form of that *bhoga* [as experienced by Brahman.] And even in your system of thought, the word *mātra* is taken in the sense of "restriction" and not in the sense of "all" because of the fact that [*Brahma Sūtra* 1.4.17] has been commented upon [by Rāmānuja] as meaning "only Brahman is capable of creating, maintaining and destroying the world." This is because the mark of equality to Brahman for the liberated soul is *only* in terms of "bhoga" [and not in the sense of being like Brahman in all ways and therefore possessing all of His powers.] (Bhogamātrasāmyaliṅgācceti sūtrasthamātraśabdasya tu manmate bhogasāmānya eva sāmyam, na tu tadviśeṣa ityarthaḥ| Tvanmate 'pi bhogamātre muktasya brahmasāmyāl liṅgāj jagadvyāpāravarjam iti vyākhyātatvād avadhāraṇārtho mātraśabdo na kārtsnyārthaḥ|)

54. "Satyakāmatvaṃ ca jagatsṛṣṭṛtvādāv ivādhikānande 'pi kāmasyaivābhāvād yuktam|" (Vyāsatīrtha 1996, 3:710).

55. See Mesquita (1997, 2000). Fisher (2013, ch. 3) acknowledges that this practice became more commonplace by the seventeenth century, but there was also extensive debate about its suitability.

56. "Vārāhe ca: Svādhikānandasamprāptau sṛṣṭyādivyāpṛtiṣv api| Muktatānāṃ naiva kāmaḥ syād anyān kāmāṃstu bhuñjate|| iti" (Vyāsatīrtha 1996, 3:710). According to Mesquita (2008, 322), this is an untraceable quote. A notable feature of this portion of the *Nyāyāmṛta* is that Vyāsatīrtha quotes many more such untraceable sources here than elsewhere.

57. Vyāsatīrtha (2000, 2:484ff.) also argues, in the "apaśūdrādhikaraṇam" of his *Tātparyacandrikā* (I, 3), against the Viśiṣṭādvaita view that śūdras cannot achieve liberation through knowledge of Brahman but only through *prapatti* or surrender. Vyāsatīrtha maintains that śūdras *can* acquire some knowledge by studying ancillary sacred literature such as Itihāsa and Purāṇa, though not the Vedic texts.

58. The inscriptions are discussed in chapters 2 and 4, respectively. For more on the boatmen inscriptions, see Verghese (2000, 19).

59. Changing social status as a result of increased economic importance was fairly widespread in fifteenth- and sixteenth-century Vijayanagara society. According to Eaton (2005, 85), weavers' economic significance won them "the right to ride palanquins and blow conch shells on ritual occasions." See also Ramaswamy (1985) for a discussion of other changes in sumptuary laws that were prompted by upward mobility in this period. These included smiths being allowed to bear insignia, play musical instruments, and plaster their homes.

60. Of course, such forms of religious, ethnic, and cultural diversity elicited similar responses in India prior to the sixteenth century as well. Finbar Flood's (2009, 4) research on transcultural communication and transregional material exchanges in North India's premodern period is eloquent on the importance of recognizing the role played by such forms of contact in identity formation: "Recent research has in fact highlighted the importance of frontier contacts for the formation or consolidation of ethnic identities in premodern South Asia, a reminder that, rather than being opposed to identity, difference may in fact be central to its construction. The historical formation and transformation of identity through such encounters also underlines that difference was not a constant (except perhaps in the rarefied world of normative rhetoric) but rather was dynamic in its emphases, contingent in its expression, and variable in its meaning."

61. See Eaton (2005, chs. 4 and 5) for a discussion of how militarism enabled social mobility in the sixteenth-century Deccan Plateau.

62. O'Hanlon (esp. 2013 but also 2012) has written extensively on Brahminical explorations of identity in the early modern period (which she tends to date to the seventeenth and eighteenth centuries) and the links of such exploration to broader social changes.

63. Clayton (2006, 58ff.).

## 6. HINDU, ECUMENICAL, SECTARIAN: RELIGION AND THE VIJAYANAGARA COURT

1. As discussed in earlier chapters, Śrīvaiṣṇavism has a tradition of prominent, highly venerated householder *ācārya*s, in addition to monastic leaders. Similarly, in Mādhva and Smārta communities, *maṭha*s were often affiliated with *agrahāra*s or communities of Brahmin families, members of which often held explicit positions of power, such as that of revenue collector, in the state administration. These other forms of authority within a given religious community likely led to power-sharing arrangements of various kinds; in other words, the *maṭha*'s power was nowhere absolute.

2. That is, up until the blatant Vaiṣṇava chauvinism of Rāmarāya's regency. Of course, as has been noted elsewhere in this book, there are inscriptional references implying that Vijayanagara kings had gurus; in Kṛṣṇadevarāya's case, one Śrīvaiṣṇava teacher, Govindarāja, is referred to in a royal edict as the "teacher of kings" and as "one's own guru." But Vyāsatīrtha is also addressed as guru in at least one royal inscription of Kṛṣṇadevarāya. See note 21, chapter 1 for sources and further discussion.

3. Most royal patronage of Jainism took place in the first dynasty or the Saṅgama period (Verghese 1995, 121). The early fifteenth-century court seems to have actively supported Islam, a fact made evident in Ahmad Khan's having dedicated the founding of a mosque in the capital city to his patron Devarāya II (Verghese 1995, 126).

4. A. Rao 2015.

5. Clayton 2006, 4.

6. Griffiths 1999.

7. Fritz, Michell, and M.S. Nagaraja Rao (1984); Verghese (1995); Eaton and Wagoner (2014), A. Rao (2015).

8. In the Tuḷuva dynasty under discussion here, Vaiṣṇava emblems in general and Rāmāyaṇa motifs in particular were important to royal self-presentation. This is evident in the placement of Narasiṃha icons at the capital's gateways; the recording of royal patronage acts that took place before Viṭṭhala as a witness; the identification of the Vijayanagara king with the epic hero Rāma during the public festival of Mahānavamī; and the placement of images of Rāma, Hanumān, Sītā, and Lakṣmaṇa in proximity to images of the king, not only in the royal capital, but in conquered forts like Raichur. (See ch. 4 for further discussion of all these examples.) Furthermore, by aligning their own iconography with that of Vijayanagara royals, *maṭhas* and *maṭhādhipatis* could also make political claims. This iconographic isomorphism was a key means of sectarian self-promotion. It was also one that was likely encouraged by the court, which relied on *maṭhas* to function as outposts of the empire in conquered regions. Examples of this, discussed in chapters 2 and 4, can be seen in Vyāsatīrtha's taking of Rāmacandra as the tutelary deity of his *maṭhas*; the appearance of Rāma and other Vaiṣṇava iconography on sixteenth-century Mādhva saints' tombs; and Mādhva installation of Narasiṃha and Hanumān icons, both within and beyond the sixteenth-century capital.

9. Morrison 2009.

10. I am thinking here of the empire's placement of *maṭhas* in refractory regions as well as of events in the *Vyāsayogicarita,* such as when Vyāsatīrtha is almost attacked but is then assisted by forest dwellers (Venkoba Rao 1926, 57). The interactions between *maṭhādhipatis* and different types of people living under Vijayanagara rule must have been highly variable, as they were contingent upon specific local circumstances. See Morrison (2009) for a study of the various ways different social and regional groups were affected by and responded to Vijayanagara rule.

11. See, for example, Rao, Shulman, and Subrahmanyam (2001).

12. For a nuanced discussion of the problems of defining early modernity in European history and the varied, vague scholarly uses of the term, see Randolph Starn's (2002) review essay. The following line hints at some of the problems Starn identifies: "Early, partly, sometimes, maybe modern, early modernity is a period for our period's discomfort about periodization"(296). Starn also notes that one of the purposes served by the term *early modern* in European history is to reinvigorate the study of the time period previously—and unappealingly— thought of as "late medieval." I would argue that this is partly what is at work in South Asian historical studies' relatively recent embrace of this term. However, I would also agree with the growing number of South Asia scholars (e.g., Rao, Shulman, and Subrahmanyam 2001; O'Hanlon 2013), who argue that it is important to look for modernity in other parts of the world besides Europe and, as O'Hanlon suggests, to identify how those non-European modernities may in fact have influenced processes of modernization in the West.

13. One example of this, discussed in chapter 3, is Kṛṣṇadevarāya's inclusion of an image of himself worshipping a Śivalingam in his newly established Kṛṣṇa temple, not far from the

temple to the empire's long-standing tutelary Śaiva deity, Virūpākṣa, in the capital's sacred center.

14. Finbar Flood 2009; Talbot 1995, 2001.

15. I agree with Talbot (1995, 2001) here, but there are additional strategies that seem to have emerged in the Vijayanagara period that suggest a much broader engagement with history to construct contemporary identity. These strategies would include sectarian institutions' use of *guru–paramparā* texts and religious biographies to document their histories. See also my discussion in chapter 2 of Rao, Shulman, and Subrahmanyam's arguments about the rise of historical consciousness in the sixteenth century as documented in *caritra* literature. Further, as Talbot herself argues and as is discussed in greater detail below, these engagements with the past as a way of dealing with the present unfolded under highly contingent circumstances; therefore, any study of them must be attentive to the particulars of the time period in question.

16. See N. A. Nikan and Richard McKeon's edition of *Aśoka* (1958) for the text of Aśoka's proclamations. See also Sen (2005) for a discussion of Aśoka's governing philosophy as a harbinger of a distinctly Indian form of "secularism." *Dhamma* is the Prakrit form of the Sanskrit term *dharma*. Both terms have a broad semantic range that includes (but is not limited to) Hindu, Buddhist, and Jain religious observances, generic righteousness, individual ethical obligations, and the connections between sacred and worldly traditions. When we speak of Aśoka's *dhamma*, we are speaking of his version of Buddhist ethics-cum-political philosophy as promulgated in his rock edicts and pillar inscriptions.

17. Bhaṭṭa 2005, 16.

18. Citing Kalhana in his edition of *Āgamaḍambara or Much Ado about Religion* (Bhaṭṭa 2005, 17), Csaba Dezső writes, "[King Śankaravarman] also deprived the temples of the profits they had from the sale of various articles of worship; simply 'plundered,' as Kalhana puts it, sixty-four temples through special 'supervising' officers; resumed under direct state management villages held as land grants by the temples; and, by manipulating the weight in the scales, cheated the temple-corporations, reducing the allotment assigned as compensation for the villages."

19. Sears (2014, 42–3) writes, "The gurus featured in the inscriptions of the Mattamayūras appear as active participants in their transactions with royal patrons, and they fully used those transactions as opportunities to increase their material resources and to renegotiate their social position within the structure of a newly burgeoning state."

20. Sears 2014, 226.

21. The full quote is as follows: "The Guru imbued the king through the ceremonies of initiation and consecration, with the numinous power of Śivahood in the exercise of his sovereignty" (Sanderson 2009, 260).

22. This is Sanderson's (2009) overall argument, but he introduces it explicitly on page 43. His discussion of the relationship between Śaiva *gurus* and royal courts spans not only the fifth to thirteenth centuries but also many different regions of the subcontinent and includes discussions of kingdoms in Kashmir, the Kalachuri rulers of what is now Uttar Pradesh, Madhya Pradesh and Rajasthan, the Tamil Coḷas, and the Kākatīyas in Andhra.

**Primary Sources: Indian Literary and Philosophical Texts (Selected)**

Appayya Dīkṣita. n.d. *Madhvatantramukhamardana.* Edited by P. Ramanathadiksita. Banaras: Chowkhamba Book Bhavan.

Aśoka. 1958. *The Edicts of Aśoka.* Translated and edited by N. A. Nikam and Richard McKeon. Chicago: University of Chicago Press.

*Bhagavadgītā.* 1986. Translated by Barbara Stoler Miller as *The Bhagavadgītā: Krishna's Counsel in Time of War.* New York: Bantam Classics.

Bhaṭṭa Jayanta. 2005. *Āgamaḍambara or Much Ado about Religion.* Edited and translated by Csaba Dezső. New York: New York University Press.

Kṛṣṇadevarāya. 2004. "Rājanīti." In *Āmuktamālyada.* Translated by V. N. Rao, David Shulman, and Sanjay Subrahmanyam in "A New Imperial Idiom in the Sixteenth Century: Krishnadevaraya and His Political Theory of Vijayanagara." In *South Indian Horizons: Felicitation Volume for Francois Gro,* edited by Jean-Luc Chevillard and Eva Wilden. Pondicherry: Institut français de Pondichéry, Ecole française d'Extrême-Orient.

[Mādhava?]. 1914. *The Sarva-Darśana-Saṁgraha or Review of the Different Systems of Hindu Philosophy by Mādhava Āchārya.* Translated by E. B. Cowell and A. E. Gough. London: Kegan Paul, Trench, Trubner.

Madhusūdana Sarasvatī. 1990. *The Advaitasiddhi.* Translated by Ganganath Jha. 2nd ed. New Delhi: Sri Satguru Publications.

Madhva. 1969. *Anuvyākhyāna, Sadācārasmṛti, Tantrasārasaṅgraha, Viṣṇutattvavinirnaya, Yatipraṇavakalpa.* In *Sarvamūlagranthāḥ* [collected works]. Edited by Bannanje Govindacharya. Bangalore: Akhila Bharata Madhwa Mahamandala.

———. 1969–71. *Daśaprakaraṇāni.* Edited by P. P. Laksminarayana Upadhyaya. 4 vols. Bangalore: Poornpaprajna Vidyapeetha.

———. 1971. *Viṣṇutattvavinirṇaya*. Translated by S. S. Raghavachar. 2nd ed. Mangalore: Sharada Press.

———. 1989. *Brahmasūtrānuvyākhyānam*. Edited by K. T. Pandurangi. Bangalore: Prabha Printing House.

———. 1991. *Viṣṇutattvavinirṇaya*. Translated by K. T. Pandurangi. Bangalore: Dvaita Vedānta Studies and Research Foundation.

———. 1994. Vols. 1–4 of *Brahma Sūtra Bhāṣya of Śrī Madhwāchārya with the Commentary of Śrī Jayatīrtha and a Gloss Thereon Bhavadīpa of Śrī Rāghavendratīrtha*. Edited by V. R. Panchamukhi Vidyāratna. Critical edition. New Delhi: Vidyaratna Sri R. S. Panchamukhi Indological Research Centre.

Nārayaṇa Paṇḍitācārya. 1991. *Sumadhvavijaya*. Translated and edited by G. V. Nadgouda. Bangalore: Poornaprajna Vidyapeetha.

Prahladachar, D., ed. 1993. *Śrī Vyāsayogicaritam*. By Somanātha. Bangalore: Dvaita Vedānta Studies and Research Foundation.

Rao, Venkoba, ed. n.d. *Śrī Vyāsayogicaritam: The Life of Śrī Vyāsarāja, a Champū Kāvya in Sanskrit by Somanātha*. Reprint of Venkoba Rao's edition, with additional materials by K. T. Pandurangi and Srinivasa Ritti. Bangalore: Dvaita Vedānta Studies and Research Foundation.

———, ed. 1926. *Śrī Vyāsayogicaritam: The Life of Śrī Vyāsarāja, a Champū Kāvya in Sanskrit by Somanātha*. With a historical introduction in English by Venkoba Rao. Bangalore: M. Srinivasa Murti.

*Sources of Vijayanagar History*. (1919) 1986. Edited by S. Krishnaswami Ayyangar. New Delhi: Gian.

*Upaniṣads*. 1962. Pts. 1 and 2. of *Sacred Books of the East*. Translated by F. Max Muller. New York: Dover.

———. 1996. Translated by Patrick Olivelle. New York: Oxford University Press.

Vidyāraṇya. 2002. *The Treatise on Liberation-in-Life: A Critical Edition and Annotated Translation of the Jīvanmuktiviveka of Vidyāraṇya*. By Robert Alan Goodding. PhD diss., University of Texas, Austin.

Viṣṇudāsācārya. 1990. *The Jewel-Necklace of Argument: The* Vādaratnāvali *of Viṣṇudāsācārya*. Translated by Edwin Gerow. American Oriental Society Translation Series. New Haven, CT: American Oriental Society.

Vyāsatīrtha. 1994–96. Vols. 1–3 of *Nyāyāmṛtam with Advaitasiddhi of Madhusūdana Sarasvatī and Three Commentaries of Nyāyāmṛtam*. Edited by K. T. Pandurangi. Bangalore: Dvaita Vedānta Studies and Research Foundation.

———. 2000–2001. Vols. 1–3 of *Tātparyacandrikā, with the Commentaries of Rāghavendratīrtha and Pāṇḍuraṅgi Keśavācārya*. Edited by K. T. Pandurangi. Bangalore: Dvaita Vedānta Studies and Research Foundation.

———. 2003. *Tarkatāṇḍavam*. Edited by K. T. Pandurangi. Bangalore: Dvaita Vedānta Studies and Research Foundation.

Yādava Prakāśa. 1995. *Rules and Regulations of Brahminical Asceticism: Yatidharmasamuccaya of Yādava Prakāśa*. Translated by Patrick Olivelle. Albany: State University of New York Press.

**Primary Sources: Travelers' Accounts (Selected)**

Nunes, Fernão. (1900) 1995. "Chronicle of Fernao Nuniz." In *A Forgotten Empire (Vijaya Nagar): A Contribution to the History of India*, edited by Robert Sewell. New Delhi: Asian Educational Services. Citations refer to the 1995 edition.

Paes, Domingo. (1900) 1995. "Narrative of Domingo Paes." In *A Forgotten Empire (Vijaya Nagar): A Contribution to the History of India*, edited by Robert Sewell. New Delhi: Asian Educational Services.

**Primary Sources: Inscriptions and Institutional Records (Selected)**

*Annual Report of the Mysore Archaeological Department for the Years 1917–1919. 1919. University of Mysore. Bangalore: Government Press.*

———. *for the Year 1933.* 1936. University of Mysore. Bangalore: Government Press.

———. *for the Year 1934.* 1936. University of Mysore. Bangalore: Government Press.

———. *for the Year 1941.* 1942. University of Mysore. Bangalore: Government Press.

*Annual Report on Indian Epigraphy, 1922–25.* 1986. New Delhi: Archaeological Survey of India.

*Annual Report on South Indian Epigraphy.* 1922. Madras: Government Press.

*Epigraphia Carnatica.* 1902. *Inscriptions in the Shimoga District,* edited by Lewis Rice. Vol. 7, pt. 1. Bangalore: Mysore Government Press.

———. 1905. *Inscriptions in the Bangalore District,* edited by Lewis Rice. Vol. 9. Bangalore: Mysore Government Press.

———. 1943. *Supplementary Inscriptions in Mysore and Mandya Districts,* edited by M. H. Krishna. Vol. 14. Mysore: Mysore Government Branch Press.

———. 1976. *Mysore District: Krishnarajanagara, Mysore, and T. Narasipura Taluks,* edited by B. R. Gopal. Vol. 5. Mysore: University of Mysore.

*Epigraphia Indica.* 1960. *Archaeological Survey of India JA 1955-JL 1956,* edited by D. C. Sircar. Vol. 31. Calcutta: Government of India Press.

*Inscriptions at Vijayanagara (Hampi).* 1995. *Inscriptions of Karnataka.* No. 8 of the Vijayanagara Research Centre Series, edited by Channabasappa S. Patil and Vinoda C. Patil. Vol. 1. Mysore: Directorate of Archaeology and Museums.

Row, B. R., ed. 1927. *Selections from the Records of the Sringeri Mutt.* Mysore: Government Branch Press.

Row, B. Suryanarain. 1905. *A History of Vijayanagar: The Never to Be Forgotten Empire in Two Parts.* Madras: Addison.

Shastry, A. K. 2009. *The Records of the Śṛingēri Dharmasaṃsthāna.* Śṛingēri: Sringeri Maṭha.

*South Indian Inscriptions.* 1932. *Miscellaneous Inscriptions from the Malayalam, Telugu, and Kannada Countries,* edited by K. V. Subrahmanya Aiyer. Vol. 7. Madras: Government Press.

———. 1941. *Kannada Inscriptions from the Madras Presidency,* edited by R. Rama Shastry and N. Lakshminarayanan Rao. Vol. 9, pt. 2. Madras: Government Press.

———. 1986. *Miscellaneous Inscriptions from the Tamil, Telugu, Kannada Countries and Ceylon,* edited by Rao Bahadur H. Krishna Shastri. Vol. 4. Madras: Government Press.

———. 1988. *Telugu Inscriptions of the Vijayanagara Dynasty,* edited by H. K. Narasimhaswami. Vol. 16. New Delhi: Archaeological Survey of India.

*Tirupati Devasthanam Inscriptions.* (1933) 1984. *Inscriptions of Saluva Narasimha's Time from 1445–1504 A.D.* Edited by V. Vijayaraghavacharya. Translated by S. Subrahmanya Sastry. Vol. 2. New Delhi: Sri Satguru Publications.

———. (1935) 1984. *Inscriptions of Krishnaraya's Time from 1509 A.D. to 1531 A.D.* Edited and translated by V. Vijayaraghavacharya. Vol. 3. New Delhi: Sri Satguru Publications.

*Vijayanagara Inscriptions.* 1986. Edited by B. R. Gopal. Vol. 2. Mysore: Directorate of Archaeology and Museums.

**Secondary Sources:**

Aiyangar, Krishnaswami. 1921. *South India and Her Muhammadan Invaders.* London: Oxford University Press.

Ali, Daud. 2004. *Courtly Culture and Political Life in Early Medieval India.* New York: Cambridge University Press.

Appadurai, Arjun. 1977. "Kings, Sects and Temples in South India, 1350–1700 A.D." *Indian Economic and Social History Review* 14(1): 47–73.

———. 1981. *Worship and Conflict under Colonial Rule: A South Indian Case.* Cambridge: Cambridge University Press.

Asher, Catherine B., and Cynthia Talbot. 2006. *India before Europe.* New York: Cambridge University Press.

Bader, Jonathan. 2000. *Conquest of the Four Quarters: Traditional Accounts of the Life of Śaṅkara.* New Delhi: Aditya Prakashan.

Bronner, Yigal. 2015. "South Meets North: Banaras from the Perspective of Appayya Dīkṣita." In O'Hanlon, Minkowski, and Venkatkrishnan, *Scholar-Intellectuals in Early Modern India,* 10–31.

———. 2016. "A Renaissance Man in Memory: Appayya Dīkṣita through the Ages." *Journal of Indian Philosophy* 44(1): 11–39.

Callewaert, Winand M., and Rupert Snell, eds. 1994. *According to Tradition: Hagiographical Writing in India.* Gottingen, Germany: Otto Harrassowitz.

Carman, John Braisted. 1974. *The Theology of Rāmānuja: An Essay in Interreligious Understanding.* New Haven, CT: Yale University Press.

Chandra Shobhi, Prithvi Datta. 2005. *Premodern Communities and Modern Histories: Narrating Vīraśaiva and Lingāyat Selves.* PhD diss., University of Chicago.

Chatterjee, Indrani, and Richard Eaton, eds. 2006. *Slavery and South Asian History.* Bloomington: Indiana University Press.

Clark, Matthew. 2006. *The Daśanāmī-Saṃnyāsīs: The Integration of Ascetic Lineages into an Order.* Leiden, Netherlands: Brill.

Clayton, John. 2006. *Religions, Reasons, and Gods: Essays in Cross-Cultural Philosophy of Religion.* Prepared for publication by Anne M. Blackburn and Thomas D. Carroll. New York: Cambridge University Press.

Clémentin-Ojha, Catherine. 2011. "Swami Shraddhananda (1857–1926) de l'Arya Samaj, un renonçant engagé." In *Convictions religieuses et engagement en Asie du Sud depuis 1850,* edited by Catherine Clémentin-Ojha, 137–63. Paris: Ecole française d'Extrême-Orient.

Clooney, Francis X. 1987. "Why the Veda Has No Author: Language as Ritual in Early Mīmāṃsā and Post-modern Theology." *Journal of the American Academy of Religion* 55(4): 659–84.

———. 2008. "Imago Dei, *Parama Sāmyam*: Hindu Light on a Traditional Christian Theme." *International Journal of Hindu Studies* 12(3): 227–55.

Dallapiccola, Anna L. 2011. "Vijayanagara and Nayaka Paintings." In Dallapiccola and Verghese, *South India under Vijayanagara*, 273–82.

Dallapiccola, Anna, and Anila Verghese, eds. 2011. *South India under Vijayanagara: Art and Archaeology.* New Delhi: Oxford University Press.

Dallapiccola, Anna, John M. Fritz, George Michell, and S. Rajasekhara. 1992. *The Rāmachandra Temple at Vijayanagara.* Vijayanagara Research Project Monograph Series. New Delhi: Manohar Publications and the American Institute of Indian Studies.

Davis, Richard. 1997. *Lives of Indian Images.* Princeton, NJ: Princeton University Press.

Derrett, J. Duncan M. 1974. "Modes of Sannyāsīs and the Reform of a South Indian *Maṭha* Carried Out in 1584." *Journal of the American Oriental Society* 94(1): 65–72.

Dhere, Ramchandra Chintaman. 2011. *The Rise of a Folk God: Viṭṭhal of Pandharpur.* Translated by Anne Feldhaus. New York: Oxford University Press.

Dirks, Nicholas. 1987. *The Hollow Crown: Ethnohistory of an Indian Kingdom.* Cambridge: Cambridge University Press.

Eaton, Richard M. 1978. *The Sufis of Bijapur, 1300–1700: Social Roles of Sufis in Medieval India.* Princeton, NJ: Princeton University Press.

———. 2000. "Temple Desecration and Indo-Muslim States." In Gilmartin and Lawrence, *Beyond Turk and Hindu,* 246–81.

———. 2005. *A Social History of the Deccan (1300–1761): Eight Indian Lives.* Vol. 8 of *The New Cambridge History of India* 1. Cambridge: Cambridge University Press.

Eaton, Richard M., and Phillip B. Wagoner. 2014. *Power, Memory, Architecture: Contested Sites on India's Deccan Plateau, 1300–1600.* New Delhi: Oxford University Press.

Filliozat, Pierre-Sylvain, and Vasundhara Filliozat. 1988. *Hampi-Vijayanagara: The Temple of Viṭhala.* New Delhi: Sitaram Bhartia Institute of Scientific Research.

Fisher, Elaine. 2013. *A New Public Theology: Sanskrit and Society in Seventeenth-Century South India.* PhD diss., Columbia University.

———. 2015. "Public Philology: Text Criticism and the Sectarianization of Hinduism in Early Modern South India." In O'Hanlon, Minkowski, and Venkatkrishnan, *Scholar-Intellectuals in Early Modern India,* 50–69.

Flood, Finbar. 2009. *Objects of Translation: Material Culture and Medieval "Hindu-Muslim" Encounter.* Princeton, NJ: Princeton University Press.

Flood, Gavin. 1996. *An Introduction to Hinduism.* Cambridge: Cambridge University Press.

Fort, Andrew O. 1998. *Jīvanmukti in Transformation: Embodied Liberation in Advaita and Neo-Vedānta.* Albany: State University of New York Press.

Fort, Andrew O., and Patricia Mumme, eds. 1996. *Living Liberation in Hindu Thought.* Albany: State University of New York Press.

Fritz, John M., and George Michell. *Vijayanagara Research Project.* University of Pennsylvania Museum of Archaeology and Anthropology. Last modified February 2014. www.penn.museum/sites/VRP/default.html

Fritz, John M, George Michell, and M. S. Nagaraja Rao. 1984. *Where Kings and Gods Meet: The Royal Centre at Vijayanagara*. Tucson: University of Arizona Press.

Galewicz, Cezary. 2009. *A Commentator in the Service of the Empire: Sāyaṇa and the Royal Project of Commenting on the Whole of the Veda*. Publications of the De Nobili Research Library 35. Vienna: University of Vienna.

Ganeri, Martin. 2014. "Free Will, Agency, and Selfhood in Rāmānuja." In *Free Will, Agency, and Selfhood in Indian Philosophy*, edited by Matthew R. Dasti and Edwin F. Bryant, 232–54. New York: Oxford University Press.

Gerow, Edwin. 1987. "The Dvaitin as Deconstructionist: Viṣṇudāsācārya on 'Tat tvam asi': Part 1." *Journal of the American Oriental Society* 107(4): 561–79.

———. 1990. Introduction to *The Jewel-Necklace of Argument: The* Vādaratnāvali *of Viṣṇudāsācārya*, by Viṣṇudāsācārya, vii-xiii. Translated by Edwin Gerow. American Oriental Society Translation Series. New Haven, CT: American Oriental Society.

Gilmartin, David, and Bruce B. Lawrence, eds. 2000. *Beyond Turk and Hindu: Rethinking Religious Identities In Islamicate South Asia*. Gainesville: University Press of Florida.

Goodding, Robert Alan. 2002. *The Treatise on Liberation-in-Life: A Critical Edition and Annotated Translation of the "Jīvan-mukti-viveka" of Vidyāraṇya*. PhD diss., University of Texas, Austin.

Granoff, Phyllis, and Koichi Shinohara. 1994. *Monks and Magicians: Religious Biographies in Asia*. Delhi: Motilal Banarsidass Press.

Griffiths, Paul. 1999. "What Do Buddhists Hope for from Antitheistic Argument?" *Faith and Philosophy* 16(4): 506–22.

Guha, Ranajit. 1997. *Dominance without Hegemony: History and Power in Colonial India*. Cambridge: Harvard University Press.

Habib, Irfan. 2011. *Economic History of Medieval India, 1200–1500*. Vol. 8, pt. 1, of *History of Science, Philosophy and Culture in Indian Civilization*, edited by D. P. Chattopadhyaya. New Delhi: Pearson Longman.

Hacker, Paul. 1995. "On Śaṅkara and Advaitism." In *Philology and Confrontation: Paul Hacker on Traditional and Modern Vedānta*, edited and translated by Wilhelm Halbfass, 27–32. Albany: State University of New York Press. First published in German in 1964.

Halbfass, Wilhelm. 1988. *India and Europe: An Essay in Understanding*. Albany: State University of New York Press.

———. 1991. *Tradition and Reflection*. Albany: State University of New York Press.

Hawley, John Stratton. 2012. "The Four Sampradāyas: Ordering the Religious Past in Mughal India." In O'Hanlon and Washbrook, *Religious Cultures in Early Modern India*, 28–51.

Haywood, John. 2011. *The New Atlas of World History: Global Events at a Glance*. Princeton, NJ: Princeton University Press.

Heras, Henry. 1929. *Beginnings of Vijayanagara History*. Bombay: Indian Historical Research Institute.

Hopkins, Steven P. 2002. *Singing the Body of God: The Hymns of Vedānta Deśika in Their South Indian Tradition*. New York: Oxford University Press.

Horstmann, Monika. 2012. "Theology and Statecraft." In O'Hanlon and Washbrook, *Religious Cultures in Early Modern India*, 52–73.

Inden, Ronald B., Jonathan Walters, and Daud Ali, eds. 2000. *Querying the Medieval: Texts and the History of Practices in South Asia*. New York: Oxford University Press.

Jackson, William J. 1998. *Songs of Three Great South Indian Saints*. New Delhi: Oxford University Press.

Keune, Jon Milton. 2011. *Eknāth Remembered and Reformed: Bhakti, Brahmans, and Untouchables in Marāṭhi Historiography*. PhD diss., Columbia University.

———. 2015. "Eknāth in Context: The Literary, Social, and Political Milieus of an Early Modern Saint-Poet." In Minkowski, O'Hanlon, and Venkatkrishnan, *Scholar-Intellectuals in Early Modern India*, 70–86.

Kulke, Hermann. 2001. *Kings and Cults: State Formation and Legitimation in India and Southeast Asia*. New Delhi: Manohar.

Lester, Robert C. 1994. "The Sāttāda Śrīvaiṣṇavas." *Journal of the American Oriental Society* 114(1): 39–53.

Lipner, Julius. 1986. *The Face of Truth: A Study of Meaning and Metaphysics in the Vedāntic Theology of Rāmānuja*. Albany: State University of New York Press.

Loewy Shacham, Ilanit. 2015. *Kṛṣṇadevarāya's Āmuktamālyada and the Narration of a Śrīvaiṣṇava Community*. PhD diss., University of Chicago.

Lorenzen, David. 1976. "The Life of Śaṅkarācārya." In *The Biographical Process: Studies in the History and Psychology of Religion*, edited by Frank E. Reynolds and Donald Capps, 87–107. The Hague: Mouton.

Ludden, David. 1994. "History Outside Civilization and the Mobility of Southern Asia." *South Asia: Journal of South Asian Studies* 17(1): 1–23.

———. 1985. *Peasant History in South India*. Princeton, NJ: Princeton University Press.

Lutgendorf, Philip. 2007. *Hanumān's Tale: The Messages of a Divine Monkey*. New York: Oxford University Press.

Mack, Alexandra. 2011. "Power Relationships as Seen through Vijayanagara-Era Temple Inscriptions." In Dallapiccola and Verghese, *South India under Vijayanagara*, 153–63.

McCrea, Lawrence. 2015. "Freed by the Weight of History: Polemic and Doxography in Sixteenth Century Vedānta." In O'Hanlon, Minkowski, and Venkatkrishnan, *Scholar-Intellectuals in Early Modern India*, 87–101.

McLaughlin, Mark. 2014. *Lord in the Temple, Lord in the Tomb: The Hindu Temple and Its Relationship to the Samādhi Shrine Tradition of Jñāneśvar Mahārāj*. PhD diss., University of California, Santa Barbara.

Mesquita, Roque. 1997. *Madhva und Seine Unbekannten Literarischen Quellen: Einige Beobachtungen*. Vienna: Publications of the de Nobili Research Library.

———. 2000. *Madhva's Unknown Literary Sources: Some Observations*. New Delhi: Aditya Prakashan.

———. 2007. *The Concept of Liberation While Still Alive in the Philosophy of Madhva*. New Delhi: Aditya Prakashan.

———. 2008. *Madhva's Quotes from the Purāṇas and the Mahābhārata: An Analytical Compilation of Untraceable Source-Quotations in Madhva's Works along with Footnotes*. New Delhi: Aditya Prakashan.

Metcalf, Thomas R. 1995. *Ideologies of the Raj*. Cambridge: Cambridge University Press.

Michell, George. 1995. "Dating of the Vidyāśaṅkara Temple at Sringeri." In Sri Nagabandinam: Dr. M.S. Nagaraja Rao Festschrift (Essays on Art, Culture, History, Archaeology, Epigraphy and Conservation of Cultural Properties of India and Neighbouring Countries), edited by L. K. Srinivasan and S. Nagaraju, vols. 1–2, 269–78. Bangalore: Dr. M. S. Nagaraja Rao Felicitation Committee.

———. 2000. *Architecture and Art of Southern India: Vijayanagara and the Successor States.* Vol. 6 of *The New Cambridge History of India 1.* New Delhi, Cambridge University Press.

Minkowski, Christopher. 2010. "I'll Wash Out Your Mouth with My Boot: A Guide to Philological Argument in Mughal-Era Banaras." In *Epic and Argument in Sanskrit Literary History: Essays in Honor of Robert P. Goldman,* edited by Sheldon Pollock, 113–35. New Delhi: Manohar.

———. 2012. "Advaita Vedānta in Early Modern History." In O'Hanlon and Washbrook, *Religious Cultures in Early Modern India,* 73–99. London: Routledge.

Misra, R. N. 1997. "Pontiffs' Empowerment in Central Indian Śaivite Monachism." *Journal of the Asiatic Society of Bombay,* n.s., 72: 72–86.

Morrison, Kathleen D. 1995. *Fields of Victory: Vijayanagara and the Course of Intensification.* Berkeley: University of California Press.

———. 2009. "Coercion, Resistance, and Hierarchy: Local Processes and Imperial Strategies in the Vijayanagara Empire." In *Empires: Perspectives from Archaeology and History,* edited by Susan E. Alcock, Terence N. D'Altroy, Kathleen D. Morrison, Carla M. Sinopoli, 252–78. Cambridge: Cambridge University Press.

———. 2011. "The Capital in Context: The Vijayanagara Metropolitan Region." In Dallapiccola and Verghese, *South India under Vijayanagara,* 46–58.

Mumme, Patricia Y. 1988. *The Śrīvaiṣṇava Theological Dispute: Maṇavāḷamāmuni and Vedānta Deśika.* Madras: New Era Publications.

———. 1996. "Conclusion: Living Liberation in Comparative Perspective." In *Living Liberation in Hindu Thought,* edited by Andrew O. Fort and Patricia Mumme, 247–69. Albany: State University of New York Press.

Narayanan, Vasudha. 2007. "'With the Earth as a Lamp and the Sun as the Flame': Lighting Devotion in South India." *International Journal of Hindu Studies,* 11(3): 227–53.

Nicholson, Andrew. 2010. *Unifying Hinduism: Philosophy and Identity in Indian Intellectual History.* New York: Columbia University Press.

Nilakanta Sastri, K. A. (1955) 1994. *A History of South India: From Prehistoric Times to the Fall of Vijayanagara.* 4th ed. Madras: Oxford University Press. Citations refer to the 1994 edition.

Novetzke, Christian Lee. 2007. "The Theographic and the Historiographic in an Indian Sacred Life Story." *Sikh Formations* 3(2): 169–84.

———. 2008. *Religion and Public Memory: A Cultural History of Saint Namdev in India.* New York: Columbia University Press.

———. 2012. "The Brahmin Double: The Brahminical Construction of Anti-Brahminism and Anti-caste Sentiment in the Religious Cultures of Precolonial Maharashtra." In O'Hanlon and Washbrook, *Religious Cultures in Early Modern India,* 100–120.

O'Hanlon, Rosalind. 2012. "Speaking from Śiva's Temple: Banaras Scholar Households and the Brahman 'Ecumene' of Mughal India." In O'Hanlon and Washbrook, *Religious Cultures in Early Modern India,* 121–45.

———. 2013. "Contested Conjunctures: Brahman Communities and 'Early Modernity' in India." *American Historical Review* 118(3): 765–87.

O'Hanlon, Rosalind, Christopher Minkowski, and Anand Venkatkrishnan, eds. 2015. *Scholar-Intellectuals in Early Modern India: Discipline, Sect, Lineage and Community*. Reprint of special issue of *South Asian History and Culture* 6(1): 1–185. London: Routledge.

O'Hanlon, Rosalind, and David Washbrook, eds. 2012. *Religious Cultures in Early Modern India: New Perspectives*. Reprint of special issue of *South Asian History and Culture* 2(2): 133–336. London: Routledge, (2011).

Orr, Leslie. 2000. *Donors, Devotees, and Daughters of God: Temple Women in Medieval Tamilnadu*. New York: Oxford University Press.

Patil, Parimal. 2009. *Against a Hindu God: Buddhist Philosophy of Religion in India*. New York: Columbia University Press.

Patton, Laurie. n.d. "Defining Hinduism." *Oxford Bibliographies On-Line*. www.oxfordbibliographies.com/view/document/obo-9780195399318/obo-9780195399318-0015.xml.

Pauwels, Heidi. 2009. "Imagining Religious Communities in the Sixteenth Century: Harirām Vyās and the Haritrayī." *International Journal of Hindu Studies* 13(2): 143–61.

Pierce Taylor, Sarah. 2014. "Sovereigns Whose Feet Were Worshipped by Kings: The Jain Maṭha and the Rhetoric of Empire." Paper presented at the Annual Meeting of the American Academy of Religion, San Diego, CA, November.

Pollock, Sheldon. 1985. "The Theory of Practice and the Practice of Theory in Traditional India." *Journal of the American Oriental Society* 105(3): 499–519.

———. 1989. "Mīmāṃsā and the Problem of History in Traditional India." *Journal of the American Oriental Society* 109(4): 603–10.

———. 1993a. "Deep Orientalism? Notes on Sanskrit and Power beyond the Raj." In *Orientalism and the Post-colonial Predicament: Perspectives on South Asia*, edited by Carol Breckenridge and Peter van der Veer, 76–133. Philadelphia: University of Pennsylvania Press.

———. 1993b. "Rāmāyaṇa and the Political Imagination in India." *Journal of Asian Studies* 52(2): 261–97.

———. 2001. "The Death of Sanskrit." *Comparative Studies in Society and History* 43(2): 392–427.

———. 2006. *The Language of the Gods in the World of Men: Sanskrit, Culture and Power in Premodern India*. New Delhi: Permanent Black.

Prasad, Leela. 2007. *Poetics of Conduct: Oral Narrative and Moral Being in a South Indian Town*. New York: Columbia University Press.

Raghotham, Venkata. 2013. "Historical Memory and Statecraft in Late Medieval South India: A Study of Krisnadevaraya's Campaigns against the Gajapati Ruler of Orissa." In Verghese, *Krishnadevaraya and His Times*, 63–80.

Raman, K. V. 1975. *Śrī Varadarājaswāmi Temple-Kāñchi: A Study of Its History, Art, and Architecture*. New Delhi: Abhinav Publications.

Raman, Srilata. 2007. *Self-Surrender (Prapatti) to God in Śrīvaiṣṇavism: Tamil Cats and Sanskrit Monkeys*. Routledge Hindu Series. New York: Routledge.

Ramaswamy, Vijaya. 1985. "Artisans in Vijayanagara Society." *Indian Economic and Social History Review* 22(4): 417–44.

Ram-Prasad, Chakravarthi. 2002. *Advaita Epistemology and Metaphysics: An Outline of Indian Non-realism*. London: Routledge Curzon.

Rao, Ajay. 2015. *Refiguring the Rāmāyaṇa as Theology: A History of Reception in Premodern India*. New York: Routledge.

Rao, Vasudeva. 2002. *Living Traditions in Contemporary Contexts: The Madhva Matha of Udupi*. New Delhi: Orient Longman.

Rao, V. N., David Shulman, and Sanjay Subrahmanyam. 1992. *Symbols of Substance: Court and State in Nayaka Period Tamilnadu*. New Delhi: Oxford University Press.

———. 2001. *Textures of Time: Writing History in South India 1600–1800*. New Delhi: Permanent Black.

———. 2004. "A New Imperial Idiom in the Sixteenth Century: Krishnadevaraya and His Political Theory of Vijayanagara." In *South Indian Horizons: Felicitation Volume for Francois Gro*, edited by Jean-Luc Chevillard and Eva Wilden, 597–625. Pondicherry: Institut français de Pondichéry, Ecole française d'Extrême-Orient.

Saletore, B. A. 1934. *Social and Political Life in the Vijayanagara Empire*. Madras: B. G. Paul.

Sanderson, Alexis. 2009. "The Śaiva Age." In *Genesis and Development of Tantrism*, edited by Shingo Einoo, 41–350. Tokyo: Institute of Oriental Culture, University of Tokyo.

———. 2015. "Tolerance, Exclusivity, Inclusivity, and Persecution in Indian Religion during the Early Mediaeval Period." In *Honoris Causa: Essays in Honour of Aveek Sarkar*, edited with a foreword by John Makinson, 155–224. London: Allen Lane.

Sarma, Deepak. 1997. "After What? Vyāsatīrtha's Arguments regarding Eligibility and Theological Inquiry." *Journal of Vaiṣṇava Studies* 5(3): 65–106.

———. 2005. *Epistemologies and the Limitations of Philosophical Inquiry: Doctrine in Mādhva Vedānta*. London: Routledge Curzon.

Sax, William. 2000. "Conquering the Quarters: Religion and Politics in Hinduism." *International Journal of Hindu Studies* 4(1): 39–60.

Sears, Tamara. 2008. "Constructing the Guru: Ritual Authority and Architectural Space in Medieval India." *Art Bulletin* 15(1): 7–31.

———. 2014. *Worldly Gurus and Spiritual Kings: Architecture and Asceticism in Medieval India*. New Haven, CT: Yale University Press.

Sen, Amartya. 2005. *The Argumentative Indian: Writings on Indian History, Culture and Identity*. New York: Farrar, Straus and Giroux.

Sewell, Robert. (1900) 1995. *A Forgotten Empire: A Contribution to the History of India*. New Delhi: Asian Educational Services.

Sharma, B. N. K. (1961) 1981. *A History of the Dvaita School of Vedānta and Its Literature*. New Delhi: Motilal Banarsidass. Citations refer to the 1981 edition.

———. 1979. *Śrī Madhva's Teachings in His Own Words*. Mumbai: Bharatiya Vidya Bhavan.

———. 1986. *The Brahmasūtras and Their Principal Commentaries: A Critical Exposition*. Vols. 1–3. New Delhi: Munshiram Manoharlal Publishers.

———. 1991. *Philosophy of Śrī Madhvācārya*. New Delhi: Motilal Banarsidass.

Sheridan, Daniel. 1996. "Direct Knowledge of God and Living Liberation in the Religious Thought of Madhva." In *Living Liberation in Hindu Thought*, edited by Andrew O. Fort and Patricia Y. Mumme, 91–112. Albany: State University of New York Press.

Siauve, Suzanne. 1959. *Les Noms Védiques de Viṣṇu dans l'Anuvyākhyāna de Madhva*. Pondicherry: Institut français d'Indologie.

———. 1968. *La Doctrine de Madhva*. Pondicherry: Institut français d'Indologie.

———. 1971. *Les Hiérarchies Spirituelles selon l'Anuvyākhyāna de Madhva*. Pondicherry: Institut français d'Indologie.

Sinopoli, Carla. 2000. "From the Lion Throne: Political and Social Dynamics of the Vijayanagara Empire." *Journal of the Economic and Social History of the Orient* 43(3): 364–98.

Sinopoli, Carla, and Kathleen Morrison. 2007. *The Vijayanagara Metropolitan Survey*. Vol. 1. Michigan: Anthropological Papers of the Museum of Anthropology.

Starn, Randolph. 2002. "Review Essay: Early Modern Muddle." *Journal of Early Modern History* 6(3): 296–307.

Stein, Burton. 1980. *Peasant State and Society in Medieval South India*. New Delhi: Oxford University Press.

———. 1999. *Vijayanagara*. New Delhi: Foundation Books.

Stoker, Valerie. 2011. "Polemics and Patronage in Sixteenth-Century Vijayanagara: Vyāsatīrtha and the Dynamics of Hindu Sectarian Relations." *History of Religions* 51(2): 129–55.

———. 2013. "Krishnadevaraya and the Patronage of Vyasatirtha: Royal and Religious Authority in Sixteenth-Century Vijayanagara." In Verghese, *Krishnadevaraya and His Times*, 262–77.

———. 2015. "Darbār, Maṭha, Devasthānam: The Politics of Intellectual Commitment and Religious Affiliation in Sixteenth-Century South India." In O'Hanlon, Minkowski, and Venkatkrishnan, *Scholar-Intellectuals in Early Modern India*, 130–46.

Subrahmanyam, Sanjay. 1998. "Reflections on State-Making and History-Making in South India, 1500–1800." *Journal of the Economic and Social History of the Orient* 41(3): 382–416.

Sundaresan, Vidyashankar. 2000. "Conflicting Hagiographies and History: The Place of Śaṅkaravijaya Texts in Advaita Tradition." *International Journal of Hindu Studies*. 4(2): 109–84.

Talbot, Cynthia. 1995. "Inscribing the Other, Inscribing the Self: Hindu-Muslim Identities in Pre-colonial India." *Comparative Studies in Society and History* 37(4): 692–722.

———. 2000. "The Story of Prataparudra: Hindu Historiography on the Deccan Frontier." In Gilmartin and Lawrence, *Beyond Turk and Hindu*, 282–299.

———. 2001. *Precolonial India in Practice: Society, Region, and Identity in Medieval Andhra*. New York: Oxford University Press.

Thakur, Anantalal. 1961. "Cannibhaṭṭa and the Authorship of the *Sarvadarśanasaṅgraha*." *Adyar Library Bulletin* 25(1–4): 524–38.

Thapar, Romila. 1994. *Cultural Transaction and Early India: Tradition and Patronage*. New Delhi, Oxford University Press.

Tobert, Natalie. 2000. *Anegondi: Architectural Ethnography of a Royal Village*. New Delhi: Manohar Publications and American Institute of Indian Studies.

Venkatkrishnan, Anand. 2011. "*Hum Hain Naye, Andaz Kyun Ho Purāṇa?* Hermeneutical Innovations in Advaita Vedānta Intellectual History." Paper presented at the South Asia Graduate Student Conference, Chicago, IL, April.

———. 2015. "Ritual, Reflection, and Religion: The Devas of Banaras." In O'Hanlon, Minkowski, and Venkatkrishnan, *Scholar-Intellectuals in Early Modern India*, 147–71.

Verghese, Anila. 1995. *Religious Traditions at Vijayanagara as Revealed through Its Monuments*. New Delhi: Manohar Publications and American Institute of Indian Studies.

———. 2000. *Archaeology, Art, and Religion: New Perspectives on Vijayanagara*. Delhi: Oxford University Press.

———, ed. 2013. *Krishnadevaraya and His Times*. Mumbai: K. R. Cama Oriental Institute.

———. 2014. "Kṛṣṇadevarāya's Pilgrimages and Temple Benefactions Linked with His Kalinga War (1513–1517 AD): Interplay of Warfare, Religion, and Assertion of Political Hegemony." In *Wege zum Heil(igen)? Sakralität und Sakralisierung in hinduistischen Traditionen*, edited by Karin Steiner, 145–58. Wiesbaden: Harrassowitz-Verlag.

Verghese, Anila, and Dieter Eigner. 1998. "A Monastic Complex in Viṭhalapura, Hampi Vijayanagara," *South Asian Studies* 14: 127–40.

Viraraghavacharya, T. K. T. 1953–54. *History of Tirupati (The Tiruvengadam Temple)*. Vols. 1–2. Tirumala-Tirupati: Board of Trustees of the Tirumala-Tirupati Devasthanams.

Voix, Raphaël. 2011. "Une utopie en pays bengali: de l'idéologie sectaire hindoue à l'édification d'une alternative communautaire." In *Convictions religieuses et engagement en Asie du Sud depuis 1850*, edited by Catherine Clémentin-Ojha, 165–88. Paris: Ecole française d'Extrême-Orient.

Wagoner, Phillip. 1993. *Tidings of the King: A Translation and Ethnohistorical Analysis of the* Rāyavācakamu. Honolulu: University of Hawaii Press.

———. 1996a. "From 'Pampa's Crossing' to the 'Place of the Lord Virupaksha': Architecture, Cult, and Patronage at Hampi before the Founding of Vijayanagara." In *Vijayanagara: Progress of Research 1988–1991*, edited by D. Devaraj and C. S. Patil, 141–74. Mysore: Directorate of Archaeology and Museums.

———. 1996b. "'Sultan among Hindu Kings': Dress, Titles, and the Islamicization of Hindu Culture at Vijayanagara." *Journal of Asian Studies* 55(4): 851–80.

———. 2000. "Harihara, Bukka, and the Sultan: The Delhi Sultanate in the Political Imagination of Vijayanagara." In Gilmartin and Lawrence, *Beyond Turk and Hindu*, 300–26.

Williams, Michael. 2011. *Mithyātva on Trial: A Mādhva Critique of Advaitin Metaphysics*. PhD diss., University of Manchester.

Zydenbos, Robert. 1991. "On the Jaina Background of Dvaitavedānta." *Journal of Indian Philosophy* 19: 249–71.

South Asia across the Disciplines is a series devoted to publishing first books across a wide range of South Asian studies, including art, history, philology or textual studies, philosophy, religion, and the interpretive social sciences. Series authors all share the goal of opening up new archives and suggesting new methods and approaches, while demonstrating that South Asian scholarship can be at once deep in expertise and broad in appeal.

*Extreme Poetry: The South Asian Movement of Simultaneous Narration*, by Yigal Bronner (Columbia)

*The Social Space of Language: Vernacular Culture in British Colonial Punjab*, by Farina Mir (California)

*Unifying Hinduism: Philosophy and Identity in Indian Intellectual History*, by Andrew J. Nicholson (Columbia)

*The Powerful Ephemeral: Everyday Healing in an Ambiguously Islamic Place*, by Carla Bellamy (California)

*Secularizing Islamists? Jama'at-e-Islami and Jama'at-ud-Da'wa in Urban Pakistan*, by Humeira Iqtidar (Chicago)

*Islam Translated: Literature, Conversion, and the Arabic Cosmopolis of South and Southeast Asia*, by Ronit Ricci (Chicago)

*Conjugations: Marriage and Form in New Bollywood Cinema*, by Sangita Gopal (Chicago)

*Unfinished Gestures: Devadāsīs, Memory, and Modernity in South India*, by Davesh Soneji (Chicago)

*Document Raj: Writing and Scribes in Early Colonial South India*, by Bhavani Raman (Chicago)

*The Millennial Sovereign: Sacred Kingship and Sainthood in Islam*, by A. Azfar Moin (Columbia)

*Making Sense of Tantric Buddhism: History, Semiology, and Transgression in the Indian Traditions*, by Christian K. Wedemeyer (Columbia)

*The Yogin and the Madman: Reading the Biographical Corpus of Tibet's Great Saint Milarepa*, by Andrew Quintman (Columbia)

*Body of Victim, Body of Warrior: Refugee Families and the Making of Kashmiri Jihadists*, by Cabeiri deBergh Robinson (California)

*Receptacle of the Sacred: Illustrated Manuscripts and the Buddhist Book Cult in South Asia*, by Jinah Kim (California)

*Cut-Pieces: Celluloid Obscenity and Popular Cinema in Bangladesh*, by Lotte Hoek (Columbia)

*From Text to Tradition: The Naisadhīyacarita and Literary Community in South Asia*, by Deven M. Patel (Columbia)

*Democracy against Development: Lower Caste Politics and Political Modernity in Postcolonial India*, by Jeffrey Witsoe (Chicago)

*Into the Twilight of Sanskrit Poetry: The Sena Salon of Bengal and Beyond*, by Jesse Ross Knutson (California)

*Voicing Subjects: Public Intimacy and Mediation in Kathmandu*, by Laura Kunreuther (California)

*Writing Resistance: The Rhetorical Imagination of Hindi Dalit Literature*, by Laura R. Brueck (Columbia)

*Wombs in Labor: Transnational Commercial Surrogacy in India*, by Amrita Pande (Columbia)

*I Too Have Some Dreams: N. M. Rashed and Modernism in Urdu Poetry*, by A. Sean Pue (California)

*The Place of Devotion: Siting and Experiencing Divinity in Bengal-Vaishnavism*, by Sukanya Sarbadhikary (California)

*We Were Adivasis: Aspiration in an Indian Scheduled Tribe*, by Megan Moodie (Chicago)

*Writing Self, Writing Empire: Chandar Bhan Brahman and the Cultural World of the Indo-Persian State Secretary*, by Rajeev Kinra (California)

*Culture of Encounters: Sanskrit at the Mughal Court*, by Audrey Truschke (Columbia)

*Polemics and Patronage in the City of Victory: Vyāsatīrtha, Hindu Sectarianism, and the Sixteenth-Century Vijayanagara Court*, by Valerie Stoker (California)